IL RIPOSO

Raffaello Borghini

IL RIPOSO

Edited and translated
with introduction and notes
by
Lloyd H. Ellis Jr

UNIVERSITY OF TORONTO PRESS
Toronto Buffalo London

Toronto Buffalo London
www.utppublishing.com

ISBN 978-0-8020-9743-9 (cloth)
ISBN 978-1-4426-1493-2 (paper)

The Lorenzo Da Ponte Italian Library

Library and Archives Canada Cataloguing in Publication

Borghini, Raffaello, 16th century
Il riposo / Rafaello Borghini; edited and translated
with introduction and notes by Lloyd H. Ellis

(Lorenzo Da Ponte Italian Library series)
Includes bibliographical references and index.
ISBN 978-0-8020-9743-9 (bound). ISBN 978-1-4426-1493-2 (pbk.)

1. Painting – Early works to 1800. 2. Sculpture – Early works to 1800.
3. Painters – Italy. 4. Sculptors – Italy. I. Ellis, Lloyd H. II. Title.
III. Series.

N7420.B7 2007 700 C2007-905352-1

This volume is published under the aegis and with financial assistance of: Fondazione Cassamarca, Treviso; Ministero degli Affari Esteri, Direzione Generale per la Promozione e la Cooperazione Culturale; Ministero per i Beni e le Attività Culturali, Direzione Generale per i Beni Librari e gli Istituti Culturali, Servizio per la promozione del libro e della lettura.

Publication of this volume is assisted by the Istituto Italiano di Cultura, Toronto

University of Toronto Press acknowledges the financial assistance to its publishing program of the Canada Council for the Arts and the Ontario Arts Council.

University of Toronto Press acknowledges the financial support for its publishing activities of the Government of Canada through the Book Publishing Industry Development Program (BPIDP).

To Eva

Contents

Translator's Preface

When Sidney Alexander published his translation of Guicciardini's *Storia d'Italia* in 1969, he explained, with another story, why he had eliminated forty per cent of Guicciardini's text.[1] People from Laconia ... Sparta ... were proverbially laconic. A Laconian was tried and found guilty of using three words instead of two. Offered his freedom if he would read entirely through Guicciardini's account of the siege of Pisa, the Laconian pleaded to be sent instead to the galleys.

I have also eliminated forty per cent of my author's text. I think this allows the reader to concentrate on what is most important in the treatise: Borghini's description of Counter-Reformation ideas about the content of religious paintings; his description of the mid-sixteenth-century reaction against the style of the *Maniera*; and, at the end of his treatise, the information he provides that updates the second edition of Vasari's *Le Vite de' piu eccelenti Pittori, Scultori e Architetori*, published fourteen years before.[2] This condensed translation of *Il Riposo* emphasizes the dramatic dialogue that Borghini's contemporaries enjoyed in his plays and that has made *Il Riposo* a model for students of Tuscan and modern Italian. This abridgement also emphasizes Borghini's description of an idyllic Tuscan countryside and manner of living. The manner of living has changed but the villa of Il Riposo, now sometimes known for its current owners as the Villa Signorini, remains largely as it was. The reader is spared Borghini's extended repetition of sixteenth-century commonplaces comparing the relative value of painting and sculpture, the seemingly endless recipes for the preparation of pigments, a long discourse paraphrasing Pliny, and many of the long monologues paraphrasing or even plagiarizing Vasari. For those averse to the galleys there is my dissertation, which translated the full text.[3] Ellipsis points with note numbers ('...[a]') indicate what is omitted. In addition, in rare cases individual words or short phrases in the text have also been excised. These ellipses are not end-noted and primarily involve Borghini's paraphrase of Pliny.

Students of the history of gardens will want to consult the full text concerning the elaborate vegetative bird trap at Il Riposo, the *uccellare*. It is described over several pages at the beginning of Book II. Scholars interested in particular artists will also consult Borghini in Italian.[4] They will find particularly helpful the analytical index that Marco Rosci appended to his facsimile edition of *Il Riposo*. In this *Indice Analitico*, organized separately by artist and by place, Rosci attempted to locate each of the 5,000 to 6,000 objects mentioned by Borghini. Giovanni Gaetano Bottari's notes to the 1730 second edition are another aid to researchers.[5] These notes, translated in the dissertation but largely omitted here, sometimes describe the subsequent location and the condition of works that Borghini had described 150 years before. In his *Indice Analitico* Rosci attempted to identify and correct many of Borghini's false attributions and other errors of fact. Bottari had attempted to do some of this in a much less systematic way. Rather than repeat these corrections and add some of my own, I have, except where Borghini's inaccuracies affect the comprehensibility of the translation, left Borghini's errors to those who are specialists in the artists he describes.

At the beginning of the first edition there is a twenty-eight-page index 'of the names of the painters, sculptors, and other persons.' Then comes a fourteen-page subject index, an alphabetical list of Borghini's marginal subheadings. The utility of these indexes to the modern reader is compromised in translation by their being alphabetized by first word (e.g., Hagesandros, Messer Cardinal Agnolo Niccolini, Agorakritos of Paros) and the fact that Borghini uses a sixteenth-century transliteration from Greek, Latin, and occasionally German. Borghini's indexes have been omitted in this translation and are replaced by a modern index at the end of this book.

In his *Prefazione* to the second edition, Bottari, who subsequently published his indispensable collection of correspondence concerning the plastic arts, the *Raccolta di Lettere sulla Pittura, Scultura e Architettura*,[6] proclaimed that republication of *Il Riposo* was necessary for two reasons. First, the artists of his time needed to be reminded how poorly they compared to their predecessors. Second, the public needed a spur to encourage them to do something about the deterioration and the mishandled restoration of their artistic heritage. Less masterful editions of *Il Riposo* appeared in 1787, 1807, 1826, and 1969 on the more utilitarian pretext that the first two editions were no longer available for purchase. When Marco Rosci published his carefully annotated facsimile edition in 1967 he put it forward as a necessary text for the study of the school of the Studiolo of Francesco de' Medici and for the study of the reaction of Santi di Tito against High Mannerism.[7]

Il Riposo has never been translated into any language. This translation makes Borghini's treatise available to students who do not read Italian but are interested in late Renaissance art and art theory, the Counter-Reformation, and sixteenth-century European culture. References to Borghini's treatise in English tend to be limited to small extracts previously translated by others or to the passages published by Paola Barrochi in her *Scritti d'arte del Cinquecento*.[8]

This translation was done from the Rosci-Labor facsimile of the 1584 Marescotti first edition. Study of the occasionally smudged and overprinted impression of Marescotti's primitive and loose type was facilitated by frequent examination of the more legible and more carefully edited second edition. The translation leans heavily on the editing of Bottari and the annotations of Rosci.

Borghini's punctuation and his spelling and presentation of proper names have been revised to make his argument more understandable and indexing more useful. This is consistent with the movement, begun one hundred years before the publication of *Il Riposo*, and firmly established by Pietro Bembo and Aldo Manuzio in their editions of Petrarch and Dante in 1501–2, to assist the reader with consistent modern punctuation and spelling.

> Sapend'io quanto di gratia si tolga alle parole nel trasportarle d'una in altra lingua, e quanto d'ornamento si spogliano i suggetti a levarli dal suo vivo fonte originale.
>
> (I know how much grace is lost from the words in transporting them to another language, and how much ornament is removed from the subjects in removing them from their original source.)
>
> Raffaello Borghini[9]

Acknowledgments

I wish my students were as indebted to me as I am to my teachers. Sumner Crosby was my first art history teacher. Vincent Scully encouraged my interest throughout a stormy undergraduate passage. Harvey Buchanan lured me away from political history. Ellen Landau was my first graduate teacher. Jennifer Neils greatly encouraged my interest in graduate study. Walter Gibson was my first graduate adviser. When I was discouraged, Edward Olszewski put me back to work and convinced me that this project was possible. In discussing possible dissertation topics, Professor Olszewski identified *Il Riposo* as a widely cited treatise that had never been translated or comprehensively studied in English and deserved a study updating the annotations that accompanied the 1967 Rosci-Labor facsimile edition. This led to a paper on the villa of Il Riposo and its original owner for Professor Olszewski's graduate seminar on 'Mannerism in Italian Art' at Case Western Reserve University in the spring of 1998. Professor Olszewski, who was also the adviser for my master's paper, patiently read and advised me on everything here.

I thank the members of my dissertation committee in addition to Edward Olszewski. Catherine Scallen's painstaking comments enriched the final form of my dissertation. Michael Altschul's avuncular good will was an inspiration to someone embarking on humanist scholarship. Recruited only a few months before the defence, because of the illness of a previous reader, Marie Lathers brought a wonderfully fresh perspective to the project. Linda Koch of John Carroll University served as an outside member of my oral examining committee. Anne Helmreich guided me through the labyrinths of garden history.

Three librarians at the Cleveland Museum of Art have been very helpful: Georgina Gy. Toth, Louis Adrean, and Christine Edmonson.

Stanley Johnston, Curator of Rare Books at the Holden Arboretum in Kirtland, Ohio, solved horticultural bibliographic puzzles.

Dr Luigi Federico Signorini of the Banca d'Italia arranged for a visit to his family's villa and was kind enough to examine and correct the part of my translation pertaining to the villa itself. Dr Giorgio Federico Signorini of the University of Florence and Mrs Signorini guided me through Il Riposo. Dr Giorgio Signorini also shared a draft of his manuscript history of the property, 'Vicende generali della proprietà Vecchietti a Vacciano.'

Denise Caterinacci of the Department of Modern Languages and Literatures at Case Western Reserve reviewed the prose introductions of each book of *Il Riposo* and also Borghini's discussion of Aristotle's theory of light and colour in the middle of Book II. Roger Manning of the History Department of Cleveland State University steered me through the military, political, and economic shrubbery of the sixteenth century. I am indebted to William Fackovec, SM, for his guidance concerning the Rosary.

Ron Schoeffel at the University of Toronto Press has been working on this book for several years. His enthusiasm, support, and encouragement would not allow the project to lapse. Anne Laughlin and Daniel Quinlan at the Press expedited publication and dissemination of this translation. Kate Baltais and Harold Otto were particularly helpful in their painstaking copy-editing of the manuscript.

I am indebted to my wife for her encouragement and advice over the many years of this endeavour. Gwendolyn Ruth Ellis took our best pictures of Il Riposo. David Bevan Ellis put up with the project.

Introduction

This is the eighth edition, and first translation, of Raffaello Borghini's *Il Riposo*. It is the most widely known Florentine document addressing the conservative iconographic issues raised by the Council of Trent (1545–63). It is also the best known Florentine statement concerning the Italian reaction against the florid style of the High *Maniera*. Sixteen years after Giorgio Vasari published the second edition of his *Vite*, Borghini focused on important issues that Vasari had avoided or ignored, or to which he was oblivious.

Vasari, at the urging of Grand Duke Cosimo I,[1] had proceeded with his usual energy to reform the physical organization of the two major religious foundations in Florence,[2] but little of the Counter-Reformation surfaced in his *Vite*. Religious decorum, in contrast, is the central message of *Il Riposo*. Borghini's treatise is celebrated or lamented as an essential document concerning the Counter-Reformation.[3]

Vasari was a heroically productive practitioner of the High *Maniera*, and his *Vite* was a paean to that style. As his second edition was being published, Vasari understandably ignored whatever reservations were emerging concerning Vasari's style. Borghini, in contrast, wrote one of the first widely read indictments of the High *Maniera* and championed those artists, notably Santi di Tito and Federico Barocci, who reacted against it.

Vasari constructed a historical model of the history of art that subsequent students employed until the last third of the twentieth century. For Vasari's first readers, however, that history ended with Michelangelo. Borghini was one of the first critics to try to deal with art history after him.

Usually contrasted with Vasari, Borghini deserves to be considered as an important figure on his own. Borghini distilled, out of the aristocratic chatter that surrounded him in the Medici grand ducal court, a few very simple criteria for judging the quality of a work of art. He then joined these principles into a system that any layman could use. Borghini's system not only determined the quality of an art object, it also determined whether the object was in the current style and, furthermore, ensured that the object conformed to the spirit of the Counter-Reformation. The subject matter of an object only needed to: (1) faithfully reflect the story it was based on; (2) show as little evidence as possible of any individuality of interpretation on the part of the artist; and (3) not be 'lascivious.' Evaluation of form and execution was even more straightforward, done simply on the basis of their mimetic achievement. This allowed Borghini to state explicitly that anyone who had ever seen anything qualified as an expert critic of the formal aspects of an image. In his discussion Borghini provided an 'unambiguous and unequivocal'[4] vocabulary for his readers. With this they could describe the iconographic and visual content, judge the quality, and make comparative judgments about works of art. Borghini would have his readers believe that the exercise of the art rhetoric he provided had the potential of making them as '*immortali*' in the arts as the practicing artists he described [458].[5]

The way Borghini applied his method of analysis was as important as his system. His discussants imagined that they were walking through the major public spaces of Florence, primarily churches, applying his system to what they saw. Thus, *Il Riposo* provided example after example of the direct application of what Borghini believed were the precepts of the Counter-Reformation, together with his interpretation of the Counter-*Maniera*.

Il Riposo has enjoyed several lives. It was the first art treatise specifically directed towards a lay audience, probably published as a handbook for the amateur collector or enthusiast The treatise contained: (1) instructions about what to look for; (2) a rapid review of Pliny and Vasari; and (3) a summary of developments in Venice and Florence in the sixteen years since the publication of Vasari's *Vite*. All of this was presented in a portable and enjoyable dialogue. Subsequently, *Il Riposo* was also used as a source of technical information concerning shop practice. The dialogue enjoyed a third life in the seventeenth and eighteenth centuries as a literary model of good sixteenth-century Tuscan, certified repeatedly as such by the Accademia della Crusca, the semi-official organization responsible for the purity of the Tuscan language then and the Italian language now. Today, the dialogue is valuable as an example of ducal Florence making the final transition from thirteenth-century Tuscan into modern Italian. Finally, Borghini's dialogue enjoys another life today as a document necessary for the understanding of its period, for the life and work of the artists of the Studiolo of Grand Duke Francisco, for Federigo Barocci, and for the sixteenth-century Venetians – particularly Tintoretto.

Borghini's Life and Writing

The life of Raffaello Borghini, the man who named Giambologna's *Rape of the Sabine,* is poorly documented. Much of our very limited understanding of the circumstances of his life depends on Borghini's poetry, and students of him differ in their very speculative interpretation of it. Borghini was probably born in 1537. He was the great nephew of Vincenzio Borghini, prior of the Ospedale degli Innocenti and counsellor and confidant of Giorgio Vasari. Vincenzio was a literary figure of such eminence that his contemporaries were not surprised when he turned down the archbishopric of Pisa so that he could continue his historical and philological studies in Florence. There is much confusion in the literature between Raffaello and Vincenzio Borghini. In the usual case Vincenzio is incorrectly credited with *Il Riposo.* Occasionally Raffaello is mistakenly credited with writings by Vincenzio.

Raffaello Borghini's father, Francesco, was a landowner with several houses in the vicinity of Pisa. He served the Medici in a variety of administrative positions and was a Knight of St Stephen. Borghini mentions his father once in the dialogue, as owner of a 'very beautiful' *Madonna and Child with Saints* 'done with great care' by Domenico Puligio [397]. Borghini's sentence suggests that his father was still living in the family home when the impoverished Raffaello was taken in by a patron to write *Il Riposo.*[6] Borghini's mother was Alessandra di Michele Buontempi.

Raffaello Borghini, born into an aristocratic and previously affluent Florentine family, became reduced in circumstances, and for this reason or perhaps because of some indiscretion, was forced to leave Florence. He probably then lived in Provence from 1572 to 1575 under an assumed name, enjoying the protection of Jean I de Pontèves, Comte de Carcès, and his wife. The count was a French general, admiral, and provincial administrator very active in the campaigns against the Huguenots. During this period Borghini may have earned his living as a dancing instructor.

Borghini probably then returned to Florence and resumed his friendship with the prominent Florentines Piero di Gherardo Capponi,

Bernardo Vecchietti, and Baccio Valori. Capponi would write the poem introducing *Il Riposo*. The dialogue was written as taking place at Bernardo Vecchietti's estate of Il Riposo. Vecchietti and Baccio Valori are two of the four discussants in the treatise.

For unknown reasons Borghini probably returned to France a second time in 1579–80, but otherwise he spent the rest of his life in Florence. As a young man he may have been connected with circles opposed to the Medici, but returning from France Borghini re-entered society in Florence around the court of Francesco as a man of letters, poet, collector, connoisseur, and writer of comedies. The Borghini family and Raffaello were typical of the Florentine aristocracy in oscillating between hostility to the Medici and attempts to insert themselves into the court and administration of the grand duchy. As a relatively young man Raffaello had addressed a poem to Archbishop Antonio Altoviti of Florence. An opponent of the Medici, Altoviti's ecclesiastical appointment had initially been blocked by Cosimo. Sometimes interpreted as an indication of opposition to the Medici, Borghini's poem may have been no more than an attempt to secure a handout from the austere archbishop. Borghini's dedication of *Il Riposo* to Don Giovanni de' Medici and the fact that *Il Riposo* reveals an intimate knowledge of Francesco's rooms in the Palazzo Vecchio suggests a close relationship with the ruling house after his return to Florence, however.

Most authors have rightly focused on the Counter-Reformation and Counter-*Maniera* as the most important aspects of Borghini's dialogue. Cristina Acidini Luchinat and Zygmunt Wazbinski, however, provide a different and important key to understanding the critical milieu that produced *Il Riposo*, a key to the audience Borghini was addressing and to the political and critical position Borghini was putting forward. Two important projects dominated Florentine discourse on art in the period between the second edition of Vasari's *Vite* in 1568 and the publication of *Il Riposo* in 1584: Federico Zuccaro's completion of the frescoes within the cupola of the cathedral of Santa Maria del Fiore and Alessandro Allori's completion of the frescoes in the salon of Leo X at Poggio a Caiano. The frescoes inside the cupola are, by area, the largest Christian fresco cycle ever completed.[7] Their size, together with the importance of Brunelleschi's dome to the self-image of the Florentines, made this a commission of great importance to the House of Medici. Allori had been a disappointed candidate to complete Vasari's work in Santa Maria del Fiore. His republican native Florentine supporters took the completion of these frescoes by Zuccaro, a Roman 'foreigner,' as an occasion for an undercover attack on the Medici. *Il Riposo* is the only contemporary published response defending Zuccaro's work, and Borghini's dialogue is thus a carefully understated defence of the Medici regime against discreet but still powerful currents of anti-Medici Florentine republicanism.[8]

Borghini made his precarious living as a man of letters. *Il Riposo* was the only thing he ever wrote about art. During his lifetime Borghini was known as a poet and, particularly, as a playwright. Although Sandra Orienti has stated that '[Borghini's] works have had no artistic significance for the history of poetry or of the theatre,'[9] her dismissal is belied by the publishing history of his work.[10] Borghini's first documented literary accomplishment was an only partially published poem in 179 octave verses, *La Veglia amorosa (The Loving Wakefulness). La Veglia amorosa* is in the genus of the allegorical-pastoral poetry of Boccaccio, Lorenzo de' Medici, and Poliziano. It provides the opportunity for a long discussion of Platonic and carnal love, which includes a perhaps overly detailed description of the nude heroine. Giulio Ferroni has said that *La Veglia amorosa,* like the paintings of Bronzino, reflected the not very repressed eroticism of the grand ducal court. Ferroni found that this erotic mood, derived from the songs of Ariosto, suffused Borghini's subsequent comedies. These comedies, although written at the same time, are quite different in tone from *Il Riposo,* where Borghini's upright discussants rail against 'lasciviousness.' Ferroni emphasized the tension pervading *Il Riposo* between Borghini's erotic Mannerist formal interests and the ideological requirements of the Counter-Reformation.

In 1572 the Spanish Franciscan Diego Serra published Borghini's *Sonetto ai Lèttori,* translated into Spanish, in a collection of poems printed in Zaragoza. Twelve years later, Borghini's first complete work printed in Italian, a translation of the *Treatise on the Origin of Jewish, Christian and Pagan Temples,* by Jean de Marconville (or Marcouville) was published in Florence in 1577 by Giorgio Marescotti.[11] Marescotti would subsequently publish *Il Riposo* and almost all of Borghini's work during Borghini's lifetime.

Borghini's first major independent work, *La Donna Costante,* a prose comedy with *intermedi* in verse, was published by Marescotti in 1578. *La Donna Costante* enjoyed a second printing in Florence and two additional printings in Venice; it was a retelling of the Romeo and Juliet story with a happy ending. A heroic–tragic quality attempted to enrich the sentimental character of the play, but this tended to get lost in the long frigid moralistic and sententious monologues that were then characteristic of Florentine dramatic practice. Borghini gave his female characters unusual prominence, probably to allow the introduction of more actresses but also to enhance the sentimental and languid tone of the play.

In 1578 Marescotti also published Borghini's *Canzone in morte della Sereniss. Reina Giovanna d'Austria Granduchessa di Toscana*, a tribute to Francesco's first wife. Borghini completed a second prose comedy with *intermedi* in verse, *L'Amante Furioso*, in 1583. It enjoyed a second printing in Venice. To modern ears, *L'Amante furioso* has some well-composed passages, particularly those involving the machinations and word play of the servants, but it is also marred by prolonged sentimental and moralistic monologues. *Il Riposo* was published in 1584. Two years later there was a *pastorale* comedy, *Diana Pietosa*, which had a second printing in Florence.

Ferroni summarized Borghini's dramatic work as 'a synthesis of moralism and hedonism' in which Borghini constructed dramatic entertainments that could be enjoyed 'in an atmosphere of controlled repression.' Ferroni located Borghini's plays, with their unrealistic stories, in the cultural history of the late sixteenth century as an example of the courtly neutralization and impoverishment of the 'sentimentality, tragedy, and paradoxical humor' that were 'the new and substantial elements of the Mannerist sensibility.'[12]

Borghini's last work published in his lifetime was a *Sonetto* included in a history of the Ubaldini family. Borghini has been associated with three other literary endeavours: a lost *Dialogue in Praise of Ignorance*, a collection of poems published in Florence by 'Filareto' in 1573, and three eclogues, also by a 'Philareto.'

Most of Borghini's surviving poetry was not published until 1822.[13] This collection included sixty-eight sonnets concerning love, religion, and morality. The sonnets were addressed to, among others, the *Il Riposo* discussants Bernardo Vecchietti and Baccio Valori. Some of the poems addressed to Vecchietti discussed his estate at Il Riposo. There was also a 'funeral *corona*' on the death of Piero di Gherardo Capponi, who wrote the introductory poem for the first edition of *Il Riposo*. There are songs dedicated to Archbishop Altoviti and the Countess de Carcès, together with a song on the death of Cosimo and a sonnet dedicated to the French Cardinal Georges d'Armagnac, which has been interpreted to suggest that Raffaelo had worked as a dancing master. The sonnets that Borghini identified in a surviving manuscript as his best evoke the atmosphere of the *Veglia amorosa* but with greater polish. The ambience is Arcadian with the real protagonists supposedly camouflaged with the fictitious names of shepherds that are often anagrams of their real names. The sentiments expressed are frequently diluted by the rhythm of the poetry.

In his dedication of *La Diana pietosa* Borghini said that he had experienced a psychological crisis from which he had been rescued by Baccio Valori. Borghini reported that Valori installed him in a villa outside of Florence and made it possible for Borghini to complete *La Diana pietosa* and *Il Riposo*. Critics are divided on whether Borghini was reporting a genuine psychological crisis or just acknowledging the assistance of a wealthy friend and patron.[14]

Giambologna had completed his *Rape of the Sabine* [71–5 and 165–9] in 1583, an event very much in the air as Borghini was completing *Il Riposo*. If Borghini's account of naming this statue is true [73], as is universally accepted by students of Giambologna, then that would be Borghini's most lasting achievement other than writing *Il Riposo*.

Over the last eight years of his life, following his return from France, Borghini's precarious financial situation gradually improved. He assembled a *Wunderkammer* that included important works of art. In 1584, after what Barocchi described as '*una vita avventurosa*,'[15] he may have professed as a Benedictine, the same year that Marescotti published his *Il Riposo*. 'His youthful fiber weakened by the adventurous life he had conducted,'[16] Borghini was buried in Santa Croce on 26 December 1588. His portrait by Ridolfo Sirigatti [22] was destroyed in Berlin during the Second World War.

The Social and Artistic Background for Borghini in Florence

Il Riposo is a flexible, very Florentine interpretation of the Counter-Reformation and of the 'new seriousness' with which the second half of the sixteenth century reacted against the hothouse artistic style of the High *Maniera*. The Florentines embraced the Counter-Reformation and the Counter-*Maniera* very carefully and with considerable ambivalence. Their response lacked the clarity and passion of Carlo Borromeo in Milan or the orthodox open-mindedness and good will of Gabriele Paleotti in Bologna. Borghini's dialogue expressed the precious and more or less strait-laced ambiance of the now-provincial court of Grand Duke Francesco.

Despite many real or rumoured personal excesses, the sixteenth-century Medici court had always been, or tried to be, upright in public. Borghini's attitude towards iconography was the official position of the ducal Medici: authoritative means ensured that art was decorous and straightforward. Fortunately for Medici political and ecclesiastical goals, this happened to agree conveniently with the final decrees of the Council of Trent. Of necessity, Borghini's standard of public decorum was flexible. The reality of the new Grand Duchess Bianca Capello was recognized without, obviously, mentioning how she had gotten there.[17] Borghini was as ambivalent stylistically as he was iconographically. Although he criticized the contorted excesses of the *Maniera* and made a case for compositional clarity and visual logic, his heart belonged to clever poses, virtuosity in execution, and lush colour. Rosci emphasized the accuracy with which Borghini described a Florentine artistic and literary community, by habit courtly and bigoted, 'inexorably pushed to the margins of history' 'and also aware, in a pathetic way, of the enormous inheritance on their shoulders, now exchanged for the pocket change of Borghini.'[18]

Brian Richardson described the characteristics that distinguished Florentine publishing during the sixteenth century. Florence had a 'strongly nationalistic and introspective climate.' Authors and editors addressed readers who, as a matter of course, were assumed to be Florentine. Most books printed in Florence were intended to promote the city and dealt with subjects that would interest Florentines. Richardson's characterization perfectly fits *Il Riposo*.[19]

If Borghini was born in 1537, his birth coincided with the final convulsive episode in the tumultuous half-century in Florence that followed the death of Lorenzo the Magnificent. This period included two rowdy expulsions of the Medici (1494 and 1527), two forceful Medici restorations (1512 and 1531), and two intervening rough-and-tumble republican episodes. The time saw Savonarola dominating Florence (1494–98), famine and plague (1496), siege and sack (1529–30), economic destitution, and several varieties of misrule. In 1537 the seventeen-year-old Cosimo established himself as the successor of his assassinated distant relative Alessandro, defeated his republican enemies at Montemurlo, received the imperial patent as duke from Charles V, and began the restrictive but pacific reign of his branch of the House of Medici that would last 206 years.

Borghini was a child and young man under the vigorous Cosimo; thereafter, Borghini was a subject of the retiring Francesco. During Borghini's life, Florence could not recover the international political, economic, and artistic dominance it had enjoyed during the thirteenth, fourteenth, and fifteenth centuries.[20] The early Medici grand dukes, however, restored their fief to local prosperity if not international prominence and presided over a final creative coda in the arts. This was a period of political passivity during which Florence obsequiously deferred to Habsburg hegemony in Italy, but it was also a period of considerable intellectual and artistic activity.

Borghini's childhood (1537–50) was, a period of consolidation for Florence. Foundations were laid for projects that would characterize the second half of the century. Cosimo's most important project was dynastic; in 1539 he married Eleonora of Toledo, daughter of the Emperor's viceroy in Naples. This produced an heir, Francesco, in 1541 and then a second heir, Fernando, to whom Borghini would refer as 'Cardinal Ernando' because Fernando only succeeded to the grand duchy on the death of his elder brother three years after *Il Riposo* was published. During Borghini's childhood, Bronzino began work on Eleonora's Chapel in the Palazzo Vecchio [535–6] and painted his *Exposure of Luxury*. Pontormo began his frescoes in the choir of San Lorenzo [78–83 and 484–5]. In Rome, Michelangelo completed the *Last Judgment* [513–14] and the Pauline frescoes [515], and Salviati painted the *Glorification of Pope Paul III* in the Farnese Palace [503]. During this period Copernicus published *On the Revolution of Heavenly Orbs*, Vesalius completed *De Humani corporis fabrica*, Ignatius Loyola founded the Society of Jesus, and Pope Paul III opened the Council of Trent (in 1545).

Borghini's childhood was a busy time for compilers and treatise writers interested in art. In Florence the last entries were made to the *Libro di Antonio Billi*, Agnolo Firenzuola published his *Dialogo delle bellezze della donne*, the anonymous *Magliabechiano Manuscript* was completed, and Benedetto Varchi published his *Lezioni*. In Venice, Marcantonio Michiel added the final notes to his *Notizia d'opere di disegno*, and Paolo Pino published his *Dialogo della pittura*. In Portugal, Francesco Hollanda published his dialogue *Tracto de pintura antiqua*. During this period Vasari was at work, apparently with the knowledge and anticipation of all Italy (Pino's *Dialogo* of 1548 indicates that Pino was aware of Vasari's monumental effort); he finally published the first edition of the *Vite* in 1550.

Borghini's adolescence (1551–56) saw some of the largest projects of the duchy completed, for better or worse. Cosimo began and completed the major military project of grand ducal Florence, his difficult and protracted siege of Siena. Pontormo died without completing his choir frescoes at San Lorenzo. Pontormo and the Medici had hoped this fresco cycle would challenge the Sistine Chapel. It did not [78–83 and 484–5]. The Medici turned to a different style when Vasari began work in the Palazzo Vecchio. Benvenuto Cellini finished the cast of his *Perseus*. During this period High Mannerism swept Italy: Salviati completed the *Story of David* in the Palazzo Sacchetti [503].

Borghini's twenties (1557–66) were in many areas a time of ending and a time of beginning: Michelangelo died, Cosimo resigned, Bronzino finished Eleonora's Chapel, the Council of Trent issued its final decrees, Vasari published the final edition of the *Vite*, and the Spanish established the first permanent European settlement in North America. When Borghini was in his twenties, his father served the Medici as *Auditore* and Raffaello produced his first known literary effort, *La Veglia amorosa*. A great flood swept away the Santa Trìnita Bridge [594], and Cosimo captured Montalcino, completing the geographical limits of the grand duchy. Francesco married Joanna of Austria the year after an exhausted and failing Cosimo retired from government. Francesco Guicciardini, shunted aside by the grand dukes, began publishing his *History of Italy*. Ammannati began working on the Pitti Palace and completed his *Neptune Fountain* [66–71, 164–5, and 593–4], and Giambologna completed his Hermes [587]. During this period, Vasari and Cosimo (whose retirement did not preclude a continuing involvement in the arts) started their reform of the appearance of Santa Croce and Santa Maria Novella, began the Uffizi, completed their redecoration of the Palazzo Vecchio [546–8], and founded the Accademia del Disegno. This was another important period for the treatise writers, in addition to Vasari. Gilio published his *Due dialoghi ... degli errori ed abusi de' pittori ...* [53–4], Cellini completed his *Autobiography*, and Dolce published his *Dialogo della pittura intitolato l'Aretino*.

Raffaello's thirties (1567–76) were a quiet time for Florence. Borghini's *Sonetto ai Lettori* was published in Spain, and his translation of the *Treatise on the Origin of Jewish, Christian, and Gentile Temples* in Florence. Cosimo in retirement was finally named grand duke of Tuscany but he, and Vasari, died five years later. Elsewhere the Spanish and Venetians overwhelmed the unbelieving Turks at Lepanto, and Catherine de' Medici struck down the unbelieving Huguenots on St Bartholomew's Day. Vasari completed Francesco's *Studiolo* in the Palazzio Vecchio (Borghini gave the credit to Buontalenti [610–11]). Ammannati finished his work on the Pitti Palace (for Borghini, 'the New Palace').[21] During Borghini's thirties Mercator published the first comprehensive map of the world, Luís Camões published *Os Lusíadas*, and Tasso was at work on *Gerusalemme liberata*. Vicenzo Danti published his *Il Primo Libro*, Palladio published *The Four Books of Architecture*, and Carlo Borromeo issued his *Instructionum*.

In his forties (1577–86), as Florence continued to slow down, Borghini entered his most productive literary period. After publishing *La Donna Costante*, Borghini apparently returned briefly to France. Returning to Florence Borghini published *L'Amante Furioso*, *Il Riposo*, and *Diana Pietosa*. Then Borghini may have professed as a Benedictine. Joanna of Austria died, and Francesco immediately married Bianca Cappello. Montaigne published his *Essays*, and Pope Gregory XIII reformed the calendar. There was a flurry of publishing on the arts during this period: Cristoforo Sorte completed his *Osservazioni* in Venice, and Francesco Sansovino's *Venetia citta nobilissima* appeared; Gabriele Paleotti published his *Discorso*; Ammannati's *Lettera agli Accademia del Disegno* was released; Lomazzo published his *Trattato*; Alessandro Lamo completed his *Discorso*; and Armenini published his *De' veri precetti*.

Borghini died in 1588, the year the Spanish Armada was repulsed. Mary Queen of Scots had gone to the block, and Francesco and Bianca Cappello had died the year before. Fortunately for Francesco and for Florence, there had been no crises during Francesco's reign. The second grand duke never perfected the perpetual motion machine that Borghini had mentioned with skepticism [613] but Francesco did build Pratolino and found the Uffizi Gallery, the Medici Theatre, and the Accademia della Crusca.

Borghini's Florentine Antecedents

Tuscan writing on the arts antedated *Il Riposo* by more than 250 years.[22] Dante, in describing the marble reliefs representing humility along the passage to purgatory, imagined the reliefs surpassing both nature and antiquity,[23] implying that an artist (as Borghini imagines Michelangelo [509]) might so improve on nature and the antique as to approach the divine. The wording of Petrarch's bequest of Giotto's *Mother and Child* to Francesco I of Carrara, his last patron, revealed that Petrarch admired Giotto's art because it appealed to the knowledgeable. This was the first suggestion in the Renaissance literature of an informed appreciation of art by non-artists. Although this idea of the informed appreciation of art by non-artists was immediately taken up by Boccaccio, the Villani, and subsequent writers, it would be two hundred years before *Il Riposo* became the first art treatise specifically addressed to lay people [127–8]. Boccaccio included a tale concerning Giotto in the *Decameron*, claiming that Giotto replaced Byzantine art with Roman art and 'brought to light again that art which had laid buried,'[24] a formula that would be at the beginning of almost all subsequent surveys of Italian art, including Borghini's [297], until the twentieth century.

The first of his Florentine act-critic forebears explicitly recognized by Borghini was Leon Battista Alberti. There was a surge of interest in Alberti in the middle of the sixteenth century with the publication of four Italian translations of his work, including two probably done specifically for use in the curriculum of the Accademia del Disegno.[25] Although Alberti's *De pictura*, which Borghini specifically cites, was noted for its lucid exposition of one-point linear perspective, Borghini stays as far away from linear perspective as possible [141 and 178].[26]

In a scheme of organization directly derived from classical rhetoric, Alberti divided painting into three parts: *circumscription, composition,* and *receptio luminum*.[27] His discussion was much more profound and detailed than Borghini's simple division of painting into 'invention, composition, pose, parts, and colour' [52], but Alberti's concept underlies *Il Riposo*. For Alberti, *circumscriptio* referred to the practice of defining objects, as Apelles was thought to have done, by means of very fine lines. This was the intellectual basis, which Alberti was the first to clearly articulate, of the Florentine linear style. For Borghini, as for Vasari and all of Alberti's Florentine successors, *circumscriptio* is *disegno*, the foundation of the visual arts that Borghini would define as 'an apparent demonstration, with lines, of that which is first conceived in the intellect of man' [137].

Alberti divided *compositio* into an ascending four-tier hierarchy of constituent parts: surfaces form members, which form bodies, which form the *historia*. Borghini uses a somewhat analogous system, inverting the order. He begins with 'composition,' which is made up of 'poses,' which, in turn, consist of 'parts.'

For Alberti, *receptio luminum* was the application of tone and hue, which, although in concept like painting by numbers and never enjoying the esteem in Florence that it deservedly received in Venice, demanded, according to Alberti, particular skill from the painter. Borghini grudgingly agrees with this in his general discussion of colour in Book II and his historical description of individual Venetian painters in Book IV.

Alberti discussed *historia*, 'invention' for Borghini, separately from his discussion of the other elements of painting. Borghini also separates his discussion of invention in Book I from his discussion of 'parts, poses, composition, and colour' in Book II. Both agreed that *historia* or 'invention' was the essence of painting, even more important than *disegno*. On our side of the Mannerist interlude, Borghini would communicate to the second half of the sixteenth century Alberti's conviction that the important elements of *historia* are decorum and clarity. Alberti also introduced, as a criterion of the quality of a painting, that it have an 'abundance and variety of objects,' a principle that Borghini frequently repeats.

Borghini agreed [140] with Alberti's initial recommendation that the artist practise by drawing from nature and avoid copying other artists. Later in life, however, Alberti recommended in *De statua*, his third treatise on the arts, the practice of copying sculpture in the training of painters, establishing an academic practice (which Borghini inconsistently commends [139]) that would continue until the twentieth century.

Alberti's idea that beauty is a harmony of parts not obtainable by mere imitation but involving a selection of the best of nature, the assembly of a compound of superior parts, is reflected in Borghini's repeated retelling of the story of Zeuxis and the Crotonian maidens, a story in which Zeuxis created a painting of an idealized Helen of Troy by combining the best features of several young models, a composite procedure derived from Aristotle's notion of the ideal. Both Alberti and Borghini used decorum in several senses. In one sense, decorum was basic to Alberti's concept of beauty, and referred to the relation between parts. Beauty required measure and harmony. Figures were beautiful only if their parts agreed with each other in size and function. Borghini repeatedly stresses this when his discussants examine the style of what they see.

In Book III of *De pictura* Alberti discusses the education of the artist. Alberti adapts the Horatian maxim *ut pictura poesis* to take the painter out of the artisan's shop and make him 'one with poets and orators,' learned in the liberal arts and drawing his subject matter from history and mythology. In doing this Alberti not only tries to make the painter a gentleman but also tried to make painting narrative. Because of a perceived need for fidelity to whatever biblical story or classical myth was selected,[28] and the need to reject whatever was unseemly or inappropriate in these stories, Alberti introduced into painting the need for decorum in a second sense, in which decorum was the relationship of the *historia* or 'invention' to the story or myth from which it was drawn. Decorum in this sense is the Counter-Reformation leitmotiv of *Il Riposo*.

After saying twice that he would like the ideal painter to be 'learned in the liberal arts,' Alberti lowers the bar and admits to the advisability of a learned adviser: 'Phidias, more famous than other painters, confessed that he had learned from Homer the poet, how to paint Jove with much divine majesty.'[29] Although Borghini attempts to elevate the status of painting, as distinct from painters, he shows no interest in the education of painters, and his basic attitude towards them is that they should do what they are told.

The imperfect reflection of Leonardo's thought, his so-called *Trattato della pittura*, was not in print before 1651. Variant manuscript versions of Leonardo's ideas, however, circulated widely in Florence in the second half of the sixteenth century. Borghini clearly used one of these manuscripts in preparing *Il Riposo*.[30]

The visual impact of the immensely energetic Giorgio Vasari dominated the artistic consciousness of Borghini and his contemporaries.[31] Borghini's life of Vasari, the third longest one in *Il Riposo*, focuses almost entirely on Vasari as an artist. Borghini's recognition of Vasari as a writer, in contrast, is fleeting and his tone towards his predecessor may be condescending. Vasari the writer receives only two very brief notices [249–50 and 550]. In one of these, however, the prologue to Book III, which introduces Borghini's lives, Borghini explains that his own historical survey will be short and suggests that 'some desiring to understand these things ... with respect to the moderns will be fully satisfied with the *Lives* of Vasari, which he wrote with great care' [249–50]. Most commentators on Borghini since the eighteenth century have touched less on the extent to which Borghini reacted to the visual presence of Vasari and more on the extent to which Borghini quoted or paraphrased biographical information from Vasari's *Vite*.[32] Although Schlosser-Magnino maintains that 'the only person who can be considered with any justice as the successor of Vasari is Raffaele [*sic*] Borghini,'[33] many critics have dismissed Borghini for his dependence on his predecessor.

Up to his discussion of Michelangelo, Borghini not only discusses artists in the same order that Vasari used but also deploys his excerpts from Vasari in the same order that Vasari used them. Then, from his discussion of Michelangelo to his discussion of Vasari, Borghini increasingly adds items to Vasari's account. In the final ninety-eight pages of his treatise, Borghini discusses artists living in 1584 (Tintoretto through Giovanni Caccini). Vasari did not give individual lives to any of these artists: Vasari mentioned twenty-four and was mute regarding eight. Borghini is particularly valuable in his discussion of these contemporaries.

In the first edition of his *Vite*, with Michelangelo alive, Vasari could position Michelangelo as the pinnacle of art. In the second edition of 1568, four years after the death of Michelangelo, Vasari was faced with the logical decline or end of the history of art. Vasari chose to avoid this problem by suggesting that, although further progress in *disegno* was no longer possible, nor attempts in that direction desirable, progress continued to be possible in invention and in colour. Unlike Vasari, Borghini never explicitly enunciates a scheme of history or historical development. Borghini treats Michelangelo as an isolated phenomenon, unrelated to the progression or regression of the arts. Borghini is oblivious to fears outside of Florence, epitomized by Armenini, that Italian art was in decline.

A reader not conditioned by Vasari might assume from reading *Il Riposo* that there is no stylistic difference between Michelangelo and Giotto. Neither would there generally appear to be any stylistic progression within the oeuvre of any individual artist. Borghini's discussion, copied from Vasari, of three stylistic phases in the work of Raphael is exceptional. So is the rare reference to individual deterioration from excessive drink, age or, in the case of Pontormo, exposure to German prints. The stylistic progression of an individual artist, as described by Borghini, is formulaic and predictable: a promising apprenticeship (sometimes preceded by the precocious drawing, say, of animals with a stick in the sand) and an intermediate period as a capable or worthy practitioner (*valenthuomo*) imperceptibly merging into mastery.

Vasari, like Borghini, defines painting, sculpture, and architecture as *arti del disegno*, with *disegno* variously used by both Vasari and Borghini to mean 'drawing,' 'design,' or both. For Vasari, in the Florentine tradition, having dealt with *disegno*, painting was almost an afterthought: 'a plane covered with patches of color on the surface ... filling up the outlines ... which ... surround the figure,'[34] echoing Alberti and in turn echoed by Borghini: 'painting is a plane covered with various colours' [170].

Vasari knew from his own creative experience how difficult patrons could be, and he weaves a fascinating history of patronage into his history. Borghini, in contrast, generally elaborates on patronage only in principle. In Book I, and in occasional asides thereafter, Borghini makes it clear that it is the patron's responsibility to keep the artist in his place as the factual transcriber of the inventions of others. Borghini briefly discusses whether the artist or the patron is responsible for errors in decorum [98–9] and reminds his readers that although the patron's association with an object may be forgotten the artist's connection with the object is always remembered. In most of *Il Riposo,* Borghini's recognition of actual patronage is limited to a simple identification of the donor, for example, 'the Chapel of the Salviati,' with an occasional effusive description of the patron, for example, 'the Chapel of Camillo Albizi, the honoured gentleman who pleases himself so much in doing courtesies, will be done to [Alessandro Allori's] design in San Pier Maggiore' [636]. Very rarely does Borghini dwell on the relationship of patron to artist. An exception is his discussion of Macchietti's unemployment on his return from Naples: 'Finally he has returned to Florence and gone to making some portraits for private gentlemen, meanwhile waiting for the occasion of showing his virtue more greatly in public. And truly they who are able should not waste time in employing him in paintings for all to see before he, who today finds himself at forty-nine years of age, is worsened by time and loses that vigour that in all men, and particularly in painters and in sculptors, at a certain time in their life is seen to be consumed' [607].

Vasari was the first writer on art to stress the importance of collections, his own collection of drawings and the collections of others. Borghini describes the collections of two of his discussants in detail [13–15 and 18–22], and in the subsequent historical sections he more briefly discusses the collections of other patrons and collectors.

An important influence on Borghini was Raffaello's great-uncle, Vincenzio Borghini,[35] whose correspondence with Vasari had urged a less polemic and more factual approach in Vasari's second edition, a more generally Italian, rather than Florentine, point of view. Vincenzio Borghini also suggested less discussion of biographical details and more discussion of works, with more detailed information concerning their locations and subjects. These ideas are reflected in the tone, character, and organization of his great-nephew's treatise.

Vincenzio Borghini was the first Florentine to explicitly consider the overall effect of a picture. In a famous simile (which his great-nephew reuses) he compares the harmony, proportion, and 'agreeable discordance' (*discordanza concorde*) of a good piece of music to that of a good painting, a piece of pictorial music (*musica pittoresca*).[36] Raffaello takes his method of evaluating the technical quality of an art object directly from his great-uncle. Vincenzio had also based his assessment of the quality of produced images on the degree of their mimetic accuracy.[37]

In the second half of the sixteenth century there was an important change in the writing of art theory. Previously it had been written mostly by artists. Increasingly it would be written by writers without workshop experience: Vincenzo and Raffaello Borghini, Dolce, Gilio, Varchi, Bocchi, and Comanini. When an artist like Armenini wrote, ostensibly for other artists, material of no immediate use in the workshop was included. This change occurred because of a new kind of reader. For the first time since classical antiquity, theory was being addressed to an educated lay audience.

Other Influences

The extremely popular dialogue guidebook *Tutte le cose notabili che sono in Venetia* was published in 1556 by Francesco Sansovino, son of Jacopo Sansovino. *Tutte le cose* went into ten editions during Francesco's lifetime and is our principle source for the paintings destroyed by the fire in the Palazzo Ducale in 1577. Subsequently, Francesco published (he was the intermittent owner of a press) his much more ambitious fourteen-volume *Venetia città nobilissima* in 1581, the first comprehensive description of a city to include its works of art. Francesco's guides were the descendents of the ancient *mirabilia*, and, like similar guides to Rome appearing in the sixteenth century, recognized Venice as a tourist destination. Borghini takes up this form in his four tours through Florence in Books I and II. Richardson points out that Sansovino and other Venetian authors played an important role in the diffusion of print and literacy in the second half of the sixteenth century by 'making history easier to read and digest by translating, rearranging and summarizing the work of classical and modern historians.'[38] This is precisely Borghini's project.

Giovanni Paolo Lomazzo's lengthy and discursive *Trattato dell'arte della pittura, scultura ed architettura*, published in Milan in the same year as *Il Riposo*, has been described as 'the *summa* of late Renaissance theory of art.'[39] Lomazzo shares with Borghini a preoccupation with the 'seven principal colours' [230–240] adapted from Aristotelian colour science. Each colour is associated with one of the seven metals, seven planets, etc. Lomazzo added the seven animals. Borghini adds the seven jewels, seven sacraments, and seven liturgical seasons of the year.

Giovanni Battista Armenini's *De' veri precetti della pittura* was published in Ravenna in 1586. Armenini wrote his treatise in response to what he perceived to be a profound deterioration in art in the second half of the sixteenth century, a theme that would be taken up by the classic-idealists of the next century. For Armenini, not only painting but nature itself was 'declining and has become so graceless and unrecognizable that, even among a great number of people, we can hardly find bodies and limbs that could be considered good without improvement by skillful men.'[40] Armenini dates this decline to the first edition of Vassari's *Vite* and attributes the decline to the failure of the great masters of the first part of the sixteenth century to teach, the absence of artistic figures of equal stature to replace them, and a general depreciation of the art of painting. Armenini's treatise, an attempt to address this problem through better education for young artists, paralleled the establishment, for the same reason, of art academies in Rome, Florence, and Bologna during the same period. Armenini's preoccupation with artistic decline does not occur to Borghini. *Il Riposo* plows forward through the later sixteenth century in full confidence that Florentine craftsmen, trained by Florentine masters and responsive to educated Florentine advisers, will continue the inevitable advance of Florentine artistic achievement.

In the twenty-fifth and final session of the Council of Trent, which dealt with painting, the council prohibited the posting in churches of images derived from erroneous doctrine that could mislead the ignorant and demanded that all impurity be avoided and that there be no attractively provocative imagery.[41] Such censure had a strong grounding in antiquity. The sixteenth century had to look no further than Pliny, Aristotle, and Plato for strong strictures against art or artists perceived to be inimical to public morality. Marcia Hall, however, considers it significant and consistent with the carefully balanced tone of Florentine religious reform that Borghini, at that time a layman, was the Counter-Reformation spokesman in Florence.[42] There the Medici implemented those strictures of the Council of Trent that advanced their interests and ignored those that did not. Cosimo, attentive to protecting the literary heritage of Florence, which was so important an element in the prestige of his grand duchy, and to protecting the Florentine book trade, which was a significant local industry, staged only two token demonstration bonfires of heretical books after the appearance of Pope Paul IV's Index in 1559. Cosimo pointedly denied the Church the destruction of all the copies that it had requested.[43]

In Florence, before the council had been called there had been Savonarola and before Savonarola there was the redoubtable Antonio Pierozzi, first prior of the reconstituted San Marco, subsequently Archbishop of Florence, and ultimately canonized in 1523 as St Antoninus. Pierozzi's *Summa Theologica* may have been more studied in his time than that of Thomas Aquinas. In it he inveighs against painters: 'when they make images that provoke to desire ... such as naked women and the like. They are to be condemned who paint things that are against the faith ... an image of the Trinity one Person with three heads ... or ... in the Annunciation ... the little boy ... to be sent fully formed into the womb of the Virgin ... or the little Jesus with a tablet of letters, when [he wasn't old enough to read]. But neither are they to be praised when they paint apocrypha, such as midwives at the Virgin's delivery or her girdle being sent down ... to the Apostle Thomas.'[44]

By 1584 no one in Florence had actually heard Savonarola for eighty-six years; it had been twenty years since the aged Michelangelo was said to have still remembered the charismatic preacher's voice. Nevertheless, Savonarola's ideas of republicanism and religious and moral reform remained very much in the culture, and the Medici were sensitive to the Dominican's ideas and to the potential political power of subsequent generations of his followers. Borghini does not, however, write Savonarola out of his history. The prior is mentioned very carefully and relatively neutrally in Borghini's life of Fra Bartolomeo [379].

In his *Sermons* Savonarola did not preach against all paintings in churches. Savonarola, like Borghini, endorsed Gregory the Great's idea of religious art as the textbook of the unlettered. What Savaronola railed against were indecent paintings, particularly when they were bad: 'no composition should be allowed which arouses laughter by its mediocrity.'[45] On one hand, Borghini echoes Savonarola's criticism of seductive religious paintings ('How disgusting are lascivious figures in sacred temples' [83]) and shares Savanorola's criticism of the portrayal of identifiable living people as religious figures in paintings [98]. On the other, although Borghini does not address the perfection or imperfection of nature, he would probably not have agreed with Savonarola, who believed that man-made art was inferior to the inherent perfection of nature.

In 1570 a northerner, Johannes Molanus, rector of the university at Leuven, published his *De picturis*, the first important publication concerning the implications of the Council of Trent for religious imagery. For Italians, however, the strictest and most lucid interpretation of the edicts of the council came from St Charles Borromeo. Borromeo had dominated the third session of the council (1562-63) at the age of twenty-four in his capacity as the Cardinal Archbishop of Milan and Secretary of State for his mother's brother, Angelo de' Medici, Pope Pius IV.[46] Borromeo's 1577 *Instructionum* outlined his ideas of what the proscriptions of the council meant in obsessive detail. Paintings should be clear and direct and move the viewer to piety. Portraits should be accurate. Non-essential animals were banned. Although Borromeo outlined the kind of iconographic obedience that Borghini promotes, St Charles is mentioned only once in *Il Riposo,* as the recipient [628] of the gift from Francesco de' Medici of a copy by Alessandro Allori of the *Annunciation of Florence* in the Annunziata.

Borromeo's friend and associate, Archbishop Gabriele Paleotti, wrote his *Discorso intorno alle imagini sacre e profane* to implement the decisions of the council in Bologna. Never finished, a draft of the *Discorso* was published in 1582. It found a wide audience throughout the Roman Catholic world. Like Zeuxis, Paleotti took the best parts of what was intellectually available in Bologna, sampling from the thought of local jurists, philosophers, scholars including Pirro Ligorio, and artists including Prospero Fontana and Domenico Tibaldi. In religious painting Paleotti carefully but firmly denounces obscurity, symbol, allegory, artistic pride, ignorance, and incompetence as sin. Paleotti, like Lomazzo, integrated form and substance in his discussion of decorum. For Paleotti, images need to be appropriate in three ways: each part of the painting must be suitable; the parts must be consonant with each other (*la debita consonanza*); and the parts must fit appropriately into the picture as a whole (to form a *bon concerto*). Thus, good narrative not only had the correct figures but also they were in the right place.[47] The 'Christian Artist' would 'imitate the truth' in clear, simple, and easily understood paintings. This was reform based on naturalism in image and accuracy of subject and would strongly influence the Carracci. Ultimately, however, the Church would reject Paleotti's straightforward imagery and turn to the Baroque style.

Borghini's Counter-Reformation message, although lacking the thoroughness and logic of Borromeo and Paleotti, is an orthodox exposition of their ideas, particularly with respect to iconography. Another newly anti-*Maniera* voice in Florence was that of Bartolommeo Ammanati. Having fallen under the influence of the Jesuits, Ammanati proclaimed in a *Lettera agli Accademia del Disegno* in 1582 that his own nude figures were an occasion for sin. Ammanati's letter was very much in the air while Borghini was writing *Il Riposo,* and Borghini alludes to it twice [110 and 595].

Marcia Hall questions how the supposed proscriptions of the council were, in fact, communicated to the artist and critic.[48] The historical assumption has been generally that the sixteenth century was a highly authoritarian environment in which ecclesiastical authorities dictated standards for church decorations. In fact, however, the Council of Trent was extremely vague about the details of desired sacred images. Although the guidelines of the council crystallized into precise norms in the writing of Borromeo and Paleotti, Hall believes that there was 'more broad-based support and less authoritarian imposition in the reform of religious art than we have been supposing.' In reviewing Hall's book, however, Charles Hope has commented: 'It is now a commonplace among art historians that the Tridentine decrees, initially at least, did not have a direct effect on the activity of artists, in the form of instructions handed down by the ecclesiastical authorities.'[49]

There was great enthusiasm in the Renaissance for the dialogue format as a means of communicating information about almost everything. This was the consequence of the enormous diffusion of the Platonic dialogue that resulted from the spread of Humanism.[50] In contrast to a prose treatise such as Alberti's *De pictura*, a dialogue, in the tradition going back to Cicero and Lucian and then back to Plato, encourages a discursive and conversational system of argument. Avanzini identifies two types of Renaissance dialogues: those, whose charm and effectiveness result from an imitation of the lively give and take of Plato's dialogues and those which use the dialogue format as a superficial veneer for a prose essay. Avanzini finds *Il Riposo* securely in the second camp and wonders how Borghini found as protagonists 'three poor Florentine gentlemen who had the patience to listen and keep silent for such a long time,' while the fourth gentleman carries on for an uninterrupted 158 pages in Book III. In Borghini's defence, however, she notes that the dialogue format is perhaps not well suited to the didactic information he intended to convey.[51]

Borghini specifically mentions Baldassare Castiglione's *Il Cortegiano* (*The Courtier*), written in 1508 and published in 1528. In *Il Cortegiano*, courtiers attending the Duchess of Urbino discuss the proper education of the ideal aristocrat. As in *Il Riposo*, the discussants are all historical persons. Although Castiglione does touch on art, his importance for Borghini is the incorporation of Castiglione's vocabulary and description of courtly manners into subsequent sixteenth-century discourse, including the discussions at Il Riposo. Borghini, however, completely misses the essential quality of Castiglione's courtier, the one that northern Europe mimicked as the pattern for civilized deportment for several subsequent centuries. This was Castiglione's *sprezzatura*, the ability to perform a difficult task with ease and elegance.[52] There is a great deal of very obvious intellectual huffing and puffing by Borghini's discussants. For them, an important indication of high quality in a work of art frequently is the expression of 'great,' or even better, 'very great care in execution.'

Paolo Pino published his *Dialogo della pittura* in 1548 in Venice. It was the first substantial theoretical art treatise by a Venetian and the first important one in dialogue format. Pino divided the elements of painting into *disegno, invenzione,* and *colore,* following the pattern of the first three elements of rhetoric, *inventio, dispositio,* and *elocutio.* His division, simpler than those of Alberti and Borghini, proved immensely popular. In the good-natured character of his dialogue Pino invented the description of the perfect painter, endlessly quoted by later authors including Borghini, as someone combining the colour of Titian and the form of Michelangelo.

Lodovico Dolce drew much of his *Dialogo della pittura intitolato l'Aretino,* published in 1557, from Pietro Aretino's letter–treatises, *Lettere sull'arte,* published in six volumes between 1537 and 1557. The *Dialogo* was a spirited Venetian polemic, but it dealt even-handedly with Michelangelo and Raphael. Dolce, a friend of Aretino, was a professional writer on a variety of subjects and, like Borghini, he was known to his contemporaries primarily as a writer of comedies. In a further parallel, the *Dialogo della pittura* was Dolce's only work of art criticism.

The *Due dialoghi ... degli errori ed abusi de' pittori* were published in Camerino in 1564, the year after the final decrees of the Council of Trent, by Giovanni Andrea Gilio. The second of the *Due dialoghi,* which has to do with art, is the only Counter-Reformation document that Borghini explicitly acknowledges [53–4 and 82]. Gilio has become notorious for his criticism of the nudity, differing ages of the resurrected, wind in the garments, Charon, Christ without a beard, Mary frightened, resurrected souls kissing, and other perceived liberties in Michelangelo's *Last Judgment.* Gilio was a stickler for decorum, condemning aesthetic extravagance and anything departing from iconographic fidelity. In contrast to Vasari, who emphasizes the importance of a graceful manner, Gilio criticizes the painters of narrative as more concerned with the demonstration of their artistic ability than with the faithful depiction of the story they are illustrating. This was a judgment that Borghini emphasizes repeatedly. Gilio also advances, and Borghini repeats after him, the idea, ultimately derived from Aristotle, that the degree of freedom allowed to the artist depends on the genre. Thus, Gilio distinguishes between the 'poetic' painter (he used

Raphael's paintings in the Villa Farnesina as an example), who is allowed a wide margin of fantasy, and the 'narrative' painter, who is expected to scrupulously follow the subject as he translates from text to image. Gilio's favourite example of dangerous individualism by a 'narrative' painter is Michelangelo's *Last Judgment*. Between these two genres of painting Gilio recognizes 'mixed' painting (here he uses Vasari's frescoes in the Cancelleria as an example), in which the painter is allowed some latitude but is expected to follow a recognizable program. Despite all this criticism, Gilio is acutely aware of the artistic achievements of his period. He concludes, therefore, with a recommendation for a 'regulated mixture,' a *via media*, which combines iconographic fidelity with the formal resources of the sixteenth century.

Rosci submits that 'the play of the parts between conversants [in *Il Riposo*] relies on its immediate model, Gilio's *Dialogo* published twenty years before.'[53] Avanzini sees the *Due dialoghi* as an important source for *Il Riposo* because Borghini's ideas of decorum mirror those of Gilio so closely and because of the close correspondence in the presentation of the two dialogues. Their common device of having the discussants retire to a pastoral location for an extended discussion over hours of idleness, interrupted only by flower smells and bird sounds, of course, has a long history in Florentine letters going back to Boccaccio.

The Treatise

Borghini's treatise takes its name from the still-existing villa of Il Riposo outside Florence, where the dialogue, decorated with descriptions of aviaries, groves, knolls, fountains, and a grotto, supposedly took place [12–18, 123, 128–35, 246–7, 250–2, 452, 459 as 445, and 648]. Claudia Lazzaro's *The Italian Renaissance Garden* is essential to a detailed understanding of Borghini's description of the surroundings and gardens.[54] The grounds of Il Riposo, other than the grotto,[55] have not been studied, and is not known whether Borghini describes actual gardens or whether he applies his imagination, enriched by the owner's plans. On one hand, the Signorini family, who now own Il Riposo, have located a report from 1583 (when Borghini would have been writing his dialogue) that describes the area around the villa as 'boschoso e selvaticho' (a woody wilderness).[56] On the other hand, the villa's south or garden entrance opens onto an imposing terrace supported on its southwest flank by a block-long two-storey retaining wall.[57] The size of this terrace suggests that the original owner may have been very active in cultivating the surroundings of his villa. Borghini's descriptions of Il Riposo probably dwelt somewhere between his imagination and the sixteenth-century reality.

The villa housed an important early art collection that included a fragment of Michelangelo's cartoon for *The Battle of Cascina*, the cartoon for Michelangelo's *Leda*, paintings by Botticelli and Antonello da Messina, and the largest collection of Giambologna's models ever assembled. Subsequently, the treatise describes other large Florentine collections, including the *Guardaroba* of Grand Duke Francesco.[58] Borghini's dialogue makes hundreds of additional references to paintings and pieces of sculpture collected by other patrons, making *Il Riposo* an important document in the early history of collecting.

Rosci sees the discussions at Il Riposo as an extremely accurate portrait of Borghini's place and period:

> With Borghini, we enter palazzetti and villas where representatives of the best Florentine society, relieved of every civil passion, share their 'delights' within a miniature shop with its little furnace and little forge [and] with a harvest of rarities of art and nature ... they admire their drawing of Michelangelo, the Flemish landscape, the Madonna of Andrea del Sarto, the Pietà or the Crucifixion of Poppi and, nearby, the little mythological and allegorical painting, a little lascivious, by the same Poppi or of some other painter of the 'Studiolo,' the family portrait by Allori, or the little bronze of Giambologna. The envy of the friends is aroused by the arrival of some drawings by Passerotti or a Saint Francis by Muziano. They discuss theory and works of art, with poorly understood ideas from Vasari and Varchi, Danti and Gilio; they discuss the latest novelties, the Salviati Chapel in San Marco, the Niccolini Chapel in Santa Croce, the recent statues of the Apostles under the dome of Santa Maria del Fiore, Giambologna's big marble group in the piazza, to which it is necessary to attribute a subject.[59]

Borghini's four historic discussants personify the social position and intellectual interests of *Il Riposo*'s anticipated readers. They each (see Personae) play a well-defined role in the dialogue. They were chosen so that each has a different focus, so that the dialogue will lead to a series of profitable confrontations. The four participants were probably all close friends of Borghini and would have been flattered to have been included.[60] The use of historical figures in a fictive dialogue was common in the Renaissance. Alberti, for example, frequently uses members of his family. Leonardo Alberti, Giannozzo Alberti, and Leon Battista himself play leading roles in *On the Family.* Alberti's criticism of the state of the Church, *Pontifex,* purportedly took place between the Franciscan Paolo di Jacopo Alberti and Cardinal Alberto di Giovanni Alberti.

Each Book of *Il Riposo* begins with a salutation to 'the Most Illustrious ... Don Giovanni de' Medici' (1566–1621; legitimized 1573).[61] The circumstances of Borghini's relationship with Don Giovanni are unknown, but more than a nodding acquaintance is consistent with Borghini's friendship with prominent intellectual and social figures such as Gherardo Capponi, Bernardo Vecchietti, and Baccio Valori. The son of Cosimo and Eleonora degli Albizzi, Don Giovanni was born between the death of Eleonora de Toledo in 1562 and Cosimo's marriage to Camilla Martelli in 1570.

Although he was only seventeen when *Il Riposo* was published, Don Giovanni epitomizes the well-educated amateur to whom the dialogue was addressed. He composed music, wrote poetry, and collected art and particularly books (including those on the Index). Don Giovanni studied at the Accademia del Disegno and in later life was very active as a patron, connoisseur, and accomplished amateur architect. The only reference in the text of the treatise to Don Giovanni is in Borghini's biography of Passerotti, where Borghini notes that a Florentine collector of Passerotti's drawings gave one of them, 'a very beautiful head of a *Gypsy Woman,*' to Don Giovanni 'who as someone who understands good things holds it dear' [567].

Borghini divides his dialogue into four books. The first deals with a general theory of sculpture and painting and the appropriate presentation of their subject matter in the context of the Counter-Reformation. The second discusses the physical technique of making paintings and sculpture and then their style in the context of the Counter-*Maniera.* The third concerns sculpture and painting up to about 1520. The fourth deals with Italian art through the early 1580s.

Each book is devoted to one day of discussion and follows a similar format. There is a prose prologue tenuously related to the succeeding dialogue. The scene is then established. On the first day the discussants ride out to Vecchietti's villa and tour his collection before lunch. On other days the discussants get up, go for a walk in the country around Il Riposo, and return to the villa for lunch. After lunch the discussants visit some interesting venue around the villa where they settle down for the afternoon's discussion. Following their discussion they walk about in the early evening before returning to the villa for supper and bed.

Il Riposo follows the style of Borghini's plays, in which the protagonists frequently become involved in long soliloquies. The discussion in *Il Riposo*, with four exceptions, is more of a series of discourses than an exchange. At the beginning of each topic the discussants establish the way they will deal with the subject: they decide that someone will discuss something; the discussant then discourses at length, with the 'elaborate humility [that] was the convention' of the sixteenth century,[62] on how inadequate he is to address his assignment; the others discourse at length on how learned the discussant is on the subject; the discussant then discourses at length. If a question is raised at the end of his long lecture, it leads to another monologue. When the topic is finally exhausted, the discussants negotiate another long lecture on another subject.

The four exceptions to the extended monologue format are in the first and second books, where the discussants move in their imagination through the public sculpture and painting of Florence, as if on a walking tour. These tours are what Schlosser-Magnino considers 'the most important and most original part of the work.'[63] Here the leader will identify an altarpiece or sculpture, someone else will make a comment, and the leader or others will respond. The format in the iconographic tours, although not rigorously followed before every object, is that one of the discussants first offers a summary of the depicted narrative as it is found in literature, Scripture, or the tradition of the Church. The artist's presentation of this narrative is then described. The faithfulness of this presentation to the narrative is then used as the standard by which to judge the quality of the piece. While Borghini may have adapted this procedure from Gilio, it is, whether Borghini knew it or not, the classical method of ekphrasis. Good examples of this are found in the *Imagines* of Philostratus the Elder, where Philostratus 'first recalls the story and then interprets the scene.'[64] Discussion is generally more spirited in the first two books; by books III and IV Borghini's interest in dialogue has waned, and the treatise becomes even more of a monologue.

Italian critics often comment on what they consider the high quality of the repartee in *Il Riposo* even as they decry the tediousness and pedantry of what is said. Discussing Borghini, many Italians repeatedly speak of the beauty and melodic richness of his style.[65] They contrast it to the compact and incisive prose of the fourteenth-century Italian writers and the clear and impetuous style of early sixteenth-century Florentine historians such as Machiavelli. Borghini's prose, with its weakness for the double or triple negative, is the style of the last part of the sixteenth century. It is 'spacious, dignified, rich in vocabulary, sonorous of adjective,

[and] overflowing with images. The sentences, rather long, are masterly conducted.'[66] (In this translation, Borghini's sentences are shortened to make them easier to understand.) This was the language of the Accademia della Crusca. Vincenzio Borghini had been the leading figure in the Crusca in the generation before Raffaello, and Raffaello's friend, patron, and putative discussant in *Il Riposo*, Baccio Valori, was a very active figure in it. The Accademia della Crusca has repeatedly identified *Il Riposo* as one of the treasures of the Tuscan language.

Borghini is rarely negative. When he is critical, his criticism is muted. Art objects are never *bello*, they are always *bellissimo*. Borghini frequently uses *bellisimo* in a sense different from the description of something that has beauty. It often indicates something done with such facility or technical accomplishment as to provoke admiration or wonder.

In his preface to Book II, Borghini states that *Il Riposo* is written, not for artists, but 'that the things that I have written, I have written for those who do not practice these [precepts] but, either for use or for delight, are seized by pleasure in knowing them.' [127–8]. This identifies *Il Riposo* as the first art treatise specifically directed to connoisseurs rather than practitioners.[67] Some read into this an implied criticism, by the aristocratic Borghini, of what they think Borghini views as intellectual presumptuousness in Vasari's *Vite*.[68]

Borghini's discussants employ a very limited art vocabulary. This vocabulary, if not specific to later sixteenth-century art, certainly operates most comfortably in Borghini's immediate period. For the lay reader this limited vocabulary makes it possible to verbalize clearly defined judgments about art objects with very limited experience. *Il Riposo* teaches its readers a socially desirable skill.

I translate the word *istoria* as 'narrative,' although it could equally well be rendered sometimes as 'scene,' 'story,' or 'history.' If, for Borghini, an *istoria* is a scene, it is a particular kind of scene, involving a narrative element, generally of a biblical or classical subject. For him there is always an element of story or history in an *istoria*, and its subject is uplifting or instructive in some way. Borghini's use of *istoria* in this sense is sometimes cited as something new, but the sense in which Borghini uses *istoria* is no different from the way Alberti had used the term 150 years before.

What is new with Borghini (and Gilio from whom Borghini takes this usage with credit, see [53-4]) is Borghini's privileging of 'narrative' painting over 'poetic' painting and 'mixed' painting. Gilio, as previously discussed, and Borghini both use 'poetic' painting to mean paintings of mythological images and subject matter taken from poetry. 'Narrative' paintings are images whose truth could be verified, which of course for Gilio and Borghini included any sacred imagery. 'Mixed' paintings involve other subjects. Borghini's use of this distinction is much more cursory and much less sophisticated but he may have played an important role in publicizing Gilio's ideas.[69] Some have seen Gilio's and Borghini's discussion of 'narrative,' 'poetic,' and 'mixed' paintings as the first instances of the privileging of academic history painting over other painting subjects.

Pliny had been preoccupied with the idea of Roman moral decline. He attributes this decline partly to the commercialization of art, by which he means art commissioned for the *luxuria* of private enjoyment in contrast to art commissioned for public edification. Pliny praises Apelles and Protogenes for refusing private commissions and admires Agrippa for proposing the nationalization of privately owned art. Borghini also strongly privileges public art. *Il Riposo* is primarily a discussion of art in public view. In his chronology of artists in books III and IV, Borghini emphasizes work in churches and other public places. A frequently unelaborated statement in *Il Riposo*, 'he also did many works for many private persons,' becomes a formula for hurrying past less readily accessible achievements before ending a biography, the penultimate comment before the date and age at death.

Borghini's privileging of public art was part of the Tuscan tradition of great art as public art, discussed in public, and publicly triumphant or the butt of civic ridicule. Art displayed publicly, subject to public criticism, was assumed to meet a higher standard than objects made for private use. Public art criticism in Italy before newspapers often took the form of poems attached to or left at the site of the art work. Borghini does not mention critical poems (such as those showered on Bandinelli's *Hercules and Cacus*) but he does mention, in connection with works he particularly values, that they 'generated much [adulatory] poetry' or some similar formula.

When the discussants begin their tours through Florence, it is immediately obvious that they will not make either a comprehensive or a random selection of the available public painting and sculpture. The discussants examine a relatively small and carefully chosen selection, frequently the kind of objects that could be commissioned in 1584. With a very occasional acknowledgment of the art of the earlier sixteenth century, these are tours of the Florentine art of Vasari and his successors: Giovanni Strada, Giambologna, Macchietti, Naldini, Santi di Tito, and Allori.[70] *Il Riposo* is a celebration of what Borghini's contemporaries perceived as the continuing vitality of Florentine art.

As the discussants apply Borghini's rules, the second one, that artists must be very careful about adding their own inventions to their paintings, is the most difficult for the reader to follow. From the discussion it appears that painters are allowed to insert some inventions of a mythological or supernatural character but not others. Borghini never clearly articulates a general rule describing which inventions by the artist are appropriate and which are not, although there are some specific situations in which the application of his rule is clear. For example, anachronistic figures are not allowed in a narrative such as a Nativity but they are encouraged in a cult image such as a Madonna and Child. The figures of donors or patrons, as such or dressed up to blend in with other figures, are particularly offensive. In any case, the less the painter adds to the image the better. The prudent painter or patron is firmly encouraged to depend on a learned adviser. Yet, for all his talk of the importance of religious iconography, Borghini can be amazingly indifferent to such iconography when describing elements of a painting with clear symbolic meaning.[71]

Borghini discusses the formal elements of art in much less detail than he discusses invention. This suggests that for Borghini the formal elements of an art object are less important or, at any rate less easy for the patron to control. For Borghini, a non-artist, it is also more difficult to discuss the form, in contrast to the subject, of an art object.

Sculptural figures are not examined as a whole. Figures are disassembled and their parts – head, legs, arms, back, and clothing – examined separately. Each part is then judged well- or ill-made. Borghini is dazzled by feats of technical virtuosity such as Properzia de' Rossi's carving 'the whole Passion of Our Lord' on a peach pit [427], Aniballe Fontana's carving on crystal [564–5], and Jacopo Sansovino's marble *Bacchus* 'which, lifting an arm in the air, holds a cup in its hand' [530]. Borghini is not uniformly negative in discussing sculpture: he defends Bandinelli's *Hercules and Cacus* and cannot sufficiently praise Giambologna's *Rape of the Sabine*. The sculpture the discussants examine, however, by Andrea Ferruci, Benedetto da Rovezzano, Giovanni dell'Opera, Raffaello di Montelupo, Bandinelli, Jacopo Sansovino, Ammanati, Vincenzio de Rossi, and Giambologna is generally not as up to date as the paintings they concern themselves with.

In painting, the essence of good composition is clarity and harmony. Borghini describes the quality of harmony by using (without acknowledgment) his uncle's musical simile (see above). For Borghini, colours 'need to be ... appropriate, matching their significance to the place, time, and persons' [183]. Borghini's interest in colour is lost in most discussion of *Il Riposo*, which concentrates on him as one more spokesman for Florentine *disegno* in contrast to Venetian *colore*. Although this is a contrast that Borghini himself encourages, as in his discussion of Tintoretto [551–8] and the Bassani [563–4], Borghini actually devotes substantially more space to colour [225–43] than he does to drawing [137–46].[72]

When the discussants debate the style of paintings, they employ the same procedure they use to examine sculpture. Paintings are not examined in their entirety but faulted for individual defects of proportion, light, and colour: 'necks are too long or too short, poses forced, parts well or less well disposed.'[73] In part this reflects a Renaissance preoccupation with proportion.

In examining an object there is frequently a discontinuity between Borghini's evaluation of iconographic correctness in Book I and his evaluation of technical quality in Book II. Paintings severely disapproved of by Borghini in Book I for their content, most notably Bronzino's *Christ in Limbo* in Santa Croce [109–10] and his *Resurrection* in the Annunziata [116], are praised for their technical execution in Book II [187] and [194]. Although the discussants find, in Book I, the 'lascivious' angel in Bronzino's *Resurrection* completely unsuitable for an ecclesiastical location, one of them says, in Book II, that he would like to take it home for his private collection.[74] Paintings by Santi di Tito that are, praised for their content and realistic colour in Book I are criticized for the dullness of their color in Book II.[75] Over the course of the tours Borghini praises only four paintings without reservation: Alessandro del Barbiere's *Flagellation* in the Corsi Chapel in Santo Croce; Santi di Tito's *Tobias and the Angel*, destined for San Marco; Allori's *Christ and the Adulteress* in Santo Spirito; and Macchietti's *Adoration of the Magi* in San Lorenzo. Borghini does not privilege content over execution or vice versa. Both are hurdles equally to be negotiated.

A drawback for the reader is that Borghini's organization puts the iconographic reading and the formal reading of the same object in two separate books. (The notes to the translation will attempt to facilitate the process of flipping back and forth between the two readings.) Hall believes that this 'redundancy of the organization reflects the tension between the religious and the aesthetic function of the work of art that existed at this time.'[76] Hope, however, believes that Hall overemphasizes this issue: ' it was, of course entirely conventional to consider *invenzione* separately from stylistic categories like *disposizione*.'[77]

Borghini's greatest inconsistency, and it is extraordinary, is in his discussion of Giambologna's *Rape of the Sabine*. Borghini's most important principle is the primacy of iconographic fidelity: the artist should not deviate from a pre-established narrative. As a consequence, Borghini's most constant criticism of artists, including Michelangelo, is of the tendency to flaunt their technique at the expense of the narrative. Then Borghini tells his self-promoting story of the naming of the *Sabine*. Giambologna, 'directed by the spur of virtue, decided to show the world that he not only knew how to make ordinary figures of marble but also many together and the most difficult that it was possible to do. Known to him was all the art of making nude figures' [72], without, according to the story, having any initial invention whatsoever. Borghini's telling of this story, as Frangenberg points out,[78] completely inverts his discussion of the primacy of invention and the desirability of technical self-effacement.

In his discussion of the statue, Borghini does not advance a sometimes-heard interpretation of Giambologna's masterpiece that is particularly adulatory towards the Medici. Roberta Olson has suggested that, despite Borghini's story, 'it is clear that the general subject, a seizure/rape, had been established' before the sculpture was begun. The allegorical reading of the statue that Olson passes on, 'the Medici (the youth) taking Florence (the woman) from the previous government (old man) and establishing a new Rome,'[79] has been thoroughly explored from a feminist perspective by Margaret Carroll, who marshalled substantial support for this reading from contemporary poetry associated with the installation of the statue.[80] What makes Borghini's omission of such a reading surprising is that the idea of allegory in support of the ruling house is not alien to him. He discusses, for example, the allegorical meaning of other Mediciophile iconography in his discussion of the frescoes at Poggio a Caino [626–7].

Borghini, as previously noted, is largely oblivious to differences in style. The discussants judge everything by the appropriateness of its content and the degree of its mimesis. There is no recognition of the major stylistic differences between the earliest works discussed in the tour, those of Perugino and Fra Bartolommeo, and more contemporary works.[81] Although there is little discussion of style, there is frequent mention of execution: *maniera* and *bella maniera*, care (*diligenza*), and experience (*pratica*). In addition the lifelikeness (*vivacita*) of figures, their grace (*gracia*), devotion (*divotione*), or spirit (*fierezza*) are sometimes important to the discussants. Hope emphasizes that Borghini, seeking the qualities of *grazia, maniera,* and *facilità*, uses the same stylistic vocabulary as Vasari.[82]

In Borghini's chronologies in books III and IV, artists are rarely recognized for any specific contribution other than for having been present and being 'very good,' 'very able,' and capable of producing objects that are 'very beautiful.' Borghini very rarely recognizes any historical progression of improving imitation of nature. Progress is episodic, identified by the very occasional discoveries of individual artists. The order of Vasari's *Vite* is followed but with inexplicable gaps and choices.[83] Siena and Pisa are ignored. Andrea del Sarto and Vasari receive greater emphasis than Michelangelo and Giotto.

Poetry concerning artists was an important part of the intellectual environment in Borghini's Florence. At the end of his life of Masaccio, Borghini includes a poem. This is a distinction that Borghini grants, somewhat inconsistently, as an indication of exceptional merit. Giotto receives a much longer life than Masaccio, but no poem. Borghini concludes his discussion of Giambologna's *Rape of the Sabine* with not one sonnet but three. The discussants find the third sonnet so obscure that it sets them off on a long explanatory tangent.

Two-thirds of Book III consists of an uninterrupted 162-page sermon on the Renaissance from Cimabue to Sebastiano del Piombo. Frangenberg suggests that Borghini changes at this point from a dialogue to a monologue because the pattern of art history he inherited from Vasari was canonical and therefore did not invite discussion.[84] Most of these lives are a simple narrative describing under whom the artist trained, where he subsequently went, and what he did for whom in what religious institution, together with a concluding note concerning his death.

Borghini's descriptions of the rare female artists in his dialogue are hair-raisingly chauvinistic: 'It would seem to me to be too great an error, and with respect to women to fall into too great a fault, if I kept silent the virtues of Properzia de' Rossi of Bologna. She, being very rare of talent and very beautiful of form, beside singing and playing instruments which she did better than the other women of her city, gave herself also – being by nature inclined to *disegno* – to carving peach pits' [427]. See also his discussion of Marietta Tintoretto [558–9] and Lavinia Fontana [568].

Early in the last book several changes become apparent in the format of the dialogue. It becomes increasingly obvious how much Borghini's historical survey, like his tours through Florence in books I and II, emphasize the sixteenth century. The historical part of *Il Riposo* is not a discussion of Italian Renaissance art, it is a discussion of later sixteenth-century Italian art with generous prologues from the early and High Renaissance. As the discussion approaches 1584, each artist receives more detailed treatment. This treatment, however, becomes less biographical and qualitative and increasingly degenerates into a formulaic listing of works, flavoured with an occasional descriptive *bellissimo*. Personal anecdotes, albeit mostly transcribed from Vasari, disappear. Borghini begins describing works in progress in his life of Jacopo Palma: 'Today he has in hand some pictures that will go into ...' [560]. Borghini's assessment of the same contemporary artists is much more blandly positive in the last book than it was during the four tours of Florence in books I and II. Vigorous criticism is missing from Book IV.[85]

Borghini devotes more space to Andrea del Sarto than to any other artist, but his biography turns out to be little more than a long list of paintings. Borghini devotes less space to Michelangelo than to Raphael, Vasari, Alessandro Allori, and Tintoretto, despite his opening comment: 'Now what will I say, it being appropriate for me to speak of the divine Michelangelo in whom is seen all perfection of sculpture, of painting, and of architecture since only he has wholly obscured the glory of the ancients and surpassed the fame of all the moderns?' [509–10].

Borghini's treatment of Bandinelli [477–80] is non-committal: an average amount of space is allocated to his life; there is neither remarkable praise nor remarkable blame. Borghini does not take the life of Bandinelli as an opportunity to aggressively promote Medici artistic interests with their tacit political implications; neither is he tempted to pass on scurrilous, implicitly republican, gossip.

The critics who are most outspoken in accusing Borghini of being a pale shadow of Vasari point to his treatment of Ridolfo Ghirlandaio [489–91]. The absence of new material for them culminates in the truncated summary of Vasari that Borghini puts in the mouth of Ghirlandaio's grandson Ridolfo Sirigatti; these critics expect something more.[86] Implicit in their criticism is that Ghirlandaio's life is actually coming from the historical Ridolfo Sirigatti. It is not.

Why did Borghini devote so much of his treatise to, and Marescotti publish, an abbreviated version of Vasari when Borghini's readers had available Vasari's comprehensive account published only sixteen years before? As previously indicated, I speculate that, with its decorative trimmings of dialogue and pastoral location, *Il Riposo* was either an attractively packaged handbook for the Florentine collector or an entertaining read for a sixteenth-century dilettante imagining herself or himself as such a collector.[87] Bound in one volume, *Il Riposo* is much more physically manageable and much less intellectually intimidating than Vasari's monumental *Vite.*

Borghini, who still considers Florence the centre of Italian art (although even Vasari had realized that the focus had shifted to Rome), begins his discussion of living artists with the Venetian 'foreigners.' We do not know the source of his information, but the tone of his description suggests that his information was derived from a visit or an unknown informant rather than a lost written source. In any case, *Il Riposo* contains information missing from Francesco Sansovino's *Venezia città nobilissima,* published three years before. Although Borghini does not completely understand the Venetians, his admiration is unquestioned and sincere. Borghini sometimes seems to relish the role of a rigidly parochial Florentine, but there is an openness of spirit in his theoretical system that allows him to praise painting outside his predominantly Florentine experience.[88] Borghini's interest in the Venetians may have been influenced by Dolce's *L'Aretino,* visits to Venice by contemporaries such as Federico Zuccaro, or simply the more cosmopolitan Italian outlook promoted by his great-uncle. Whatever the reasons, *Il Riposo* is an indication of increased Florentine interest in Venetian art sixteen years after publication of the second edition of Vasari's *Vite.*

Borghini's biography of Tintoretto was the second to be written. Although no doubt influenced by Tintoretto's productivity, Borghini's biography of the Venetian is longer than he gave any living artist except for Alessandro Allori. The discussion of Tintoretto consists largely of lists of works, in one case extending over two and a half pages [551–4], a list that is only interrupted by another list of his paintings in the Scuola di San Rocco. At the beginning of Tintoretto's biography Borghini qualifies his admiration: 'he took for his principal master the works of the divine Michelangelo, not concerned with any expense in collecting his figures from the Sacristy of San Lorenzo and equally all the good models of the best statues that were in Florence. Therefore he himself acknowledged that he did not recognize any except the Florentine craftsmen as masters in the things of *disegno.*'[89] And at the end, 'Tintoretto, today finding himself sixty years of age, neither therefore fails to virtuously do his best but also studies, taking great pleasure as someone who recognizes good things in having some models of the excellent Giambologna nor, however old, does he tire in imitating them' [558]. Borghini's brief notice of Marietta Tintoretta (Robusti) [558] is the first mention of her in print by a contemporary.

Borghini's description of artists at the end of Book IV is the oldest contemporary discussion of the most influential masters then in Florence, many of whom, like Giambologna, Borghini knew well. Particularly important is the information Borghini provides concerning the inexhaustible Giovanni Strada and the energetic Bernardo Buontalenti, who apparently took the place of Cosimo's Vasari as Francesco's favourite agent for the arts.

The essence of *Il Riposo* is Borghini's discussion of invention, the most important of his five parts of painting: invention, composition, pose, parts, and colour. Invention is most important for him because it is the only part the artist does not control. Invention gives the adviser or patron control over the painting. According to Borghini, Horace was correct when he elevated the status of painting to that of poetry, but problems developed when he was interpreted by 'those dissolute painters' to mean that painters had the same licence as poets to modify the expression of the narrative. Borghini divides invention into two parts: 'inventions derived from others, and those that come from the artisan himself.' Inventions derived from others are to be followed. Those from the 'artisan himself' are best if done in consultation with advisers and not by 'chance or whim.' The Counter-Reformation and the grand dukes did not encourage 'chance or whim.'

So, what of all this has been left behind? As indicated in the Translator's Preface, forty per cent of Borghini's original dialogue-treatise is missing in this edition. Everyone who has had anything to do with *Il Riposo* since the seventeenth century, no matter how highly they have esteemed the dialogue, has suggested passing over major portions of Borghini's masterwork. This includes, more recently, my dissertation adviser, every member of my dissertation committee, my editor, my anonymous readers, and me. The basic criteria I used for inclusion or exclusion of material in this edition were whether or not I thought the material advanced or detracted from Borghini's exposition of Counter-Reformation and Counter-*Maniera* principles and whether or not I thought the material advanced our understanding of Borghini's period.

Almost all of Book I, Borghini's discussion of iconography, is retained. The only parts excised are most of Borghini's derivative prose preface and his discussion of the *paragone*; the former because it is boring and almost incomprehensible and the latter because Borghini took it almost verbatim from Varchi.[90] More material is excised from Book II, Borghini's discussion of the formal aspects of the Counter-*Maniera*. In his discussion, Borghini included a good deal of technical studio information along the lines of '*Tracing paper of many kinds, how it is made and how it is used*,' together with many recipes for pigment manufacture. This material is excised, together with a long description of one of the elaborate bird traps at Il Riposo.

Elimination of ancient and Renaissance lives from Book III and Book IV is more substantial and subjective. The thirty-page history of ancient art that Borghini paraphrases, guided by Vasari, from Pliny's *Natural History* is removed. All of the most major Renaissance figures (Giotto, Masaccio, Donatello, the Bellini, etc.) are retained together with enough of the second tier (Cimabue, Luca della Robbia, Uccello, etc.) to retain some of the flavour of Borghini's original. Also retained are all of the other artists that Borghini mentions in books I or II (Domenico Puligo, Andrea Ferucci, Benedetto da Rovezzano, etc.). Borghini begins to include material in his biographies in Book IV that is absent from Vasari. Retained are all of Borghini's lives that contain such material.

The History and Appreciation of the Treatise

Schlosser-Magnino claims that Francesco Bocci's *Le Belezze della città di Fiorenza* of 1591, an important early guide to Florence, largely accepted and spread the critical judgments made in *Il Riposo*.[91] Further, Schlosser-Magnino believes, *Il Riposo* 'contributed greatly to the diffusion of [Counter-Reformation] ideas in the literature of Florence.'[92] There were scattered positive references to *Il Riposo* during the century following its publication. Then the adverse criticism begins. Filippo Baldinucci, artistic adviser to grand duke Cosimo III, articulates what would be the principle criticism of Borghini over the next three hundred years: he is an 'utter fat head' (*solennissimo capocchione*) for his dependence on Vasari and a bad and hasty copyist at that.[93]

Early in the eighteenth century, Giulio Negri, in his *Istoria degli scrittori fiorentini*, praises Borghini's literary style.[94] This becomes a frequent theme among Italians. In Spain, Antonio Palomino de Castro y Velasco writes that *Il Riposo* was part of Velázquez's core library and that Borghini's dialogue shared part of the credit for Velázquez's reputation as a 'learned painter.'[95] By 1730 the rarity of the first edition induced

Francesco Maria Gabburi to underwrite a second edition.[96] Ably edited by Giovanni Bottari, the second edition of *Il Riposo* was of such quality that it became the definitive and most legible edition, but also increasingly rare. Later in the century Tiraboschi commends *Il Riposo* in his *Storia della letteratura italiana* as a work in which 'precepts of painting and sculpture are joined to history,'[97] but della Valle comments that 'Borghini puts one to sleep.'[98] In response to the increasing rarity of the second edition, a third edition of exceptionally poor quality was published in 1787. The following year Angelo Comolli described the publishing history of *Il Riposo* up to that time.[99]

The fourth edition of *Il Riposo* was published in 1807 and the fifth edition in 1826–27. This fifth edition was the most used edition of the treatise until the publication of the facsimile first edition annotated by Rosci in 1967. It is unclear why there was this outpouring of editions of *Il Riposo* in the later eighteenth and early nineteenth centuries: three new editions in forty years. Evidently there was a continued market for the treatise in Italy, coupled with the unavailability of the first two editions and the inadequacy of the lamented third edition. As Italian interest in *Il Riposo* as a historical and technical treatise decreased, there was an increased interest in it as a good example of sixteenth-century Tuscan.

It is also unknown why Borghini's dialogue has never before been translated. The absence of translation may explain why, with rare exceptions,[100] only Italians discussed *Il Riposo* before the twentieth century. The most likely explanation is that during the sixteenth, seventeenth, and eighteenth centuries, when the dialogue might have enjoyed a popular audience outside of Italy, northern readers and publishers were discouraged by its Tridentine message. By the twentieth century, when the treatise would have lost its appeal to a general audience, many foreign students of the sixteenth century read Italian. The seventh and last printing of *Il Riposo* was published in 1969 in Germany as an unannotated facsimile of the first edition.

Despite Anthony Blunt's dismissal of Borghini as 'just worthy of mention,'[101] there are five pieces of important scholarship concerning *Il Riposo* written in the twentieth century.[102] The first is Julius von Schlosser(-Magnino)'s essay in his *Die Kunstliteratur* of 1924. He considered Borghini's story of the naming of Giambologna's *Rape of the Sabine* 'one of the most memorable documents of this epoch.'

Elena Avanzini wrote the only monograph on the dialogue, *Il Riposo di Rafaello Borghini e la critica d'arte nel '500*, in 1960. There is much romantic speculation in what Giulio Ferroni calls 'her curious little book'[103] but also more archival research than anywhere else. Rosci, Barrochi, and Frangenberg defer to Avanzini on several of the few known details of Borghini's life while expressing reservations concerning some of the information she believes she extracted from Borghini's poetry.

In 1967 Marco Rosci edited a facsimile of the first edition of *Il Riposo* with a second volume of extremely helpful notes and an essay. This was the most important event in the history of the treatise since the publication of Bottari's second edition in 1730. Rosci's introductory essay is the most fluent, incisive, and extensive critique of the limitations of *Il Riposo* ever published.

In her *Scritti d'arte del Cinquecento* published in 1970, Paola Barocchi includes three substantial excerpts from *Il Riposo*. These contain much of the theoretical essence of the dialogue. In her usual fashion, Barocchi carefully identifies Borghini's sources for each excerpt. For many authors over the past thirty years Barocchi's excerpts in the *Scritti d'arte* have been the principle source of citations to *Il Riposo*.[104]

In 1990 Thomas Frangenberg published "Fundiert reden' Raffaele Borghinis *Riposo*,' a chapter in his *Der Betrachter*, a book concerning the relation between image and viewer in the sixteenth century. Frangenberg's essay is the most perceptive study of *Il Riposo* available. Straightforward concerning Borghini's limitations, Frangenberg nevertheless gives *Il Riposo* a positive review, concluding that the dialogue is 'one of the most important source texts of the Cinquecento.'

Conclusion

Borghini's treatise is valuable to the modern reader because it illustrates how the Florentines applied the iconographic ideas of the Counter-Reformation and the stylistic ideas of the Counter-*Maniera* to their art. To the extent to which Borghini speaks for later sixteenth-century Florence, and *Il Riposo* is the major Florentine document available to us, the Florentine response to the Counter-Reformation was only modestly vigorous and the Florentine response to the 'new seriousness' of the Counter-*Maniera* was half-hearted and ambivalent.

Like most Renaissance writers, Borghini relied heavily on the writing of others. Although he gives his predecessors and contemporaries little credit, probably few, if any, of the ideas in *Il Riposo* originated with Borghini. Nevertheless, the commonplaces that Borghini compiled, tirelessly repeated by him and others, probably reflect values and ideas accepted in his time without question.[105]

Borghini's accomplishment was modest compared with Vasari's, but he plays an important role in confirming and transmitting the aesthetic canon established by his predecessor. In addition, Borghini promotes figures only touched on by Vasari: Tintoretto, Veronese, Barocci, Federico Zuccaro, Giovanni Strada, Giambologna, Buontalenti, and the other artists of Francesco's Studiolo. Borghini is also important as a populizer of the Counter-Reformation ideas of Gilio, Borromeo, and Paleotti.

Personae

Bernardo Vecchietti, the owner of Il Riposo, initiates and controls the discussion. The others defer to him as their host. Vecchietti discusses Counter-Reformation iconography in Book I and Renaissance art from Cimabue to the early sixteenth century in Book III.

The historic Bernardo Vecchietti, banker, litterateur, and collector, was Giambologna's first patron. As an artistic adviser to Francesco, Vecchietti oversaw the project for the equestrian statue of Cosimo in the Piazza della Signoria. Federico Zuccaro thanked Vecchietti for his influence in getting the commission by including Vecchietti's labelled portrait in Federico's fresco in the cupola of the Duomo.[1]

Ridolfo Sirigatti, maternal grandson of Ridolfo Ghirlandaio, is described in *Il Riposo* as a practising artist. Sirigatti discusses style and technique in Book II and all of the material in Book IV, which deals with Italian art after about 1520.

The historic Ridolfo Sirigatti was actually described by Herbert Horne as 'a great *amateur* of those times.'[2] An important Medici bureaucrat and only sometime sculptor and painter, Sirigatti was an important collector who 'gave' the two Botticelli paintings of *Judith* and *Holofernes*, which are now in the Uffizi, to Bianca Cappello. His destroyed portrait of Borghini, mentioned in Book I [22], was in Berlin. Ridolfo Sirigatti may have been the father of Lorenzo Sirigatti, famous as the master of Pietro Bernini, father of Gian Lorenzo.

Baccio Valori is the savant. He deals with philosophical bits and pieces such as the theory of light and the iconography of the colours. From time to time he adds a comment intended to be sage.

The historical Baccio Valori was described by Cochrane as '[among the latter day] Atticuses and Varros ... [a] wealthy, humane, and urbane

Maecenas.'[3] A doctor of law and librarian of the Laurenziana, Valori represented Cosimo in the Accademia del Disegno. Valori was the builder of the unkindly nicknamed 'Palazzo dei Visacci,' the 'Palace of Ugly Faces' (Palazzo Altoviti), decorated with the images of fifteen famous literati in the form of low-relief herm busts, on the Borgo degli Albizi. Borghini had a close financial and literary relationship with Baccio Valori. In addition to serving as a financial guarantor for some of Borghini's financial problems, Valori installed Borghini in a suburban retreat of Valori's where Borghini completed *Il Riposo* and *La Diana Pietosa*. Valori's portrait bust by Giovanni Caccini is in the Museo Nazionale.[4]

Girolamo Michelozzi is the foil. His false steps allow the others to emphasize points by correcting him. This makes him a principle player in the church tours in books I and II. In the course of these discussions Borghini rather clumsily attempts to have Michelozzi gradually improve his understanding.

The historic Girolamo Michelozzi war the most obscure of the four discussants in *Il Riposo*. Apparently a friend of Borghini, Michelozzi was a member of a distinguished Florentine family.

IL RIPOSO

by Raffaello Borghini

IN WHICH PAINTING AND sculpture are discussed, the most illustrious painters and sculptors, and the most famous of their works are mentioned and the principle things pertaining to these arts are taught.

To the Most Illustrious and Most Excellent Sig. Master,
the Most Singular
The Signor Don GIOVANNI *de' Medici.*

FLORENCE
Printed by Giorgio Marescotti 1584
With permission of the Superiori

TO THE PAINTERS AND SCULPTORS OF FLORENCE

Piero di Gherardo Capponi

As in sweet shyness the painted face of
Nature admires the beautiful rare work
So precious and dear from your hand,
The Arno longs and hopes and gives itself to you in defeat;
From this writing, where sculpture and painting
As the living spirit of art, appears to you,
All, reading to learn, before working,
To give life to marble and substance to feigned shadow
Then manifest as well carved and painted:
Here and there a new Polyclitus,
Art with similar guidance erects a canon.
Certain that in this way superb Flora
Decorates her facades and streets most beautifully
Her soul flies to the heavens where virtue abides.

Book One

TO THE MOST ILLUSTRIOUS,
AND MOST EXCELLENT LORD
Master, your most singular
Signor Don GIOVANNI
DE' MEDICI

Whenever I think carefully (Most Illustrious and Most Excellent Lord) about the marvellous works of nature, – so beautiful, varied, and useful – I find them every hour more admirable and more worthy of greater consideration. One gazes at the infinite light of the Sun, the fluctuating brightness of the Moon, the wandering stars, and the octave heaven.[1] There are so many shining resplendent little flames spread over its ultramarine blue. Each narrowly turns in sweet harmony as they run their course. Among them, in their very gentle drift, there is no discord. Who can raise his eyes to these supernal spheres without his thought turning to imagine [2][2] the benign universal Mother [Nature]?[3] She is much more full of excellence and of perfection than human intellect understands. But wait! One lowers one's face to earth and to those things which are closer at hand. Who does not see the charming flowers, the green new grass, and the sweet fruits that please us, cure us, and nurture us? These she produces in her wisdom, her grandeur, and her liberality. We wish to roam more widely through [the World's] grandeur. Then we are able to consider the broad seas, the running rivers, the murmuring fountains, the wide meadows, the magnificent mountains, the charming gems, the rich metal mines, and so many species of birds, fish, and terrestrial animals. With infinite Divine Providence, she marked off and ordered her noble magistery. (She separated the confusing elements and created unity from disunity. She put the earth in the centre of the World and gave laws to the sea. She spread the air like a delicate veil and made the fire gust to the highest place. She imposed perpetual and infallible order on the Sun, lord of the planets, power and strength of all living things. She distinguished the years, the seasons, the months, the days, and the hours.)

But of all the marvels that she has scattered throughout all the world one can see that she wanted to take particular care in one. To show the final sign of the perfection of her hand, she created man. He is a microcosm of all. In his making were collected and included all the works, all the marvels, that she had made in the whole universe. [3] All things nature created are in him, or were made for him ...[4]

But, leaving these subtle considerations, one who would want to recognize the excellence of man in more material things will consider [man's] marvellous efforts in the discovery of the many arts and sciences. One will clearly see how much [man] has of immortality and of the divine. Besides the things discovered for the decoration and for the convenience of human life – not satisfied with superb palaces, charming gardens, various and delicate foods, draperies of silk and gold, of having trod the earth, ploughed the sea, flown through the air, and passed through all the heavens[5] – [man] has also wanted, almost as if he were nature himself, [10] to make the most excellent works of these appear as human works. And he has done this with sculpture and with painting, imitating the heavens, fire, air, water, earth, beasts, and men.

I am myself familiar with a discussion, not unworthy of being repeated, of these two very beautiful and very noble arts of painting and sculpture. It occurred between four gentlemen (according to what one of them recounted to me), and I hope to make it known to your Most Illustrious Excellency in my simple style. You are occupied, with much praise at every moment, in more weighty and more important studies. But I hope when you turn and pause to deign to read [my treatise] it will delight you, as a virtuoso and lively spirit. [Further I hope] that students of these fine arts will obtain a more than mediocre profit from it. But before passing further forward, I believe it would be well to make clear how and where the discussion of these things took place.

I say, therefore, that one evening last May, Bernardo Vecchietti and Ridolfo Sirigatti, a Knight of St Stephen, availed themselves of the coolness in the Piazza of San Giovanni, where the nobility of Florence idle. [Vecchietti] is a Florentine gentleman greatly recognized by our Grand Duke and by all men, not only because of the wealth that he possesses but for his virtues. After much discussion between them, Vecchietti turned to Sirigatti and said: 'One has not any doubt that all those of you, who, among other delights, please yourselves in the [11] study of design and the practice of sculpture and painting, take little pleasure in attending only to the needs of the body. Nonetheless, it does not seem an unsuitable thing sometimes to give ease to the mind and restoration to the spirits with some honest amusement for the body. Such activities, which are a consolation to the spirit, allow one to carry on more strongly. I say that I think that perhaps you are quite weary from giving yourself to the study of design and from bringing to perfection your beautiful [sculpture of] Venus. And I myself, because of many troubling thoughts finding me again, would judge it well done, if you would be pleased to do me such a favour, that we go to my villa to take some air and take a truce from the many cares of the city. And meanwhile you could give me some good advice about some things of mine.'

'I would not be able to give you any good advice to improve the organization of your things,' Sirigatti responded. 'You have a very good understanding of architecture, and could err little, having been endowed by nature with singular judgment. But I will come quite gladly – something I've been wanting to do for a long time – to see your villa. I understand it is not only abundant in the benefits of nature and well cultivated with all possible skill, but also decorated by you with the very rare things that you have notably made. Therefore, to put into effect the desire that I have of seeing it, [12] I will gladly accept the virtuous pastimes that you offer me in this. At a subsequent time of your choosing, I will depart.'

While they chatted in this manner, the excellent Doctor Messer Baccio Valori, of most noble blood, and Girolamo Michelozzi, both Knights of St Stephen, arrived unexpectedly. And after exchanging greetings, Vecchietti told them what they had been talking about, that he and Sirigatti were going to the villa. He urged them strongly to accompany them, citing additional reasons why they should not refuse. In addition to the obligation that they had to him, and how pleased Sirigatti would feel, there would spring, from such a courteous exercise, an occasion of common satisfaction to all. The two knights, as very much gentlemen, after thanking them and having made clear how much they would be obligated to Vecchietti and Sirigatti for this, happily accepted the invitation. And so they agreed to put themselves on the road the next day.

Vecchietti's Villa[6]

After attending mass the following morning, they mounted on horseback in the coolness [of the morning] and proceeded without pause to Il Riposo. This is the name of Vecchietti's villa. This place is, going to the right out of the Porta San Niccolò, about three miles from Florence across the very clear little stream of the Ema at Vacciano. The villa faces southeast, somewhat above the plain, on a charming little knoll. Different fruit and many productive vines are, in addition [13] to the utility they represent, a marvel to see. There are pleasant and fruitful slopes. Groves of cypress and laurel arouse in everyone a solitary reverence with their thick shade. Very clear waters are heard to murmur softly. Little meadows are covered with the freshest and most delicate grasses, coloured and marked by many sorts of charming flowers.

The well-arranged villa has spacious halls, tidy and ornate rooms, bright loggias, very fresh water in great supply, and cellars full of wonderful wines. But what attracts everyone's attention are the rare paintings and sculpture that one can see there.[7] The famous cartoon of *Leda* from the hand of Michelangelo is there,[8] and a fragment of a cartoon, also by Buonarroti, of the wars in Pisa that were to be painted in Florence in the palace.[9] There is a dead man's head done in great detail by Leonardo da Vinci, the drawing by Benvenuto Cellini for the model of the *Perseus* in the piazza, four very beautiful sheets by Francesco Salviati, two drawings in his best manner by Bronzino, a very beautiful painting by Botticelli, and a picture in which there are painted two heads by Antonello da Messina, who introduced working with oils into Italy. Many wax, clay, and bronze figures by Giambologna in different poses represent different figures such as prisoners, women, goddesses, rivers, and famous men. It would take too long to recount the several things by many other painters, particularly [14] some very beautiful landscapes by Flemish painters.

But a great marvel to see is a study with five shelves where small statues of marble, bronze, clay, and wax are arranged in beautiful order. Fine stones of many sorts are arranged there, vases of porcelain and of rock crystal, seashells of many kinds, pyramids of precious stone, jewels, medals, masks, fruit and animals frozen in very fine stone [fossils], and so many new and rare things coming from India and from Turkey as astonishes whoever sees them. Beyond some further rooms, in another part of the villa, is a similar study completely stocked with silver and gold vases and prints and drawings by the most excellent masters that sculpture and painting have had. Precious distilled waters and very efficacious oils are there, many retorts, very beautiful knives from the Orient, Turkish scimitars worked in various ways, and a large number of cups and different porcelain vases.

From this first floor one descends below to three rooms. Here Vecchietti retires when he praiseworthily wishes to exercise his own hands in crafts, at which he is highly skilled. The first room is completely encircled with models by Giambologna and with statues by other masters, paintings, and drawings. The second is full of a variety of iron tools, and the forge is there with everything pertaining to work with it, with many tools that serve a mathematical function. The third has the lathe with all its accessories, [15] and many works of ivory, ebony, mother-of-pearl, and fish bone made with great artifice on the lathe by Vecchietti himself.[10] In sum, all the things that could give pleasure to the body and nourishment to the mind are found in this villa.[11]

Having arrived, the noble company relaxed for a while in beautiful quarters, taking repose while enjoying refreshments. Then all went to see the things [I have] described and much else that for brevity I have kept silent about. These gave them the utmost satisfaction, and after a great deal of discussion about these things, they finally reached a great hall. And there they saw the tables set with very white tablecloths and with goblets that appeared to be of silver and everything covered with broom flowers. Washing their hands, everyone went to sit down. There were delicate foods and very fine wines (since this was a very excellent area for their production) quietly served by servants. But then, as the table was cleared, having discussed various things, feeling the air rather fresh, they went out onto a little lawn. This faced towards the north but was protected from the north wind by a gentle hill in front of them surmounted by a well-sited chapel. Having spent some time there, Baccio [Valori] turned to the others and said:

'In every season of the year the midday nap is not good for your health, although it is less harmful in the summer because the days are so long. Nevertheless, beyond the sleep that is necessary for the nourishment of the body, I believe that sleeping should be avoided by those who wish to live longer. [16] Therefore, if you would care to take my advice at this time, I would say it would be appropriate, to leave sleep lying behind the curtains of our beds. We should walk to some place not far from here and rest there in the shade in the coolness of the grass passing this unseemly part of the day with some pleasant discussion until the Sun, lowering itself to the top of these mountains allows us to walk around in the coolness.'

All were greatly pleased by the proposal made by Valori, and Michelozzi immediately added: 'This is not a suggestion to ignore. But where we go, so that the place offers us a cool shade, will be up to Messer Bernardo [Vecchietti] to decide. He knows every most pleasant corner of this place.'

'This hill that is before us,' responded Vecchietti, 'has on its highest crest a chapel and a broad shady meadow over which a soft breeze is always felt. And much of the country can be seen around it. There we would be able to be rather comfortable, if at this time its pleasant slope does not seem steep to you. Alternatively, it mighty be of lesser annoyance to descend to that closer place where a very clear fountain surges.'

'The weather is cool,' Sirigatti said, 'and the rays of the Sun, being hidden among the clouds, do not offend us. Therefore, I would think it well done, if it does not displease the others, to climb the little mountain. It seems certain to me that there should be some beautiful paintings in the chapel that would be a great pleasure to see. [17] In addition, we should value it greatly to begin our first diversion in seeing, and revering the sacred things.'

All praised the recommendation of Sirigatti and immediately proceeded with slow footstep on the road towards the summit of the little mountain. When they got there they found the place more pleasant, cooler, and more comfortable than they had imagined. They had arrived in a meadow, in the form of a theatre, coloured by thousands of varieties of flowers appearing to them like a very charming carpet, inviting everyone on it to rest themselves. This was thickly surrounded by a tall garland of cypresses and thick grass, shaded by the cypresses which looked almost black. The view that is seen from this prominent place is very beautiful. The well-cultivated country about Antella is seen where the Sun rises and the Certosa and Galluzzo where it sets. Fiesole, Pratolino, and Florence are where the coldest wind blows on us, and Prato and Pistoia lower down and to the left. And from where the warmest breath of midday comes are Lappeggio and Marcignano beyond the Grassina River and, higher up, San Giusto a Monterantoli. The carefully studied chapel, surrounded by cypresses,[12] is located at the entrance of the beautiful circle. The *Ascension of Our Lord,* with the Apostles and some very beautiful angels in the vault, are painted within it in fresco by the hand of Francesco di Goro Pagani. If death had not taken him so suddenly from the world, he would have become a most excellent painter. The four gentlemen reverently entered. Then, after the proper prayers to God, [18] and having examined and praised the beautiful pictures, they went back out into the green theatre. And they were not satisfied by [only] a short look around at the very beautiful views. Finally, sitting down on the tender little grasses in the coolest part, Sirigatti began to talk in this way.

'I had heard the beautiful things of Bernardo described. Now, in seeing them, I come to understand that, contrary to what is said about them, their reputation remains a great deal less than their reality.'

'[But] those, who look at your things,' Vecchietti immediately responded, 'come to recognize that they make others marvel. Not only are they so numerous but among them are things done with your own hand of a greater beauty than those of the most excellent masters they are competing with.'

Michelozzi, turning to Vecchietti said: 'You greatly increase in me the desire that I have always had to see the rooms of Messer Ridolfo [Sirgatti].'

'Therefore,' Vecchietti responded, 'you have not seen very beautiful things, worthy to be considered by every beautiful spirit. But, as we will return to the city, if it will be your pleasure, we will go to see them together. While I often go there, I never go there that new paintings and sculptures are not put before my eyes.'

'You honour me too much,' said Sirigatti, looking at Vecchietti, 'since my things are worth little. But even so, you may at your pleasure, together with the others, have them at your disposal.'

'It will be a very great favour to me,' added Michelozzi enthusiastically, responding to [19] Vecchietti, 'to be there in your company. You would make known to me, by your graciousness, that which I do not understand. I know that out of modesty Ridolfo would not speak about [his things]. But, if the discussion does not bore you, since here we are reduced to waiting for a fresher hour, I would be very grateful, and perhaps it would not bother Messer Baccio, [for you] to discuss some of it.'

'A discussion by Bernardo is precious to me at all times,' responded Valori. 'But now for your satisfaction, and because he will make the heat pass by us without boredom with this material, it will make me particularly thankful. And knowing his generous nature I am certain that he will not fail to satisfy us.'

'I will always exert myself to satisfy you to the extent that my abilities allow,' Vecchietti answered. 'But I will leave others to judge the effect that results. The many and very beautiful things of Sirigatti are arranged in his rooms as objects for the eyes. They are placed to delight those who are welcomed there, for which I think they are truly to be praised. As for the pleasure to [your] ears transported there, as for all things inappropriately used, in this they lose grace and value, giving little delight.

'Since it is your wish that I describe them in this way, I will not describe them in order – they are very well organized – because that would be too long. Rather, following what memory brings back to me, I will speak briefly, in obedience to you, of [only] some things. And thus I say, in describing each of them, I will begin in this way.

'Ridolfo has five rooms, [20] each different and decorated as you will hear. In the first there are a thousand heads, arms, legs, torsos, and other parts of statues, of which all the walls are full, and models of horses and other animals that are placed on shelves. There one sees the *Night*, the *Dawn*, and the other figures of Michelangelo that are in the Sacristy of San Lorenzo, of full scale and made of plaster with great care.[13] The second contains many different things. There are ancient marble heads and figures, some little paintings of very beautiful Flemish landscapes, a clay model of St John the Apostle by the hand of Sansovino, and a large cartoon by the hand of Michelangelo, displays of lifelike dried-out fish, mother-of-pearl mollusk shells and other sea-shells, vases of jasper and crystal, ivory and ebony lutes, harpsichords, viols, zithers, flutes, and other musical instruments, and very beautiful books of music of many kinds and of introductions to the lute. The third room, of all the others the most beautiful and most abundant, is richly decorated with three friezes. The first, next to the completely painted ceiling, is divided up by many pictures by Andrea del Sarto, Jacopo Pontormo, Perino del Vaga, Puligo, Domenico and Ridolfo Ghirlandaio, and Albertinelli. Between each picture are wax models, a braccio high,[14] and ancient bronze figures of many styles [*maniere*]. The second frieze is composed of eight pictures by Francesco Salviati and of two very beautiful views by Alessandro [21] del Barbiere. Between these paintings, bronze figurines by Giambologna and other worthy men are placed on beautiful shelves – from which medallions and ovals of jasper, bloodstone, amethyst, agate, and many other stones hang. Around the third frieze is a shelf on which there are many bronze and marble statues and ancient and modern heads that are placed between many painted pictures by ancient masters,[15] some drawings by Bronzino and by Taddeo and Federico Zuccaro, and two very beautiful sheets of new inventions by the Flemming Giovani Strada. The fourth room, which has a devout bronze Crucifix at its primary entrance, is devoted to the study of belles-lettres. There are countless books on various professions. And there one sees the busts of the most famous ancient and modern philosophers and poets. And there are three great spheres, two of wood, one the terrestrial globe, the other the celestial, and the third of brass demonstrating the spherical rings, and a beautiful timepiece that sounds the measurement of the time hour by hour. The fifth room, where he retires to paint and draw, is also decorated with many sketches, models, and a very beautiful picture by Andrea del Sarto.

'Ridolfo has done many things of painting and sculpture himself. Among others is a marble head of his father portrayed from life that resembles him greatly. Another equally is of his mother. On this, besides appearing as if it were alive, it is a marvellous thing to see the very thin veil that he has done on her head that [22] hangs onto her shoulders, every part separate from the neck and done with so much care that it is transparent. In painting I have seen the portrait of his very dear friend Raffaello Borghini. It lacks only speech to make it seem alive. He now has in hand, having completed all the limbs, a larger-than-life marble Venus with a Cupid at her feet. Very great grace is already seen in this. The wax model, studied from life, promises that she will have to be a figure of all beauty and perfection. But because, as I said a little before this, these things are made more to see than to hear about, I will, with your good grace, refrain from speaking more about them.'

'One would expect nothing less from the graciousness of Bernardo,' Sirigatti said. 'But when Messer Girolamo [Michelozzi] deigns to come to see my things, clearly he will be able to recognize how much greater is [Bernardo's] oratorical skill than [my] weak accomplishment.'

'For now it would not occur to me to respond to this,' Michelozzi added. 'But I should greatly thank Bernardo, who has satisfied my question. He has given us the opportunity, which it did not displease you in taking, of consuming this very warm time in talking about painting and sculpture. Having seen the rare things that he has of painting and sculpture and this painted chapel, and then also having heard the things of Sirigatti discussed, with the good grace of you others, I would ask him if it would please him to discuss some of these fine arts [in general]. [23] Learning from this will make me thank him for having gratified my desire.'

'You need not be grateful to me,' Vecchietti replied. 'When I discussed your suggested subject I spoke without preparation, knowing you to be astute. But, liking the subject very much, I would not refuse a beautiful occasion to discuss what you have put before us. Ridolfo, however, understanding both the arts, is expected to speak of them.'

'Talking about something is fundamentally different from the experience of putting it into practice,' Sirigatti responded. 'There are many painters and sculptors who have done things that cannot be criticized but who cannot discuss what they have done. Therefore, if one had to make a model or figure here, perhaps I could not refuse because of some experience that I had had in it, in being the first to put it into practice. But now, having only to discuss them, you, who every day have the ancient and modern books at hand and that which is found here [Vecchietti's collection] and find yourself every hour next to princes and great men where such things are discussed, are more suited, it seems to me, to the first place.'

'Forgive me, I pray you,' Valori added irrepressibly, 'if I change the relative position of things between you with too much audacity. Much time is uselessly lost, however, and many opportunities of life denied us through respect and ceremony. I would not wish that now, out of a desire to humour each other, we should lose, through inexperience, this beautiful [24] occasion that we are handed to discuss painting and sculpture. And I offer, with the help of Girolamo, to so straightforwardly arrange things among you that no one will have just cause to complain.'

'Very gladly,' immediately replied Michelozzi. 'I will help you in any way I can, provided that the thrust of our discussion today deals with things of the fine arts, about which for a long time I have wanted to have detailed understanding.'

'I,' added Valori, 'if it is not displeasing to you, would have it that Bernardo discuss those parts of painting and sculpture that pertain to philosophy, poetry, and history. And it falls to Ridolfo to discuss those things that pertain to the painter and sculptor in the practice of their arts.'

'Truly, you have organized things so well,' Michelozzi said, 'that no one, the spirit tells me, being by nature most gracious and our being given this special opportunity, could refuse such an honourable undertaking.'

'You have done such in your words,' Sirigatti responded. 'As for me, I feel weak under such a heavy weight and want to put it down immediately. But, to obey you, rather than get out from under the weight, which would displease you, I will carry it forward.'

'It would be a very improper thing,' said Vecchietti, 'if I alone appeared to disagree with you three. But I protest to you, that you are very deceived in your opinion in thinking that I could discuss things that are worthwhile on this subject. [25] And I will be worthy of being excused if I, pulled by others, stumble along that road where I cannot go of my own strength. But you, Baccio, to whom by study such discussion is more fitting, even though more serious subjects are your profession, if you are going to be here while we toil, I do not know how you will view things done here. Gravitas is left in town, and the familiarity of our practice here is such that many things that in the city would be unsaid are very appropriate here.'

'On the contrary, I have already shown that I do not want it to be me,' added Valori. 'I have divided the subjects between you with so much boldness so that it seems to me that who can do it better will. Therefore, start the desired discussion so that I will not fail when the occasion presents itself to speak.'[16]

Definition of sculpture and painting

Vecchietti responded: 'Sculpture and painting are arts of which one removes the superfluity of the material and the other adds onto it that which is judged appropriate, making what was in the mind of the craftsman appear. Both imitate the natural and artificial things that exist or that could exist. And they have in common four factors, which are: the material, the formal, the efficient, and the ultimate. The material is that of which everything that is made is made. The formal is that which gives the essence to something. The efficient is he who makes it. And the ultimate is that reason which invites the craftsman to make it, for glory or for gain. And, as the formal cannot exist without the material, so, neither can the agent without the ultimate, which is more [52] noble than all the others because everything [that is done] is done for its goal. And this is as much as it seems to me one can say about the definition of these arts ... Nothing else remains for me to do now, if I am not mistaken, but to divide them appropriately into their various components.'

Which are the components of painting and sculpture

'I would divide painting into five components:[17] invention, composition, poses, parts, and colour. Sculpture [is divided] into the first four, and only that many when scenes are done in bas-relief. When statues are only done completely in the round, composition is not needed, but only the other three, that is invention, pose, and parts.'

'Please discuss these components more broadly for us,' Sirigatti said, 'since I intend to touch on them in my discussion.'

'I call invention,' answered Vecchietti, 'that narrative or fable, or that man or god, that the painting or sculpture represents. Composition is that beautiful order that is made of many figures, animals, landscape, and architecture. [In composition] all things appear well distributed, with their dress and place appropriately well positioned and well ordered. Poses are those actions and gestures that the figures make, either in sitting or standing upright, stooping, waking up, or other actions that speak more fully of the invention, the person, or the place. Parts are those proportions and measure [53] that there are among the parts of the figure, thus appearing neither too long nor too short nor in any way crippled. Colouring is not only that charm and delicacy that [colours] show when mixed with care and well laid on but also their meaning and appropriateness to those people and those places to which they are applied.

Invention is the only one of these five components that most of the time does not derive from the craftsman. The other four all depend on his judgment. Therefore, I will leave them to Ridolfo and will say something only of invention. It is something that often depends on narrative or poetry. It seems not a little to me that the sculptors and the painters, taking too much licence, have erred in invention.'

'You speak the truth,' Valori added immediately, 'and I remember having read a dialogue by Messer Giovanni Andrea Gilio of Fabriano. In it he shows many errors the painters made in invention, and particularly Michelangelo in his marvellous *Judgment*.[18] You have probably seen this discourse.'

'Yes truly,' Vecchietti answered, 'and if I remember, he divides painters into three manners: poetic painters, narrative painters, and 'mixed' painters. This is a division that does not displease me. As he would have it, when the painter represents the things of poets, he should take the invention from them. When he paints narratives he should observe the truth of them. And when he paints [54] landscapes or other things that depend neither on poetry nor narrative he is given rather more latitude. These have acquired the name 'mixed.'[19] But it is not, therefore, reasonable that in the warmest part of midday he represent mountains full of snow or orange and olive trees and cedars on the coldest mountains of the north.'

'I am of the opinion,' Michelozzi said, 'that many painters believe they are able to do whatever most pleases them, moved by the words of Horace in his *Poetics*, that to painters and to poets is given equal power to invent what is to their liking.[20] And, following the sound of these words they would have a very broad field, more to unfold their own concepts than to show the inventions of others.'

'What you say is unfortunately true,' answered Vecchietti. 'And many are those who err. They use the shield of the authority of Horace in these verses, more from having heard them from others than understanding what they intend to say. And perhaps they are not familiar with what Horace added a little later:

But not that tame animals should mate with the savage,
charming little birds with horrid snakes,
and innocent lambs with cruel tigers.[21]

But since these dissolute painters want to excuse themselves by having the same authority as the poets, I am pleased to concede it to them. But let's see if they don't go too far, and if poets have as much authority and freedom to invent as they seem to believe.'

Of the authority of poets and of painters

'Poets [55] would have it that many people have been transformed into trees, rivers, springs, stones, and wild beasts. But this is not accomplished by human doings but by the will of the gods. And then these fables are not completely accurate. They only describe the outward appearance, rather than describing even a crumb of the great substance within. It will be seen if poets are enlarged or diminished after having invented these things, putting forward such fables. It is certain that good authors have not done this. Nevertheless, many are those painters who, painting things, change the identity and the figures. In addition to that, at their convenience, they invent new things, or take away things already established, or paint them to the contrary.'

The painting of figures in the air without wings to be an error

'The poets, with their great authority, have not made mortal men fly through the air without wings or without some winged thing that could carry them, unless they are moving by the magic arts. And, therefore, one reads that Bellerophon, wanting to go through the air, rode the horse Pegasus, which had wings. And Perseus was given wings by Mercury. And Ariosto, very aware of this, had his hippogriff rise, making him first ridden by Ruggerio and then on a longer course by Astolfo. But in this the painters are held more accountable, since there are those among them who have made men fly through the air without wings. They could not have Daedalus and Icarus try to flee the labyrinth, as the poets showed, without something that would be able to support men in the air, assembling it of feathers and wax. And it was this [56] that failed Icarus and forced him to fall into the sea.'

'Forgive me if I interrupt you,' said Michelozzi smiling. 'Perhaps the painters value the authority of Boccaccio where he says that Alberto da Imola flew many times at night without wings for the love of Donna Lisetta.'[22]

All laughed at these words, and Sirigatti added: 'I believe that on such occasions not only the painters but all other men would want them, so that they would not have to come to the second experience of Alberto when he flew from the window into the canal.'

'Bernardo, it also follows from your reasoning,' said Valori, 'that those without wings, should the opportunity present itself, would avoid launching themselves into the air in flight.'

'Not only humans,' Vecchietti continued, 'but even gods. The poets not having wanted that they go through the air without any means of supporting themselves. Therefore, they have given them wings, chariots pulled by various animals, and clouds, which, descending to earth, support them. Giulio Caccini is a young man who, in addition to the excellence of the music with which he appears in every famous place, is graced with handsome and modest manners. He had a modern painter, of whatever name, complete a picture that another Flemish painter had left unfinished. In it Apollo is seen flaying Marsyas, together with some beautiful landscapes. There, not having room to do anything except in the air, he did, to make them appear rather distant, the nine Muses on a cloud in the act of looking at [57] the well-done spectacle of Marsyas.'

'Since they are held up by the cloud,' said Sirigatti unrestrainedly, 'he should not have done wrong.'

'On the contrary,' Vecchietti replied, 'it seems to me that he has doubly erred in this. First, by having the nine Muses there. And I do not know how he came up with such a thing. Minerva and Midas, King of Lydia, were said to have been the judges of this. And according to the true judgment of Minerva, Apollo won, so that Midas, in ignorance favouring Marsyas, had his ears turned into those of a donkey. And Marsyas was skinned for it. For this, they say, the nymphs and the satyrs having wept so much that a river was born, it took its name from Marsyas. Others say that the nymphs, the fauns, and the satyrs of the country were the judges of it and that the river that we spoke about began from the blood of the flayed Marsyas. Therefore, it is clearly seen, for the first error, that the Muses did not have anything to do here.

'Then I cannot see how the Muses, for the first time, have now been able to crowd onto the clouds only to observe Apollo flaying Marsyas. [The Muses] always have their meetings on earth. Never, from what I have seen, are they in the sky or in the air. The exception was when they foresaw the downfall of certain cloisters in the Pyrenees in which they were confined. In order to flee, so that they not be taken by force, they were perhaps allowed by the Gods to fly out rather than the young women coming to shame.'

'Your comments are subtle, [58] Bernardo,' Sirigatti replied. 'Because, not being able to make figures except in the air, I believe he put the Muses here to enrich the picture with figures, because [the painting] concerns a poetic subject and because, as you know, [the Muses] are called Camenae.[23] But if he had not done this here, what would he have been able to do? How could he have done better?'

'I answer you first,' Vecchietti responded, 'that mine is not subtlety but truth. And then that things inappropriate and against order are first found to impoverish and not to enrich paintings. [The painter] could well have located [his painting] on Mount Parnasus. This is in Phocis, where the fable of Marsyas was found. But he did not judge it appropriate to have the Muses come in the end to Phrygia, as was the case. Therefore, others should not have allowed him to give the Muses this awkwardness. There was no shortage of judges in Phrygia who were able to judge this. As for what should have been painted here, it only being possible to do figures in the air, it is one's duty to only do things that can possibly be in the air, like birds or truly figures that are painted with wings such as Victory and Virtue coming to crown Apollo. And here you could add Pride and Arrogance, which they tie up and defeat.'

'Could he not also,' said Michelozzi, 'put Apollo here on his chariot in the sky, in the act of arriving in Heaven victoriously? That, perhaps, would be closer to the sense of the fable. It would be possible to place the figure gracefully within the rays of the Sun. One could make of these, different effects in the air and embellish [59] the chariot with four horses and other things pertaining to the Sun, lightening it up with some birds.'

'I told you before,' Vecchietti responded, 'that painting is the imitation of natural and artificial things that are or that could be.[24] And, therefore, there should not be painting in a picture that is different from what the eyes see represented in those things that we can see in one view, such as having Apollo in the air and [also] on the ground flaying Marsyas. He cannot be in two places at the same time. We cannot see the same person at one time in two places.'

'I have also seen,' Michelozzi added, 'many narratives in fresco and many panels[25] in oil where several things are done by only one person. In the courtyard of the *Annunziata*, by the hand of Andrea del Sarto, there are three different deeds of St Philip seen in only one picture. Although I do not know why it could not be done, since in the foreground view he has made his figures larger. Then the same, St Philip is seen in more distant places, not really being in the same place. And equally, Alessandro del Barbiere has done a very beautiful panel that is in San Brancatio [Pancrazio], where there are three episodes concerning St Sebastian. The first, in the nearest view, is when he is put in the tomb. He is beaten at the column in the second. And the third, when he is shot at with arrows, appears in the distance and is very beautiful to see.'

'I will not deny you,' Vecchietti replied, 'that many painters have erred in [60] this. Consider what little verisimilitude there is if we would be able to see one person three times in one view, with the same body being in three places. And how possible is it that one is shown alive and dead at the same time? When the painters want to paint so many episodes they should divide their wall or their panel into more pictures and do in every picture its episode. And in this they would conform with a good heroic poet who undertakes in each poem to treat only one deed of one knight and then, wanting to have others speak, has them speak in episodes.[26] Thus, [the poet] is seen to divide each incident from the beginning. Similarly the painter should divide his narrative into several pictures and not confuse all together, a thing repugnant to art and nature. Therefore, I hold it a very grave fault to paint the same person in the same picture many times, even if he is shown close by and then far away. The eye, gazing at natural things, is able to enlarge its view enough to be able to see men, women, animals, trees, mountains, and rivers all at once. It does not set apart one of these things in several places. In nature itself something cannot be at any time in more than one place.'

'The painters,' Sirigatti said, 'try as much as they can to demonstrate the excellence of their art. They energetically paint many episodes, to have the opportunity to do more poses and so that the painting fills up the canvas.'[27] [61]

'When painters,' Vecchietti added fervently, 'wish to show the excellence of their art, they paint fables or narratives that follow their subject without changing them. They do not find in them something of their own [imagination]. For example, wanting to show various poses and human effort, Michelangelo imagined some soldiers, washing by a river, hearing the trumpets and drums calling them to the battle [of Cascina].[28] Therefore, marvellous gestures of dressing and getting out of the river are seen in them and the hurried preparation to fierceness as the requirement of war calls them.

'But because I have not previously shown [as much as I would like] how the poets do not enjoy as much licence in this as the painters think, it would please me to say a few things more to set apart those who wish to use the same authority. It is not permitted for [the poets] to trespass the rules imposed on them, as it is not appropriate for painters to represent the things invented by others differently than wanted by those who invented them in the first place.'

Things inappropriate to poets and to painters

'The poet is the imitator of the deeds of others. What praise of good poetry would we believe that he merited if the poet, making a prince speak, made him say those words that a cowardly and ignorant servant would say? And if he [had] an idiotic person [speak] with the majesty that would be appropriate for a king or an emperor in the course of his affairs? And if he put in the mouth of a modest and noble matron, or a pure young virgin, the licentious words of an infamous woman? Equal [censure] [62] would come to the painter should he wish to transform the order of the narratives or of the tales already received from the world, or [make] inappropriate the attributes or the clothing of the figures that he wished to place in a painting. Feeling himself highly valued in the making of nudes, Bronzino did this in his narrative in fresco of St Lawrence [in San Lorenzo].[29] He had the Emperor tormenting the martyr [while] surrounded by his barons [who were] all nude or covered with few drapes, something very unsuitable to people who serve high princes. Also unfortunate are those virtues, gathered there in the form of very beautiful women sitting among the other people. And in addition it pleased him to do them seen individually in the air and in other places. There are also some poets who, having developed some beautiful description of the celestial arc or of the dawn, it appearing to them that they have done a beautiful thing, put it in each of their writings although it has little purpose in being there. Some painters do this. Painting a cypress or a dog or other thing well, they want it seen in every painting that they do, even though it is not appropriate. And in this it can be conceded that the painters and the poets, with equal praise, are in equal repute.'

'Truly,' Michelozzi said, 'from what I see every day, the authority of poets is not as great as others think. Granted that no work appears to me to be more rehearsed and in every least part more thoughtful than that of the poets. And in great sorrow one sometimes sees a sonnet that, [63] while it is well constructed, passes through the hands of those who presume to understand poetry without taking it in.'

'From two causes,' Vecchietti answered, 'if I am not mistaken, one is able to say this. The first is that truly there are few today who write according to the rules of poetry, and then only when they come to speak of nature. They think that only the born versifier is able to write adequately, as many painters are given to understand that doing figures of well-composed parts and beautiful colours suffices to become known as worthy men. They have not considered the context in which they paint. All their stories or fables are done to the contrary. The second is that many put little into their [own] work. Only by criticizing many of the things of others are they thought to have obtained some understanding. And because [poets] never read poetry they grimace and shake their heads as if they always see things unworthy of their wisdom.'

'Ah, how much better it would be,' added Valori, 'rather than these discussions of the work of others, if they employed the time that they spend in finding new arguments to offend those who try to please the world in undertaking to work. Then many would recognize the difference there is between wasting words on the deeds of others and going to work and making the concepts of the mind appear with order.'[30]

'Let us not abandon [the visual artists] for the poets,' said Sirigatti. '[The poets] know very well how to defend themselves from malignant comments with their verses. Continue with our discussion [64] of the inventions of the painters and the sculptors. I have in mind putting some of these ideas into practice when I can. I now understand that I should observe how they [should] be derived from others rather than, from the liberty with which I use them, pretending they are something of my own.'

Invention divided into two parts

'You have in your words,' Vecchietti responded, 'mentioned two things of great importance, that is, inventions derived from others and those that come from the artisan himself. And in truth it would seem to me that inventions suitable to the painter and to the sculptor should be divided into these two comments of yours. The inventions that the painters or the sculptors take from the poets or the historians should not otherwise be represented than as the authors themselves write and direct.[31] Those inventions that the artisan himself develops can then be expanded over a larger field as they please.'

'Please,' Sirigatti added, 'so that I quite understood these two kinds of inventions, give me some examples of what you call invention: that derived from others and that which can be attributed to the craftsman himself.'

What is invention that proceeds from others

'An invention that proceeds from others – not wanting to separate myself from the fictions of the poets –,' Vecchietti said, 'is that fable, which was first told by Ovid and others, represented by Titian in the person of Venus and Adonis with other things. And from [the poets] it is said that Adonis, when he was propositioned by Venus, threw himself on his knees at her feet. He thanked her [65] for having deigned to concede her divine beauty to a mortal man and was quite ready, with reverence, to serve her. From this it appears that Titian failed in the invention. He showed Adonis fleeing from Venus, who is in the act of embracing him. Here most [authorities] desire that they embrace each other. And when she, having to go up into Heaven, advised him to abstain from going to hunt fierce wild animals, she from him, and not he from her, departed, flying towards the sky. And then he, wretched one, little observing her instructions, proceeded to his unlucky death that she so bitterly mourned. Therefore, it can be seen that Titian took to himself that licence that painters should not take.

'A well-observed invention can be called that of Michelangelo, in the very beautiful figure that he did as the *Night* [in San Lorenzo].[32] Besides doing her in the act of sleeping, he put a moon on her forehead and a nocturnal bird at her feet.'

Night as painted by the ancients

'These things demonstrate night, even though they were painted otherwise by the ancients. Granted that [the ancients] showed her as a woman with two great black wings, enveloped with a mantle full of stars with a garland of poppies on her head. This was an image that Buonarroti well knew to be more proper to the painter than to the sculptor. And while the *Dawn, Day,* and *Dusk* are not only beautiful but marvellous, primarily for their pose and the composition of their parts, nevertheless I do not know what to say of the invention. They did not have, when they were finished, any of the attributes that the ancients gave them [66] to make them known. If the names that Michelangelo had for them were not already known, I do not know that I could see that any, while well conceived, would be able to be recognized.[33]

'As also the figures made, as *Equity* and *Rigour,*[34] for the new Uffizi by Vincenzo Danti of Perugia cannot be recognized by their attributes. Cannot be seen as who they are, it is said, because from the principal view from the street some of the things they have in their hands are hidden. Whoever wishes to see them needs to take the trouble to climb up to where the figures are placed.'

'If [Danti] did the attributes corresponding to the finished figures,' Sirigatti said, 'I would not call this an error of invention but rather of carelessness, in not knowing in which place to erect them appropriately.'

'You are correct,' Vecchietti responded, 'because such things truly are necessary. Those who will see these figures where ordinarily they are to be seen will not see any demonstrable sign of who they are. They will imagine that the craftsman had either left the invention in the chisel or, it would be better to say, in the marble, or truly might have wanted to represent nothing more than a man and a woman.'

'It is certain that not to see the appropriate attributes in figures brings very great annoyance to those who look at them,' Michelozzi said, 'since it cannot be guessed who they are. It is not less important, I think, that the attributes facilitate the devotion of those who are accustomed to see them.

'Ammanati did the twelve signs of the Zodiac on the wheels of the chariot of his Neptune in the Piazza.[35] I do not know if it comes from my limited [67] understanding or from being a new invention that I am unable to imagine what the signs of the Zodiac have to do with Neptune. Also I do not remember having seen [Neptune] elsewhere with garlands of pine. Therefore, do me the favour, Bernardo, of telling me your opinion about such a thing.'

'I am afraid,' Vecchietti answered, 'that my opinion with respect to the celestial signs would rather add to your doubt instead of giving you any good resolution.'

To whom the ancients gave pine

'As for the pine, this reminds me that I have read that it was given by the ancients to the great Mother Goddess. The very beautiful youth greatly loved by her, Ati, was transformed, in dying, into a pine. Also Valeriano in his *Hieroglifici*[36] and Cartari in his *Imagini degli Dei*[37] would have it that the pine was devoted to Pan, god of the shepherds. They said that Piti, the nymph loved by him, was transformed into a pine. But I believe that they are deceived since Piti – as Benedetto Curtio Sinforiano says in his *Libro degli Orti*[38] – was not transformed into a pine but into a spruce. This is a species of pine and very similar to the fir. [The spruce] was consecrated to the god Pan and not the pine. The ancients also preferred the spruce to the pine, noting that [the spruce] was beautiful, tall, straight, and always green, appearing to invite people to put themselves under its shade. And then [there was] the often great injury to those hit by falling pine cones. Also the pine was given to Bacchus and to Neptune. [68] These gods are occasionally seen with this attribute. And Plutarch gives the reason in his *Symposiaca*,[39] saying that the pine is appropriate to Bacchus. He is the god who created these trees. Casks are caulked with pitch made from the sap of pines. The ancients flavoured their wine with pitch, which they called *vino picato*, and held to be excellent. And finally because those lands where there are many pines produce very good wines because, Theophrastus says,[40] pines are more often in places where the ground is full of gravel and there the vines, because of the drainage, come to perfection. [Pines] are equally dedicated to Neptune. Like Neptune, they rise above the mists. They make ships from pine. And pitch, without which ships could not possibly plough the sea, is made from the sap of the pine. The ancients also crowned the victors of the Isthmian games, dedicated to Neptune, with garlands of pine. Therefore, for all these reasons, you can clearly understand that the pine is appropriate to Neptune.'

What celestial signs are and why they are imagined in the sky

'But I do not know what to say about the celestial signs. These were imagined in the Zodiac by the first astrologers to show the course of the planets and the movement of the Sun. Perhaps these signs were not anything other than stars separated into twelve parts, every part occupying thirty degrees in length and twelve in width. They came to form the circle of the animals perhaps, it is said, because the influence of the stars have some correspondence with the nature of the animals that gave them their name. [69] Perhaps those ancient poets, who made up stories, wanted to imprint the deeds of mortals on the sky in this way. Perhaps the position of such stars has some similarity with the form of these animals, and it was the occupation of the astrologers to impose on them some name. And under this circle [of signs], without ever failing, the Sun passes by the ecliptic forming the year, divided into twelve months by the twelve parts that it transcribes.[41] Thus, I do not know how it happened that the twelve signs were put on the eight wheels with Neptune signifying the sea.'

'As you know,' Sirigatti said, 'the poets imagine that when the Sun falls below the horizon, it goes to lie down in the sea. And similarly I believe it is possible to say of the celestial signs that, when they set, they go down into the sea to lie down. And consequently Neptune, as their caretaker, could be decorated with them.'

'Yes, but consider Ridolfo,' Vecchietti answered excitedly, 'that it might not be necessary to take this other than as you have devised. Some could believe that Neptune made prisoners of his guests [the celestial signs], leading them at the wheels of his chariot as in a triumph. This, however, would suggest betrayal rather than the glory of Neptune.'

All smiled at this comment, and Valori added: 'I would believe that it can be said that the celestial signs have been given to Neptune because the greater part of them either depend on the sea or exert some important effect on it. And while there are many that [70] have no relationship with the sea, in this the style of the poets is followed. They are used to taking the part for the whole, so in this they are taking the whole for the part.'

'And which signs are those that depend on the sea,' Michelozzi asked, 'and are thus in high ascent?'

'The Ram, the Bull, the Crab, the Scorpion, Capricorn, Aquarius, and the Fish,' responded Valori. 'The Ram is because Neptune was transformed into one when loving the maid Theophane. She, to be more comfortably enjoyed, was transformed into a sheep. And from their union the Ram with the golden fleece was born on which Phrixos passed over the sea with Helle. She fell into the sea and gave it the name Hellespont, and Neptune remembered her in creating the peony. The Bull is because

Jupiter, transformed into one, passed over the sea with his beloved prey, sheltering in Crete to happily enjoy his love. The Crab is for being a water creature and for having restrained the flight of the nymph Garamantide, while Jupiter amorously chased her. The Scorpion is for having killed Orion, born of the urine of Jupiter, Neptune, and Mercury. He presumed, with so much arrogance, to kill all the animals of the Earth. Capricorn is because its rear half is a fish and because the god Pan transformed himself into one and, jumping into the water, escaped from the cruel anger of Typhoeus. Aquarius and the Fish are because they were nurtured in the sea and from the sea they have their essence. [71] Venus and Cupid were transformed into fish in the Euphrates River to flee from the fury of the aforesaid giant [Typhoeus]. Therefore, all these signs having something to do with the sea, it does not appear perhaps inappropriate – taking the whole from the part – that the celestial signs be given to Neptune.'

'You have discussed these new attributes of Neptune with beautiful acuteness,' Vecchietti replied, 'but I suspect that Scorpio has misled you into giving the wrong judgment. Having killed Orion, one-third the child of Neptune, for fear that the father, whoever he was, would take revenge for the son, he would not dare as you [would have it] to be an attribute on [Neptune's] chariot. And even if Jupiter, also the father of Orion, took [Scorpio] to heaven for this deed, [Jupiter] perhaps did this to demonstrate how much, as universal judge, he hated [Neptune's] arrogance. He would not, therefore, put [Scorpio] by his side, as now is seen with Neptune. And if you would say that he leads him as in a triumph, I would respond that it should be equally so for the other attributes that are put in the same place. This is something very disgraceful, since they had not deserved becoming prisoners.'

'Since we have talked enough about Neptune,' Michelozzi said, 'say something, Bernardo, about the very beautiful statue by Giambologna, done as the *Rape of the Sabine*.[42] And please make this narrative known to me and perhaps, in addition to this, other [narratives] that are related to it.'[43]

'Giambologna demonstrated,' Vecchietti responded, 'how excellent he was in his art by making many large and small figures of bronze and endless models. [72] Some envious craftsmen, not being able to deny that in such things he was extremely rare, admitted that he was very capable in making graceful figurines and models in various poses with a certain charm, but that in setting to work on the great figures of marble, in which true sculpture consists, he would not be able to succeed.

For that reason, Giambologna, directed by the spur of virtue, decided to show the world that he not only knew how to make ordinary figures of marble but also many together, and the most difficult that it was possible to do. And known to him was all the art of making nude figures: demonstrating the weaknesses of old age, the strength of youth, and the delicacy of women. And so he produced, only to demonstrate the excellence of his art and without selecting any subject, a fiery youth who abducted a very beautiful young girl from a debilitated old man. And having almost finished this marvellous work, it was seen by the Most Serene Francesco de' Medici, our Grand Duke. And admiring its beauty, he decided to put it in that place where it is now seen. Therefore, because the figures could not go out [of the studio] without some name, he urged Giambologna to find some invention to call his work. And he was told, I do not know by whom, that it would be well done to follow the narrative of the Perseus of Benvenuto [Cellini]. He might intend the abducted girl for Andromeda, the wife of Perseus. The abductor was her uncle Phineus. And the old man was Andromeda's father Kephus. [73] But Raffaello Borghini happened to be one day in the shop of Giambologna and saw to his great delight this beautiful group of figures. Hearing the narrative of what it should represent, [Borghini] showed signs of surprise. Giambologna, noticing this, strongly pleaded with [Borghini] to say what he thought of this. [Borghini] concluded that in no manner should [Giambologna] give such a name to his statue but that it would be better adapted to the *Rape of the Sabine*. Which narrative, having been judged appropriate, gave its name to the work.'[44]

'Why was it not possible to use the narrative of Andromeda,' Michelozzi asked, 'since it would compliment the Perscus that is beside it?'

'Because,' Vecchietti said, 'from that would follow many errors.'

The narrative of Andromeda

'The first one would have been of the narrative. Andromeda was never abducted by Phineus or anyone else. It is true that Phineus, while she was being married, came into the room with armed men to kill Perseus. Nevertheless, not only did he not touch the young girl to put his thoughts into effect, but he was transformed by Perseus, with the head of the Gorgon, into stone. The second error would also be of the narrative in showing Kephus, father of the young girl, struck down by Phineus. This never happened. The third would be committed in going against what was observed by the ancients and the moderns in raising statues to gods, famous heroes, and brave captains. And here a statue would be raised to Phineus, a man of dark reputation who was ruined and killed in attempting this very enterprise.[45] [74] The fourth would be in demonstrating little invention. One would appear to have stolen the concept from the Perseus of Benvenuto. Further, it would be recognized as turning everything upside-down because, in this narrative, Perseus should be taking the initiative, raising himself up against the reputation of Phineus his enemy. Also, this would require an adjustment because all the other statues of the Piazza have different narratives rather than only one. [Giambologna's group] should also follow the same organization.[46] The fifth error would be that it made it possible to imagine Phineus taking the young girl in his arms to lead her away. It would not be possible, therefore, to say that any good result followed from this act, rather we would be forced to concede that his thought had been foolish and dishonourable. Therefore, to avoid all these errors, the task was to find a more proper and more noble narrative, such as that of the Sabines.'

'I am now very satisfied,' Michelozzi said, 'that such an invention was not used. Please do not mind, however, telling me briefly how the abduction of the Sabines happened and how it is appropriate to this statue.'

The narrative of the Sabines

'After Romulus had built and occupied Rome,' Vecchietti responded, 'not having women, he sought to convince others to want to join their young girls in marriage to the young Romans. He was refused this. Therefore, he thought with astuteness of obtaining that which he could not achieve by asking. And therefore, [75] with great preparation, he gave orders to celebrate Consular games in honour of the equestrian Neptune[47] and made a public proclamation about it. For this reason, many people gathered to see the festival and the new city, among whom were the Sabines with their women. And while they were all intent on looking at the festival, the young Romans, as they had organized it among themselves, abducted all the young Sabine girls, from the arms of fathers and from the laps of mothers. Among whom, being carried away by some comrades of Talassio was a very beautiful girl. And when asked whose girl she was, [the Romans] responded "of Talassio and to Talassio we lead her." And therefore, since this marriage would have a happy outcome, the Romans became accustomed at a wedding, as the Greeks invoked Hymen, to call out the name of Talassio.'

Talassio, Roman god of weddings

'Therefore [Giambologna] intended the abducted young girl as this Sabine. And the abductor represents Talassio who, while he did not publicly take her away himself, he did abduct her for himself and took her virginity in private by force. And [Giambologna] showed the old man below as her father, the story saying, as I have said, that they abducted them from the arms of fathers. And one can then consider Talassio as the Romans, prevailing over the Sabine people represented by the old man. And the parts of these people in embrace is imagined as the rape of the Sabine because truly, of these two people were made one, in Rome, which then became so powerful.'

'With great pleasure have I understood how the Rape of a Sabine is appropriate to this beautiful statue,' Michelozzi said. [76] 'Now it will be possible to continue our previous discussion.'

'It seems to me these things have been covered rather well,' Sirigatti added, 'how invention is derived from other people and how craftsmen are not to alter, neither to amplify nor diminish, any part of it. It remains for me now to understand that invention which, as something of his, the painter is able to expand without fear of being reprimanded for not having observed the narrative or the fable.'

'This field is very broad,' Vecchietti responded, 'but nevertheless we need to go over it with great judgment.'

Invention proper to the craftsman

'I would term it the invention of the craftsman to show the four seasons of the year, not with figures of the gods as was done by the ancients but, according to the incidents that every season brings with itself. In winter the painter would be able to show ice, snow, hunting, fires, and other similar things to his liking and other seasons in this way. He does them with more or less plentiful figures, according to what most pleases him, provided he does not show mature grapes in the spring and heavy heads of wheat swaying in the fields in the fall. The craftsman can do in these, and represent as his invention, costumes and clothing at his whim, hunts, battles, dances, new brides with much company, baths in which are seen lascivious women and amorous young people, little boys' games, and endless other similar things that it would be a very difficult thing to recount, thus appearing to advance here every day with new inventions. But if you want [77] two beautiful examples of this, look, Ridolfo, at those sheets that you have in your study by Francesco Salviati where he has drawn very well, of his own invention, the ages of the world and the seasons of the year and that canvas of Federico Zuccaro, of very beautiful and charming invention, placed in the Sala Grande of the new Uffizi.'

'I am now greatly satisfied,' Sirigatti said, 'concerning these two examples of invention, but what will we say of sacred paintings?'

Of sacred paintings

'We will say that the paintings and ornaments of the Church,' Vecchietti continued, 'are the scripture and the lessons of the common man. And therefore St Gregory the Great said, rather than adoring paintings, some are learning by adoration the narrative that is there in the painting since "the painting shows to the unlearned looking at it what scripture teaches those who study the sacred pages."[48] We note that the unlearned see in the paintings that which comes from God and read in them that which [they cannot read] in scripture. Every painter who wants to paint sacred images should not only know these words but consider them very well and, after considering, diligently observe them.'

'Please tell us in more detail,' Michelozzi said, 'what, in the invention of the sacred narratives, it is appropriate for the painter, who wants to do them, to observe.'

Three things that need to be observed in sacred paintings

'Three things mainly,' Vecchietti replied. 'The first is to paint the inventions derived from the Holy Scriptures simply and purely, as the Evangelists or [78] other Holy Doctors of the Church have written them, so that unlearned people, desiring to see something in the pictures, faithfully receive the Holy Mysteries in their minds. The second is that [painters] add to their inventions with very great consideration and judgment. It is not well to add to every narrative. Rather, not being well done most of the time, it reveals disgrace and great unsuitableness. The third, which should always be observed in their paintings, is modesty, reverence, and devotion so that those observers looking at them, instead of being moved to penitence, are not instead moved to lasciviousness.'

'If it would not trouble you to make it more clear,' Sirigatti intervened, 'give us some examples where the three things that you have discussed were badly or well observed.'

The Deluge poorly painted[49]

'It seems to me that Jacopo Pontormo,' Vecchietti said, 'who had been a worthy man in his other works, observed these poorly in the choir of San Lorenzo. Having painted Noah going out of the ark, as he was promised by the Almighty after the Deluge, as is seen by the rainbow, he has not faithfully represented the invention of the sacred narrative. And that which he has put there of his own cannot in any way have happened. And one does not come to speak of modesty and reverence, rather very great immodesty is seen.'

'I believe that he has done so many of these nude bodies,' Sirigatti responded, 'to demonstrate the excellence of his art in different poses, as you truly see here.'

'This is the error [79] common to all painters,' Vecchietti added, 'to want more to display their whims than to observe the sacred narrative and have respect for the holy temple of God where they paint it.'

'Please tell us how Pontormo has failed,' Michelozzi said, 'in the narrative of the Deluge. The ark is seen on the mountain and Noah, with his children and grandchildren, are reverently speaking to God. And then below one sees the dead bodies appearing in different poses according to how they were left by the receding of the waters. This would not appear to be a very inappropriate thing to those who have it well in mind.'

The narrative of the Deluge

'The sacred narrative says,' Vecchietti responded, 'that having rained forty days and forty nights, the waters that flowed over the whole world began to diminish after a hundred and fifty days and the ark grounded on the mountains of Armenia on the twenty-seventh day of the seventh month. And the first day of the tenth month the mountains started to appear. Then, forty days having passed, Noah opened the window of the ark, sending forth the raven, which did not return. And, therefore, he let loose the dove, which, not finding a place to land because waters were still everywhere, returned to the ark. Then, Noah having waited seven more days and then sending out the dove again, she returned towards evening with a branch of green olive in her mouth. And letting seven more days pass and sending out the dove, she did not return. Therefore, Noah opened the roof [80] of the ark and saw the surface of the land to be dry. And the Lord spoke to Noah, commanding him to go out with all the animals and with his children. When they were on the ground they built an altar and on that humbly made a sacrifice to God. He spoke to Noah, blessing him and his children and promising not to disperse mankind again with the flood and showing them the rainbow as a sign of the covenant.

'Now, if Pontormo had wanted to show this narrative when Noah went out of the ark to make the pact with the Lord, I ask, where is the altar on which he made the sacrifice and where are the many animals that had gone out of the ark, which would have enriched the narrative and given charm to the picture? And why did he make Noah nude as if he had got out of the water, little different from those that are still seen in [the water]? And, I ask, who made these men still alive, seeking to escape from the waters on horses and those others who are noted saving themselves. I do not know how they held onto life for so many months among the impetuous waves and storms. And then, since they are living, they would also have increased the fountainhead of humanity. This is against what the Lord determined, that only Noah and his own would resume from the beginning. Nor is it possible, where there are such men, to say how the Deluge transpired. [Their presence] would be greatly inconsistent with all the rest that is seen here, showing as it does the time at which the Deluge not only had stopped but also the waters to a large extent had receded. [81] So, you see how many errors the painters make, thoughtlessly displaying their opinions in pictures.'

The Last Judgment badly painted

'What will you say,' said Michelozzi, 'of the *Last Judgment*, also by Pontormo, which is next to the *Flood*?'

'That is done,' Vecchietti answered, 'by the same master with the same whims, and without observing any of the three things we have discussed. Scripture says the terrible Judgment, when it happens, will be done in the valley of Jehoshaphat. And the angels will take up the ashes of the dead from all parts of the world and carry them to that place. There Our Lord will stand in majesty among the angels, much more resplendent than the Sun. And all the ashes of the dead being about there, together with the bodies of those who have died up to then, the Archangel Michael according to some, or truly the Redeemer of the world himself, with great voice, as he already called Lazarus, will call the dead, who will be resurrected. And then, in an instant and indivisible moment, the marvellous mystery of the Resurrection will be accomplished. And all the dead will be resuscitated nude as they were born and as Our Lord was resurrected nude. The Resurrection will not take place with people clothed. And all who died as children or as elders will be resurrected at the perfect age of a man of thirty-three years and of that stature that they were or that they would have been at that age. The accidental defects that the body would have had will be taken away. And because the bodies will be glorified, the elect will be more beautiful, more brilliant, [82] and more resplendent. The wicked will be more ugly, more dark, and more deformed. But because Giovanni Andrea Gilio of Fabriano has written broadly of this concerning the *Judgment* of Michelangelo in that dialogue of his, *Of the Errors of the Painters*,[50] I believe my having said this little will suffice to show how far from the truth is the painting of Pontormo. In it, as you know, he has made a great mountain of ugly bodies, a filthy thing to see, where some are shown resurrected, others are being resurrected, and other corpses are lying around in immodest positions. And up above [Pontormo] has done some *bambocci*[51] with very forced gestures playing trumpets, and I believe that he wants them to be recognized as angels.'

'Why cannot they be recognized as angels,' Michelozzi asked, 'since they are in the air, calling with sound the dead to the Resurrection?'

How angels should be painted

'Because,' Vecchietti replied, 'angels should be painted as very beautiful young people, modest and with wings. These make them different from other young people and demonstrate in them promptness and speed in carrying out the precepts of God. Such a manner is always used to paint them, although, being spirits without body, they really do not have wings. Isaiah saw Seraphim with wings, two that veiled the face of the Lord, two the feet, and two with which they flew. A little later he added: "And one of the Seraphim flew to me."[52] And in his vision Ezekiel said that the sound of the wings of the Cherubim was heard, and then a little later continued, "and then [83] the Cherubim spread their wings."[53] Also, very beautiful young people should be painted because one reads in the scripture that they always appear as such, and because they are different from evil demons, which should be painted ugly and frightful.'

'If I have noted your words well,' Michelozzi said, 'you have said that we all will be resurrected nude and of an age of thirty-three years like the Saviour of the World. From which it should be observed, one can say, that a great fault was committed by Federico Zuccaro in the *Judgment* that he painted in the Dome of Santa Maria del Fiore.[54] There all the saints and the elect are seen dressed and of different ages.'

'You still have to remember,' responded Vecchietti, 'that I included modesty and reverence among the three things that I said were appropriate for painters in the painting of the holy narratives. And now I tell you more strongly that it is a much more appropriate thing in following these to alter the invention of the sacred writing rather than, in observing it, to give sign of little reverence and little devotion.'

How disgusting are lascivious figures in sacred temples

'And the Greeks, to demonstrate how important modesty is in paintings and to remove every foolish thought from the minds of those who look at them, painted only war and nothing else. And, taking this modesty into consideration, Homer has Ulysses take a branch of a tree full of leaves in his hand in order to cover his shameful parts when he wakes up nude outside the forest to the sound of feminine voices. And the Romans, who lacked the light of the holy faith, [84] nevertheless demonstrated a distaste for immodest paintings. The work of the painter Arellio, while it was very beautiful as art, was taken out of the temples because of his being often enamoured of infamous women and having painted in public the goddesses worshiped in those temples as the nude portraits of his loves. They, even though they had the attributes of the goddesses, were recognized as dishonest women as much as for effigies. Therefore, for the lasciviousness that they demonstrated, his efforts had a short life. Now, what should we do, who observe the true and holy Religion? Is it not our task to try with every effort so that the Holy Church is decorated with modest and devout images? Such incite, in passers-by, remorse for their failings rather than awaking their carnal senses to lasciviousness. And therefore, although Christ was resurrected nude without any drape around him, this invention [here] is nevertheless very beautiful, painting him, to veil, for modesty, his shameful parts.'

The Judgment *in the cupola well considered*

'But coming to Federico Zuccaro, I say that it was very well done to paint the elect in his *Judgment* clothed. First, it observes that modesty that above every other thing should be the use in the Church of God. And then because the different dress shows the different classes of the people. This would be difficult to recognize in nude figures, in addition to this [nudity] demonstrating little reverence and devotion. As for having done the saints of different ages, those old and those young, as not being in conformity with what [85] the Scripture says, it does not seem to me a thing worthy of blame. The different ages make it much easier to recognize the saints for who they are than in other ways of painting that one is accustomed to where, being all of one age, they cannot be differentiated one from the other. Then, his having made the damned in Hell all naked and tormented greatly pleases me. The lost do not have any adornment but are stripped of every benefit and should appear deformed. It is quite true that Zuccaro took too much licence where he represented punishment of the sin of lust. He should not so immodestly have revealed how the demons were able to touch the immodest parts of the women. This, in any non-sacred and private place would have been ill-conceived, and certainly not in a public and holy temple.'

'In this so great and marvellous painting in the cupola,' Michelozzi asked, 'are there other inventions than those derived from the sacred writings?'

'There are those of the craftsman himself,' Vecchietti answered, 'which seem to me very appropriate and easily explained.

Inventions in the painting of the cupola

'But because I know that Baccio has detailed information of all the inventions that are in this painting, he will be able do us the favour of briefly describing their organization. And thus you will be able to recognize the proper inventions in them.'

'You are as able as I to memorialize such a thing,' Valori responded. 'But since it pleases you, I will not avoid gratifying you with what I remember. However, I will not be constrained [86] by a detailed description because our discussion would be too long.

'The cupola, as you know, is divided into seven surfaces plus the principal one, which is that which is above the tribune of the Sacrament.[55] Below the enclosure of the moulding that goes around the lantern – where the

Four Evangelists and the Prophets of the Old Testament are – [the greater] part represents the time that is mentioned in the Apocalypse and signifies the Church Triumphant.

'[On the surface above the tribune of the Sacrament] two angels are seen, one of whom unfolds the document that says, "Here is the man." And the other one shows the written titulus that was posted above the Cross of Christ, "I.N.R.I."[56] And the Saviour of the World follows closely, seated on His throne. Surrounding Him are the Choir of Seraphim shown with their red wings and the Choir of Cherubim with their blue wings, according to the use received from the Church. On the right hand is the Glorious Virgin and, kneeling on the left, St John the Baptist. There one also sees an angel who thrusts a nail into a great ball covered with stars representing the *primum mobile*.[57] This shows that on this day the celestial motions will be stopped. Farther down from there are Faith, Hope, and Charity as triumphs, having accomplished their mission. Thus, the Church Militant is stripped by angels of the arms with which it fought and dressed in triumphant vestments. There lies great Mother Nature with the four seasons, not having their properties any longer. Time is shown broken in its course and Death – between two little boys, one [87] signifying death from natural and the other death from violent causes – with its sharp scythe already dulled.

'On the wall that is above the new sacristy, two angels support the Cross of the Lord, the first of the seven mysteries of His Passion. And one sees near them the Choir of Thrones seated on a white cloud. And following them are the Apostles and the Patriarchs. And then [come] the blessed of the peacemakers in the middle of whom is placed Wisdom, given by the Holy Spirit, and the virtue of Charity. And in the lower part the sin of Envy, represented by the hydra, is punished in the Inferno.

'An angel with the lance, the second mystery of the Passion, is seen on the highest place on the wall that lies above the old sacristy. And the angels denoting the Virtues are there, wearing sallets[58] on their heads and with red crosses on their armour. Martyrs of both sexes triumph there. And the gifts of the Holy Spirit, Fortitude and the virtue of Patience, are there, placed in the middle of the blessed of those that were persecuted. And below in the Inferno are punished those who have sinned in Anger, shown to us as bears, animals with a great appetite for vengeance.

'On the wall that is over the Chapel of the Cross, the angel above holds up the column, the third mystery of the Passion. And the choir of angels called the Powers, dressed in white gowns and priestly habit, are above the bishops and the priests who control the spiritual discipline of the Church of God. There the blessed of the meek are seated, having [88] the Intellect on the right, given by the Holy Spirit, and, on the left, the virtue of Prudence. And in the Inferno the appropriate suffering is shown for those left dominated by Sloth, signified by the camel.

'The wall, below which is the Chapel of St Anthony, has the angel with the sponge in its hand, the fourth mystery of the Passion. There are the angels called Dominions, with books in their hands and radiance about their heads. Nearby are the Doctors [of the Church] and the prophets and the blessed of those that have used much abstinence and fasting, with Science given by the Holy Spirit and with the virtue of Sobriety. And below in the Inferno come the afflicted who have sinned in their Gluttony, represented by Cerberus.

'On the wall that lies above the Navicella, towards the Annunziata, the angel is seen who shows the nails, the fifth mystery of the Passion. The Archangels are painted dressed in white, garlanded with flowers. And below these the virgins and religious persons and the blessed of those of clean and pure heart are accompanied by the Piety given by the Holy Spirit and the virtue of Temperance. And in the Inferno the punished who have been conquered by Lust are shown as pigs.

'The wall that is seen above the Navicella, towards the Canonica, shows the crown [of thorns], the sixth mystery of the Passion. And the angels called Principalities with crowns on their heads and with sceptres in their hands are above the emperors, kings, dukes, and other secular princes who have ably administered their realms. [89] And nearby are the blessed who with mercy for human misery have tempered the rigour of justice. In the middle of these are the Counsel given by the Holy Spirit and the virtue of Justice. And in the Inferno, those villains given to the prey of Avarice are afflicted, shown as poisonous toads.

'The robe, the seventh mystery of the Passion, is seen on the last wall, which is set in the middle, above the nave. And the angels with wings are nearby all the Christian people, called by the Church the holy people of God, and the blessed of the poor of Christ. And put in their midst is the Fear of God, given by the Holy Spirit, and the virtue of Humility. And in the Inferno, Lucifer appears shown as Arrogance.

'And those open books that are held aloft by the angels, which you see on all the walls, signify those of pure conscience who conform to the virtues that are exalted on that wall. The open books held by some little monsters lower down correspond to those living with stained consciences, who are shown to us as appearing punished below.'

Here, Valori keeping silent, Vecchietti, turning towards Michelozzi, added: 'Now, among all the things that you have heard, you should be able to easily examine the very beautiful inventions of the craftsman himself. These, from what I am made to believe, square very well [*molto ben quadrano*] with [our understanding of] the Universal Judgment.'

'Do you confirm, Bernardo,' Michelozzi asked irrepressibly, 'what is said, that these inventions were developed by Don Vincenzo [90] Borghini, then Prior of the Innocenti, and not by Zuccaro?'

'This is true,' Vecchietti replied, 'and I know very well that few others than Don Vincenzo Borghini, who was very well lettered, would have been able to organize this great painting as well. But this has little import to what I have wanted to say, which is that all the inventions that are seen in the sacred narratives, other than those that are taken [directly] from the scriptures, might be, however the inventor wished, identified as the craftsmen's own invention. One notes that most of the time who has painted [the picture] is known, and not who has developed [the invention]. And it would be much better if the painters – who do not read or understand the sacred writings – would consult with the theologians when they want to paint the divine narratives. And they should not do them by chance and their whim, since everything that is based on these is badly done. Equally in this way, in doing things well understood, they would themselves acquire all the honour and glory.'

'You speak truly,' Sirigatti responded. 'But it often happens that the sacred narrative is so bare and so stripped of figures that the painter, deciding to put in the work what the inventor did not decide to write into it, adds many things in order to give grace and fullness to his work.'

'That is well done when things are added that are not inappropriate to the principal narrative,' Vecchietti said vigorously. 'Thus, I would praise, in the panel of *Christ on the Cross* in Santa Maria Novella by Giorgio Vasari,[59] [91] the virtues, of his invention, which he has put around the sacrosanct body of the Lord. When he, then, put [the virtues] in the air, he added wings to them.'[60]

'Now we have entered Santa Maria Novella,' Michelozzi said, 'where there are so many beautiful paintings that could be very useful to us by their example. I would think it well done, before leaving, to note in each panel the three things we have discussed, how they are observed for better or for worse, as models and to clarify what we have talked about.'

Concerning the panels of Santa Maria Novella

'Therefore to begin, if it does not bore you, what do you think, Bernardo, of the panel by Bronzino, in the very beautiful Gaddi Chapel, of the young girl resuscitated?'[61]

'For me,' Vecchietti answered, 'he has, speaking of the [first] two inventions we discussed and of modesty, exceeded himself. He has observed the inventions of the sacred narrative. It says that Our Lord sent away the throngs, keeping with him only the apostles Peter, James, and John and the father and the mother of the young girl. He said to them: 'I tell you that she lives for you.'[62] And, taking her by the hand, He returned her to life and ordered that they bring something to eat. All of this is seen very well expressed in the painting. He has then, appropriately, inserted his own invention. Here, Fame is done in the air with wings, sounding the trumpet to manifest the miracle. She has another trumpet in the other hand to show, perhaps, that she now sounds the trumpet to compare the good and the true and now the trumpet to compare it with the evil and the false. Yet, he [92] has not wanted to show an angel, since the breast appears more that of a woman. Rather, perhaps, he is considering her as Fame. The ancients, however, would have painted her in another way. That is as a woman dressed in a thin veil with wings, with her body all covered with eyes, ears, and mouths, and only one trumpet in hand. But because such a figure is not very appropriate in a sacred narrative it is well done to show her in this way, showing a celestial messenger who does the office of this Fame. And, considering her as an angel, one can say that the two trumpets are shown in the two manners of the trumpets given to sound at the Universal Judgment. One to call the chosen to the Resurrection and the other the damned. These people, though, who appear in the distance striving to want to see, to be able to be there, since they are not in the same place where Christ is, perhaps it would have been better for them not to be there.[63] He has also observed reverence and devotion, making the women modest and with their breast veiled and Fame also covered with drapery.'

'He did this panel in his old age,' Michelozzi said. 'And perhaps it is so modest to purge the reputation for lasciviousness that he had acquired in his other works.'

'And also perhaps,' added Valori, 'to show that the elderly are given to proceed more modestly in their work than the younger in theirs. As the Tuscan poet said: "What in youth fails is less shameful."'

'Both reasons are good,' Sirigatti said. 'When we come [93] to speak of the other works that he did, perhaps we will find some excuses in his defence. Meanwhile, let us not, if you please, neglect following the order begun among us. And Girolamo, who has with beautiful deliberation conducted us into Santa Maria Novella, continue, if it is your pleasure. Begin by organizing the discussion of the pictures that are there.'

'I will continue,' Michelozzi responded, 'to take the opportunity to ask Bernardo to make us aware of which are the well-observed sacred narratives. And because I know how great are his manners and how much he is valued in this, without expanding into many words, perhaps for my part he will find it necessary to say what I see in the panel of Giorgio Vasari. In this he has painted Our Saviour resurrected from death,[64] surrounded in the air by many angels and, on the tomb, the angel whose shining aspect makes the soldiers that stand on guard fall down. And in front are four Apostles who devotedly regard the resurrected Saviour above them.'

A Resurrection of Christ not well painted

'It seems to me the sacred invention is greatly altered in this painting,' Vecchietti said. 'None of the Apostles were present when Our Lord was resurrected. So I do not know how four are done here, if not to make the unlettered – most of whom do not [carefully] look at painting – believe something that surpasses the requirement of what is read in the holy documents. And if He had been seen by the Apostles at the Resurrection, it would not then have happened that He appeared to the Magdalene, to Cleopas, to Luke, and to all [94] the Apostles together. All of these things are the very greatest mysteries that sacred theology contains. But then, I judge that he has put the angels that he has done surrounding the Redeemer of the World there to enrich his work. Where God is, there are angels. So it seems to me that the remainder of the panel is very well observed.'

'We pass then,' Michelozzi said, 'to the other panel of Giorgio, where he has portrayed the Sacred Virgin demonstrating the Holy Order of the Rosary.'[65]

'For some time I have wanted to know,' Sirigatti added, 'who organized the Company of the Rosary and what the crown of five Our Fathers and fifty Hail Marys signifies. Therefore, it should not be difficult for you, Bernardo, to briefly say something about it on this occasion.'

On the Rosary of the Virgin

'You have put a very large field before me on which to speak,' Vecchietti responded. 'Many, many are the considerations of the Most Holy Rosary and endless the miracles that the Glorious Virgin has done through it. And very great are the benefits and the blessings following from it to those who are inscribed in that Company. But to satisfy you in part, I will condense into a few words what I now remember about it. I say, therefore, that about the year of the incarnation of Our Lord 1200, St Dominic, inspired by the compassionate Mother of Our Saviour, who was always concerned for the health of mortals, discovered a way of sending prayers to God by saying fifteen Our Fathers and one hundred and fifty Hail Marys.[66] This way [95] of praying was called the Psalter of the Blessed Virgin, having been constructed in imitation of the one hundred and fifty psalms of David the prophet. And these prayers were so arranged for a long time in the Church of God, to the great profit of the souls following them. But the ancient serpent, enemy of our health and good behaviour, cooled the souls of the devotees of the Holy Rosary. And he dispersed the tears from their eyes so that through negligence such an agreeable and salutatory prayer almost went into oblivion. Then, about the year of Our Lord 1460, the Queen of Heaven appeared to a Brother of St Dominic, a holy man and doctor of the sacred Scriptures named Brother Alano della Rupe of Britain. And She exhorted him greatly that he preach and urge the people to resume and renew her holy Psalter and Rosary.[67] He, receiving the very holy vision, so accurately adopted it that many, including many princes and lords – among whom one of the first was the Holy Roman Emperor Frederick III – entered with great zeal into this beautiful order of prayer. It was approved by the Papal Legate Alexander, Bishop of Forlì, and then confirmed by Pope Sixtus IV. He conceded five years and five quarantines[68] of indulgence for every crown of fifty Hail Marys that was said. Then Pope Innocent VIII [granted] plenary indulgences in life and death. And Pope Leo X [granted] the indulgences of the Stations of Rome[69] to all those who were inscribed or would be enrolled in this company. If the Psalter [96] of the Virgin Mother of God is said, that crown contains one hundred and fifty Hail Marys and fifteen Our Fathers, the Rosary only fifty Hail Marys and five Our Fathers. The very Holy Psalter and the whole Rosary of the Bride of the Creator of the World is then composed and ordered of fifteen Our Fathers and one hundred fifty Hail Marys. In all these constitute fifteen decades [*decine*], signifying the fifteen mysteries of Our Lord Jesus Christ. Now this little that I have said about it will be enough for now. Those who would wish to enter into the miracles that have come from this holy prayer and describe all the other things pertaining to it would be unable to finish and our original discussion would remain incomplete.'

'Truly,' Sirigatti added, 'I have taken much pleasure in understanding the origin of the Rosary. Now continue, if you please, to say something that occurs to you about the panel of Giorgio Vasari representing this Rosary.'

'This painting depends,' Vecchietti responded, 'almost entirely on the invention of the craftsman himself. It does not seem to me that it is possible not to greatly praise the invention. I see he has made the Mother of the Highest Good in the act of receiving all those who kneel in this holy prayer and the angels who, holding her skirt wide, give comfort to those who wish to flee the falsehood of the world and shelter under her.'

'Since enough has been said about this, we proceed then,' Michelozzi said, 'to the *Samaritan* of Alessandro Allori.'[70]

'This is worthy [97] of consideration and very charming,' added Vecchietti, 'and it seems to me truly that the narrative is well observed and the other parts appropriately represented. Some say, though, that the Samaritan and the little boy are drawn too softly and lasciviously.'

'To this it can be responded,' Sirigatti said, 'that the Samaritan is in the lascivious dress that she wore before she knew the true God. And softness is less inappropriate for a little boy than for a man because the sensual appetite in much less aroused in childhood.'

'The temptations of the enemy of the human generations are great and subtle,' added Valori. 'He twists away at every least occasion where he learns he can. Thus, I would esteem it well done, as Bernardo has said, if all the figures that are put in the sacred narratives were done modestly, and not only the women and the men, but also the little boys and the angels, be covered with charming drapery.'[71]

'Since we do not have anything else to say about this, I see before my eyes,' Michelozzi said, 'the panel of the Flemming Giovanni Strada. St John the Baptist is painted baptizing Our Lord.'[72]

A Baptism of Christ poorly drawn

'I do not know,' Vecchietti said, 'how some [of these figures] were found present at this very holy mystery. The angels that he has done here, for reasons already discussed, are fine. And so are those figures that are seen above the bank of the river in different poses, since they appear very distant from the place [98] where Christ is baptized. But those three figures that are here close by, with faces drawn from life, one of whom motions towards the baptism, are a very inappropriate thing. And they are discordant from the truth and I am amazed that the painters are induced to make such great errors.'[73]

'Do not pour all the water on the poor painters again,' Sirigatti added emphatically. 'As you know, for the most part they paint to earn a living. And those who have them do the paintings say, "I want this in here and these figures," little considering if they are appropriate there. And when the painter says he does not want to do it there, in addition to laughing at such a thing, they would give the business to another painter. He, out of need, would not look at it so carefully. And I can be made to believe that the figures that you describe here were done by Giovanni Strada for the satisfaction of the patrons who wanted the portraits to appear there in their memory.'

'I believe all this that you say without any doubt,' Vecchietti responded. 'It does not follow from this, however, that the fault is not a fault and that it is not seen to appear from the hand of the painter. And one can presume what you have said every time something is without logic. In time, however, the things that are in the mouths of these and those are lost, and the paintings are kept. Thus, it is not astonishing if the errors are attributed only to the painter. I equally do not greatly praise those who have public paintings done and do not consult with those who understand such things. [99] [These patrons] only trust in their own judgment and the whim of painters who intend to demonstrate their art more than the narrative.'

'We pass ahead at this point,' Michelozzi said, 'to the panel of Jacopo di Meglio, where St Vincent and Our Lord triumphant are painted.'

Confused paintings

'This is an invention of his whim,' Vecchietti responded. 'If he wanted to do the Triumph of Christ, other circumstances would have been sought than those that are here. And if he had wanted to do St Vincent considering the mystery of this Triumph, he would not have happened to do St Verdiana here. She was many years after St Vincent. He was martyred in the time of Emperor Diocletion, while St Verdiana died the year of our health 1242.[74] And the other figures that are here are not appropriate, either to a Triumph of the Saviour or to a speculation of St Vincent. In any case, St Vincent considering the Triumph of Christ, being surrounded by so many people and specially, as there are here, young women, is repugnant to reality. Neither do I know why the Angel Raphael and Tobias, who are from a narrative in the Old Testament, not appropriate with the others, are done here.'

'If I was correct in the reasoning given above,' Sirigatti added, 'that the patrons of the panels are the reason that the painters do inappropriate things in their works, I would say that the fault for the errors of this panel came from its patrons. I note the many portraits from life that are seen here of men and women and of the patron himself that [the patron] has had done. [100] Therefore, it can be believed that the painter did it more to gratify others, by portraying the payer, than for his own satisfaction and the observation of the narrative. But then, as all the ways this has been badly done have already been said, I do not know what more I can say in his defence.'

'The panel of Girolamo Macchietti, I believe,' Michelozzi said, 'will give you material more to praise than to blame. St Lawrence is seen devotedly receiving his martyrdom on the grate, and the fiercely deranged tyrant imposing his unfair sentence.'[75]

'Truly I would not know how not to praise this,' Vecchietti answered. 'As you have said, St Lawrence is devout and is seen on the fire partly roasted. And the tyrant shows cruelty and the other figures are well placed and modest. The angel who carries the palm of martyrdom has all the circumstances that belong to it.'

'Everything pleases me in this picture,' repeated Michelozzi, 'but I marvel greatly of Girolamo [Macchietti], that he put such great peril in it.'

'And, how so?' Vecchietti interjected.

'Do you not see,' Michelozzi replied, 'that [St Lawrence] is put close to the Emperor, among these idolatrous men, so that they can recognize, to his peril, that he is Christian?'

'Yes!' rejoiced the company at the pleasing comment of Michelozzi.

Vecchietti continued: 'This is an important thing, that all men seek in various ways to live longer than they are able in this world. And when they clearly recognize [101] that the body, as something very alive, unfortunately quickly fails, they strive with all diligence to live for fame. By writing narratives and poetry, by doing famous deeds in war, by building superb palaces, and by means of sculpture and painting, they seek to become immortal. But few are those, alas a thing undeserving of humanity, who, with their good works and with celestial considerations,[76] procure for themselves the eternal blessed life.'

'You speak the truth,' Michelozzi said, 'but if you agree we will continue our discussion. There appear before us three panels worthy of consideration for their beauty by Batista Naldini. The first represents the *Nativity* of Our Lord, the second when the Glorious Virgin went to purify Herself in the temple, and the third when Christ was taken down from the Cross.'

A Nativity of Christ poorly painted

'In the panel of the *Nativity*,'[77] Vecchietti responded, 'there are some things there that should not be there and others that are missing without which the story is incomplete. The two apostles and the bishop that are seen there should not be painted there because there were neither apostles nor bishops when the Saviour of the World was born. There never could have been, such ranks not yet being known to the people, there not having been such orders. Then, the ox and the ass are missing here. I say missing here because he has made them appear distant, the muzzles only, in a shadow, as in a hole. They are seen with great searching, with great difficulty to the eyes, as if they were not there. And these took part [102] in the birth of Christ and are as necessary in this narrative as the principal figures that need to be painted if one wants it to be complete. He has done as his invention the angels and Virtues in the air with wings, surrounding the great God. They show that all the Virtues came to the world when He was born, bringing them with Him for the welfare of humanity. They seem to me well done, with beautiful ornament and in concordance with the narrative.

'The panel of the *Purification* seems to me quite well observed if it were not that in the air there are two angels, one of which, being without wings, looks like a child falling to the ground, although the other is shown with feathers to keep himself in the air.'[78]

'Have you seen,' Sirigati said, 'the panel newly done by Francesco Poppi, concerning the same narrative, which is going to be put up in San Piero Scheraggio?'[79]

A Purification not well painted

'I have seen it in his house,' responded Vecchietti, 'and I do not know why that beautiful young woman that he has painted beside Simeon is put there. This should have been Anna the Prophetess, who was a venerable old woman and not a graceful young woman.'

'I also considered the same thing when I saw her,' Sirigatti responded, 'and I asked Francesco [Poppi] himself why he had done that beautiful woman there. He told me that he had done her as Anna. But, not having wanted to put an old woman who would give little pleasure to the eye in the most beautiful aspect of his panel, he therefore, had done that young woman there. And that, even if some [103] wanted to say that Anna was missing there, if they looked up in a corner of the panel beside the Madonna, they would see a face of an old woman that they could take for Anna if they wished.'

'You make me want to laugh,' added Vecchietti. 'And one is forced to say he was right, being still a young man, in wanting to see a fair young girl rather than an old woman burdened by her years. And I will allow myself to take the old woman that he has done in that corner for Anna as he wishes, even as I believe that she cannot be known as her since Anna was at the side of Simeon and not of the Virgin. But to please Poppi, who is a worthy man in his art, we will accept for now that beautiful young girl.'

A Christ deposed from the Cross painted without devotion

The others could not restrain themselves from laughing and Vecchietti continued: 'But passing to the other panel of Naldini in which there is the *Deposition* from the Cross,[80] I say that it pleases me. But it would have pleased me much more if the body of Christ had had more evidence of the flagellation and of death than it has. This appears to be a body coming out of the bath rather than one taken down from the Cross.'[81]

'Keep in mind,' Michelozzi said, 'that the Marys washed and anointed Him with precious ointments. And Naldini has made him so soft to show when he was washed and anointed.

'But what will you say of the panel of Alessandro Allori in Santa Maria Nuova, where Christ is seen taken down from the Cross in the arms of the angels?[82] This is the most beautiful body that it is possible to see.'

A deposition from the Cross badly painted

'I will say,' Vecchietti responded, 'that this is his invention, which does not have to do with the narrative. [104] Having to show the mystery of Christ when He was taken down from the Cross, it is necessary to show the people who took him down, that is Joseph, Nicodemus, and the others.[83] And while the angels can be there, as I have said at other times, they should not be as principals in this case. Joseph and Nicodemus and the Marys took down the very holy body of the Saviour from the Cross. After having bathed Him with tears and washed Him with precious waters and anointed Him with sweet smelling ointments, say the Scriptures, they wrapped Him in a white sheet and put Him in a new tomb. From which He was not moved, but resurrected by His own virtue. So this would not have been the time for the angels to take Him by the arms by themselves, as is seen in this picture, without the men and without the women who took Him from the Cross and then placed Him in the tomb. The evangelical text also says that the Jews, going to take down the Cross because their festival followed the Crucifixion, broke the legs of the thieves. Seeing that Christ was dead, they did not do anything else with Him except that Longinus opened his ribs with the lance. And then Joseph and Nicodemus with the others took Him from the Cross and buried Him. How then has Alessandro done the two thieves if both were dead and had broken legs? One holds himself up by [extending] his bent knees, seemingly supported by them and the other hangs from the cross with only one arm, without being tied or nailed. [105] And he has done the good thief, who is on the right, in a desperate pose. This is against what the sacred scripture says, that he expected to go to enjoy Paradise through the very truth that he had been promised. The body of Our Lord, which is beautiful, pleases me, because the body of Christ was very handsome. For being so soft and delicate and for having more of life than of death in many parts, I will not say anything. All the painters have always decided to paint it [in this way] to more demonstrate their art rather than to move others to devotion.'

'Perhaps he has not wanted to represent,' Sirigatti added, 'as others think, a Christ taken down from the Cross, but has wanted the pious Christian to imagine Christ dead in the arms of the angels, as he is also seen in the arms of God the Father in many paintings. This is not an inappropriate thing, even if it is not read in the scriptures that God the Father ever took Him in His arms.'

'I will not say,' Vecchietti responded, 'that it is not possible to have Christ in the arms of the angels and also in the arms of God the Father, particularly when one wants to show the Trinity. I would not blame that of Alessandro if all he had done was a Christ in the arms of the angels, but he did it here next to the empty Cross and on each side the thieves still on the cross. These are clear signs showing that Christ had been removed from the Cross a little before. Thus, he needed, either to completely follow the mystery of Christ when he was taken down from there, or truly, as you say, something newly imagined, [106] without mixing one with the other, discordant in both.'

'Enough is said of this,' Michelozzi said. 'We return to the panel of Santi di Tito[84] in Santa Maria Novella where Our Lord is portrayed raising Lazarus.[85] This picture appears to me very beautiful, very well observed, and very modest.'

'You tell the truth,' Vecchietti responded, 'and it pleases me greatly, because I see in it the sacred narrative well described. I see reverence and devotion and the things of the craftsman himself very well arranged.'

'Therefore, there does not remain anything else for us to discuss in this church,' Michelozzi added, 'other than the *Conversion of St Paul* by Bastiano of Verona.'

'If you will,' Vecchietti responded, 'let us not also try to speak among ourselves about this since it seems to me of a manner very far from the others and not necessary to be enumerated among them. Therefore, as a different way of painting, we will leave it by itself.'

'If we want to find a broad field to battle,' Michelozzi said, 'we need to make a leap to Santa Croce where there are, as you know, many beautiful panels.'

'Yes, but I fear,' Vecchietti responded, 'that the contest will be as tiring as past battles. One will hazard a great risk, in the new melee, of reporting defeat. Perhaps it would be better to look back at [previous] honours rather than accepting new invitations to fight with the danger of losing all.'

'Rather, it would be a very great shame,' Michelozzi responded, 'to abandon the enterprise on the eve of obtaining victory. [107] And then, having so victoriously passed forward, not wanting it to be said of you, what was said in the splendour of the Tuscan language:

Hannibal conquered often, yet he knew
Never the fruits of victory to obtain.[86]

Therefore, the more difficult is the battle, the more you ask kind spirits to not abandon your noble-minded enterprise.'

'Girolamo has spoken so well through the mouth of Petrarch,' said Valori, 'that it would be difficult for you to contradict him, Bernardo.

And, for my part, it appears to me that I should follow him in this, to do as he wishes.'

'And I cannot begin to believe that [Vecchietti] will gainsay you or Girolamo,' Sirigatti added. 'He would not, because of being friends of both, and because, being prudent, he would not flee from the occasion of acquiring praise and giving us some part of his very impregnable doctrine.'

'I will not do it for that, nor be able to if I wished,' Vecchietti responded. 'But I will do it to not fail to please you since all three [of you] are in accord in one wish. I hope that the immediate desire of satisfying you will raise me up, where ignorance could make me fall.'

'From the shadows that are beginning to grow larger from these cypresses,' said Valori, 'you can appreciate rather clearly that the Sun is setting towards the west. Therefore, wanting to bring a close to this our first discussion, of invention pertaining to painting and sculpture, it is necessary that we hasten our footsteps if night is not to fall while we are on the road.'

Concerning the three statues on the tomb of Michelangelo

'On first entering Santa Croce,' [108] Michelozzi interjected, 'there appear before my eyes the three marble statues on the tomb of the previously greatly praised Michelangelo Buonarroti. You are able to say something about this, Bernardo, if you please.'

'It will be for Ridolfo to touch on these,' Vecchietti responded, 'when he is ready to discuss the poses and the parts of figures. With respect to the invention, it seems to me that the first statue, by Giovanni dell'Opera, represents *Architecture* because of the rule and triangle that it has for attributes.[87] That in the middle by Valerio Cioli with the hammer and chisel is *Sculpture*.[88] The third, of Battista del Calvaliere, when seen from the front, also seems to refer to sculpture, because it holds a rough model in its hand. But those who look at the foot of this figure, on the right, will see brushes, bowls, and other things pertaining to the painter. Therefore, it is clearly intended to be *Painting*.'[89]

'I want to tell you' Sirigatti added, 'the reason for these attributes that appear to demonstrate two [different] things. It was planned in the beginning by Don Vincenzo Borghini, Prior of the Innocenti, that painting be put in the middle. And sculpture would be where the statue of Battista del Cavaliere is today and the statues were commissioned in this way. And Battista was the first to begin to work the marble and had already been well started on his statue, having done that model in its hand that is seen today. Then the heirs of Michelangelo begged the Grand Duke to do them the favour [109] that sculpture should be put in the middle, as Michelangelo was of greater excellence in that mode than in any of the others. And he always had more esteem for it and held it in greater merit.[90] And His Highness conceded them what they asked. Battista, who had already arranged his figure to put it in place in the corner where it is seen today, could not put it in the middle. It was necessary that his statue, that up to then had been as sculpture, be transformed into painting. And he did this by doing those attributes that are seen at its feet. Neither did he want to remove the model from its hand, in which he was right, so as to not to give disgrace to his figure that had already been almost finished in that pose. The others, who were very behind with their statues, easily accommodated themselves to what was done to the project. Therefore, do not be astonished by the statue of Battista if it seems to show two arts in the attributes that it carries.'[91]

'It is very important to me to have understood how this came to be,' Vecchietti answered, 'since it was difficult for me to believe in what way this figure was supposed to have been made.'

Concerning the panels of Santa Croce

'I am at a standstill,' Michelozzi said, 'confronted with the panel of Bronzino where he has shown *Christ in Limbo* and feel very great pleasure in gazing at the delicate parts of those beautiful women.'

'We have already discussed,' Vecchietti responded, 'how badly done are sacred figures made so lascivious. Now, I tell you once more that they are inappropriate, not only in the churches but in every other public [110] place. They give a bad example and induce vain thoughts in the mind. And the craftsmen who have done them feel their hearts consumed in old age by belated thoughts of conscience. The sculptor Bartolomeo Amannati appropriately confessed this in his published letter to the Academicians of the Accademia del Disegno. He said that he had done badly in having done many nude statues and accused himself as not worthy of excuse but asked God to forgive and support others to not fall in so serious a fault.'[92]

Lascivious paintings inappropriate in church

'In your delight in gazing at these lascivious women, you confess yourself how little praise Bronzino deserves in this work. And I am sure that whoever stops to look carefully at this painting, considering the softness of the parts and the charm of the faces of these young women, cannot but feel some stimulus of the flesh. It is a thing completely contrary to that which one should have in the holy Temple of God.[93]

'And in this Francesco Salviati did much better in his *Deposition from the Cross* close by.[94] Besides having observed the narrative well, he has made the women modest and devout. Although it is true that the body of Christ, coming down from the Cross, should be more lacerated and more evilly transformed. This would move to greater devotion and greater consideration of what the Redeemer of the World suffered for our guilt.'

'There are three panels in this church by Giorgio Vasari,' Michelozzi said. 'One shows the *Road to Calvary*.[95] [111] Another is when, appearing to the Apostles, He was touched by St Thomas.[96] And the third is when the Holy Spirit came from Heaven in tongues of fire.'[97]

'I do not know what to say about these with respect to the invention,' Vecchietti answered. 'It seems to me rather well explained, although in the panel of the Holy Spirit he has made the Queen of Heaven a young woman, appearing the age of twenty or more, and she should have been about fifty. I will now pass, without saying more, the panel of Jacopo di Meglio where Christ is seen above, shown to the throngs by Pilate when he said, "Here is the Man." He appears to be a statue that is placed on a dado of stone.'

'What will we say,' Michelozzi added, 'about the panel of Andrea del Minga where Christ is praying in the garden?'

'Many would have it,' immediately replied Sirigatti, 'I do not know if from envy or because of little love for Minga, that this panel is not all his. They say that he was helped by Stefano Pieri in the colour, in the landscape by the Flemming Giovanni Ponsi, and that the drawing is by Giambologna.'

'It went out under the name of Andrea,' Vecchietti said, 'and, they can say what they want, we should hold it as his, and it is very well done and well observed, as you see.'

'Here near it,' followed Michelozzi, 'is the panel of Alessandro del Barbiere that shows Christ beaten at the column,[98] a very copious painting and full of invention if I am not mistaken.'

'It pleases me greatly,' Vecchietti responded, 'as much for the invention [112] of the Sacred Scripture as for that of the painter himself. He has enriched it with a beautiful building and many figures. But it would give more devotion if the body of Christ showed the bruises of the beating by those scoundrels.'

'It seems to me that the *St Francis* of Battista Naldini is very full of emotion and devotion,' Michelozzi added. 'The dead Christ in the arms of God the Father, however, by Girolamo Macchietti seems to me to have too much life and this God the Father is too fierce.'[99]

'You are right,' Vecchietti responded, 'and I like this figure less than the others that Girolamo has done. And a dead body does not make the impression that this one does. But the invention is very well observed in his other panels, very modest, and very charming, as in the *Assumption* that he has done in the Carmine.[100] And his panel of *The Magi* in San Lorenzo pleases me more.[101] There one sees the Glorious Virgin with a very beautiful face, showing the greatest modesty.'

Concerning the panels of San Lorenzo

'Since we are in San Lorenzo,' Michelozzi said, 'tell me something of the panel of Rosso where one sees the *Marriage of the Madonna*.'[102]

A wedding of the Madonna with figures inappropriately painted

'I say that he has made a great dissonance,' Vecchietti answered, 'in making a monk present here. The orders of monks were not yet established at that time. Therefore, I would judge more observant, with respect to the holy invention, the panel, also of the *Marriage of the Virgin*, by Francesco Poppi in San Niccolò.'[103]

Concerning the panels of Santo Spirito

'Therefore, you will like less,' Michelozzi added, 'the other panel [113] of Rosso in Santo Spirito, where the Genetrix of the Supreme Good is seen with the Little Child in her arms, surrounded by many monks, bishops, and male and female saints.'[104]

Paintings in which it is allowed to portray figures of different times

'On the contrary, this does not displease me,' Vecchietti responded. 'And it does not seem to me that it is possible to blame it. It is not done to demonstrate any mystery derived from the sacred writings but only for the contemplation by the Christian faithful of the Mother of the Saviour of the World with the Little Child in Her arms. All people of any time, being of any state or grade one wishes, can come to this contemplation. When a dead Christ is portrayed without any other mystery or a Virgin with the Child, as are seen in many pictures, it is possible to add some modest figure, as pleases the painter. That Christ or that Virgin is not considered in a narrative mystery, but is done for remembrance and for contemplation. But in Rosso's panel of the *Marriage of the Madonna* one sees her marriage expressed, and one recognizes that he wanted to represent that event. Therefore, the monk cannot be there nor can the other things be there that are now present.'

A Christ appearing to the Magdalene poorly painted

'Thus, Bronzino has also been unsuccessful,' Michelozzi added, 'in the panel where he has Christ in the clothes of a gardener appear to the Magdalene.[105] He has done two other women there close to her, and the scripture says that He appeared to her alone.'

'Who doubts that in this he has not failed?' Vecchietti responded.

'Before we leave [114] Santo Spirito,' repeated Michelozzi, 'let us say something of the *Adulteress* of Alessandro Allori.'[106]

'It satisfies me greatly,' added Vecchietti, 'and particularly this woman who shows shame and repentance for the sins she committed.'

'This reminds one,' Sirigatti said, 'of the panel of the *Ascension* by Giovanni Strada in Santa Croce.'[107]

'Yes, but first [let's] say something about the panel where Christ is painted sending away the merchants from the temple,' Michelozzi added. 'This is by this same Strada.'[108]

'I do not know what else it is possible to say,' Vecchietti responded, 'other than that it well observes the three things we have been talking about.

'The Holy Scripture says, about the mystery of the Ascension, that the Redeemer of the World, having appeared to the Apostles and having discussed a good deal with them, was seen by them to rise in the air. And a bright cloud covering Him, He disappeared before them and suddenly two men dressed in white came and spoke with them.'

The Ascension of Christ in which figures are missing that of necessity should be there

'Now if the two angels dressed in white who appeared to speak with the Apostles had been in this panel, since Christ has been raised from the earth, the rest would please me greatly.'

Concerning the panels of the Carmine

'There is also a panel of the *Ascension* in the Carmine by Battista Naldini,'[109] Michelozzi said, 'over which one should not pass in silence.'

'He placed St Lena and St Agnes there,' Vecchietti responded, 'who came into the world quite long after the Ascension of the Lord, and [he did] the Virgin Mary as a young woman of eighteen or twenty years. [115] I do not know how that could be appropriate, in addition to also omitting the angels there who should speak to the Apostles.'

Ascensions in which there are figures that should not be there

'I know that he did the two saints that are in front,' Sirigatti said, 'to please the patrons of the panel. And, while you have said that this does not merit an excuse, it is also worthy of consideration, as the patron has greater guilt in it than the painter.'

'This is true,' Vecchietti responded, 'and we know it because it is near to us [in time]. But it will not be near to those who come along many years from now. They, not knowing so many justifications, will attribute everything to the painter, as we do in the old pictures and statues that we see.'

'Do not let other considerations make us forget,' Sirigatti added, 'the panel by Santi di Tito of the *Nativity* of Our Lord in Girolamo's chapel.'[110]

A Nativity of Christ with figures that could not be there

'From what has been said,' Michelozzi responded immediately, 'I myself can deliver the judgment against it. The St Jerome and St Anthony could not be there since they were many, many years after the Nativity of Christ. And perhaps my father's portrait, in the person of St Anthony, and mine, in that of a shepherd,[111] shows too much presumption. My father was pleased in this and he wanted it to be done in that way.'

'I would not judge,' Vecchietti responded, 'that your portrait demonstrates any presumption, rather modesty and humility, since you have been done as a shepherd going to adore the Saviour of the World.'[112]

In Santa Croce

'Two panels remain for us [116] in Santa Croce, both by Santi di Tito,' said Michelozzi, 'one of the *Resurrection* of the Lord[113] and the other when He blesses the bread before the two Apostles in Emanus.'[114]

'I esteem both worthy of praise,' Vecchietti responded, 'for the observation of the sacred narrative, for modesty, and for the things there proper to the painter, which are well arranged.'

'Speaking of the Resurrection,' Michelozzi added, 'has made me remember a panel by Bronzino showing this mystery in the Annunziata.'[115]

Concerning the panels of the Annunziata

'Please let us not speak about it,' Vecchietti responded, 'because there is an angel there so lascivious that it is something unsuitable.'

'If I had that beautiful figure at home,' Michelozzi said, 'I would value it greatly and hold it in high value as one of the most delicate and soft figures that it would be possible to see.[116] However, since it does not please you to discuss this, at least we will not keep silent about the panel of Giovanni Strada in which Christ is on the Cross, speaking to the thief.'[117]

'This panel is among those that please me greatly,' continued Vecchietti. 'I see there well explained all that the sacred narrative says. And it is very copious in [the painter's] suitably presented inventions. Death and the ancient serpent are chained to the Cross to show that the death of Christ slayed death and the infernal enemy, taking us back to happy life from miserable death.'

'Everything is fine, but does it not appear to you,' Michelozzi said, 'that the body of Christ is rather delicate, for such great suffering?' [117]

'You are right,' Vecchietti answered. 'He could be rather more blood-stained. But you need to consider that he has imagined him alive and that the vital spirits still sustain the parts when alive and no longer do so when one is dead. And even more that, speaking to the thief at that point, He was thinking about His glory more than His Passion.'

'Since we have come to this point, before we proceed to discuss other things,' Michelozzi said, 'I would be grateful to hear your opinion of the panel by Francesco Poppi in San Michele Visdomini, which represents, so it is said, the *Conception of the Glorious Virgin*.'[118]

Painting of the Conception of the Virgin to be recklessness, and that it should not be painted

'I do not know,' responded Vecchietti, 'who first had so much boldness as to want to paint the Conception. It is not described or defined in the sacred writings. And for myself I esteem it a great temerity to paint it, as it would also be not without arrogance to want to paint Solomon in glory and Enoch in Heaven, portraying the place where they were, the clothing they had, and the food that nourished them. But when it is agreed that the Conception should be painted, I believe that much caution would need to be taken, which I do not see in this panel. And I do not know why Adam and Eve were done in such forced and immodest poses, rather than with humble and modest gestures. They demonstrate either the hope of being freed from the chains of sin by the Conception or truly giving thanks to the Genetrix of the Supreme Good, if they want [118] to consider her as already conceived. And those thin cords coming out of the mouth of the serpent that resemble lines of string and tie up those ancient fathers are also lacking in verisimilitude. Therefore, I would praise more in this, the invention of Giorgio Vasari on this same subject in his panel in Santo Apostolo.[119] There he did Adam and Eve and the other Fathers attached by their arms to the trunk of the tree of sin. But to tell the truth, I would conclude that until the Holy Church has determined more about the Conception, it should not be painted in any manner.'

'We have not said anything about the marble Apostles,' Michelozzi said, 'that are by the hand of worthy men in Santa Maria del Fiore.'

'Ridolfo will touch on them in his discourse,' Vecchietti responded, 'discussing their poses and parts. Invention in a single figure is a simple thing and particularly in the Apostles, which are so numerous and have been carved so many times.'

'I am also eager to know,' Michelozzi replied, 'if there is anything particular to consider in painting prophets, martyrs, confessors, and Apostles.'

How prophets, martyrs, confessors and apostles and other saints should be painted

'The difference is,' said Vecchietti, 'that prophets are to be painted with scrolls of paper in their hands, to show that the law, which at that time was written on tablets of stone, was wrapped in shadow, in imagination, and in obscurity. The Apostles should be given open, not closed, books. This demonstrates their evangelical authority [119] already written in scripture. It clearly denotes the fluency and the clarity of the law of the Evangelists to have been open and preached to the whole world. The four Evangelists are given the four animals seen in the vision of the Prophet Ezekiel as attributes: the winged lion to St Mark; the ox to St Luke; the angel to St Matthew; and the eagle to St John.

St Peter is painted with his keys, St Paul with the sword, St John with the poisoned chalice,[120] St Andrew with his cross, and, in sum, all the Martyrs with those instruments that were used for their martyrdom. Martyrs can also be shown with a palm in their hands as a sign of their glorious victory, like non-martyred virgins with the lily signifying their virginity. This also in Confessors is an indication of their pure self-restraint. But I would close our discussion here at this point with the authority of Corrado Bruno, since the fresh breeze invites one to take sweet recreation in the shady hills. Hear what he says about paintings and sculpture that are placed in sacred temples.'

How the sacred paintings should be that are placed in churches

'Sacred images are to be utilized so that, not the dreams, or the fables, or the profane things of curious men, but the true and holy narratives are offered to the people. Many, many times vain things are heard preached and seen painted in the Church of God, not without great offence to the faithful of Christ. Ecclesiastical writings, [120] therefore, should be true and not false, to teach and not to deceive, and to confirm the minds of those who read and not to dissuade them from compassion and mercy. In the same way, the sacred images are not to be false, but true, not lascivious, but modest and, in sum, arranged so accurately that the Holy Mysteries of Our Lord, or the glorious deeds of the saints, are reduced to memory. It is as if again they were put before the eyes of the beholders, moving their minds to piety and holy living and not, instead, arousing them as many modern paintings do, to foolish and lascivious thoughts.

'But by now the hour is late and very suitable to go to enjoy the view of this beautiful country. Because I have spoken, spontaneously, taking simply from what I remember of this material, it would seem to me time, with your good grace, to put an end to our discussion for today. And tomorrow, Ridolfo will discuss the other things pertaining to the painters and the sculptors. As someone who is very qualified in this by learning and experience, he will make up for everything through his courtesy that I, in my weakness, have missed.'

'You have put me in such great depth,' Sirigatti responded, 'that I fear, as an inexperienced swimmer, that I will remain entirely submerged if I am not helped. I do not have the strength that others require of me in order to give them any help. Rather, if it is attempted, it might take both of us to the bottom rather than get us to the other side. [121] But you, having crossed this sea, have already bravely placed your feet on dry land. At my great peril I am required to enter here. When you see the absence of strength that supports me, it will not be too difficult to extend a hand to pull me up. Otherwise, in vain I would be unable to surmount this obstacle.'

'The interchange between you,' Michelozzi said, 'is more a sign of temerity than of prudence, but I will trust at this time the confidence of friendship. And, Bernardo, grant me a favour before we leave so that I, who desire to know, will retain until tomorrow what by chance could flee the mind but, in another time could perhaps help me to remember what has happened up to now.'

'Not being here on dry land, as you call it,' Vecchietti responded, 'and it being again necessary to dive in, being already weary, I will run a great risk of not being able to stay afloat. But for all this, I cannot fail Girolamo, desiring with everything of mine to be able to gratify him.'

'It would be a great pity if you wet a foot,' Michelozzi added, 'since without leaving the shore you will be able to satisfy my desire. I am eager to know why many sculptors and painters, and particularly Bandinelli, did the ancient serpent, between Adam and Eve, with the head of a charming damsel.'

Why the ancient serpent is given the face of a damsel

'This is the invention of the craftsman himself,' Vecchietti answered, 'noting that the Sacred Scripture simply speaks of the snake. No [122] mention is made in any place that it has another head than that which snakes are accustomed to have. In his first appearance [the Devil] took on an aspect of benevolence to then be able to get the woman to want to do his wickedness. Because the serpent put it in his mind to first deceive the woman, I think that people imagine him with the face of woman. And perhaps they also give him the face of a young girl to show that great deceptions and betrayals are often hidden under a beautiful and delicate face.'

'There is too much malignant invention of this kind against women,' Michelozzi added. 'Nor I will ever be able to praise such revelations about them. Why could they not leave the head of the serpent as it is, according to the story? If they wanted to increase the horror of the sight, why not make it the head of a man instead? Granted that seeing a man more pleases a woman, who would not be pleased by a woman, but it does not follow from this that deceptions are hidden under a beautiful face. Rather, when I gaze at the beautiful face of a woman it seems to me that every good and happiness breathes from her. And one is given to believe that a beautiful woman is of greater goodness and faithfulness than a deformed one. Beauty – as I understand has already been said by a scholar – gives indication of temperance of humour from which the uprightness of living well is derived and is born. It seems to me that beneath the beautiful face of a women it is more possible to demonstrate purity and simplicity rather than [123] deception and betrayal. And, therefore, the angels are painted with delicate and feminine faces.'

'Fraud and sirens,' Sirigatti responded, 'are also painted with the faces of damsels.'

'There is not time,' said Valori, 'for tension over this. It would have us speak too much apart, one from the other. Enough, that Girolamo has reason to defend the women. They have rational and immortal souls, as have men, and many benefits and many comforts are born into our lives from them.'

Vecchietti getting to his feet at these words, all the others rose. They walked out of the little meadow and over the pleasant hills, discussing this theme for a good while, enjoying themselves in the freshness. But the crickets already stopping their song, they returned to the villa and dined with delight. And then, having refreshed themselves with pleasant discussions in the breezy air on the green grass, the hour to go to sleep having already overtaken them, each took himself to his room.

Book Two

Many are the virtues, Most Illustrious and Most Excellent Lord, [124] that men have who are notable and worthy of praise. But above all the others, I have always esteemed, to be the most worthy of praise, that which moves itself to do things for the benefit of other people. A prince who, with his authority, seeks to govern universally. A wealthy man who supports the needy with his resources. A wise man who comforts the afflicted with faithful consul. A lettered man who instructs the ignorant with the arts and sciences. A plain man who, [125] serving faithfully, lessens in great part for his lord, the labour and discomfort that human life carries. What could be desired more commendably and more usefully?

What if every man strove as much as he could – closing his ears to the false flattery of Avarice and Envy – to help others intelligently. The very many laments of the people who are badly treated, of the poor who are abandoned, of the princes who are deceived, and of the rich who are badly served, would immediately end. And that proverb which is now held false, that man to other men is a god, would be known to be true.

This so noble thought, to help others, shows its effects more greatly among those who abound in the blessings of fortune. Many times it does not deign to concern those of humble heart, devoid of superb dress, who show their concern by writing for others. They are not among those who, to show their good intention serving others, help others with riches and favours.

I desire, however inadequate my strengths are, to pass not unusefully the time that the Supreme Giver of All Good has allowed me to enjoy the beauty of the earth. Being left by fortune with a closed hand from being able to employ the generous virtue of liberality, and being true to my mind by having denied every occasion for fame, I have resorted to the pen as less subject to the rages of the mind's cruel storms. I do as much as I can, so that others receive that benefit whose value is recognized, not by me, [126] but by others. And perhaps it will seem to some, who sense in themselves a greater power, that I am not of little or no value and not, therefore, someone to be despised. Not little is given those who give everything that is in their power to give.[1] And if everyone also did this, I do not think that one could ever see this as an occasion to regret that anyone kept something to themselves.

Some will perhaps say that there are more astute observers of the deeds of others who, from their own experience, are better judges than I in discussing painting and sculpture. Not knowing the practice of these arts, [they say], I can teach much less about them and consequently bring nothing useful to the world. I will respond to these things in two ways as [would be] better than the poisonous teeth of envy that moves them to criticize the works of others, leaving them to bite and to tear.

For the first, I will say that if good and true things about these arts are uncovered in these writings of mine and taken by people to use in their work, few will take care to know if I myself, in writing about them, examined them by putting them into practice. The goodness or evil of [preachers] does not help others' well-being, but the good precepts of those who show others the way to Heaven greatly help their listeners. Similarly, great benefit will be made of the things that I write by those who wish to put them to use, but neither profit nor injury [to them from the fact] that I know or do not know how to put these [precepts] into practice.

For the second, I will respond [127] that many are those arts, such as the seven liberal arts and almost all of the manual arts, which would be badly described by those who do not practise them. How will those who have not learned or practised their precepts be able to speak of grammar or astrology? Or how can one describe riding horseback, playing a musical instrument, or building a wall who does not know how to hold the bit of a bridle, tune the instrument, or manipulate a T-square or a plumb line?

But this does not apply to painting and sculpture. These arts not being anything other than the imitation of nature,[2] whoever really understands the effects of nature will also be very able to discuss painting and sculpture. I say to discuss them, but not to put them into practice. As nature establishes the proportions of the parts and of the colours that pertain to making a man handsome and well formed, so one [can] recognize such parts when they are assembled in a well-rendered figure. But one would not know how to make [the figure] appear real, noting that making something seem real comes more from practice than from science.

Therefore, a man is able, although he is neither a painter nor a sculptor, to discuss sculpture and painting well and with usefulness for others. Some worthy painters or sculptors will say, perhaps, that those things that I have written about were created by capable men of the art and, therefore, that to write about them is superfluous or of no value. To this I will briefly respond, saying that the things that I have written, I have written for those [128] who do not practise these [precepts] but, either for use or for delight, are seized by pleasure in knowing them. Therefore, they who create will not read this. And those who understand it or know its discussion are welcome to put it aside. But many are those men who, living comfortably, although they may not practise the arts, are able to judge them. And they take great pleasure in caring to discuss them in depth, as were the gentlemen who were discussing painting and sculpture with Vecchietti.[3]

The Sun had chased every star from the sky and the humid shadows of the night from the earth. [The gentlemen] arose and amused themselves with light footstep for a good distance through the soft hills, over the dewy lawns, accompanied by the sweet songs of nightingales on saplings cheerfully singing the first hour of the day. But, already feeling that the solar rays were warming them, they finally turned their footsteps towards a place in the delightful garden above a beautiful little meadow covered with the finest of grasses, amusing themselves until the time to eat. That coming, everything being casually laid out as Vecchietti liked it with the greatest discretion, they put to table, and, with very great and beautiful and quiet order, good and delicate foods were served.

But when, after dining with pleasant discussions, they had rather taken to lying down, Michelozzi said, turning to the others: 'I have seen not very far from here a little grove on the top of a little hill. It [129] appears almost in the form of a fortress. While I believe it is an *uccellare*,[4] nevertheless, from what can be seen of its outside from afar, it is no ordinary thing. It seems to me done with great expense and great art. Therefore, if we would go over there together, perhaps we would be able to see something that we would be very grateful to have seen. And perhaps we will find a cool and comfortable place for the discussion that today is given to Ridolfo.'

'You will see,' responded Vecchietti smiling, '– if you are not restrained by the heat, the hour, and the little climb that make the way appear tiresome in climbing the low hill – an *uccellare* that I have constructed. I have spent so much time and money on it that I know not whether I should say I have built it to catch birds or to be caught like a bird. When you find yourself in it you will certainly decide that you are not lacking coolness and ease.'

Everyone getting to their feet at the end of these words, they concluded it would be well to go there and, protected by umbrellas, slowly took the path. Discussing various things, hardly noticing the effort that, at such a time, the easy climb required, they reached the top of the pleasant hill ...[5] Reaching here and, having with great astonishment diligently considered and greatly commended everything and finally making themselves comfortable ... the noble group kept silent.

Michelozzi began in this way. 'This wonderful and cool place is very favourable for the discussion that Ridolfo will provide. The thick shade of these leafy saplings brings us to a certain solitary silence that invites us to listen to his words. Only the inventions of the painters and the sculptors were discussed yesterday. It is yet necessary to speak of composition, poses, parts, and colour – things that will take much time if we want to completely discuss them. I believe it would be well to begin our discussion.'

'Not being able to discuss such things completely,' Sirigatti responded, 'but only to touch on some small parts of them, I should not like to give myself too long a time for discussion. [136] I know that [describing] the technique of making these things will fail me, something that one would not allow to pass by without comment.'

'Excuses here are not sufficient,' Michelozzi said, 'to relieve you of an obligation that was promised us yesterday. And we greatly appreciate how very much you are able to offer us. Since it is time to favour us, I desire that you, step by step, describe today, beginning with the first principles of the painter and sculptor, all those things that they do to become capable men in their calling.'

All the others confirmed what Michelozzi said. And turning towards Sirigatti, they prayed of him that he not wish to fail to do this, which he answered in this way.

'For myself, I will not avoid trying with all my power to satisfy you, but you will see here how I have been able to accomplish what is necessary. If it does not displease you, I will hold to this order in my discussion. First, I will speak of drawing as a common and necessary principle to the painter and sculptor. I will follow this by discussing those things more appropriate to the sculptor, until the hand, following the intellect, discovers and makes known in the marble that which was first in the mind [*idea*] of the craftsman. Turning then to the painter, since he embraces more parts, I will more broadly discuss his things, not leaving the trail of my discussion until all of the painter's colours are put in context.'

Each of them greatly commended Sirigatti's organization. And then, keeping silent, they applied themselves to waiting for him to tell them these principles. Since there was a good deal [137] to it, should he delay, he began in this way.[6]

What drawing is

'Drawing does not seem to me to be other than an apparent demonstration [*dimostrazione*], with lines, of that which is first conceived in the intellect of man and imagined in the mind [*idea*]. This, wishing to make it appear with appropriate means, requires that with long practice the hand become accustomed, with pen, with charcoal, or with pencil to obey what the intellect commands.[7] But to come to this point, many methods are sought by beginners to help them along the path of drawing. Some draw on certain little panels of boxwood or fig, others on sheets of parchment, and others on sheets of cotton. All these things, however, are first suitably prepared, which I will omit talking about so as not to be too tedious in my discussion ...[8]

'In the beginning it is necessary to portray easy things, little by little accustoming oneself to do well the outlines, the features, and the shadows. These things it is possible to understand more with practice than with words ... Then, having had some practice with these things, it will do well to begin drawing with the pen. This, while it is more difficult, is much more beautiful and [done] by people more familiar with the art. And, wanting to do well in drawing, it is well to portray three-dimensional figures of marble, of plaster, or of other things. Since these are immobile, they give great ease to those drawing.'

What should be portrayed from nature and not imitated from the style of others

'Then, when the hand becomes well assured, one can draw from nature. And practise a great deal on this, since the things that come from nature are those that give honour. And [140] those who desire to become capable men are not given to imitate the manner of others, but nature herself, from which other things get their appearance. It would be great folly, being able to have pure water from its source, to go and take that which was diffused in altered channels.

'It is possible to draw with the pen alone, letting the sheet provide the highlights. This method is very difficult but very suitable in training the hand. But wanting to draw with more charm, by putting more figures together, and to demonstrate some narrative, it will be very appropriate to draw in chiaroscuro on coloured sheets. These provide the middle tones, the pen making the outlines or features and diluted ink making a soft hue that veils and shades the drawing.'

White for doing the highlights

'Highlights are then added with a fine brush, dipped in white mixed with gum.'

How cartoons are made

'And when one wants to make the drawings for use in great works of painting, it will be very useful to first make cartoons ...[9] They are drawn on with charcoal on the end of a rod, transposing all that which is in the smaller drawing and increasing it in proportion. And if there are buildings or perspectives there, these are magnified with the grid. The perspectives first, however, are drawn on the sketch in their correct measure, meeting at a point, with the intersections and recessions taking the eye back as it should. [141] These things being very difficult and taking a great deal of time to understand,[10] I will leave them aside and wholly cease speaking of drawing. It seems to me concerning this that I have said as much as one can understand with words and as much as there is to see of my understanding.' ...[11]

'It seems to me, however, that you have taught much that is appropriate concerning drawing,' Michelozzi responded. 'Therefore, proceed to your post to introduce me to the things of the art of sculpture.'

Principles of sculpture

'Once you have had substantial experience in drawing,' Sirigatti said, 'you can begin to make some heads or figures in profile in low relief in clay. Having only this view is easier for beginners. Then, you will be able to pass further forward to making, also of clay, some narratives in low relief and then some heads in the round. And finally, clay figures completely in the round can with charm be admired completely all around. These things having succeeded, it is necessary to pass to larger works. Take a piece of sandstone or marble and start to remove the superfluous material little by little with the chisel until one uncovers a head or figure in low relief. And then, taking heart, do heads [147] in the round and finally figures. Be warned, when you want to make figures of marble, to first complete your carefully done and well-considered model of clay. And then, proceeding to take away the marble, always take care to leave much behind, for any difficulties that can develop there.'

Saying this, Sirigatti keeping silent, Michelozzi said: 'The instructions that you have given me are too universal and [are] for people practised in the art. Therefore, I would be very grateful if you dealt more with the details. Teach me how clay models are made, how figures are fired, and how they serve as models to transfer into marble. And, also, tell me the rules for measuring human parts and other detailed precepts for making beautiful and graceful figures.'

'You expect so much of me here,' Sirigatti responded, 'that I am very afraid you will end up feeling deceived. But I will do my share to partly satisfy your desire as much as I am able. And I will continue to discuss what I understand. Many times in speaking, however, more real ignorance is demonstrated than esteemed wisdom.'

'You are right when too much is discussed without order or understanding outside of its allotted time,' immediately added Valori. 'But you will only briefly, in a very appropriate period [of time], treat material that might require a long discussion. You are asked to systematically analyse things that you not only understand but have put into practice. One cannot doubt [148] what it was said that Apelles said to Alexander the Great about this. Alexander was in the rooms of Apelles and speaking without judgment and without understanding of many things pertaining to the arts. Apelles told him, "Please be quiet. Even the more regarded shopboys here who grind my colours, when silent or speaking inappropriately, do better than you."'[12]

'I see that it is better to obey and show what little I know than to disobey and hide my ignorance,' Sirigatti responded. 'You all are of a will that by discussion I make my small worth apparent. Therefore, following your will in this, I say that clay models that are made with the intention of being saved and that are fired in furnaces are made in this way.

Models of many kinds

'Taking the least sandy clay[13] that can be found and softening it with water, it is well pounded. Then one begins to form the figure from the legs. These are made solid, like the arms and the neck. But the torso is made hollow, and also the head. And while the figure is being made, those parts that are up in the air are propped up as necessary. And the toothed spatula made of iron and other spatulas[14] are used in rough modelling to go into places where it is not possible to put the fingers, as between the hair and in other places. And it is necessary to caution that if one part dries before another, particularly an arm that is attached to the figure by hand, the clay, which contracts on drying, may break or crack. [149] Therefore, it is necessary to keep all the parts equally soft with wet rags so that everything dries at the same time. And cleaning is done that a soft rag around the finger, or better, with a sponge. And when only faces are done, the head and the breast are left empty.[15]

'Then the model that is done as a pattern for a figure that is to be made of marble is done in a different way. It is composed of a thin skeleton of lumber over which straw is gently tied. And first some clay mixed with straw is put over the parts of the figure, holding it together with string. Then sandy clay is taken, because this contracts less, and, being softened with water, it is mixed with shearings. And then the clay with the shearings is applied, little by little bringing the figure to perfection. And, wishing to dress it or put some drape around it, some red linen is cut, or something else if a thicker drape is desired, and dipped into slip. And it can be smeared over with clay to give it more strength. And equally it is possible to dip it in liquid limbellucci glue, which will give it more grip when dry. And then the drape is arranged as the craftsman most likes it.

'Also, if small models of wax are being made, you mix together tallow, turpentine, the very finely ground wheat flour that flies around the mill in the milling of wheat, which the sculptors call *fucello* flour, and cinnabar red to give it colour. And some add some pitch, because [the wax] has more strength and is firmer when [150 as 136] it is dry, and it makes the colour black. These models are very helpful for studying, as much from other good figures as from nature, since the wax always waits and one can remove at any time that which does not please. And these also serve whomever wants to cast them in bronze. Such things not really being sculpture, I will omit discussing them.

And, since it seems to me that I have said enough now about models, I will not continue further.'

'I remain completely satisfied up to here,' said Michelozzi, 'now that you have told me how to begin to carve marble. However, tell me the proportions [*misure*] that are appropriate for a good figure and all those things about this that are worthy of consideration.'

'Proportions,' Sirigatti responded, 'are a necessary thing to know, but we should consider that it is not always appropriate to observe them. Figures are often done in the act of bending down, waking up, and turning. In these poses, now they are stretched and now the arms are raised. So that, wanting to give grace to the figures, it is necessary in some places to lengthen and in some other places to shorten the proportions. Such a thing cannot be taught, but it is necessary that the craftsman learn it with judgment from nature.'[16]

The proportions of the parts

'But the proportions that are to be observed, except in the cases mentioned above, are these.[17] In the first place, the face of a man is divided into three parts. The first is from the beginning of the hair to the beginning of the nose, and this is called a "forehead." The second is from the attachment [151 as 149] of the nose to its end. And the third is from the point of the nose to the point of the chin. From the middle of the nose, between the two eyes, to the end of the length of the eyebrow is a forehead. From the end of the eyebrow to the beginning of the ear is a forehead. From one ear to the other, spanning both the ears is a "head."

'All of the proportions of the face are also in the hand. From the knuckle in the middle of the index finger up to its end is the same distance as from the point of the chin to the joining together of the lips. And this is the same as the width of the mouth and also as long as the ears and the nose. From the last knuckle towards the nail of this finger up to its end is the width of the eye and also the distance from one eye to the other. The middle finger of the hand is as long as the space from the ear to the nose. And the distance from the point of the nose to the beginning of the ear is as much as that from the point of the chin to the eyebrows.

'Most sculptors are used to making the figure nine heads high, measuring in this way. Two heads make the shin. Two are from the knees to the testicles. The torso up to the fontanel of the throat is three. One is from the chin up to the top of the face. One consists of the throat, together with that part on the back of the foot above the sole. These all come to make the number nine.

'Then the arms are attached to the shoulders and from the fontanel of the throat to their attachment on each side is a head. And the arms have to have a length of four heads. Two heads are measured from the point of the shoulder [152] to the elbow. Another two heads are from the elbow down to the knuckles where the fingers are attached. And the hand is as long as a head. And from the point of the ear to the fontanel of the throat must be a head. And the width of the thigh is the same as the face in profile. And this is as much as I [can] remember to tell you about proportions.'

Here, Sirigatti having kept silent for some time and the others waiting for him to continue, he resumed his discussion in this way: 'Many are the precepts that are given the good sculptor. They make his figures delightful to look at and to have a certain grace so that in any view they are not seen to lack something that does not please those who look at them. This advice is much better learned in putting it into practice than in hearing it discussed. However, I will not fail to note some of this that can be learned from discussion.'

Advice given the sculptor in the making of statues

'First, it is of great importance to locate the head properly above the shoulders, the upper trunk on the hips, and the hips and the shoulders above the feet. Then, when a figure is done in ordinary pose, the shoulder on the side of the leg that is weight-bearing should be lower than the other shoulder. And, wanting the head to turn towards one side, it is necessary to turn the torso so that the [other] shoulder is lifted. Otherwise, the figure would be quite awkward. And, when it happens that the torso is resting on the leg that is weight-bearing, avoid not having the head turn towards that side. To give such grace would be a very difficult thing. And if the figure shows the strong side, [153] then make it a habit that the fontanel of the throat is right over the fontanel of the ankle of the foot that is weight-bearing. And when [the figure] comes forward the hollow can also be somewhat on the inside but not on the outside [of the foot]. When you have a figure that is planted on its feet without moving, throwing an arm forward towards the chest, there has to be as much natural or accidental weight thrown behind. And I say this of every part, other than the fixed parts, that sticks out from the whole. One also notes that the muscles of the arm swell and grow larger on gripping the hand and do the opposite on opening it. And a man in moving fast or slowly always has that [hip], which is holding up the body, lower than the other. It is also a good precept, when figures are made to sit, to work to make them sit upright and their heads rather small. This will make them more graceful. And for all figures, so they will have more grace, make it a rule to make the hands that hang down large and the feet small.

'When it is necessary to make any figure clothed or covered with drapery it will be very well to make it thin because the clothing makes it bulky. And above all take care that the parts without drapery do not give offence. And heads that have beards are made rather small, since the beard makes them appear large. And it is a very praiseworthy thing to try to arrange the drapery so naturalistically that the nude is recognized underneath. Because it is very difficult to give grace to figures, have them raise the arm of the weight-bearing leg. The ancients did this [154] many times, and it is something of theirs that is good to learn. Whoever wants to do this, however, is advised to study it well. Since it is not possible to do all views of the figure beautifully, capable men have also made use of arranging a drapery over those less beautiful parts. This covers them so that only those parts that have grace remain uncovered. It should also be considered that, looking at the figure in profile, when the leg cannot be thrust behind neither can the torso be directed behind. If the leg truly comes forward then it is possible for the torso to come forward. And if, going down the proportion of the legs, they are made longer, they will appear better. Making them short would be a very great disgrace. Other than this, I do not know what to say here, except that the figures of men should be a little broad in the shoulders and the attachment of the arms strong. Those of women should be narrower in the shoulders and wide in the hips.' Having said this, Sirigatti kept silent.

'If the hand were as fast to obey the intellect,' Michelozzi now said, 'as [the intellect] is fast to learn the precepts of sculpture from your words, I would believe that in little time I would make myself known as a good master. But I will say with the Tuscan Poet: "The spirit is willing, but the flesh is weak."'

'The arts and sciences are undertaken by means of words,' Vecchietti added. 'Although the words follow from the practice, many times words have done what works cannot do.' [155 as 137]

'You are right,' immediately replied Michelozzi. 'In cases of love, humble entreaties have often done more than deeds to soften a heart of diamond.'

'True, being expressed by a man as handsome and fortunate as you,' Sirigatti responded energetically. 'But for myself, if I hadn't been helped by the secret of drinking gold, words would have been in vain in finding the remedy of love.'

'We will depart too much from our first path if you now want to dispute what has more merit in love,' said Valori. 'It would seem to me much better that you continue your discussion of sculpture and painting. It is now in the fullness of bearing fruit. Ridolfo has uncovered beautiful precepts that not only can help one do things but also judge those things that others do. And you will remember that the time is brief "with more to do and the day advances."'

'Baccio is right,' immediately added Vecchietti. 'And if we consider well the utility that the discussion of Ridolfo could bring, we will pray that he wishes to continue with his lecture, turning everything over to him.'

'As Pythagorus taught his pupils well, it is a very reasonable thing,' Michelozzi replied unrestrainedly, 'that the disciple keep silent a long time before daring to respond to the teacher. Therefore, I will not now respond to Ridolfo for having given me the title of handsome and fortunate. Together with you, I will ask him that he continue [156] to instruct me in the things of sculpture.'

'You honour me so much more than is appropriate,' replied Sirigatti. 'I cannot do other than try to obey, to pay part of the obligation that I have to you. But, as you say that I should continue with my discussion on sculpture, I will begin by coming to an understanding of my ignorance. It seems to me that I have said enough about this, and that I have said enough of what you seek of me.'[18]

This having been said and Sirigatti keeping silent, Michelozzi began to speak in this manner: 'I do not believe that there is anything more that I want to know about sculpture. But I would think it highly appropriate, before you proceed to consider painting, to have a brief discourse concerning the marble statues that are publicly seen in Florence. This will ground me soundly in the precepts learned [about sculpture] and make a universal judgment about them,'

'I commend to all the suggestions of Michelozzi,' and, continuing to speak, Valori turned to Sirigatti: 'This work is quite appropriate for you. You more truly understand the names of the sculptors who have done the statues and the shortcomings and perfections that these have.'

'You burden me with a weight that I do not feel fit to carry,' Sirigatti responded. 'Other men than I would need to judge the works of so many capable men. Their names, and nothing more, I can quite well speak here.'

Concerning the statues of Santa Maria del Fiore

'We enter, if you please, into Santa Maria del Fiore,' Michelozzi said. 'And tell me by whose hand are the statues that are there and the beautiful parts that you recognize in them. And then I will ask you what occurs to me about them.'

'You also desire that I plough in this sea that has no bottom or shore,' [replied Sirigatti]. 'I have decided, no matter where I have to follow, that I will gratify your desire. Therefore, to begin, I say that entering into Santa Maria [159] del Fiore there is represented before my eyes the *St James the Great* of [Jacopo] Sansovino. It is a very beautiful figure, lifelike, well studied, and of good pose.'[19]

'You will quite allow me to say what it is, how it appears to me, and what I have understood some artists to say about each figure,' Michelozzi said promptly, 'not with the intention of blaming anyone but to discover the truth, and to provide material for our discussion.'

'On the contrary, we asked that you come, not for you to say what we allow you,' Vecchietti responded emphatically, 'but rather that you speak freely.'

'Since the authority is given to me,' Michelozzi said, 'beginning to take advantage of it I say that all of what Ridolfo has said is true. This is a very beautiful statue. Nevertheless, that fold in the drapery that it has above the right leg seems awkward. And the head, while it would be widely held as beautiful, it seems that those who specialize in art would prefer it to have more style [*più maniera*].'[20]

'As for the fold in the drapery,' Sirigatti responded, 'do not marvel that it looks badly. This is not a defect of Sansovino, who made a rich drape here that descended down to the ground. The figure was broken in handling, and it is from this that it happened that it appears poor in that part. Then, it seems to me that it is not possible to desire the head to be more beautiful. And a good master is not always required to draw in style [*maniera*]. He can sometimes demonstrate his knowledge making things finished and delicate.

'But continuing further forward, I see the *St Andrew* of Andrea Ferruci of Fiesole.[21] His statue, while not to be [160] compared with that of Sansovino, is not, however, to be blamed.'

'I quite see,' Michelozzi intervened passionately, 'that the affection that you have for the sculptors makes you speak discreetly here. It is not that you do not recognize that this figure, besides its weakness of manner and its having very confused draperies on the back, has one hand larger than the other.'

'I had not recognized so many defects here,' Sirigatti responded. 'And I know that this same Andrea did the portrait head of *Marsilio Ficino* that is very commendable in this same church.[22] But, returning to the statues, I find myself before the *St Peter* of the Cav. Bandinelli. This was done by him when he was young. The experience that is in his other things is not seen here. Nevertheless, it shows very great vitality.'[23]

Here he kept silent a while and, seeing that Michelozzi did not respond, resumed his discussion, saying: 'Now comes the *St John the Evangelist* of Benedetto da Rovezzano.[24] I would praise this figure but I fear that Girolamo will not give me the opportunity.'

'You do well,' Michelozzi said, 'since who is it that does not recognize the weak manner of this figure and cannot see that it has short thighs and a large head?'

'Now come two figures,' continued Sirigatti, 'about which you cannot speak if not in praise. And these are *St James the Less* and *St Philip*, both of Giovanni dell'Opera.[25] They are beautiful, well studied, and in the best possible poses.'

'Truly [161] they please me,' Michelozzi added, 'and much more the *St James* than the *St Philip*. They seem two very commendable statues to me even though some say that the *St James* would have been better covered or draped below the elbow on the right arm. An arm so bare, next to all the other clothed parts, shows poverty.'

'It seems to me,' replied Sirigatti, 'that this quite beautiful uncovered arm, which is different from the other parts, gives grace. The moods of men are different, and it is a very difficult thing to try to make everyone content. But what will you say of the *Adam and Eve* of Bandinelli.[26] These are two figures worthy to be imitated. Much study was given to the torso and arms of Adam. And while the breast and body of Eve could have been made a little more beautiful, you see how very well both are posed.'

'All agree,' Michelozzi said, 'that the Adam, by being made to stand too short in comparison to the Eve, has need of the rather high clogs that are seen under his feet.[27] But you will not give so much praise to the God the Father that is on the altar. It shows more marble than art.'[28]

'All the craftsmen who labour,' Sirigatti responded, 'do not make their works of the same perfection. And this figure, having to be so large and surrounded with much drapery, was a difficult thing to give grace to. Those who consider it well will find it beautiful. But if you want to see a very beautiful figure, turn your eyes to the dead Christ on the altar by the same Bandinelli.[29] Come now, I see [162] that you do not have anything to tell me here. Therefore, I will pass to the *St Matthew* of Vincenzio de' Rossi.[30] This statue is made with great care and very well worked. And for that it appears to me worthy of praise.'

'I have heard various things said about this,' Michelozzi responded, 'as all do not think so. Some say that it is not well posed, others that the shin of the leg is short and the thigh long and poorly attached.'

'Talk is very easy and the work very difficult,' Sirigatti said, 'When Bandinelli put his beautiful statues in public, who could blame them more? Now that he has died, his excellence is recognized. And everyone who spoke badly of him has retracted. But since nothing remains for us to see in Santa Maria del Fiore, where does it seem to you that we should go for material for our discussion?'[31]

'In San Lorenzo, if you like,' Vecchietti answered. 'There you will have much to say, and a few things on which it will be up to Girolamo to comment.'

'I see that I will acquire the reputation of being too critical by wanting to discover the truth,' Michelozzi said. 'But why? Is it not better to be blamed for truth in hand than praised for flattery?'

'If you said both at once,' added Valori, 'it would immediately have finished our discussion. Girolamo, however, deserves praise. By showing us how it appears to him and to others, he provides the opportunity to consider the truth.'

Concerning the St John Baptizing Christ over the door of San Giovanni

'But whose was the first hand on the two statues above the door of San Giovanni where Christ is baptized by St John? They seem very beautiful to me.' [163]

'They were done by Andrea dal Monte à Sansovino,'[32] answered Sirigatti. 'Because he did not leave them completely finished, Vincentio Danti of Perugia, as you know, then completed them.[33] And as you see, they are worthy of consideration.'

Concerning the statues of the sacristy of San Lorenzo

'But what will I say on entering the [new] sacristy of San Lorenzo, since I see *Dawn, Dusk,* and *Duke Lorenzo* by the hand of the divine Michelangelo on the left? These figures, with the verisimilitude of their parts, greet me, although their mouths are shut. And what will I respond to them? If they are not fortunate marbles, which were worked by the hand of an angel [*Agnolo*], they are not either among the things described as insensible. They are among the living and immortal. But if I turn my eyes to the right I will keep quiet to not wake the *Night,*[34] who has the *Day* and Lord *Giuliano de' Medici* nearby while she sleeps. These are all figures of this same Michelangelo, in which art is seen to be not less than nature.'

'Here I cannot [speak] if not to help you praise them,' Michelozzi added. 'I would conclude that all those who wish to become capable men in sculpture should make these their study. And they should seek with every effort to grasp this beautiful manner. But by whom are the other three figures that I see beside the door?'

'The unfinished *Madonna with Her Child* in Her arms,' Sirigatti responded, 'is also by Michelangelo. It well shows his excellence. The *St Cosmas* is by Fra Giovanagnolo Montorsoli,[35] a very beautiful figure as you see and worthy to be beside that of such a great master. The *St Damian* [164] in a very good manner,[36] which shows the emotion of devotion in its face and in every part shows signs of having been carved by a master's hand, is by Raffaello di Montelupo.'

'You are right,' Michelozzi responded, 'but it seems to many that the right arm of this figure is rather thin.'

Concerning the statues of the piazza

'Perhaps it came from a defect of the marble,' Sirigatti responded, 'such as happened to Michelangelo in the shoulders of his *David* that it is in the piazza. Therefore, he did it with the intention of putting it in a niche, so that one could not see the defect of the shoulders. Then it was put, to his mild dissatisfaction, where it is now seen. Nevertheless, it is one of the most beautiful figures that it is possible to see.'[37]

'Since you leaped to the piazza,' Michelozzi said, 'tell us something of the other marble statues that are there.'

'What can I say,' Sirigatti continued, 'if I do not praise to the sky the Hercules that has Cacus under him by the Cav. Bandinelli?[38] The parts of these two figures have all the muscles and all the understanding that art seeks.'

'Yes, but some say,' Michelozzi added, 'that the Hercules should have a fiercer pose and not display such little interest in the enemy that he has between his feet.'

'Some imagine this,' Sirigatti responded, 'as Hercules in the act of fighting with Cacus. And they are deceived, because he has already conquered him and Cacus has been made a prisoner. Therefore, Hercules victoriously stands up straight, without looking at him. I then see Amannati's *Neptune*.[39] This, being in the customary pose, the parts [165] well proportioned, and with very beautiful figures of sea monsters at his feet, it seems to me that it is not possible if not to praise.'

'If I have kept the precepts that you gave me well in mind,' Michelozzi said, 'you told me that the shoulder of the leg that was planted should be lower than the other.[40] And that, wanting to make the head look towards that side, it is necessary, wanting the figure to have grace, to make the torso turn so that the [other] shoulder is lifted. And I have observed that the *St James* of Sansovino gives this same impression. But I see that Amannati's *Neptune* has the shoulder of the planted leg higher than the other, and that it looks to that side, without having the torso move at all.'

'And it seems to me, if I am not entirely wrong,' Vecchietti added, 'that Ridolfo said, when he spoke of the proportions, that from the hollow of the throat to the outside of the shoulder on each side should be a "head." And in this figure I am shown a greater space from the fontanel to the right shoulder than from that to the left shoulder.'

'This can appear, but not be,' Sirigatti responded. 'Being turned to the left side, the face blocks the view of the space of this shoulder, while the other is uncovered. But I do not intend to respond so much to one feature.[41] Now, since it is not our intention to speak of those of bronze, there is not another figure left for us to speak about in the piazza except for the beautiful group of Giambologna.[42] This seems to me done with so much art and so much care that I do not believe it is possible to desire something more finished. [166] And the many poems done about this have made it widely known, and particularly a sonnet of Bernardo.'

'Please recite it for us, I pray you,' Michelozzi said, turning towards Vecchietti. 'It would make me very grateful to hear verses done about such beautiful statues, and particularly yours, which I know are of such great value.'

'Not because of their value,' Vecchietti answered, 'but so as not to neglect the deserved praise of Giambologna, I will not omit reciting for you my weak sonnet. Many other beautiful spirits better than I have written about this. This is mine:

Among the most famous, most appreciated, and rare
 Marbles and bronzes, which more than elsewhere
 Decorate Florence, to whom surrender in carving
 Athens and Rhodes and their works so brilliant.
Among those of honour, not of avaricious riches,
 The great Etruscan prize is given very worthily
 to the live marble of Bologna,
 Who expressed emotion in so many and varied ways.
Elderly weakness appears oppressed in these,
 Virile young furore, abducting also,
 Fair youth as not seen elsewhere.
From the Quirinal comes the prey and the unfortunate
 Sabine with such art and charm
 Sculpture, that in live stone sighs and moves.[43]

After they had greatly commended the verses of Vecchietti, Michelozzi added: 'He reminds me of a sonnet done about the same [167] statues by Vincentio Alamanni. In addition to being a Senator of Florence of some reputation, [Alamanni] knew and greatly loved the belles-lettres and particularly poetry. And I will recite it for you provided that Ridolfo promises to recite one, which pleases me greatly. It was done by Piero di Gherardo Capponi, a man of very beautiful spirit, great virtue, and very noble manners.'

'Recite that of Alamanni,' Sirigatti said, 'and I will not fail to have you hear that of Capponi.'

'I am ready,' Michelozzi responded, and said:

While I contemplate the beautiful marble and perceive in it,
 Issuing from above to inflame the young desire
 To abduct chaste woman, abducts me also
 I feel the marble itself within and without.
But if you have a spirit in a stone, and motion engraved
 Yes lifelike, my noble Bologna;
 Quite giving you security from eternal oblivion
 Your name to live long and near.

Three faces in a spiral are in view,
 Desire, fear, pain, in loud voice and clear
 Of who presses, and who flees, and who is saddened;
That work so rare which the pious Grand Duke,
 Astutely recognizes, granting it the highest honour.
 It also amazes less experienced people who examine it.[44]

All greatly liked Alamanni's sonnet. Satisfied that praise was given to it, Michelozzi said, looking at Sirigatti, 'Now it is your turn to recite.' He, enthusiastically began in this way: [168 as 192]

An abduction was not what the maker intended
 To portray in marble; but to show a charming and beautiful
 Woman, in lovely actions to appear so
 Nude and lascivious, that every heart would burn for her.
An ardent youth seeing her, impressed
 Kisses on her lips and fixed his gaze on her;
 Then turning to the loving star
 Begged to become a new Pygmalion.
The Goddess, in compassion gave life to the marble limbs;
 But when he embraced her, now separated from her master,
 A spoil to the predator, she returned to stone.
When the fearful sculptor sees (is it as he believes?)
 The lover in grief, in amazement he implores,
 What a marvel it is that everyone seemed to be alive?[45]

Valori and Vecchietti greatly praised the sonnet of Capponi as new in concept and well expounded. But Michelozzi who, among them, was thinking to himself, said turning to Sirigatti, 'The sound of the verses pleases me greatly, but I am forced to confess that I have not quite mastered the subject. Therefore, I ask you to talk briefly about it to me.'

'It is not surprising that what is apparent to some seems rather obscure here,' Sirigatti responded. 'In his way, Capponi imagines a new fable in his sonnet. He says that the master did not propose to do an abduction in marble, but only a very beautiful and lascivious young girl. That, having finished with the most delicate parts, a youth [169] saw that beautiful statue following its completion. And enflamed by amorous desire for its beauty, he embraced it, begging Venus to do him the favour of making it come alive, like the ivory statue that Pygmalion made. And [Capponi] says that Venus, to gratify the youth, gave life to the marble limbs. Therefore, having obtained the gift, he pressed the young girl to his breast, wanting to carry her away. But the virgin, seeing herself the prey of the young man, fearing to lose her virginity, was frozen by fear and became marble again. The youth, conquered by sadness, seeing himself deprived of every hope, was transformed into stone. And the master who had carved the woman, was distraught because the young man did not bring her to him when he saw her alive. Taken by great surprise and astounded by what now happened, seeing them turned back into marble and hardened into cold stone, he was himself petrified. And, therefore, he says at the end of the sonnet, "What a marvel it is that everyone seemed to be alive?" He wants to say that a little before, all had been alive.'

'Now that I understand it,' Michelozzi said, 'I praise it greatly, seeing in it such a new and beautiful invention.'

And the others then repeated many things about it. And finally, leaving the discussion of this, Sirigatti said, 'If it is with the good grace of all of you, it would seem to me that I should bring the discussion of statues to an end. From what was said, one can easily make a judgment about other things. If I entered into a discussion of the many ancient and modern statues [170] that are in the Palace of the Most Serene Grand Duke Francesco, in the superb Pitti Palace, and in other places, it would limit ahead of time our day of discussion. And we would propose in vain to speak about painting.'

All agreed with what Sirigatti said and Michelozzi continued: 'You have made me, with your words, not only knowledgeable in good figures but almost a sculptor. I would also hope to not have less profit from your discussion of painting. Since we await it with great desire and attention, you can begin at your pleasure.'

'Painting,' Sirigatti responded, 'the essence of which Bernardo identified, is defined to be an imitation of nature. The craftsmen augment this into an art by adding what they judge appropriate to make the concept appear that was in the mind of the maker.'

Definition of painting with respect to materials

'I believe that, considering it with respect to materials, one can say that painting is a plane covered with various colours on the surface of a wall, panel, or canvas. By virtue of lines, shadow, light, and a good drawing it shows a figure modelled, strong, and in relief.'

Three ways of painting

'This is put into effect working in three ways. And these are: working in fresco, in tempera, and finally in oil.'[46]

Painting in fresco

'It is the task of whoever wishes to paint in fresco to plaster as much of a wall as suffices for work on one day. You will want to tone down the whiteness with sand and with a little black so that it appears a third colour.[47] Greatly delaying putting the colours on the fresh lime makes a certain coating that heat, [171] cold, and wind cause to speckle and stain the whole work. It greatly helps to frequently bathe the wall. Having put down the plaster, the cartoon is fitted over it or a piece of [cartoon] countermarked, to know the next day the next piece that follows. And then with a stylet of iron or ivory or other hard wood ... proceed to trace over the profiles and outlines of the cartoon. This tracing sinks into the lime because it is fresh and receives all the lines. And then taking away the cartoon, one paints around these, not making them less distinct, with earth colours tempered with clear water. And the white is baked Travertine. And it is necessary in this work to proceed with great judgment. The wall, while it is soft, shows the colours in one way, while when it is dry it makes another effect. And above all be careful to not have to retouch anything with colour that has *limbellucci* glue or egg yolk or gum or gum tragacanth.[48] Then the wall will not show its brilliance, and the colours will become blurred and in a brief space of time will become black. Therefore, whoever paints in fresco completely finishes his work every day, without having to retouch in *secco*, so that in this way his paintings have a much longer life and he will have from them the reputation of a greater master.'

Painting in tempera

'Painting in tempera can be done on a dry wall, on panel, and on [172] canvas. Wanting to paint on a wall that is dry, it is mopped with white and given two coats of warm glue. Then, the tempera is made in this way. Taking egg yolk and beating it very well and mincing a twig of soft fig in it, colours of every sort are tempered with this material. All are good for this work except for white made of lime, which is too strong. However, the blues, which turn green with this tempera from the egg yolk, need to be tempered with gum or *limbellucci*.[49] One can also make the tempera for all colours with *limbellucci* glue. This is done today in Flanders, where one sees such beautiful canvases of landscapes done with similar tempera ...[50]

'Over a [gesso] panel attach your cartoon, and between the cartoon and the picture, a white sheet of the same thickness, coloured with charcoal dust on the side that is placed over the gesso. And proceed, pressing down on the outlines as I have described at other times. And you will see your design there on the panel and the cartoon will remain intact. And then you will be able to begin painting with colour at your pleasure.'

How canvas is prepared

'But if you want to paint on canvas, there you will apply a coat or two of size and then begin colouring. And fill in the texture of the cloth well with the colour. And the Flemish canvases, which can easily be rolled up and carried everywhere, are done in this way.'

Chiaroscuro

'Whoever wishes to paint on walls in chiaroscuro needs to cover the field with *terretta*.[51] Apply three colours, each one darker than the other, *terretta*, umber, and black, to make the shadows and the modelling. And these are highlighted with Sangiovanni white, [174] dazzled with *terretta*. And in all chiaroscuro, green, yellow, and every other colour are used in the same order. And to make the colour bronze, mix umber with vermilion and, as with other colours, temper it with water. And the same thing is done on canvas, except that the colours are tempered with glue, egg, or gum.'

Painting with oil

'To pass now to painting with oil, it can be done on wall, panel, canvas, and stone.[52]

'Trace the cartoon or the sketch onto [the prepared wall] and [then] apply the colours tempered with walnut or linseed oil. Walnut, in which it is well to mix a little varnish, is better because it is thinner and will not yellow the colours. Bring your work to completion with care, it not being necessary to varnish it ... But whoever wishes this painting in oil to last awhile on the wall, puts it on a wall of brick and not of stone. Stones soften in time, sending out humidity and staining the painting, while the bricks do not retain so much humidity.

'Whoever wants to paint in oil on panel, prepares it and applies gesso … Apply the priming that one most likes. Then, trace the cartoon or the drawing with tailors' white chalk or with [176] reduction charcoal, either of which are easily erased. And colour with colours tempered with walnut oil and nothing else. And equally the same order is followed in wanting to paint on canvas except that it is necessary first to adjust it in one of two ways that I will describe.'

How canvases are prepared for drawing on in oil

'The first way is to apply one layer of size and then two of priming, leaving each layer to dry. For the second way, take some Volterrano chalk and some of the superfine flour called *fucello,* in equal parts. These materials, put in a little pot with glue and linseed oil and brought to a boil, are united together. And then this mixture is put on the canvas and flattened and spread out over everything with an iron rod. And when it is dry you paint on it. But the first way is better if the canvas has to be transported to other countries. Canvases done in the second way, with chalk, would crack in many places in being rolled up.

'Those who prefer to use colour on stone will find certain slabs very good that are found on the coast of Genoa. On these it is only necessary to put the priming and then work, colouring with care.

'I have now briefly discussed the three principal methods of painting. Painting, as you very well know, was divided yesterday into five parts by Bernardo and he has happily treated invention. I would delude myself greatly if I were to promise too eagerly to manage to speak of composition [*dispositione*], poses [*attitudini*], parts [*membra*], and the colours [*colori*].[53] [177] I will follow these things in the order that was devised by him, saving myself to speak of colour at the end, because the other parts are learned first in design and because its discussion would take too much from the others. And I will do all with brevity, since there is a great deal to speak about concerning these things over and above what I have been able to master. More time than what remains to us would be required [to discuss everything].'

Everyone commended the words of Sirigatti and then, keeping silent, waited for him to resume his discussion. Thus, keeping silent for a moment, he said: 'Composition is, among the many important things that the painter does, very difficult and, among the difficult, very important. In it is the knowledge and the good judgment of the craftsman principally known.'

Precepts in composition

'One takes, therefore, great care when one does a narrative. Proceed to arrange and segregate the figures, the buildings, and the landscape, making one see more figures within it than is [naturalistically] possible, but not entangling them so together that they seem confused. Do not imitate some who, wanting to be shown making many figures in a painting, paint two or three large figures in front and then many heads above heads. This thing is not suitable in art and does not give pleasure to those who look at it. Rather, it is necessary to avoid placing large standing figures in the front because they cut off the view of those behind and occupy a great part of the field. The astute painter, however, tries to make the figures in front either bending down or seated or in some low position so that space remains [178] for other figures, buildings, and landscapes. Do not do as a painter, of whose name I keep silent, who, having to paint a picture of animals, put an elephant and a camel in the foreground in a way so that there did not remain room for other animals. And the others that he did there displayed only a small part of their bodies.

'It is suitable then to arrange, with art, the elderly, the young, women, perspectives, and animals in places that are most appropriate for them. Give clothing to people that is appropriate to the age and to the class that they are given to represent.

'And particularly, always make it so that one sees [only one] plane where the figures are placed.[54] And do not do as certain painters who put a narrative on a plane with its landscape and buildings and then rise up to another plane and do a different narrative with a perspective different from the first and then pass on to a third, something worthy of very great disapproval. But whoever wants his works to be praised makes it a habit to set the point [where the prospective lines converge] at the eye level of the observer. And develop the principal narrative on that plane and then, little by little, begin to diminish the figures.

'And perspective that is laid out in the painting is to be divided into three parts. The first involves the diminution that is made in the size of the bodies at different distances. The second is that of the colour of these bodies. And the third is the reduction in the detail of the figures and of the borders that the bodies have at different distances.

'Thus, if figures appear in a form smaller than the others, this happens because they are distant [179] from the eye. And, as a consequence, there is much air between them and the observer. This prevents the discernment of the details of these objects. Therefore, it is necessary that the painter make small figures only rough and not finished because otherwise it would be against nature, teacher of art.

'And when landscapes are painted, be advised that the lower parts of the mountains should always be made darker than the higher, and in this same way the mountains above mountains. The air is thicker and darker the closer it is to the earth and thinner and more transparent the higher it is. Therefore, the lower parts of things large and tall, which are distant from the viewer, will be made less well seen. They are seen on a line that passes through, interrupting, the densest air. And the summit will be made better seen. It is seen on a line – even if the eye is in the thick air – not so interrupted [by dense air]. It terminates on the high summit of the thing seen, which is in the thinnest and most transparent air. Thus, it follows that this line, although it [ends up] farther from the eye, moves so much more from point to point through a thinner quality of air that it makes things more visible.

'Finally it is necessary to arrange everything so naturalistically that it is created in harmony and unity. As harmony that delights the ears results from varied voices and from different chords, in the same way, pleasure and content for the eyes are created from the many parts arranged in the painting showing charm and judgment.'[55]

Concerning poses

'But passing to poses,[56] I say that these need [180] to conform in everything to the narrative and to the person that they illustrate. Therefore, it is necessary, painting the sacred narratives, to make grave, modest, and devout, not fierce or forced, the poses of patriarchs, prophets, saints, martyrs, the Saviour of the World, the Queen of Heaven, and the angels. But it will be very appropriate to make those of tyrants and their ministers fierce and cruel. [Do not make them] immodest and lascivious. This takes away the devotion that one has in gazing on the saints that are near [the tyrants]. When wars and arguments are painted, then you are able to play with forceful, vigorous, and terrible poses. When doing things of love, make a habit of doing soft, delicate, and graceful poses. It is appropriate neither in the young nor in the old to show quick and fierce actions. Such gestures are unseemly for their limbs. It is also unsuitable to show young women in activities showing their legs apart. I would also counsel the painter that, having to make a single figure, he avoid foreshortening in part or completely. In narratives and in battles it will be possible to do this to his liking. And I would greatly desire that he take great care not to repeat the same faces, the same clothing, and the same poses in the same narrative. These are something found in almost all the painters and especially in making the same faces.'

Concerning parts

'As for the parts, while it is true that their proportions were discussed when sculpture was spoken of above, it is a necessary thing for every painter to know them. [181] Much judgment needs to be used putting these into place. The different poses of the figures put the parts in different positions and show different foreshortenings.

It is necessary to help these with shadow and with light, the proportions now shortened and now lengthened according to whether this is seen to have a good effect on that part, so that the natural action is represented. And also do not give a delicate damsel the limbs and the muscles that are appropriate for a fierce man nor, I tell you, the softness of the parts of a youngster to men already mature. Do not give muscles with too much prominence to a figure that is thin. Thin men never have much flesh on their bones, and where there is little flesh there cannot be greatness of muscle. And above everything, take care that all the parts together have a certain balance and especially where you separate them where they are connected together. This is not seen in individual parts.'

Concerning the colours

'Now needing to treat colour, within which light and shadow are included, a long subject is handed to me to discuss. I will dispatch it with the usual brevity, saying that the colours are of very great importance. And in spreading them the painter needs to take great consideration and care, noting that the depth and the shallowness of the figures' modelling is created by them.

'And it is particularly important to know how to catch the light and put in the shadows. If someone is portraying from nature, he needs to take the light from the north, in order not to have it vary. And if [182] it is also taken at midday, have the windows covered, so that the sun does not make changes. And the light needs to be caught from above in a way that every object makes as long a shadow on the ground as its height. And always, when portraying from nature, try to have the light strong and high up. Portraying with a light lower down, the portrayals change their aspect, hardly making it possible for things that are done to be recognized.[57] If figures are imagined in the sun, make it a habit to make the shadows dark and the lights strong and brilliant and the shadows that are impressed on the ground precise. Imagining them in a cloudy time, it will be appropriate to make little difference between the lights and the shadows and not to make any shadows at the feet. If figures are represented in the house, make a great difference from light to dark and make the shadows on the floor. But if they are painted in a white room with a covered window it is necessary to make little difference between the light and the shadow.[58] And if the room is illuminated by fire, it will be appropriate to make the light turn to red and the shadows dark, projecting onto the wall and onto the floor. And if the figures will be partly illuminated by the fire and partly by other light, it will be necessary that those in the other light have a strong light and those by the fire, reddish.

'The borders of figures are not done with any colour of the background itself. I mean to say that the profile should not be obscure between the background and the figures. And the background also should be done with care. Therefore, if the figure is bright, it is praiseworthy to make the background dark, and if [183] the figure is dark to make the background light.[59] The material that clothes the figures should have the folds arranged in such a way as to encircle the parts of those people that they clothe. And they should [hang] so that the illuminated parts are not set in folds of dark shadow or the shadowy parts in bright [light]. The outlines of these folds should flow on each part around the part that they cover. But they should not [flow] in a way that cuts them off or so that the shadow that should be at the bottom [of the fold] is on the surface of the dressed body. And the shadows put between the folds of clothing that surround the bodies are much darker than those that the eyes [actually] see in the concavities in which such shadows are produced. The eye understands this when it moves between the shadowy and bright part of the figure. Great modelling will be achieved by arranging the painting so naturalistically that that part that is illuminated ends in something dark and the dark part ends in something bright.[60]

'Then, the colours need to be finely and thinly ground, charming and cheerful, and appropriately matching their significance to the place, time, and person. And in a painting it is necessary to give it here brightness, there darkness, life and pallor. Nevertheless, the capable painter will so arrange it and veil it that he makes altogether a united composition. He will see this done if he uses the brightest colours in the first figures that are in front. And then, as he moves farther into it, he will proportionally diminish the brightness in such a way that the last figures are all much [184] darker than the others. And those few that are bright will appear veiled in a certain way to appear to the eyes to be going further away.

'Now I have discussed what little I know about the four parts that Bernardo left me. I should consequently be absolved of every promise that I have made and every obligation that came to me about it.'[61]

'Slowly,' Michelozzi said. 'How do you want me to evaluate the precepts and the admonitions that you have given me, to put them into operation, if I do not know what colours are? I do not know their nature, have no information of their differences, do not know how to make those that are artificially made, and also do not understand their meaning. Therefore, tell me and teach me all these things. In such a way you will fulfil your promise and, loosening you of every obligation, bind me so that in truth I will always be beholden and obliged to you.'

'Girolamo is right,' Vecchietti emphatically added, 'and deserves to be satisfied in the honest things he asks. But I would think, if it does not displease you, that we should make firmer the precepts that Ridolfo has given to us, before starting to deal with colour. We [should] consider if the four parts discussed by him have been well observed in the panels that are in the churches in Florence. In this way one will come to have good experience and good judgment in painting.'

'Bernardo has certainly thought well,' responded Valori, 'although Girolamo will have a rather serious wait [185] until this is finished, before knowing what he desires about colour. Thus, if Ridolfo likewise will not seem to be bored, imagine we are going through the churches where the good paintings are. Tell us first of your thoughts about the panels that we find. And subsequently be willing to discuss what you will with respect to the subject of colour.'

The proposal of Valori was greatly commended by Vecchietti and Michelozzi and, when they were silent, Sirigatti said: 'It will not bore me at all to obey you, since my work corresponds to your hopes and perhaps [if you hear] as much as is in me, I will not fail.'

Concerning the panels of Santa Croce

'Here, obeying you, one enters into Santa Croce. At first sight I am presented with the very beautiful panel of Francesco Salviati where he has portrayed Our Saviour taken down from the Cross.[62] Here you can see a well-considered composition, putting the short figures ahead of those that are tall. Almost all are seen complete and their parts suitably posed. The poses are appropriate, and especially those of the tallest figures. And the parts appear almost completely faithful to nature and particularly the body of Christ. And the colouring is done with all the art that is appropriate.'

'Nothing more is being said in front of Sirigatti?' Michelozzi asked, turning to the others. 'Gentlemen, if some of us do not speak out, Ridolfo, as a partisan of the painters is going to praise them to the skies. And we will not uncover, as is our desire, any poorly observed parts in any panel. Therefore, since the others keep silent, [186] if you will, I will say about every panel those things that some artists have been heard to notice as errors. I am very eager to hear the thoughts of others about painted panels when they have gone out [of the studio]. And I will also state my opinion about them so that more from me, than from them, can come the error. From this I will learn more of the practice. I have no intention of contradicting what [Sirigatti] has said. I would not want to do this in any way, but this will more completely uncover the truth and to give you occasion to discuss.'

'Certainly speak freely,' Sirigatti responded. 'As you do not wish to contradict the things that I will say, neither do I also wish to contradict you or others. It is a pleasure to understand all.'

The other two lauded Michelozzi and heaped praise on him for proposing what he had said, and Vecchietti added: 'Thank goodness we come to the point, and now, Girolamo, leaving ceremony aside, what do you think of this panel of Salviati?'

'For me, it is very beautiful,' Michelozzi responded. 'Nevertheless, some things are there that do not end pleasingly. The pose of the Magdalene appears to be done rather as a pose of humour than of sorrow. And the Madonna is as large sitting down as one of the Marys that is standing beside Her, and their feet are placed on the same plane. If the Virgin stood up it would make Her disproportionately large in comparison with the other women that are there. And Her head would reach to the middle of the body of the Christ.[63] In [187] its other parts, it appears to me very worthy to be praised.'

'I have already decided, as I said, not to answer you,' Sirigatti said. 'Therefore, I will pass to the panel of Bronzino representing *Christ in Limbo*.[64] In it I see a very beautiful composition, graceful poses, parts well understood, very charming colours, beautiful complexions, faces very well done, portraits from life, and all very studied and done with great art.'

'I do not have anything to say about this,' Michelozzi responded, 'other than that I see Baccio is greatly delighted in looking at it, as I am also, as I consider it beautiful and charming.'

'I am delighted to gaze at these beauties that were given to us by the Supreme Donor of all Blessings,' Valori added enthusiastically, 'as long as we look at them in an appropriate way. And I consider how much we are obligated to the Donor for such a great gift. But you should not hesitate to state your opinion [even] if you have to say something against such a beautiful thing.'[65]

'I like your Platonic opinion,' Michelozzi responded, 'and if everyone looked at it with such intention, some would not happen to make sacred paintings in any other way. But I do not know that this continence and this saintly thought – contemplating things that so greatly allure the senses – penetrates others, or if it lasts for long in those transfixed.'

'Do not let us be diverted from our straight path,' Vecchietti said, 'as the road is still long, and the time is brief. Here we are, Ridolfo, in front of the panel of the *Resurrection of the Saviour* by Santi di Tito.'[66]

'It seems to me,' responded [188] Sirigatti, 'that this panel is done with great drawing and with good poses. Great emotions of fear are seen in the figures that are shown fleeing.'

'It is certain,' said Michelozzi, 'that this panel is well done and perhaps of the best that Santi has done. Nevertheless, that pose of Christ, in which His left side hangs down so much, has a *je ne sais quoi* [*un non so che*] that mars some of its grace. And the colour might be more lively and more charming.'

'You will not say this about this other one that is also by Santi,' Sirigatti said. 'Here Christ is breaking bread at Emmaus.[67] There are very beautiful colours here, the figures graceful, and the composition very well considered.'

'I believe that Santi wanted to show in this painting,' Michelozzi added, 'that he coloured well when he wanted to but that more depends on drawing than [depends] on beautiful colours. Also, that figure dressed in blue is held to be rather large in proportion to the others.'

'This which follows, where St Thomas touches Christ, is by Giorgio Vasari,'[68] said Sirigatti. 'And, if I am not wrong, it has good composition and good colouring.'

'Do not go further,' responded Michelozzi, interrupting him. 'I have understood that St Thomas and St Peter have poor poses, that there is not great artifice [*artificio*] about the figures, that the draperies are poorly composed, and that some figures, which are placed on the same level as the columns, are hardly less tall than the columns. Now, we can speak of the following panel of the *Ascension*.'

'This is by [189] Giovanni Strada,'[69] Sirigatti responded, 'and, as you see, very well organized. It shows Christ and the Madonna, affectionate and devout, and they have good poses, the parts are well composed, and the colour cheerful and applied with art.'

'All pleasing,' Michelozzi responded, 'except for the poses of the two angels at the extremities of the corners. They show fear, where they should show joyfulness.[70] And the short figure, which is seen in the middle, is seen placed on a level very low in comparison with the level where the other figures are placed.'

'Now follows,' said Sirigatti, 'the panel of the *Holy Spirit* by Giorgio Vasari.[71] Here one sees many good faces and a rather dazzling choir of angels that are shown very well. And the colour could not but be praised and there are here, as you see, many figures.'

'Yes, but poorly organized,' immediately added Michelozzi, 'and that seated old man is done in a pose with little grace. But what will you tell us of the panel of the *Trinity* by Girolamo Macchietti?[72] He so greatly satisfied all in his other works as much as he appears to have failed in this. Christ has a living pose and God the Father shows too much fierceness, and the colours are neither very well arranged nor very good.'

'This is a very difficult art,' responded Sirigatti, 'and is not always successful. And all the masters have made things better and worse. But this is not, however, as bad a thing as you make it. Consider well the drawing that is in it and that the invention does not [190] provide material that allows the demonstration of his art. But we pass to the other side and you can put in mind the *St Francis* of Batista Naldini.[73] Try to imagine a more appropriate pose and a face with more emotion and with more devotion.'

'One cannot say otherwise,' Michelozzi repeated, 'but the pose of the little brother who is next to St Francis does not seem to me to be very good.'

'The panel that now follows is of Andrea del Minga,' Sirigatti said, 'where Christ is portrayed praying in the garden and the disciples sleep.[74] I would not know if not to greatly praise it.'

'The painting can be praised,' Michelozzi continued, 'and also Andrea del Minga if he, contrary to that which is said, had done it by himself, but we pass to another.'

'This, of *Christ at the Column*,' Sirigatti said, 'is by Alessandro del Barbiere.[75] In it you can see a well-ordered composition, appropriate poses, the parts well arranged in their places, the colours charming, and the perspective moving inward with beautiful order, offering delight to the eye.'

'It is true that many well-observed parts are seen there,' Michelozzi said, 'and altogether I like it a good deal.'

'That which follows, where Christ is seen shown by Pilate to the people, is by Jacopo de Meglio,'[76] Sirigatti said. 'And it seems to me very copious.'

'Yes, but the copiousness produces tediousness,' Michelozzi responded. 'It is, according to what those who understand [art] say, poorly organized in composition, the architecture confused, the women without grace, and Christ badly posed. And the legs of that [191] figure dressed in yellow, who is in front, are not appropriately together. And particularly the right leg does not seem to be connected to the torso, and the figure as a whole is of disunited parts. But we see this other, which is the only thing remaining for us to see.'

'This, where Christ is seen carrying the Cross, is by Giorgio Vasari,'[77] Sirigatti responded.

'Thank goodness enough has been said up to here,' Michelozzi immediately added, 'since good organization is not seen here, rather, the figures seem glued together. And the Magdalene, the Madonna, and St John appear to be wrestling. Christ does not show emotion in carrying His Cross and turns to St Veronica with too much strength, and the horses that are here are not very well drawn.'

'You will see one of his panels that will not give you so much to say,' Sirigatti responded, 'and you will perhaps agree with me to praise it.'

In Santo Apostolo

'What will you make of that which is in Santo Apostolo,' Michelozzi asked, 'which represents the Conception of the Blessed Virgin?'[78]

'This is [Vasari's],' Sirigatti added, 'and I esteem it very beautiful and done with great art and consideration.'

'And I hold it the most beautiful panel that Giorgio has done,' Michelozzi responded. 'And if he would have continued with this manner and care, his things, which do not please me, would have pleased me much more. But now, what paintings will we discuss since we have left Santa Croce?'

In the Church of Santa Maria Nuova

'We could imagine ourselves going to the Annunziata,' Vecchietti said. 'In passing we could glance at the panel [192] of Alessandro Allori in the Church of Santa Maria Nuova where Christ is painted in the arms of the angels.'[79]

'In this picture one sees great diligence,' added Sirigatti, 'and the parts are well understood and the colour very beautiful.'

'One thing appears that satisfies little,' Michelozzi responded. 'That is the chalice showing the blood. It is shown as a gold chalice that is not transparent and put in a place where the line of vision is from below. If it had not already been made to overflow, according to the rules of perspective, one should not be able to see [the blood].'

In the Annunziata

'I will follow our route,' said Sirigatti. 'But before we enter the Annunziata I should speak of the two very beautiful figures, done by Jacopo Pontormo,[80] that are above the door of the courtyard. In the cloister are those of Andrea del Sarto,[81] Rosso,[82] and Franciabigio.[83] In these the whole diligence of art is seen. These are truly figures to be copied and imitated by those desiring to do well. I will not be able to give them, other than that, the worthy praise that is appropriate to them. [Otherwise,] we will not end what we are doing and will conclude it today leaving our discussion incomplete.'

'You speak the truth,' Michelozzi responded. 'It is never possible to fully praise beautiful things such as these. Therefore, you may enter the church at your pleasure as the journey that remains for us to finish today is yet very long.'

'I will not say anything, since Bernardo did not speak of it yesterday, about the panel of Alessandro Allori,'[84] Sirigatti said. 'Although very well done, it is something copied from Michelangelo. [193] But I will pass to the panel of Giovanni Strada where Christ is still alive on the Cross speaking to the thieves.[85] The Glorious Virgin, with St John and the Marys, is at the foot of the Cross with an endless throng of Pharisees, partly on foot and partly on horseback. And the figures are organized with so much judgment that the first ones, bending down, leave space for the second to be seen and almost all can be enjoyed completely. And as many, however, are not compressed on each other, they make together a rich and very beautiful mixture. The poses are appropriate and particularly that of the Madonna who shows great emotion in crying. The parts are well understood and the colours very beautiful.'

'Here I have nothing to tell you,' Michelozzi added, 'if not that this pleases me more than almost any other work of this Strada that I have seen.'

'Under the organ,' Sirigatti said, 'I see a Christ surrounded by some saints and prophets by the hand of the Frate [Fra Bartolomeo] with well-integrated beautiful poses and good colouring.'[86]

'Yet, do not omit saying,' Michelozzi responded, 'that the figures are somewhat short.'

'The *Deposition from the Cross* that is seen close to here is by Pietro Perugino,'[87] Sirigatti added, 'a work worthy of consideration with beautiful poses and very well coloured. And while all the figures are good and well understood, those above are even better. And particularly great art is seen in the Christ and altogether are well spaced and well positioned. But, [194] since I see that you have nothing to tell me here, I pass behind the choir to the panel representing the *Resurrection of Our Lord* by Bronzino.[88] Here there are many figures in different poses and two very delicate angels are seen, the colour good, and [the figures] well spaced.'

'Do not say so much that nothing remains for me to say,' Michelozzi added. 'According to the opinion of many, the left leg of the Christ is too bright. The fleeing soldier dressed in red is too tall. The angel's leg that is planted on the gravestone should have been turned away. And it seems to me that the other soldier in the yellow uniform is reduced to nothing in the waist.'

In San Marco

'In San Marco,' Sirigatti said, 'there are two panels by the hand of the Frate with beautiful and devout poses, although the colouring is rather raw. But very beautiful, also by the same master, is a figure of a seated *St Mark*. In manner it has grandeur, well-composed parts, well-understood drapery, and well-considered colours.[89] Nor, as well, do I wish to pass in silence the *Angel Raphael and Tobias* by the hand of Santi di Tito.[90] In this picture, in addition to every other beauty, one can recognize that he colours well when he wishes to do so.'

In San Lorenzo

'But there not being anything else here, we take ourselves to San Lorenzo. There, on entering I see on the right hand the *Wedding of the Virgin*, by Rosso.[91] Here appears an easy and beautiful manner, graceful poses, figures that appear three-dimensional, and very good colouring.'

'Everything pleases me,' Michelozzi responded, 'but some would have wanted the faces of the women [195] rather more beautiful and the hands of these saints that are in front, a little larger.'

'Next comes the panel of *St Gismondo*, by Giorgio Vasari,'[92] Sirigatti said. Very plentiful figures are in his usual manner and well coloured.'

'We pass forward,' Michelozzi said, 'as we have seen enough of his things and will see others of them in Santa Maria Novella.'

'I have before me by the hand of the Frate,' Sirigatti continued, 'a panel in chiaroscuro where St Anne is with many saints and angels. It is done with devout poses in a beautiful manner, appearing three-dimensional. But after this I see the *Three Magi*, who present offerings to the Saviour of the World, who is in the arms of the Glorious Virgin,[93] surrounded by many other figures. This is a work of Girolamo Macchietti in a very beautiful manner, very three-dimensional and with charming colouring. And the faces of the figures please me greatly and particularly that of the Madonna. And all seems to me well understood and organized with judgment. Now, if we want to consider all of the many figures of Jacopo da Pontormo in the choir, I doubt that it will take us much time.'[94]

'You are right,' Michelozzi added immediately. 'One can say in few words what I have heard said many times. There is no artifice here, no colour, no organization, and no grace. And the poses are almost all in an unsuitable and immodest manner and only some muscles are good. But the figures below by the hand of Bronzino are very good and well understood. [196] For that reason it amazes me greatly that Jacopo Pontormo, who was such a capable man and who had done so many figures commended by everyone, seems to have lost his gift in this work.'

'Sculpture and painting,' Sirigatti responded, 'are very difficult arts. They require steady judgment in order to observe carefully and a practised and firm hand. Time weakens and consumes all these things.

Therefore, every sculptor and painter who studied in youth and worked in maturity with praise should retire from doing public work in old age. And, leaving the world, he should turn his mind to heavenly concerns. One notes that all human activity finally climbs up to a certain level. Here it is usual for men, having arrived almost as at the top of a mountain, wanting to pass further forward, to descend downward. Therefore, many works are seen by capable men, done when age begins to fail them, much different in grace and in beauty from the things that they first did.

'But we are looking at the narrative in fresco of St Lawrence, by the hand of Bronzino.[95] This was done with great diligence, well finished, and well understood in the many nude parts.'

'This work was done at the time,' Michelozzi said, 'when you said that he should have stopped working. It is no wonder that it is unworthy in composition, lacking in three-dimensionality, unpleasing in the poses, and weak in colouring.'

In Santa Maria Novella

'But it seems to me time that we take ourselves to Santa Maria Novella, where one will not lack themes to discuss.'

'I note [197] just now,' Sirigatti said, 'that you have arrived and will consider the panel by Girolamo Macchietti where St Lawrence is on the grill.[96] In this I see a very beautiful and copious composition, very great drawing, appropriate poses, the parts of the body well placed, the colours well applied, beautiful perspective, the figures with emotion, and all full of artifice and worthy of praise.'

'You are right,' Michelozzi responded, 'and everyone likes it greatly, and particularly those of the art rather praise the king with the other figures who are around him. And they say that the one stoking the fire is well foreshortened and that the St Lawrence is a well-understood figure. But, on the other hand, that soldier who is in front seems too tall. And, according to the rules that you described, that the brightest colours should to be given to the figures that are more to the front, the yellow robe of the king has come to be coloured too brightly. In front of him a soldier has yellow stockings of a darker colour.'

'The panel that follows,' Sirigatti said, 'where the *Nativity* of Our Lord is painted, is of the hand of Batista Naldini.[97] It seems to me to have a beautiful manner and its colour is very charming and delightful, and here he has done the night very well.'

'What you say cannot be denied,' Michelozzi spontaneously added, 'but this composition of the *Nativity* seems unfamiliar to many and recognized a great pity for that by those who consider it well. The Child seems rather large to me, as are also the knees of the saints that are in front. And those [198] of the angels are so big and their drapery pulled up so that they appear swollen.'

'The *Purification* that is seen nearby is by the same Naldini,'[98] Sirigatti continued. 'Here the organization is very beautiful, the perspective done with good judgment, and the colours excellent and well applied.'

'This pleases more than the other,' replied Michelozzi, 'and particularly in the composition. But I also see the swollen knees in some figures. And I marvel that this man, who is so capable in this, has developed this habit of making the knees so large.'[99]

'You will like this other more, also of the same master, where the dead Christ is taken down from the Cross,'[100] Sirigatti said. 'This *Deposition* is done with great art, the poses well arranged, the body of Christ very beautiful, and the coloring excellent.'

'You are right,' Michelozzi replied, 'and it is believed that this is the most beautiful work that Naldini has done. Nevertheless, he has not wanted to avoid giving that old woman who sits in the corner swollen knees.'

'The *Raising of Lazarus* is by Santi di Tito,'[101] Sirigatti continued, 'and I judge this a beautiful panel. The figures have so much life and the faces are very beautiful, the gestures very appropriate, and it is copious of organization, one seeing there figures of many kinds, perspectives, and landscapes.'

'Yes, but you refrained from saying,' Michelozzi added, 'that the colouring is not very commendable. And you do not care to speak of the *Conversion of St Paul* that follows, because it is a work so commonplace and of such a weak manner that you find in it [199] little of merit.'[102]

'In the beautiful Chapel of the Cav. Gaddi, the panel in which Christ appears resuscitating the young daughter of Jairus of the synagogue,' Sirigatti said, 'is by the hand of Bronzino.[103] It is done with great care, with good organization, and with very beautiful colouring. The mother of the young girl particularly seems to me very well portrayed.'

'You are right,' Michelozzi replied, 'because as a good orator you only praise those things that are appropriate for your defence of the painters. You seek to pass over in silence those things that might bring to you some impediment. For example, Christ is not well placed. His left arm is a very great disgrace. And Jairus of the synagogue does not have a very good pose.'

'I have already said,' answered Sirigatti, 'that as much as I can, I do not want to contradict you. Instead, I will take myself to the panel by Giorgio Vasari where Christ is on the Cross, surrounded by many figures, well organized, and vividly coloured.'[104]

'And it seems to me,' said Michelozzi, 'that the Christ has its arms pulled too far apart. Therefore, I would judge such a pose to be unnatural.'

'The *Resurrection* of Our Lord that is seen here close to this,' followed Sirigatti, 'is also by Vasari,[105] done with beautiful composition and good colours. And that angel that appears in the radiance with much grace particularly pleases me.'

'I like everything about it that you say,' Michelozzi responded, 'but the pose of Christ seems to me rather forced. [200] And St Andrew and St Damian, where he placed the two saints in front, do not seem, following what was said with respect to the plane, either standing or kneeling. If they were standing on that level they would be short of leg, and if they were kneeling they would appear too tall.'

'I have learned so many beautiful things today,' said Valori, 'from the good judgment of one, as a connoisseur of the beauties of paintings, and from the good memory of the other, as an industrious conservator of the sayings of others and wise on his own. From now on perhaps I will be able to discuss painting with greater depth.'

'And I also,' added Vecchietti, 'will proceed to consider the works of the painters with greater taste. But we continue, please, our discussion, while the time, the place, and the good grace of these Signori are favourable to it.'

'The *Madonna of the Rosary*,' Sirigatti continued, 'is also by Giorgio Vasari.[106] Very beautiful composition is seen, the Glorious Virgin is very well portrayed, and the colour [is] very charming.'

'Everything satisfies me,' responded Michelozzi, 'except for that woman who is below in the front here. She has an arm that if it were a little larger would have been out of proportion for a giant.'

'The panel where the Samaritan woman is portrayed speaking to the Saviour of the World,' Sirigatti said, 'is by Alessandro Allori.[107] It has very well-composed organization, the woman very charming, the little boy with a very beautiful face and delicate parts, the landscape well arranged, and the colour not possible to desire better.'

'This [201] panel,' added Michelozzi, 'is very charming and has a certain majesty that rather pleases and delights. But on considering it then in detail, there are seen some things that annoy many. The head of Christ is of dull wax. And the Samaritan woman, as fair as that figure is, nevertheless, is not able with her left arm to manage to cover, because it shows, her left breast. And she can only uncomfortably keep her bucket from falling, having to support it on her leg, which is planted, and holding it loosely with her hands.'

'One now comes to the *Baptism of Christ*, by Giovanni Strada,'[108] Sirigatti said. 'Here, besides the well-considered organization and the very charming colouring, a very beautiful landscape is seen with very naturalistic waters, and a lively radiance in the sky, and three faces rather well portrayed from life.'

'The landscape is certainly very beautiful and charming,' Michelozzi responded. 'The face of the angel dressed in yellow, however, and that of the other angel holding that drape in its hand have little grace. And the torso of Christ, by the way, seems to some quite short.'

'The panel that follows between the doors,' Sirigatti continued, 'is by the hand of Jacopo di Meglio. I do not know if we should call it a panel of *St Vincent* or of the *Triumph of Christ*.'[109]

'Please,' Michelozzi added energetically, 'allow yourselves to tell me what it is that I [should] understand about this. The leg of Christ, which goes behind, does not seem to be planted there. And the torso of the woman who has her child next to her cannot [202] be made out. And the old man who is in the front has a crippled left hand. And, in sum, one concludes that in all there is little design.'

'Since we are finished with Santa Maria Novella,' Vecchietti said, 'we can go on to the Ognissanti.'

In the Ognissanti

'I never go into this church,' Michelozzi responded, 'that I do not lose my taste for painting. A panel is there by Carlo da Loro that could serve as an example. In it one sees all the parts of what we have talked about badly observed. Besides having badly located all the figures, he has put in the front a great ugly nude woman who displays all her behind parts and occupies more than half the panel. And then he has placed her above the Madonna, as if he had put her over Her shoulders. The other figures have forced and inappropriate poses, and their parts are poorly composed and without any design. Perhaps it is well that we go on to Santo Spirito, where we will see beautiful things and have a larger field to discuss.'

In Santo Spirito

'It is wonderful to consider the panel of Rosso,' Sirigatti said, 'where there is the Glorious Virgin with Her Child in Her lap and other figures.[110] All are of a beautiful manner, facile and graceful, with very great three-dimensionality, good poses, good colour, and very beautiful drapes.'

'Truly, this is a work to like and to be imitated,' Michelozzi responded. 'Nevertheless, some curiosities appear. The St Sebastian, while it remains a very beautiful figure, has a rather short neck and one would like for the hands of that seated saint to be a little longer.'

'The Christ appearing to the Magdalene in the form of the gardener, [203] by Bronzino,'[111] Sirigatti added, 'is done with great care and with very beautiful colour.'

'Please do not say in addition,' Michelozzi responded immediately, 'that the poses are too forced and without devotion so that every other thing that you praised to me about this would be obscured.'

'We pass then,' Sirigatti said, 'to the *Adulteress* of Alessandro Allori,[112] a panel where many figures are seen with good composition, appropriate poses, and beautiful colours. And particularly pleasing to me is the woman found in sin who, besides being very well adorned, is arranged in that pose which shows the shame of her error.'

'Proceed also forward,' Michelozzi responded, 'as I willingly grant you everything you have said.'

'This other panel, where the martyrs are seen, is also by the same Alessandro,'[113] Sirigatti added. 'And I believe it is possible to give it the same praise, and particularly the nude parts are very beautiful.'

'Let us not move so quickly,' Michelozzi responded, 'as this pleases me rather less than the other, for not having such beautiful organization and for some poses being there that do not greatly satisfy. But the nude parts are truly beautiful, as you say. What will we say, however, of the panel of Giovanni Strada, where Christ appears sending away the Pharisees from the Temple?'[114]

'We will say,' Sirigatti responded, 'that the composition is done with great art, one seeing so many figures well arranged in such a small panel, with different poses, good three-dimensionality, and beautiful colours.'

'It would seem to me [204] that what we have seen here could be enough for us,' Michelozzi said. 'However, being near the Carmine, we could glance at some panels that are there.'

'While I am almost tired of discussing and have yet to satisfy you concerning colour,' Sirigatti answered, 'I will do this gladly so that you truly are satisfied here, provided that [after] talking about these one does not pass further on.'

'You are agreed,' Vecchietti added, 'that something also should briefly be said about the very beautiful ceiling of the Palace of Grand Duke Francesco.'

Of the ceiling of the Sala Regia of the Grand Duke of Florence

'You have [only] said what can be said with brevity,' Sirigatti responded immediately. 'This is to say that it is very beautiful and was done by Giorgio Vasari with very great judgment, study, art, and care.[115] Thus, it is seen full of beautiful inventions, well observed of composition, considered and graceful in the poses, of parts of the body well formed, and very charming in colour. And if truly the excellence of the painter is recognized in it, even more is the magnificence of Grand Duke Cosimo in having commissioned a work so great and so rich without sparing any expense. Thus, it would require a long time for whoever wished to speak of it in detail, and also of the narratives and of the statues that decorate all the walls of the great room.

'Two more figures by the hand of Lorenzo Sabatini of Bologna are very beautiful, painted in fresco on the vault ascending the staircase of that palace, one representing *Justice* and the other *Prudence*. In these good drawing is seen, great three-dimensionality, and [205] beautiful colouring, in sum, well observed in every part. Who wishes then to discuss the room of Francesco Salviati, in which the *Triumph of Camillus* and other narratives are painted, and where the whole excellence of painting is seen,[116] would take on too great an enterprise and perhaps such a thing would not come easily to an end.'

In the Carmine

'Therefore, returning to the Carmine, I see the Bearer of the Saviour of the World rising to Heaven, painted in a panel with the Apostles by the hand of Girolamo Macchietti with beautiful organization and the figures are of well-arranged parts and poses with three-dimensionality and with good drawing.'[117]

'Everything pleases me,' Michelozzi responded, 'but the colour could be more charming, as also that in the panel by Santi di Tito of the *Nativity*,[118] which nevertheless, rather pleases me.'

'You are able to be pleased,' Sirigatti added, 'because it has good design and in every part is done with consideration. The other panel, worthy of not being passed in silence, is by Batista Naldini, representing the *Ascension of Our Lord* with many saints,[119] where it is possible to see beautiful composition, appropriate poses, the parts of the body well composed, and the colouring very beautiful.'

'The pose of Christ does not please many,' Michelozzi responded, 'but the other things rather satisfy. And the lower figures particularly please me greatly.'

'It seems to me that there has been enough discussion on these subjects,' Vecchietti said. 'The Sun with its gilded chariot full of splendour has come down a good way from the circle of midday. [206] [I hope] that time remains – before he lays his blonde head in the lap of Thetis – to proceed comfortably for amusement among these charming hills. Thus, it would seem to me well done, if you would be in agreement, that [we] begin to discuss colour. The Sun below the horizon in the west, when it comes, like us, to the end of its day, reflects its rays into the air and paints it with a thousand charming colours. So we, painting from the science of colours, will be able to end the discussion of painting this second day.' ...[120]

Michelozzi continued in this way: 'Signori, it seems to me that there is much time for us to advance, before the Sun, approaching the horizon, makes the longer shadows appear from the trees. [Only then can] we proceed through the more pleasant coolness and entertain ourselves in these pleasant hills. Bernardo was very wearied yesterday in speaking of the inventions of the sculptors and the painters to our great satisfaction and profit. Today, no less, Ridolfo discussed the other things ... It would seem to me, if you approve, to give an end to this day's work [*per dar fine a questa giornata*][121] and a good conclusion to our discussion, [225] that we advance to spend this little time in discussing the significance of colour.

'While it takes much time, I have wanted to know about this and also it will not be an inappropriate subject for the painters [who read this book]. And for this part, so that it will be something well divided and ordered, it would seem to me that you should turn to Baccio. He delights in and turns the pages of many books, in addition to his studies of the law, of belles-lettres, and of refined concepts. Not concerned with what common people say about colours, he will easily be able to tell us their true meanings. Thus, we will be able to deal in good judgment when considering paintings, devices, liveries, weapons, and [other] undertakings.'

'The comments of Girolamo are certainly very good,' Vecchietti said. 'Our discussion would remain very imperfect and with little use to the painters if the meaning of colour was not treated. It is something not only proper but necessary to those who wish to put painting into practice if they do not wish social gradations, dress, the ages of men, the weather, and the seasons to be represented with very great inappropriateness. Therefore, I am positive I can believe that Baccio, to give perfection to our discussion and to please Girolamo and also the rest of us, will not fail to make manifest to us the meaning of colours if we ask this of him.'

'You have little need to ask,' answered Valori, 'since I am very ready to please you by arranging myself to your will. But, as you put unexpected material before me [226] to be discussed, I do not know how I will be able to satisfy you. It has been some time since I interrupted similar studies. I will, however, put myself to the test to produce something rewarding for you, if I can, about some of the things that I remember.'

'I do not doubt for a moment,' Vecchietti responded, 'that the desire that you have to serve others has not reduced your memory of these things that could be useful to and altogether delight us, as you suggest. But, because time does not force you to restrict to brief words so beautiful a subject, would it please you for now, abandoning every excuse, to favour us by beginning your discussion.'

At these words Valori gathered himself and, looking at the others who attentively waited for his words, in this way with a sweet manner had them listen. 'Colour and what gives rise to it would be a very beautiful and very fine subject to be discussed. In the elements, in the plants, in the stones, in the metals, in the animals, and in men such a variety is seen that you would want to report and talk about it according to its nature and its effects. I might be given to investigate these things another time than what is given me. They are more appropriate to the philosopher than to the painter and to the knight, and little appropriate to our purpose. Therefore, I will leave them aside. I will declare, with brief words only, what colour is, without proceeding through other philosophical considerations separately. This will make simply apparent to you only what I understand is necessary to the painter about the meaning of colour.' [227]

What colour is

'The Pythagoreans would have it that colour was not anything other than surface. The Platonists thought it light. Aristotle, taking almost the middle way, said that colour is a boundary of the form. It is not, as Pythagoras wanted, part of the form as the surface would be. Nor is it a form without boundaries, as light would be according to the thinking of Plato. Rather, it is a boundary of the shining form. Therefore, following the opinion of Aristotle, we will say that colour is a boundary or a limit of the bounded shining form. But, so that this is made more clear, it is known that a natural form is understood as something that receives colour, odour, and all the other things that come under the senses. It exists in three dimensions, length, width, and depth. The philosophers postulated five natural forms, the heavens and the four elements. The animals, plants, and metals, which are created from the elements, follow their nature in many qualities. The heavens are raised as the primary form of this order of forms by not having any colour. They are clear and transparent in that part where there are no stars. And the stains of the Moon are none other than a deprivation of light or parts of the Moon that are not as thick as the others.'

The heavens were not coloured

'I conclude finally that the heavenly bodies, while they seem coloured, do not have any colour. Transparent bodies cannot truly have colour, since they are the heavens. Thus, the colours proceed from the qualities of the elements: from the warm, the humid, [228] the cold, and the dry. And because the celestial bodies do not participate in these, consequently they have no colour. Otherwise, they would be capable of being generated and corruptible.'

The elements do not have colours

'The three things then, that rotate under the heavens, as uncircumscribed simple and transparent bodies, do not really have colour. And the Earth, while it is a solid body and has its surface and margin, does not, however, have any colour. It does not contain, in relation to itself, the four qualities generating colour. Although some have it that it is white, or rather, pale like ash.'

'Please, because this subject is rather obscure to me,' Michelozzi said, 'give me some examples of what are bordered and unbordered luminous forms.'

'Some forms are found,' Valori responded, 'that are bordered in themselves. They receive their own boundaries from their own shape, as a stone, a piece of wood, a horse, and a man. Some other bodies, in the same way, are not bordered. They do not have any shape, such as the water in the rain and the water running in a river. If they also have boundaries, these do not proceed from them, but from the form that contains them. Some forms are also transparent. They do not have any light in themselves, nor any shape to receive it, as the water and the air. And other forms, also transparent, which are found to be circumscribed or we would say with a shape, only have light on their surface, like a piece of marble, wood, gold [229] or iron, or as a mountain, a valley, a lowland, a beach, or similar things. And, therefore, when it is said that colour is the border, it is understood that it is on the border of something or on the surface of whatever body is solid and circumscribed.'

Definition of colour

'We will repeat, therefore, concluding that true colour is not anything other than a quality on the surface, or on the border, of solid and circumscribed bodies. And likewise, the colours that art makes in imitation of nature, as in clothes, in draperies, and in other textiles, we will manifestly say to be certain and true colours. Equally are those that are shown in painting on paper, canvas, panels, and walls. There are two principles that contribute to produce the colours. One of which is light, truly the formal principle, and the other transparency, the material principle, of which by now enough has been said. It will not take us far from our principal intention, before we move ahead, to briefly recall what light is.'

What light is

'In the second book of *De Anima,* Aristotle says that light is the expression of a transparent thing. And, in his treatise on the senses and the sensorial, he would have it that the light on a transparent form is coloured by impingement. And this last definition should not, however, appear discordant with the first. It has to be understood to contradict the second in similarity and not in essence. It is not true that light, of its own essence, is colour. Rather, but by a certain similarity. Colour makes the transparency on bodies coloured and lighted concurrently. Clearly, it is seen [230] that the transparent body, if it is not struck by the light, does not shine. Therefore, it is possible to consider, when it is said that colour is by impingement, that it is such because, while it is proper to the thing coloured, it becomes visible through an extrinsic cause that is the Sun or other light. As also the transparent light comes from the extrinsic cause that is this same Sun or other light. Therefore, it is clearly seen that both proceed from extrinsic causes.

'But I have said enough for now about this. It is our intention, as soon as possible, to come to the meaning of colour. I do not want to deal with it in those ways that are appropriate to the philosopher, but rather in that which is expected by painters, gentlemen, and princes. I will not follow further for now the opinion of Aristotle. He has proposed only white and black for primary colours and all the others, as sharing with them, in between.'

There being seven principal colours

'But I will say, following Cassaneo and other famous authors, that there are seven principal colours. They are yellow, white, red, blue, black, green, and purple. All the others, as derived from these, I will call mixed. And it pleases me also, for the significance of colours, to follow the opinion of the previously mentioned authors for now, as well as conforming sometimes with the common use. Thus, the painters in painting and gentlemen in making devices and liveries have a larger field on which they can unfold their concepts.'

Meaning of gold and of the colour yellow

'But coming to the colours, I say that the first one is the colour of gold. This can be considered as the metal or [231] simply as the colour yellow. This is more noble than all the others for the material that it represents. Gold is the most perfect of all the other metals. It is naturally bright, shining, virtuous, and comforting. Reduced to a drink by physicians, it is given to patients near death as a final comfort. And gold is not only the most noble of the other bodies, but their lord and prince. It is contaminated or diminished by neither earth, water, air, or fire, nor burned by sulphur, as are the other bodies. Beside this, it represents the Sun, most noble light, since its rays are shown as the colour of gold. And it is clear to everyone that nothing is more welcome nor more joyous of the light. And, therefore, the Holy Scripture says that the just and holy man will be like gold and the Sun. And Our Saviour Jesus Christ, when He was transfigured on Mount Tabor, appeared to the Apostles resplendent as the Sun of golden colour. And because gold resembles the Sun in many things, the ancient laws prescribed that no one would dare to wear gold or gilded things who was not born or made noble.

'The colour of gold signifies wealth, nobility, greatness of spirit, steadfastness, and wisdom. It also resembles the topaz among the precious gems. Among the seven principal virtues it denotes Faith, the Sun among the planets, gold among the metals, Sunday among the days, August among the months, adolescence up to fifteen years among the ages of man, and the very Holy Eucharist among the seven sacraments. [232] And the Church Militant, bride of Our Saviour, is to be dressed in vestments of fine gold, David saying that the Queen on the right was dressed in gold vestments. Placed on men, the colour yellow demonstrates wealth and enjoyment; on women, jealousy; on children, playfulness; on houses, wealth; and on standards and insignia, the desire for victory.'

'Therefore,' Michelozzi responded, 'the proverb of the common people is not true that says that whoever wears yellow looks forward to a fall. Nor equally could one say the verses of Ariosto are true when he says, speaking of Bradamante,

> These counsels seemed the best
> To the damsel. And immediately a device
> As if on arms, that wish to inflict
> Desperation, and desire to die.[122]

'If the common people simply mean the yellow that I discussed above,' added Valori, 'there is not any doubt that they are mistaken. But if they take for yellow that colour that Ariosto describes – which I will speak about when I come to discuss mixed colours[123] – then the device of Ariosto is as well done as the words of the people are very true.'

Meaning of silver and of the colour white

'But we pass to discuss the second colour and metal that can be considered as silver and as the colour white. This is the most noble colour after yellow, as silver is the most esteemed metal after gold. White denotes [233] victory, and therefore, the ancient triumphers were dressed in white and they were drawn on chariots by four white horses. But to speak of it in a more elevated way, the Scripture says that when the Redeemer of the World was transfigured on Mount Tabor, he had on garments brighter than the snow. And equally, He came out of the sepulchre triumphantly, dressed in white. And St John the Evangelist foresaw the martyrs shedding their blood in snow white dress. And the angels at the Resurrection and at the Ascension were seen in white vestments.

'White signifies learning, purity, innocence, justice, and rectitude. It resembles crystal, the stars, rain, snow, hail, the rose, and the lily. It also demonstrates eloquence, where it is necessary to speak in a snow white and pure style. It represents the pearl among gems, water among the elements, silver among metals, the phlegmatic among the temperaments, youth up to seven years among the ages, Hope among the virtues, the Moon among the planets, Monday among the days, January among the months, and Baptism among the sacraments. It shows chastity in women, virginity in young girls, justice among judges, and humility in the rich. The Holy Church uses white hangings on the feasts of the holy confessors and of the non-martyred virgins, for their purity and innocence, and also on the feasts of the angels and on all the feasts of the Glorious Virgin Mary, on the Nativity of Christ and of St John the Baptist, and in the consecration of churches, [234] and at other times which, not to be too long, I avoid mention. The colour white incorporates all the colours and is incorporated by none of the others. And it is also very divisive and harms the sight. For this reason it caused great injury to the soldiers of Marc Anthony returning from making war on the Parthians by a long trip covered with very high snows; thus, many of them lost their sight there.'

Why white harms the sight and why not

'But it is known that there are many kinds of white such as that of the snow, purified chalk, milk, pearls, ivory, fine marble, and the white flesh of women. And while the white of the snow and of chalk is divisive to the sight, the white of milk, pearls, and these other things do not have this effect. Rather, with a certain bright whiteness, they give charm and delight. And this happens because such whiteness carries with it a hidden sanguine mixture.'

Meaning of the colour red

'But now it seems to me time that we discuss red, the third colour. This is the first colour without a metal. And it represents to us, among the elements, fire, the most noble of all and, after the Sun, the most bright and resplendent. And the ancients esteemed the colour red so noble that they directed by law that no one was able to wear clothing dyed with that colour who was not noble. In the sacred literature red signifies the virtue of love, martyrdom, and the blood constantly shed by the holy martyrs. It resembles thunder and lightning, the ruby among the precious stones and the poppy among flowers. It demonstrates audacity, stature, boldness, and, sometimes, disdain [235] and anger. It denotes copper among metals, Charity among the virtues, Mars among the planets, Tuesday among the days, July among the months, summer among the seasons, maturity up to fifty years among the ages, the choleric among the temperaments, and Confession among the sacraments. The colour red is also taken for the good luck of those who wear it. The Holy Church uses red hangings on the feasts of the Apostles, of Evangelists, and of Martyrs for the blood shed for love of the Passion of Our Lord Jesus Christ, also on the feast of the Innocents and also at other times that I do not now remember.'

Meaning of the colour blue

'Therefore, I will proceed to talk about blue, the fourth colour and the most esteemed after red. This represents the air, the most noble element after fire. [Air], by being thin, penetrable, and fitted to receive all the luminous influences is what, without which, one would not be able to live on the Earth. Blue resembles the sky when it is serene and the sapphire, stone of very great virtue. And it shows the very ardent zeal of religion. Hence, Jeremiah, crying in his lamentations, describes how anciently the priests were richly dressed in the service of the temple: "Their priests were whiter than the snow," and added in conclusion, "They are more beautiful than the sapphire."[124] And Tobias, wanting to show the very great value of the sapphire, seeing in his mind the walls of Heaven in the form of a city, said that its gates were of precious sapphire. [236] And St John also said the same thing in his Apocalypse. Blue signifies beauty, chastity, humility, holiness, devotion, gentleness, loyalty, and good reputation. It denotes Jupiter among the planets, Justice among the virtues, Wednesday among the days and, according to others, Tuesday, autumn among the seasons, September among the months, the sanguine among the temperaments, youth up to fifteen years among the ages [but see page 149], tin among the metals, and Confirmation among the

Holy Sacraments. But what was said about it suffices for now and we come to the colour black, which is the fifth.'

Meaning of the colour black

'This is the least noble of those discussed above, more approaching the darkness. As Bartolus says in his treatise on arms, the colours that more closely approach the light are more noble.[125] And Aristotle, in his book on the senses and the sensible, would have it that colours are more or less noble according to whether they more approach white or black. From that it follows that black is the most base of all the other colours and sometimes is used as a synonym for bad. Therefore, the ancients were in the habit of marking what was good and commendable with white chalk and marking what was bad and blameworthy with charcoal.

'Yet there is no shortage of those who say the colour black is more noble than white. They allege that black always maintains its condition, and throw out that white incorporates things in itself. And white, being more convertible into others, comes to be more easily transformed, corrupted, and soiled, and consequently less noble. In addition to this they say that black resembles the diamond, the stone that [237] appears to many more precious than any other. And that, among the many kinds of eagles, the most black is the most worthy. This fixes its eyes on the Sun and is queen of all the birds. And black is very exalted in the Sacred Scriptures where it says, speaking of the Glorious Virgin in the Song of Songs: "Dark I am, yet lovely."[126] And it continues, close to this, "His hair is black as a raven."[127] Also valued in this is the authority of Virgil who says: "The white privets fall, and the black violets are gathered." Resembling this is the lover's yearning since, among the beauties of women, the principal one is eyes and eyelashes of black. It is said that from the glance of two black beautiful eyes shines a soft splendour accompanied by a flaming love. It reaches out with so much charm to the eyes that receive it that, enamored by that charming light, having put every other thought into oblivion, they search, transformed, in the image of so much beauty.

'But leaving the discussion of its nobility, we come to its meaning. The colour black demonstrates sadness, simplicity, constancy, culture, and steadiness. It denotes the diamond among stones, iron among metals, the earth among the elements, Saturn among the planets, Prudence among the virtues, final old age or death among the ages of man, melancholy among the temperaments, winter among the seasons, December among the months, Friday among the days, and Extreme Unction among the sacraments. Black, when it is very dark, impedes the sight. The Holy Church uses black hangings on Days of Supplication [Rogation] and on Days of Affliction [238] and of abstinence for sins and on other occasions that I will not speak about now for coming to discuss the sixth colour, green.'

Meaning of the colour green

'This, because it does not share much of black, is not as ignoble as the colour black, although it is less noble than the other colours. And some would have it that, because it is not numbered among the four elements, it is the least esteemed of all. Nevertheless, it represents trees, plants, lawns, verdant new grass, and leafy hills, things very joyous and delightful to the sight and should not, however, be held in low esteem. It signifies joyfulness, love, gratitude, friendliness, honour, goodness, beauty, and, according to the common opinion, Hope. Among the precious stones it is likened to the emerald. Among the virtues it demonstrates Fortitude, Venus among planets, lead among the metals, youth up to thirty-five years among the ages of man, Thursday among the days, spring among the seasons, April, dark green, and May, bright green, among the months, and Marriage among the sacraments. Green is a very great comfort to vision and supports it and soothes it when it is tired, and therefore, the eyes are greatly pleased and satisfied by the colour green. The Holy Church uses green hangings during the octave of Epiphany, on Septuagesima, on Pentecost, during Advent, and on ordinary and week days.'

Meaning of purple

'But it is time to discuss purple, the seventh and last colour. Mixing the six previously discussed colours together one comes to make purple, which is that colour that today is called crimson or cochineal. Some [239] consider it a colour and others not, wanting it rather to be among the mixed and in-between. And even if it is a colour, it is the least noble of all,[128] being composed of all and not having anything of its own virtue but that which it receives from others. Others would have it that it is of all the most noble, since all participate in it. And, anciently, the kings and emperors used purple dress to preserve their royal and imperial dignity when they went out in public. The first one who wore it was Tullus Hostilius, third king of the Romans, although Pliny says that Romulus used it first.[129] Isidore would have it, in his book of *Etymologies*, that the word purple is derived from purity and that it is resplendent.[130] And Messer Giason Maino shows in his treatise on colour how much merit purple has.[131] And St Jerome, in his sixth sermon, treating the Annunciation of the Glorious Virgin, says that when She heard the salutation of the Angel Gabriel, his very beautiful face became as wool, dyed of purple blood. Priests were anciently dressed in this colour, as the cardinals are dressed today.'

Two kinds of purple

'One finds two kinds of purple. Artificial is made, as was said, mixing together the other six colours. The other, natural, is made from the blood of a sea conch called purple [*porpora*] about which Pliny writes extensively, in the ninth book of his *Natural History*. And in ancient times, no one not a prince was allowed to dress in this purple. Today, this colour is made very beautifully with crimson and with cochineal, [240] as all those who practise the art of making textiles do very well.

'This colour signifies the grace of God and, in the world, dominion over many people, wealth, abundance of blessings, and liberality. It is likened to the ruby and the amethyst among the precious stones and the violet called the Pisan violet among the flowers and, of other flowers, the carnation. It represents Mercury among the planets, Temperance among the virtues, free mercury among the metals, old age up to seventy years among the ages of man, Saturday among the days, November among the months, and the Ordination of Priests among the sacraments. This is as much as it is convenient for me to say about the seven principal colours.

'Now, whoever wishes to speak of all the mixtures and compounds and give them their meaning would have a wide field to discuss. And perhaps he would find a very arduous and little used path that others would not be made to believe. Very few are those authors who write about the meaning of mixed colours and, moreover, they treat them briefly. But I, to not let our discussion be so truncated, will come to say something briefly about some of the more known mixed and in-between colours.'

Yellowish-green

'And first I will speak of that bleached yellow colour that many call yellowish-green. This is made of a weak white colour that is inclined rather towards red and is mixed with green. And this is that colour, if I am not wrong, that is understood when it is said, "Who wears yellow, looks for a fall," and that Ariosto intended to describe very well when he said: [241]

It was a surcoat of the colour,
That remained on the leaf, that is bleached,
When it is removed from the branch, or when the sap,
Which made the tree alive, is absent.[132]

This colour signifies lost hope, distrust, deception, and desperation.'

Pallido[133]

'Another colour, which is called *pallido*, is very similar to this, but is rather darker. And the face of a man becomes this colour moved by some accident, as from a great fear, excessive worry, or immediate suffering. It denotes betrayal, deceptive cunning, and a change of mind.'

Deep blue

'Deep blue is a colour in-between [the colour of] water and air that more approaches air. This colour resembles sky and air. It signifies goodness, courtesy, friendship, good manners, and, according to the common people, jealousy.'[134]

Mauve

'Mauve is another colour that is much like deep blue, but brighter. This denotes beautiful speaking, graceful thought, and fine talent.'

Rose pink

'Rose pink, which is very similar to rose, is a charming and beautiful colour, like the vermilion cheeks of a young woman. It is composed of red and white, indicating a person of good constitution, pleasant, bold, and kind. It signifies elevation of mind, health, and beautiful concepts.'

Purple violet

'Purple violet is produced from material that is derived from water and earth and is a colour in-between red and deep blue and is a sign of coldness and of melancholy. It signifies [242] friendship, love, loyalty, integrity, gratitude, and sweetness.'

Tan

'Tan is a colour in-between red and black, and tans are found of many kinds. Tan commonly signifies great heart, courage, harsh thoughts, grief, rage, and suffering. The tan that tends towards white and is so faded that it appears almost yellow demonstrates contrition for past errors, the end of innocence, simulated joy, and clouded justice. The tan that has purple violet is a very charming and pleasant colour denoting troubled love, simple courtesy, and false loyalty. Dark tan, which is composed of black and tan, demonstrates pain, imagination, and melancholy deprived of any consolation. The tan that has grey, made of these two colours, signifies little hope.'

Blue that has purple violet

'The blue that has purple violet shows fidelity in the things of love, learning, good manners, and sweet courtesy.'

Cream of peach

'The colour cream of peach [*fior di pesco*], which is like a faded complexion, signifies deteriorating wealth, little nobility, and having lost heart.'

Grey

'Grey is a colour in-between white and black, and there are many kinds of grey. Those that are inclined more towards the dark demonstrate hope, patience, consolation, simplicity, and praiseworthy manners. And those that are closer to white signify poverty, enmity, and desperation. The grey that tends towards purple violet is a good colour, demonstrating hope of love, toil gladly undertaken, patience in friendship, and simple loyalty. Bright grey splattered with small dots of red demonstrates [243] hope of having immediate joyfulness, patience in contrary things, and suffering without pain. The grey called ash-grey, for being the colour of ashes, signifies annoying thoughts and troubles leading to death. Dark grey tending towards black denotes hope for one's thoughts [that one's wishes come true], fear together with hope, and joyfulness turned into grief. Some would have it that silver-grey demonstrates humility and to have been deceived.

'While it would be possible to say many other things, I do not know anything else for now to tell you about the colours in order to give copious material for the painters in painting. It also seems to me that I would go out too far in continuing [to describe] certain common uses. Beside which, it already seems to me time to proceed to enjoy this beautiful country. [Time] to give the limbs, cramped together from sitting so long, in agreeably moving, and the eyes, in looking at the green and flowered lawns, that satisfaction that we have given the ears up to now in discussing.'

'You have given us so much to enjoy,' Vecchietti responded, 'that I do not know what more delight we will be able to enjoy today. Weakness and faintness [from sitting down so long] do not seem to us to compare with the consolation that we have received from your words. It only remains to give some relief to the body, while the mind stays intent on enjoying your beautiful and learned discussion. Thus, I would esteem it well done to put into effect what you have suggested.'

'We have had two days with so much pleasure and profitable discussion of sculpture and painting. For me, nothing is left to be fulfilled,' Michelozzi added, getting up, 'provided that, [244] in order to give a good conclusion to our discussion, this material is followed up tomorrow and, if necessary, also the next day, by speaking of the most excellent painters and sculptors and of their most famous works ... up to our time. To recount the works of so many capable men who extended over so long a period of time would require more leisure than that of a day or two, if we were able to discuss every manner. Thus, we will need to speak briefly and only of the most illustrious.'

All the others already risen to their feet and going out of the grove, Vecchietti responded: 'Girolamo's remarks are very beautiful and truly will give a certain perfect and necessary ending to our discussions or, as the proverb says, seal the letter of our writing. But perhaps it will be more difficult to put [his proposal], some of which will be my responsibility, into effect than was appreciated at first glance. And I, for myself, do not recognize in myself the strength sufficient for such an enterprise.'

'The excuse not asked for,' Michelozzi immediately responded, 'is an inevitable accusation. I know that such work appears heavy to you and the others. But I have also thought, because it will be lighter for each, if the others do not disagree with my thoughts, of dividing the work of these two day ... [245] Bernardo is someone who greatly understands design and has contended with the worthy painters and sculptors. He will be able to deal with those who came to be known while working with excellence from Cimabue up to the time that Perino del Vaga flourished. Ridolfo has detailed information about those *eccellenti* who have passed to another life and those living today. I would crave that he take the ... part in which those craftsmen should be discussed who have worked from Perino up to our time and [those who] continue to operate with praise.'[135]

'Your division,' said Valori, 'not only is not to be refused by we others but, as very commendable and suitably divided, is to be held dear and followed. I believe that neither Bernardo nor Ridolfo will be bored pleasing you, even though almost all the difficulty falls on them. For the reasons that you said, it is better they discuss such material, as well as to give some conclusion to the work we have done these days. And also they would not know, being asked of an honest thing, how not to desire to be able to please others.'

'Let us help,' said Vecchietti enthusiastically, turning to Sirigatti, 'since these people are in accord against us. And I know them to be of such power and worth [246] that only with difficulty would we be able to defend ourselves in this [if we did not].'

'For myself, I do not wish,' Sirigatti responded, 'to contest these things from which it is not possible to obtain any victory. And I find myself more suited to obey those who are greater than I, rather than to oppose the wishes – hoping to be freed of any effort – of those who would have me do something else.'

'You want to vanquish it rather than be vanquished,' Vecchietti added, 'since, recognizing that you cannot defend yourself with argument, you try to make it, with courtesy, remain lost. But I have decided to continue with you in this enterprise. You will see me joined with you to go to war under this standard, which you will do most willingly.'

Many polite words were said about this and repeated. And meanwhile, they descended, foot by foot, down towards the river Ema. Arriving there, they saw two of Vecchietti's workers in waist-high water. One searched with a pole into those parts where he knew that fish were hidden. And the other was seen to scoop them up, to the very great pleasure of the gentlemen who attentively stopped to look at the many fish they took. And the fishermen, realizing the delight that they had in seeing them take the fish, began to take and throw the best towards them. [The group] took marvellous pleasure in these fish wriggling on the green grass and made a contest of who could catch them first.[136] And so they enjoyed themselves among the trees above the bank of the river until the sun [247] was completely under the horizon.

Then all took themselves with slow step back to the house, the country folk having gotten out of the water with their gourds full of fish. And, washing their hands, they sat down. There the delicate food came, and there the wines were optimal and precious. And the setting was beautiful and very praiseworthy without any pretense and without tiresomeness. But then the tables were cleared and for quite a while they were entertained with pleasant discussion. And, after some of the night had passed and the gentlemen excused themselves with modest words, finally each, proceeding at his pleasure, went to rest.

Book Three

Not all writers, Most Illustrious and Most Excellent Lord (even as they strive so that their writings commonly please) obtain universal praise from everyone. Rather, very few are those, even if they have written with great skill, who are not deprecated in great part by many. And if every man who intended to do something waited until he was sure it pleased everyone, it would frequently happen that he would not leave any sign of having travelled through [249] this mortal life. It is almost impossible, while doing everything that is possible to serve and to please, to proceed in a manner that satisfies everyone. Very few are those authors who are not criticized in some part by someone. Therefore, one should not (dismayed by the thought of not pleasing all) [deprive the world] of some beautiful thought by not explaining one's beautiful concepts on paper. And recounting these discussions the four gentlemen had, I fear more than anything else, not only not to please all but to satisfy few. It is very well known that in telling the truth one acquires the odium of many. And while it does not seem reasonable to me to say otherwise than what is necessary about what happened, I would much more gladly keep silent than to write about them. Man is more a friend of leisure than of beneficial works. But then, asked to do it by someone whose desires I would never contradict,[1] I set about faithfully retelling it as I was told by others.

So, to whom it pleases, excuse me if I speak too freely in some places. I have written in brief summary the lives of the … modern sculptors and painters, and also those of today, many of them for the first time. And if there are those who say that I have left some behind, do not blame me that I do not recount the things discussed by others, or the four gentlemen. They did not discuss anything other than what I wrote. On the contrary, blame instead the brief time that restricted their discussion, not giving them leisure to be able to mention everything. And if someone, [250] desires to understand these things still more broadly ... he will be fully satisfied with the *Lives* of Vasari, which [Vasari] wrote with great care.[2]

But, returning to the noble brigade who were honourably enjoying themselves at Vecchietti's villa, I say that the four gentlemen arose the third morning. (The blonde Apollo with the golden mane had just appeared over the horizon.) And, invited by the fresh airs, they marched over the dewy lawns and went to contemplate with delight the beautiful and fertile country, taking pleasure in the beautiful place. But then the sun, climbing towards the circle of midday, to a large extent dissolved the morning freshness, and they returned to the villa. And there they dined at the appropriate hour, being served with good order. Because of the brightness of the sun, and because everywhere every breeze was calmed, a long day was anticipated. All in accord, to flee the heat, they transferred to the cool grotto where a very clear fountain surged with great copiousness of water.

Vecchietti's fountain

This crystalline water comes out in a large spring at the foot of the hill on which the *uccellare,* on the part to the east, is set. The grotto was constructed with great artifice and all charmingly painted inside. Falling in a great oval basin [the water] makes a delightful sound to hear. Above the basin that receives the water is a very beautiful nude marble damsel, done by Giambologna, in the act of leaving a cave. One hand is put to her delicate breast. [251] The other one holds up a sea conch from which the water rises and, seeming like quicksilver, falls back down into the basin. And this beautiful woman is portrayed as the Fata Morgana (for whom this spring was anciently named).[3] There is an ample grotto, decorated on the floor with beautiful *compartimenti* of crushed stone. Next to this is a separate room with many reservoirs for different fish. And above this are arranged some little rooms where it is possible to prepare food properly for those who might wish to eat their meals in the main, cool room of the grotto. Now the water – I mean, that of it which overflows from the [brim of] the basin – [after] leaving the grotto through a hidden conduit becomes visible again outside of [the grotto] in a pleasant fountain. This gives comfort to wayfarers and refreshes thirsty horses, falling crystal clear into a great basin. And, passing from there by covered channels into a wider basin, it is collected to accommodate the women washing their laundry. Not less plentiful and generous, it abundantly flows further down into a long channel for the lowly little sheep and other beasts.[4]

The gentlemen arrived here and diligently considered and greatly commended everything. Entering the grotto, they came to see verses carved on a little marble tablet. Approaching them, Valori, the others stopping attentively to listen, recited, reading to them with a beautiful manner: [252]

Were it possible, O Wayfarer
To work with all studiousness and care,
So that this fountain in place of pure water
Should pour out excellent and noble wine,

Colour yet of Garnet and of Ruby
These waves would have; but if nature forbid this,
You are able to extinguish the thirst, temper the heat
Satisfied with the sweet crystalline humour.

And if all around trees, plants, or stems
Pleasant shadow offers you, or fruit, or flower,
Or this cave at times beneficent repose;

One could say: he would have more adorned his Repose,[5]
With a greater sign of love towards us,
If more life and more strength he had from Heaven.

As Valori ended reading, he turned towards Vecchietti with a sweet manner, congratulating him that he had constructed so beautiful a sonnet. And many were the words that were said by everyone about this. Finally, settling himself down to sit, Michelozzi turned towards the others and began to speak as follows: '*Signori*, the obligation that we owe to Bernardo is great, not only for the many courtesies that he has shown in allowing us to enjoy this, his comfortable estate, but for the beautiful opportunity that he has given us to discuss painting and sculpture. Of these fine arts I have learned so many beautiful secrets and so many good precepts. Thus, for myself, I will dare to move ahead so as not to leave behind what we have done, to my satisfaction, in discussing painting and sculpture.' [253]

'I am indebted and obliged to you who have favoured me [with your presence],' Vecchietti answered. 'And I will always do what you wish and serve you at your pleasure with those things that you call mine but which really are yours. I have learned many things of great benefit from our discussion. And with respect to it continuing among us, I should thank you if you would begin and if you others would discuss what it is that is good.'

'To bring an end to words,' immediately added Sirigatti, 'we are not here today to enter into praise of that work which is not yet completed. But rather, according to how things were organized by you yesterday, to discuss the ... modern sculptors and painters. For this, since it is perhaps not as brief as some have thought, it would seem to me, if it is your desire, that it would be possible to begin.'[6]

'Truly Ridolfo is right,' said Valori, 'and it will be to you, Bernardo, to proceed with the enterprise that is already seen leading to an honourable end.'

'The craftsmen of these beautiful arts were so many,' Vecchietti answered, 'and the works that they were commissioned to do so endless. Wanting to discuss all of them and all of those would be the task of many days and not this little time that remains to me. I will briefly recount here only those whom I remember as the most excellent and of their works the most praised.'

Vecchietti's organization was commended by all but, as they then kept silent, he proceeded to speak in this way: 'Long ago, through wars and ruination, miserable Italy, who had been queen of the world, was many times made a servant by foreigners [288] and barbaric people. Sculpture and painting, together with their craftsmen, lay almost buried.'

Cimabue

'Then, as God willed it in the year 1240, Giovanni, surnamed Cimabue,[7] was born in Florence of the noble family of the Cimabue to return painting to the light.[8] Recognizing a beautiful talent in him, his father had him taught his first letters with the intention that he apply himself to his studies. But instead of attending to these, feeling himself led by nature, he drew men, horses, buildings, and other fantasies all day on sheets and on books. Fortune would favour putting his inclination into practice. The Florentines called some painters from Greece at that time to re-establish the art of painting in Florence. They, among the other works that occupied them in the city, began the Chapel of the Gondi in Santa Maria Novella, which Cimabue, abandoning every other activity to see these masters work, never left.

Therefore, seeing this, his father, satisfied with these painters, gave him to them so that he could learn the art. In this he advanced so much that to a great extent he surpassed his masters. And he greatly improved that rough ancient manner of the Greeks of that time and would add grace and perfection to the art. Among other things he painted a panel that was put up in Santa Trinità, in Florence, in which there is a *Madonna with Her Child* in Her arms surrounded by many angels adoring Him in a golden field. [289] He also did a great wooden Crucifix for Santa Croce, where it is still seen today.

'Then, transferring himself to Pisa, [Cimabue] painted *St Francis* in a panel that was held to be very beautiful. He recognized in it a certain quality in the demeanour of the head and in the folds of the drapery that had not been practised in the Greek manner up to then. He also did an *Our Lady with Her Child* in Her lap and many angels in a field of gold on a large panel that was put in the Church of San Francesco. He painted *St Agnes* on a little panel and, around her, all the narratives of her life in small figures. This work today is above the Altar of the Virgins in San Paolo, in Ripa d'Arno.

'Thus, the name of Cimabue spreading everywhere, he was called to the Umbrian city of Assisi. There, in the Lower Church of San Francesco, he painted some narratives of the Queen of Heaven in fresco on four walls in the great tribune above the choir and the four Evangelists larger than life on a part of the vault.[9] [He painted] Jesus Christ, the Glorious Virgin, St John the Baptist, and St Francis on another part, the Doctors of the Church on another, and on another he did gold stars on a field of ultramarine blue. He also painted many narratives on the walls of the church from the Old Testament, starting from the beginning of Genesis, and the deeds of Our Lady and of Jesus Christ.

'Then, returning to Florence, [Cimabue] painted, in the cloister of Santo Spirito, which was painted in the Greek manner by other masters, the *Life of Christ* on all the [290] part towards the church. In figures done in greater size than had ever been done up to that time, he did the *Glorious Virgin* with many angels in a panel that was put up in Santa Maria Novella, between the Chapel of the Rucellai and that of Bardi di Vernio. And this work was so marvellous to the people, who had never before seen anything better, that it was carried from the house of Cimabue with great pomp, to the sound of trumpets and with great rejoicing in the order of procession, to the church. There he acquired from it a brilliant name, much honour and great reward. And it is said that while Cimabue was doing this panel outside of Florence, in a district next to the Porta San Piero, King Charles the Elder of Anjou passed through Florence. And, among the other honours that were done him, he was taken to see this painting. There, in showing it to the king, because it had not been seen before, all the men and all the women of Florence gathered to see it with the greatest festivity. Therefore, for the happiness [*allegrezza*] that had overcome them, they called that place the Borgo Allegri. This has always retained the same name, when with time it was enclosed within the walls.

'Cimabue did many other works that I will not discuss because the time does not allow it. Finally, having almost resurrected painting, he died at the age of seventy years. His portrait, by the hand of Simone Sanese,[10] can be seen in the chapter house of Santa Maria Novella, done in profile in the *History of the Faith*. His figure has a thin face, a small reddish beard, [291] and a hood on the head that is wound around, around and under the throat, as it was done in those times.'

Giotto

'Giotto[11] learned the art from Cimabue. He was born in 1276 in the countryside of Florence, fourteen miles from the city in a town called Vespignano, of a peasant father named Bondone, who worked the land. This boy was, by nature, so cheerful that [his father] called him Giotto.[12] And, as he saw him seeming to be of a good spirit at ten years of age, he had him watch a flock of sheep. And while they were at pasture, pushed by his inclination towards the art of design, [Giotto] always traced over the ground, drawing something in the dirt or in the sand.[13] So it happened that one day Cimabue, finding it necessary to go from Florence to Vespignano, found Giotto drawing a sheep from life with a sharpened stone on a clean stone while his sheep grazed. Therefore, stopping and greatly marvelling, Cimabue asked him if he wanted to apprentice with him. The boy responded that he would very gladly, provided that his father approved. Then Cimabue asked this of his father and, obtaining it from him, they left together for Florence. There [Giotto], helped by nature and taught by Cimabue, in a brief time not only equalled his master but left him behind by a great distance. He did away completely with that rough Greek manner, entirely resurrecting painting. [292] He introduced copying from nature. This had not been used for more than two hundred years and, although some had tried, had not been happily done. In sum, it was [Giotto] who gave light to the good manner of painting and did endless and very beautiful works.[14] All of these I will not recount to you, as it would be too long, but will briefly discuss only some here.

'The first figures done by [Giotto] were in the choir of the Badia of Florence. Among these an Our Lady at *The Annunciation* by the Angel Gabriel, in which she seems full of fear, as if she wishes to flee, was held to be very beautiful. And in that church he also painted the panel of that chapel.

'And he painted four chapels in Santa Croce, three between the sacristy and the high altar and one on the other side. The *Life of St Francis* is seen in the first chapel, which is the Bardi. In the second, of the Peruzzi, are narratives of St John the Baptist and of St John the Evangelist. In the third, of the Giugni, the martyrdom of many Apostles appear. In the fourth, of the Tosinghi and the Spinelli, is the *Assumption of the Glorious Virgin Mary.* He also painted many other narratives of the Queen of Heaven. But, noted among the others for great beauty was that in which She hands the Little Child to Simeon. In this is seen the great emotion in the old man on receiving the Saviour of the World and the beautiful pose of the Child, almost as if He had fear of him, in turning back to His Mother. Many beautiful and varied figures by his hand are also seen in the same church: in the Chapel of the Baroncelli, above the tomb [293] of Marsuppini, above that of Leonardo [Bruni] of Arezzo, in the brothers' refectory, and on the armoire of the sacristy.

'Also, in the Chapel of St John the Baptist, in the Carmine, he painted the whole life of that saint in many pictures. [He painted] a narrative of the *Christian Faith* in fresco in the Palace of the Guelph Party. In this the portrait of Pope Clement IV, who created that organization, is seen giving it his arms, which it still retains today.

'Then, [Giotto] left Florence and went to Assisi. There he painted in fresco in the Upper Church of San Francesco, underneath the gallery that goes around beneath the windows on both sides of the church, thirty-two narratives of the deeds of St Francis. He conducted them very happily, so that he acquired a great name from them. And very beautiful among the others there is that narrative where a figure is bent to the ground, drinking from a fountain. It shows very great expression in drinking and seems to appear almost completely alive.

'In the Lower Church he painted the walls above the high altar, and all of the vault where the body of St Francis is and its four corners with beautiful and new inventions. And there one sees *St Francis Glorified in Heaven,* surrounded by those Virtues that guide him to Paradise. Obedience puts its yoke on the neck of a monk, who is kneeling before her, and the bonds hanging from the yoke are drawn by some hands to Heaven. And Obedience, with a finger to her lips, enjoins silence and has her eyes turned to Christ, [294] who sheds blood from His side. And in her company are Humility and Prudence. Chastity, who will be conquered by neither the kingdoms, nor the crowns, nor the palms that some promise her, appears in another place on a very strong fortress. At her feet is Purity, washing nude figures. And Fortitude leads people to wash and purify themselves. Near Chastity is Penitence, sending winged Love away with a scourge and making Immodesty flee. In another part, Poverty is seen stomping on thorns with bare feet. And a dog barks behind her, a little boy throws stones at her, and another approaches her with a stick. And while Christ takes her hand, she is married to St Francis, Hope and Chastity being present, not without mystic meaning. Giotto portrayed himself in these narratives, which were very well done. And he painted, above the door of the sacristy, a *St Francis Receiving the Stigmata* with very great emotion. This figure, of all the others that he did here, was held to be the best.

'Returning to Florence, [Giotto] painted a panel in which there is St Francis with many beautiful landscapes and narratives from his life. Today this is in San Francesco in Pisa. Being called by the Pisans as a result of this work, he painted the *Narrative of Job* in six parts, in fresco, in the Campo Santo.

'The fame of the excellence of such a man, therefore, spread everywhere. Pope Benedict IX of Treviso [Benedict XI] sent one of his familiars to Tuscany to become familiar with the things of Giotto in the spirit of having him do some paintings in St Peter's [295]. Coming to Tuscany, and having spoken to many masters and having drawings from them, the familiar finally found Giotto working. And apprising him of the thoughts of the Pope, he asked him for a drawing to send to His Holiness. Giotto, who was very courteous, took a sheet of paper. And, holding his arm at his side almost as a compass, with a brush dipped in red, he turned his hand on it to make a circle so true in proportion and circumference that it was a marvellous thing. And smiling, he told the familiar, "Here is your drawing." [The familiar], thinking himself mocked, said, "Do I get to have another drawing than this?" "This is enough and more so," Giotto answered. "Send it together with the others, and you will see if it will be recognized." The familiar, seeing it would not be possible to have another, sent it together with the other drawings, saying that it satisfied the requirement. Therefore, from this the proverb was born: "You are rounder than the 'O' of Giotto." Recognizing his virtue, the Pope sent for him and did him many honours. He had him paint five narratives from the life of Christ, in the apse of St Peter's, and the principal panel in the sacristy, and many other figures outside of St Peter's. And a panel of a great Crucifix coloured in tempera in the Minerva was held to be very beautiful.

'By the death of Pope Benedict, Clement V was created Pope in Perugia. Then, taking himself back to Florence, Giotto was forced to move with [Clement] to Avignon, where this Pope transferred the Apostolic Seat. And in that city [Giotto] painted [296] many beautiful works as well as in other places of France.[15] Then, returning to Italy, he painted a chapel for the Scaligieri Lords in the Church of the Santo in Padua and some figures for Messer Can [della Scalla] in his palace in Verona, and particularly, his portrait and a panel in the Church of San Francesco. And for the Este Lords, in their palace in Ferrara and in Santo Agostino, [he painted] some paintings that still are seen there and in Ravenna, arranged by Dante Alighieri, some narratives around the Church of San Francesco for the Da Polenta Lords.[16] [He painted] other figures in Arezzo for Piero Saccone, others at the request of the Castrucci in Lucca, and narratives from the Old Testament and of the Apocalypse in many chapels in Santa Chiara for King Robert in Naples. And, for brevity, I pass over many other paintings in other places. To please the Lord Malatesta in Rimini, he did many beautiful works in the Church of San Francesco and, among the others, the narrative of the blessed Michelina, which was the best thing that he did up to then.[17]

'Then, returning to Florence, [Giotto] painted many other things that I will not discuss. And on 9 July, 1334 the foundation of the Campanile of Santa Maria del Fiore was laid. For this Giotto did the model and some of those narratives in marble, where the beginnings of all the arts are. The panel on the high altar of the noble Valori family in San Procolo is of his hand, where the Glorious Virgin is seen on a field of gold with the Child in Her lap, set between four saints [297] among whom are two bishops. And two angels above the Madonna, done with care, lift some curtains in beautiful poses. A little later, he went again to Padua and did other works there.[18] And in Milan he painted many things that are scattered over the city.

'Returning finally to his country, having lived as a Christian and worked excellently in painting, [Giotto] died in the year 1336, not only to the great sorrow of all of his fellow citizens but of all those who had known him and heard his name. His effigy, as you know, carved in marble and erected through the effort of the Magnificent Lorenzo de' Medici the Elder, can be seen in Santa Maria del Fiore, with some verses under it by the divine Agnolo Poliziano. These, because I know they are very well known to you, I will not otherwise recite for you. I have spoken rather at length of the things of Giotto because it was truly he who brought painting back into the light. Of the others who will follow, I will speak briefly so that I can say something of all the most excellent in this little time that is granted me.'[19]

'Up to here I have not mentioned any sculptor because none came to me that could enter into the choice of good masters that we have been assigned to make.'

Luca della Robbia

'Now I appear before Luca della Robbia,[20] born in Florence in the year 1388, who was so adept in sculpture that it is worthwhile to remember him. Five little marble narratives of his hand can be seen on the campanile of Santa Maria del Fiore on the side towards the church, portraying five Liberal Arts. He also did the decoration of the organ above the sacristy in that temple. On the plinth one sees some choirs of musicians, carved in marble, who sing in different ways. And above this ornament he did two nude angels of gilded metal and also the bronze door of this sacristy, where one sees many beautiful sacred narratives.

'[Luca] worked with great diligence but then, considering that in making these things he had lost [308] much time and advanced little, he left marble and bronze. He gave himself to making figures of clay, having found a method in which these were defended from the insults of time. And this was by giving them a covering of a material made with tin, lead, antimony, and other minerals and compounds, heated in a special furnace, then put over an unglazed figure, preserving it for a long time. And the first work that he did in this way was a *Resurrection of Christ* that was put in the arch over the bronze door that he had done for the sacristy. This pleased so greatly that the wardens of Santa Maria del Fiore had him make, in a similar manner, that *Ascension of Jesus Christ* that can be seen there yet today. This is over the door of the other sacristy, where Donatello had done the decoration of the other organ.

'Then Luca added to this invention to give it colour, which was held to be a very beautiful thing. And he made many works in this manner for the Magnificent Piero di Cosimo de' Medici, and he also made some for the merchants who sent them, to their great profit, to various parts of the world. But the most notable work of this kind that left his hands was on the vault of the Chapel of San Jacopo in which the Cardinal of Portugal is buried in the Church of San Miniato al Monte. There the Four Evangelists are seen and, in the middle of the vault in a tondo, the *Holy Spirit*. He did the marble tomb in San Brancatio of Messer Benozzo Federighi, Bishop of Fiesole. There [309] this bishop is seen laid out, portrayed from life, and three other half-figures and some festoons of fruit and of leaves so lifelike and natural that one could not have painted them more beautifully with the brush on a panel. But this man, who was very active finding new inventions, was taken from the world by death while he laboured to adorn it with his beautiful talent.'

Paolo Uccello

'Paolo Uccello was highly valued in painting animals and particularly birds, from which he acquired the last name of Bird [*Uccello*].[21] He spent a long time in discovering the rules of drawing perspective to a point, and of perfecting the manner of where figures place their feet on a plane, and making them foreshortened and decreased little by little so that they proceed to disappear. If, instead, he had devoted himself only to painting, he would perhaps have climbed to a greater perfection of the art than he did. [The following] are his most commended works. The *Annunciation* and a building, in fresco, worthy of consideration, which in that time was the first that was shown with a beautiful manner, are in a chapel beside the side door in Santa Maria Maggiore. And in the cloister of Santa Maria Novella is the *Creation* of the animals of every sort and the narrative of the first parents, when they were created and when they sinned, with many trees and landscapes. [Also there] is the *Deluge* with the ark of Noah, where the dead bodies, the tempest, the fury of the winds, the flashes of lightning, the trunks of the trees, and the fear of the men are seen, done with great diligence. And under [310] this narrative is the *Drunkenness of Noah*, with the scorn of his son Ham, where a cask is seen in perspective that curves towards every side, held [to be] a very beautiful thing. And nearby is the open Ark from which the birds are seen going out, flying foreshortened in many ways, and many other figures.[22]

'In memory of the Englishman Giovanni Acuto [John Hawkwood], Captain of the Florentines, [Uccello] did a horse on which this captain is mounted in Santa Maria del Fiore, in chiaroscuro the colour of green earth. In a picture ten braccia tall, in the middle of the wall of the church, he drew in perspective a great sarcophagus under the feet of this horse. This work was, and is, held to be very beautiful for a painting of that sort, even though there is a very great error there. The horse moves both legs [in the same direction] on each side, which in reality horses cannot do. [Uccello] also painted in green earth the loggia that faces west above the garden of the Monastery of the Agnoli, where he did the narrative of St Benedict. He did the vault of the loggia of the Peruzzi in fresco. And above every corner he painted the four elements represented by four animals, a mole for the earth, a fish for the waters, a salamander for fire, and a chameleon for the air. And because he had never seen one, deceived by the similarity of the name, he did a camel instead of a chameleon.[23]

'Finally, he was commissioned to do, over the gate of San Tommaso in the Old Market, that same saint touching the chest wound of Jesus Christ. And having [311] said he wanted to show how much he was worth in that work, [Uccello] put a lock on the narrative so that no one could see his work. Therefore, encountering him one day all alone, Donatello said to him, "What work is this of yours that you hold it so closely?" Paolo replied, "You will see it soon enough." Having then finished the work and uncovering it, falling in with Donatello, [Donatello] was asked by Paolo what he thought of it. [Donatello], after having considered it carefully, replied, "What should I say, if not that now, when it should be time to cover it, you uncover it?" Paolo, grieving greatly at this response, withdrew to his house. Humiliated, he did not dare to go out anymore, attended to perspective, and lived poorly up to the eighty-third year of his life. And I have already done this epitaph about him:

Although Paol was fortunate in painting men;
In doing animals with his brush
He flew so high that not only of bird [Uccello]
His last name deserved, but of Phoenix.

Lorenzo Ghiberti

'It is not our intention to discuss sculpture except that which has been carved. I do not wish, however, to pass in silence, as it comes before my imagination, the excellence in casting of Lorenzo di Bartoluccio Ghiberti of Florence.[24] And to show how much was his virtue in this art, I will not say more than that he made the bronze doors of San Giovanni that face [312] towards Santa Maria del Fiore, a very singular work and not ever praised enough. And equally of his hand are the other doors, also of bronze, facing the Misericordia [Bigallo][25] and the *St John the Baptist* and the *St Matthew*, grand figures, that are in two niches of Orsanmichele. And he also did many other bronze works in Siena and in Florence, all worthy of praise.'[26]

Masaccio

'Masaccio from San Giovanni di Valdarno[27] learned the art of painting from Masolino. All the painters who [immediately] came after him and [all] who came thereafter should be obligated to him. It was he who first opened the path to the good and modern manner of painting and left behind to a large extent the hardness, the imperfections, and the difficulties of the art. He was the first who initiated beautiful poses and who gave boldness, lifelikeness, movement, three-dimensionality, and natural grace to figures. And he did the foreshortening much better for every sort of view than any other who had been before him.

'Of [Masaccio's] hand is seen a panel in tempera in which there is an *Our Lady with the Child* in Her arms in the lap of St Anne in the chapel that is beside the door in Santo Ambrogio. And he painted the *Annunciation* and a building full of columns thrown in perspective, with very beautiful organization, in San Niccolò Oltrarno. And in a fresco on a pillar opposite one of those that support the arch of the high altar in the Badia, *St Ivo of Brittany* is shown within a niche so that his feet are foreshortened as seen from below. And there are seen, on a cornice at the foot of this saint, widows, orphans, and beggars helped in their need by this saint. And he painted the *Virgin Mary, St Catherine, and St Julian,* with some little figures from the life of St Catherine and other narratives in the predella, on a panel in a chapel in the corner by the side door in Santa Maria Maggiore. [314]

'Then, transferring himself to Pisa, [Masaccio] painted a panel in the Church of the Carmine. In it there is the *Glorious Virgin,* surrounded by many saints, and at Her feet She has some little angels playing music. And below, in small figures in the predella, the three Magi offer gifts to Christ with other little narratives of saints. Here there are seen some horses drawn from life, of which it would not be possible to desire anything more beautiful. Then, taking himself to Rome, he painted the *Passion of Our Lord* and the narrative of St Catherine the martyr in fresco in a chapel in the Church of San Clemente. And he did many other panels in tempera in many places of that city.

'Finally, returning to Florence, [Masaccio] was commissioned, Masolino having died, to finish the Chapel of the Brancacci that Masolino had left incomplete in the Carmine. Before putting his hand to that, he did the *St Paul* that is next to the bells to show the improvement that he had made in his art. And this figure appeared to lack only speech and nothing more to show life. And in it is understood the cleverness of foreshortening the view from below [*di sotto in sù*], a marvellous thing, not being better done by anyone. This Church of the Carmine was consecrated while he was attending to this work. And, to leave this in memory, he painted, in green earth in chiaroscuro above the door within the cloister that goes into the convent, the whole festival as it had occurred. And there he [315] portrayed an endless number of citizens, all in mantles and hoods, who came behind in the procession. Among them he did Filippo di Ser Brunelleschi in wooden shoes, Donatello, Masolino [*sic*], and many others. This work had great perfection with a sure observation that distinguishes these from those. One sees the men, five and six to a row, becoming smaller in proportion, and all placing their feet on one level, so well foreshortened in line that one could not make it more natural in any other way.

'Returning then to his work in the Chapel of the Brancacci, [Masaccio] continued with the narrative of St Peter started by Masolino. And, among the other things worthy of consideration is that where St Peter, to pay the tribute, found the money in the belly of the fish on the instructions of Christ. One recognizes the portrait of Masaccio, who appears alive in the person of one of the Apostles who is in the back. One recognizes the ardour of St Peter and the attentiveness of the Apostles surrounding Christ with gestures as vivid as nothing else, and many other things that for brevity I pass over. But I do not want to avoid saying that in the narrative where St Peter baptizes, a nude shivering among the others being baptized, demonstrating the great cold and done with very beautiful three-dimensionality, is greatly commended. In sum, this work of his is such that all the capable men of the art who were after him were made excellent in studying it up to Raphael of Urbino and Michelangelo Buonarroti, not to speak of the others. This work was not [316] entirely finished by him, since death interrupted him, cutting the thread of his life when he was twenty-six years of age, when it was hoped to see of him stupendous and marvellous works. Baccio here has of his hand a very beautiful portrait of Baccio

Valori the elder. Masaccio was buried in the Carmine in the year 1443, and Anibal Caro wrote this epitaph for him.

I paint, and truth appears in my picture,
The expression, the animation, the giving of motion,
I gave them emotion, I will teach Buonarroti
And all the others, and only from me you learn.

Filippo Brunelleschi

'I will also not omit making a brief remembrance of Filippo Brunelleschi of Florence,[28] since he did a few things in sculpture, although he gave himself to architecture. In this he was very excellent, as he demonstrated in the dome of Santa Maria del Fiore done under his direction and to his design, the Church of San Lorenzo, and a thousand other buildings that I do not name to not go outside of our interest. He originally learned the craft of the jeweller and then gave himself to sculpture and made a very beautiful *St Mary Magdalene* of linden wood that was put in Santo Spirito. This was burned by the fire in that temple in the year 1471, along with many other notable things.

'He was a close friend of Donatello who, having finished a wood *Crucifix* that is seen today [317] in Santa Croce showed it to [Brunelleschi], asking [Brunelleschi] to say how it appeared to him. To this Filippo responded that [Donatello] had put a ploughman on the Cross. This answer seeming strange to Donatello, [Donatello] told him, "If it were as easy to do as you think, my Christ would seem to you Christ, and not a ploughman. However, take some wood and also try to make one yourself." What he said bore down severely on Filippo, and he was quiet many months until he completed a wood *Crucifix* of the same size as that of Donatello, and then he showed it to him. Therefore, on considering the artful manner that Filippo had used in the torso, in the arms, and in the legs, [Donatello] was amazed and not only declared himself defeated but also considered it a miracle. That *Crucifix* can still be seen today in Santa Maria Novella, between the Strozzi Chapel and that of the Bardi di Vernio. In sum, this man was of very beautiful talent, a marvellous jeweller, excellent sculptor, good mathematician, and very rare architect. He died at the age of sixty-nine years in 1446. He was buried in Santa Maria del Fiore, and his bust in marble, portrayed from life by the hand of his student Buggiano, was put up in that church inside the door to the right, going out to the Piazza of San Giovanni.'

Donatello

'Donato, who was called Donatello,[29] was born in Florence in the year 1303 [*sic*] and was raised in the house of Ruberto Martelli and, applying himself to design, became a most excellent sculptor. The first work that [318] he did to demonstrate his marvellous talent and understanding of the art was an *Annunciation* of sandstone that was erected in Santa Croce in the Chapel of the Cavalcanti. There six putti are seen in the decoration holding some festoons and holding onto each other with their hands. And the Virgin shows fear at the sudden greeting of the angel and turns with very modest reverence. The drapery of the angel and of the Virgin is done masterfully with very beautiful folds showing underneath the nudity of many parts which up to then had not been done. In sum, this work was done with so much artifice that it is not possible to desire more from the design, the chisel, and the execution.

'Then [Donatello] did, in the Temple of San Giovanni,[30] the tomb of Pope Giovanni Coscia, on which the deceased in gilded bronze is seen reclining. And Hope and Charity are there in marble by his hand, and there his student Michelozzo did Faith. A *St Mary Magdalene* of wood, showing penitence, a very beautiful and well-understood figure, is also by the hand, of Donato in the same church. His works, all worthy of praise, include an *Abundance* of hard sandstone on a granite column that is in the Old Market and a prophet *Daniel* of marble and a seated *St John the Evangelist*, four braccia high, on the facade of Santa Maria del Fiore. And in the church he decorated the organ, which is above the door of the old sacristy, with rough figures that, to see them, appear to be truly alive. There, [319] it can be said that he worked as much with judgment as with his hands. Many things that are done appear beautiful in the rooms where they are done that then, when they are taken from there and put in another place and another light or lower or higher making different views, succeed very distantly from how they first appeared.

'On the facade of Orsanmichele [Donatello] did the statue of *St Peter* for the Butchers' Guild, *St Mark the Evangelist* for the Guild of Linen Workers and Pedlars, and *St George* in armour for the Armourers' Guild, a wonderful figure. And he did the same saint on horseback killing the dragon in low relief in marble on the plinth that holds up this tabernacle, and that work is easier to greatly praise than to imitate. There are four statues by him on the campanile of Santa Maria del Fiore, two of which were portrayed from life. One is of Francesco

Soderini as a youth. And the other is of Giovanni Cherichini, today called the "*Zuccone*." This is a very rare thing and among the best that he did. He did a bronze *Judith* who has cut off the head of Holophrenes. This is still seen today, under the arch of the loggia of the Piazza looking towards the new Uffizi. And, in the courtyard of the palace of the Very Serene Grand Duke Francesco, a nude bronze *David* who has Goliath under his feet is of his hand. And in the clock hall of this palace is another *David*, of marble, who has the head of the dead giant between his legs and the sling in his hand. He did eight medallions of marble, where ancient cameos, the reverse of medals, and some very beautiful narratives are portrayed, on the frieze between the [320] windows and the architrave, over the arches of the loggia in the first courtyard of the palace of the Medici. There are many bronze and marble statues by him in the house of the Martelli and, among others, a *David* three braccia high and a marble *St John*, completely in the round, a very rare thing. This figure was so valued by Ruberto Martelli that he made a legal agreement that he could neither sell it, lend against it, or give it away without great prejudice.

'There is a marble tomb done by [Donatello] in Sant' Angelo a Nilo in Naples, where three figures in the round are seen holding up the sarcophagus with their heads, on which a very beautiful narrative is carved in low relief. In Prato, a city ten miles from Florence, he did the marble pulpit from which the belt of the Glorious Virgin is displayed [to the people]. And he carved a dance of little boys on it so beautiful and so lifelike that it astonishes whoever looks at it. He did a bronze horse mounted on which was a figure in memory of Gattamelata in the Piazza of St Anthony in Padua. This work in the casting, as in every other part, can be compared to whichever one pleases of the most praised ancients. And on the predella of the high altar in the Church of the Brothers Minor of that city he carved the narratives of St Anthony of Padua in low relief. All the perfection of art is seen in the many figures and perspectives and the three Marys mourning and, in another part, the dead Christ. He gave the Florentine people in Venice a [321] *St John the Baptist* of wood, done by him with great diligence. He did a marble tomb in the Pieve of Montepulciano with a very beautiful narrative.

'And there are two little bronze doors in low relief, in the sacristy of San Lorenzo in Florence, with the apostles, the martyrs, and the confessors, and, above these, some flat niches in one of which are *St Lawrence and St Stephen* and in the other *St Cosmas and St Damian*. Seen by his hand in the collection of the Very Serene Grand Duke Francesco is an

Our Lady with Her Child in Her arms on a marble in *relievo schiacciato*[31] of which a more beautiful thing cannot be seen. [Also there] is a bronze picture in low relief in which there is the *Passion of Our Lord* with many figures and another picture, also of metal, in which Christ is seen on the Cross with other figures pertaining to the narrative. And, in the study of Her Very Serene Highness there is a bronze *Crucifix*, also from the hand of Donato, not only very beautiful, but miraculous. In the house of the Capponi and of Jacopo Capponi, a very nice young man, is a marble picture of *Our Lady* in half-relief, held in very great merit. As, equally, is another in which there is a half-length *Our Lady* in low relief in the house of Giulio de' Nobili who, as a virtuoso and understanding such things, holds it very dear.

'Donato did many other things that, to not be too long, I will leave aside. I say only that it was truly he who resurrected sculpture and who gave light to those who then came to [322] work in a good and praiseworthy manner. There have been few, however, who have been able to arrive at his excellence. He died at eighty-three years in 1466 and was buried in the Church of San Lorenzo, next to the tomb of Cosimo de' Medici the elder. And many Latin and Italian epitaphs were done. But for now I will remember only a sonnet that Messer Ruberto Titi, doctor of law and a young man of great value in the belles-lettres, has done about him which is this:

While it gave grave injury to the mocking of time,
 That he took his marbles and bronzes to completion,
 Which with chisel and wrist and strength
 Have been living many, many years;

To make them illustrious deceptions on this page
 Is not impossible for you; since great
 Praise for this light and serene spirit
 May carry your name to more sublime locations.

And it is of the works such work most rare,
 That while some of your writing or discussion
 Itself is raised to such a longed for level.

Alive your merit, gives life and illuminates
 His name, of whom you write your page;
 So that it gives Donato eternal glory.[32]

Fra Giovanni Angelico

'I will not omit mentioning Fra Giovanni Angelico of Fiesole[33] of the Order of Preaching Brothers. He, while he was of the very holy life, was also a capable man [324] in painting. He painted a panel in which there is *Our Lady with Her Child* in arms and some angels and saints that was hung in the major chapel belonging to Cardinal Acciaioli in the Certosa of Florence. Close to this are seen, also of his hand, two other panels: the *Coronation of the Madonna* in one, and a *Virgin with Two Saints*, done in very beautiful ultramarine blue, in the other. He painted the *Passion of Jesus Christ* in fresco on a wall of the chapter house of San Marco and beside it all the saints who were heads and founders of orders. And below this work, in a frieze above the panelling, he did a tree that had St Dominic at the foot. On this in certain medallions surrounded by branches were all the popes, cardinals, bishops, saints, and masters of theology who up to then had been in the Order of the Preaching Brothers, where many portraits from life are seen. He also did many other paintings for this convent. In the first cloister is a greatly praised *Crucifix* with St Dominic at its foot, and a narrative of the New Testament is in the dormitory. And the panel of the high altar in the church is his, in which there is the *Glorious Virgin* who moves those who see Her to devotion. And in the predella are narratives of the martyrdom of St Cosmas and St Damian in very beautiful little figures.

'In San Domenico, in Fiesole, he painted the panel of the high altar, which was then retouched and worsened by others and a panel in the same church in which there is the *Virgin Annunciate* with the angel and Adam and [325] Eve. And also another panel [is there], perhaps of the most beautiful that he did, where Jesus Christ is seen crowning Our Lady in the middle of a choir of angels and within an endless crowd of male and female saints, a work in truth deserving great consideration for the different and devote poses that are there. In the Chapel of the Annunziata in Florence, which Piero di Cosimo de' Medici had commissioned, he painted the counters of the cabinet, where the silverware is, with little figures done with great care. Of his hand are the panel of the *Deposition from the Cross* that is in the sacristy of Santa Trinità and the *Annunciation* that is in San Francesco outside the gate to San Miniato. [He did] the panel that is seen in the office of the Guild of Linen Workers and Pedlars and the panel on the high altar in the church of his order in Cortona. [Also his] are the panel where there is a dead

Christ in the Confraternity of the Temple in Florence and the small-figure *Paradise and Hell* on the right going towards the high altar in the church of the monks of the Agnoli.

'Called then to Rome by Pope Nicholas V, [Fra Angelico] painted the chapel of the palace where the Pope hears mass and a panel in which there is an *Annunciation* for the high altar in the Minerva. Today, this is attached to a wall at the corner of the choir. He painted many other things for this Pope. Therefore, the Archdiocese of Florence being vacant, he deserved that the Pontiff, judging him worthy of this dignity, offered it to him. But he very modestly begged His Holiness to ask [326] another, since he did not feel himself fit to govern the people. And his order had a monk fond of poverty, learned of government, and fearful of God who would be much better suited for this than he was. And he said this was Brother Antonino of the Order of Preachers who, the Pope approving, was made Archbishop of Florence, a man who, for his holiness and very clear doctrine, deserved to be canonized a saint. And so Fra Giovanni – something that time has come to erase – conceded this honoured degree to another who he judged more appropriate to it. And having lived piously, he died in the seventy-eighth year of his life in 1455 and was buried along the side entrance next to the sacristy in the Minerva in Rome, in a round marble tomb on which is seen his portrait from life.

'The painters, up to this time having painted on panel and on canvas in tempera, recognized that this way of painting was unstable and in many ways imperfect. It was not possible to clean the paintings which became soiled from much handling. And, while many suffered a long time trying to discover a better method, no one among them, however, succeeded.'

Giovanni of Bruges, first to discover painting in oil

'In Flanders a Giovanni of Bruges,[34] a painter greatly esteemed in those parts [*in quelle parti*] and who also amused himself with the things of alchemy, understood the imperfections of tempera colour. He discovered, after many experiments, that tempering [327] the colours with walnut and linseed oil gave a very strong tempera. This, when dry, not only did not fear water but gave liveliness and lustre without other varnish and brought colours together more than ordinary tempera. Thus, very happy with this invention, he began to do many works coloured in this way, among which was a panel that was sent as a gift to King Alfonso I of Naples. This, for the many well-done figures that were in it and for its charming new manner of colouring, not only was very dear to the king but also all the painters of the kingdom went to see it and praised it greatly.'

Antonello da Messina

'Among these was an Antonello da Messina,[35] a person of beautiful spirit who was rather valued in painting. Marvelling at the beautiful way of colouring, leaving all his other affairs, he took himself to Flanders. He neither held back presents, nor other modes of courtesy to obligate men, until he became familiar with Giovanni of Bruges and learned from him the way of painting in oil. He returned to Italy with this secret, settling in Venice, where he did many pictures in oil according to what he had learned in Flanders. These, for their new way of painting, were held very beautiful in that time. And having acquired great fame, he finally did a panel that was hung in San Cassiano, a parish of that city. And while he was living, Antonello was very esteemed for having brought so rare a secret to Italy. He taught this to many [328] others, so that it spread wider and wider, and today it is seen transformed into the greatest perfection. You have seen a small painting by the hand of this Antonello in my house, in which he painted the head of St Francis and that of St Dominic. I hold this very dear for the beauty of the work and for the memory of such a man. But this, for now, is enough for us of Antonello da Messina.'[36]

Gentile and Giovanni Bellini

'Gentile and Giovanni Bellini, famous painters in that time, were born of the Venetian painter Jacopo Bellini.[37] Gentile painted the miracle of the Cross of Christ [about] a relic held by the Scuola della Croce [San Giovanni Evangelista]. This miracle was this. The Cross was thrown, by I do not know what accident, from the Straw Bridge into the canal. Many, for the reverence that they had for the wood there of the Cross of Christ, threw themselves into the water to retrieve it. But, as it pleased God, no one was able to retrieve it except the prior of that scuola. Gentile painted, then, the narrative of this miracle, drawing many houses in perspective on the Grand Canal, the Piazza of San Marco, and a long procession of men and women behind the clergy. Many were thrown into the water and others in the act of throwing themselves in, with very beautiful poses and all the other things pertaining to this narrative. He did these paintings on many canvases, and they gave him a great name.

'Therefore, the *Signoria* commissioned many pictures from [Gentile], also on canvas, for the Sala del Gran Consiglio. The Pope is seen presenting a wax candle to the Doge, with other figures. The Emperor Barbarossa graciously receives the Venetian ambassadors and then disdainfully prepares himself for war. The Pope blesses the Doge armed to go against Barbarossa. And there is a naval battle with many inventions and other narratives that it would be too long to describe. Two portraits by Giovanni Bellini having been taken to the Grand Turk during this [time], he wrote to the Signoria of Venice that they send him this master. [342] Therefore, the Signoria, because Giovanni was already elderly [*sic*], and to not deprive themselves of such a man, sent him Gentile who Mohammed, who was now emperor, viewed very favourably. And he had him do some portraits. And, greatly rewarding him and giving him a favourable letter addressed to the Signoria, he sent him back to his country where he returned, assigned 200 scudi per year as an annuity for as long as he lived. And, having done some other works, he finally passed from this to the better life at the age of eighty years.

'His brother Giovanni painted many things. Among these are a panel in which there is *Our Lady with Other Saints* on the altar of St Catherine of Siena in the Church of San Giovanni [e Paulo]. Great drawing and very beautiful colour are seen in another panel in the Church of San Giobbe, with the Madonna seated and the little Child in Her arms and other saints. The *Glorious Virgin with Many Saints* is in a panel in the Chapel of St Jerome in San Zaccaria. And he did many other works that, for brevity, I will pass over. In the Sala del Gran Consiglio he painted four narratives. In the first, Frederick Barbarossa is bent over in front of the Pope to kiss the [Pope's] foot. In the second, the Pope says mass in San Marco and, in the presence of the Doge and of the Emperor, grants a complete and perpetual indulgence to those visiting the Church of San Marco at certain times. In the third, the Pope in a rochet[38] gives an umbrella to the Doge, having first given one to the Emperor. In the fourth, the Pope, the Emperor, and the Doge, [343] coming to Rome, are met by the clergy and people of Rome, where there is seen the cityscape of Rome and many other beautiful things. Giovanni also did many portraits from life for many lords and princes that were highly valued and greatly commended. Bembo makes mention of him in that sonnet that begins: "*Oh image mine celestial and pure.*"[39] And Ariosto also, in the beginning of the thirty-third canto of his *Orlando Furioso*, numbers him among the most famous painters of his age.[40] Consumed by age, he died at ninety years, having done a great deal and with great praise.'[41]

Sandro Botticelli

'Sandro Botticelli[42] was of the same time. He was the son of a Mariano Filipepi, a citizen of Florence. And although he was sent to school by his father to have him study, or at least to learn the abacus, nevertheless, he was not content with any master since he easily learned everything. Finally, despairing of him, his father put him, for his master, with a jeweller who was called Botticelli from whom Sandro acquired his last name. And applying himself to drawing, he made a resolution to turn to painting and, therefore, was sent to be with Fra Filippo of the Carmine, in that time a very excellent painter, [351] and in a brief time became a capable man.

'He painted a panel in the Chapel of the Bardi in Santo Spirito, one for the nuns of the Convertite [Santa Elisabetta] and one for those of San Barnaba. And in the Ognissanti he did a very beautiful *St Augustine* in fresco in competition with Domenico Ghirlandaio, who did a *St Jerome*. In San Marco he did a very well-executed panel in which there is the *Coronation of Our Lady* with a choir of angels. He did many things for Lorenzo de' Medici the Elder and particularly a life-size *Pallus* above a device of branches spouting fire and, equally, a *St Sebastian*. He painted a *Pietà* with very beautiful little figures beside the Chapel of the Panciatichi in Santa Maria Maggiore. And there are two pictures of his hand at Castello, the villa of the Most Serene Francesco de' Medici. In one is the *Birth of Venus* with breezes and winds that conduct her to land with cupids. And in the other is another Venus, decorated with flowers by the Graces as a symbol of *Spring*. And he did many pictures with many very lively figures. They are framed with walnut trimming going around a room in the house of Giovanni Vespucci in the Via de' Servi, today belonging to Sig. Giovanni de' Bardi de Vernio, a very virtuous and courteous gentleman. And he did a panel in which there is an *Annunciation* for the monks of Cestello. And a panel is his of the *Assumption of Our Lady* for Matteo Palmieri in San Pier Maggiore, and this Matteo is portrayed there kneeling with his wife, with endless numbers of figures, with the regions of Heaven done with the different categories of [352] the saints identified. A very beautiful little panel of his hand, three-quarters of a braccio high, with little figures of the narrative of the Magi, was put in Santa Maria Novella. The first of the Magi is the portrait of Cosimo de' Medici the Elder, father [great-grandfather] of Pope Clement, and the third is Giovanni, Cosimo's son, and this work is truly admirable and rare.

'Then, taking himself to Rome, called by Pope Sixtus IV, [Botticelli] was made head [*capo*] of the painting of the [Sistine] Chapel. There he did many narratives himself such as when Christ was tempted by the Devil and other narratives from the Old Testament and some holy popes in the niches above. From these he acquired a great deal of profit and honour. Then, returning to Florence, he put himself to illustrating Dante and representing Hell, and this was issued in print. He did many pictures for many people. Francesco Trosci – an astute man of great judgment and, therefore, used in many negotiations by our Grand Duke – has one. In this [Botticelli] painted the *Virgin with the Child* standing on the ground, supported by an angel, next to which is St John as a child and a very beautiful landscape.

'Not having many of these, Ridolfo gave two little panels together to our Grand Duchess, the Most Serene Sig. Bianca Cappello de' Medici. In one of which Holophernes, surrounded by his astonished barons, is painted in bed with his head cut off, and in the other, Judith has his head in a sack. [Ridolfo] understood that Her Highness, as [353] someone who is most virtuous [*virtuosissima*],[43] wanted to decorate a study with paintings and ancient statues. He judged these little works of Botticelli to be worthy of appearing next to the others that Her Highness has arranged there. But, to return to Sandro, he finally passed from this life in the year 1515, having lived seventy-eight years, and was buried in the Ognissanti.'[44]

Andrea Mantegna

'Andrea Mantegna[45] was born in the country around Padua and from boyhood looked after the sheep. He was then taken to the city under Jacopo Squarcione, attended to painting, and left his master behind by a great distance. At age seventeen he painted the panel of the high altar of Santa Sofia di Padova. And then he worked in the Chapel of St Christofano in the Church of the Eremitani Brothers of St Augustine. There he did the Four Evangelists, which were held very beautiful, and the narrative of St James with many portraits from life [of figures] dressed in spotless armour as burnished and splendid as the real thing. In Verona there is a panel of his on the altar of San Christofano e Santo Antonio, some figures on a corner of the Piazza della Paglia, and another panel for the high altar for the Brothers of Monteoliveto in Santa Maria in Organo. He did a picture of *Our Lady* with certain angels singing that is a very beautiful and rare thing that is today in the library of the Badia of Fiesole.

'[Mantegna] did a little panel with not very large but very beautiful figures for the Marquis Lodovico Gonzaga in Mantua, which was put up in the chapel of the castle. And he painted the *Triumph of Caesar*, in a hall for the same lord, with many beautiful figures and animals. And it is truly the most beautiful work that Andrea ever did, with very great organization of perspective. [357] He placed the plane where the figures stand higher than the level of the eye, showing only the lower part of the figures and concealing the upper part. Therefore, the marquis, greatly liking this work, in addition to every other prize, made him a cavaliere.

'Then called by Pope Innocent VIII, he went to Rome and painted a little chapel in the Belvedere with so much care that it appeared illuminated as in a manuscript. Among the other figures, there is very beautiful one that removes a stocking from the inside out by crossing his shin over onto his other leg with a pose that shows this effect very well and was held in that time a marvellous thing. He did at the same time an *Our Lady* in a little picture with the Child sleeping in Her arms. And in the landscape, enclosed by a mountain, he painted some stone-cutters quarrying stone in some caves, done with so much care that it appears almost impossible that art can do so much with the brush. And this picture is found today belonging to the Most Serene Francesco de' Medici who, as a connoisseur of good things, holds it very dear. Mantegna did many other works that I pass by for brevity. He painted and built himself a house in Mantua which he honourably enjoyed until he left the present life when he was sixty-six. He died in 1517 and was buried in Sant' Andrea, where his portrait is seen in bronze over his tomb.'[46]

Pietro Perugino

'But we pass on to speak of Pietro Perugino.[47] He was born in Perugia of a poor and humble father. And desiring to make some progress in painting, he moved himself to Florence and became an excellent painter under the instruction of Andrea Verrocchio. And so much credit would his things have [363] that the merchants began to buy them up and to send them to different countries to their great profit. They were scattered not only over Florence and throughout all Italy but also through France and through Spain. There is a panel by his hand in Santa Chiara in Florence of charming colour in a devout and very beautiful manner in which there is a dead *Christ with the Marys*. And it is said that Francesco del Pugliese wanted to give to the nuns of this church three times as much money as they had paid for it, and have another similar done by the same master. But they would not have it because Pietro said that he did not believe he would be able to do another to compare to it. There are three panels done by him in San Giovannino degli Ingesuati, next to the Porta San Piergattolini. In one is *Christ in the Garden* and the sleeping Apostles. Christ in the lap of the Madonna surrounded by four figures is in another. And a *Crucifix* with the Magdalene at its foot and other saints is in the last. He painted *St Jerome* in penitence in a panel in San Jacopo tra' Fossi and a dead Christ with St John and the Magdalene on the wall in fresco above the steps of the side door of San Pier Maggiore, very well preserved up to today. A panel in Cestello in which there is a *St Bernard* is his and, in the chapter, a Crucifix, Our Lady, and other saints. [He painted] the lower part of the panel in the Annunziata where there is the *Deposition from the Cross*, the upper part having first been done by Filippino. Giovambatista [364] Deti, a gracious gentleman who pleases himself with the belles-lettres, has a large picture of his in which there is the Madonna, with the Child in Her arms marrying St Catherine. And another saint is there and St John putting a stick in the mouth of a monster. And the background is completed with a landscape, a truly beautiful work and done with great care. The panel of the high altar in the church in Vallombrosa is of his hand, where there is the *Assumption of the Glorious Virgin*. He painted a large panel in San Francesco in Siena that was held very beautiful and another of a Crucifix with some saints, in Santo Agostino. An *Assumption of Our Lady* with the Apostles is on the high altar in the Piscopio [Duomo] in Naples and a *Madonna* in the air with some standing figures for San Giovanni in Monte in Bologna.

'Then called to Rome, to his great glory, by Pope Sixtus IV [Perugino] worked in the [Sistine] Chapel together with the other masters. But the things that he did there were then pulled down to make the wall for Michelangelo's *Judgment*. Also in Rome, he did a narrative of two martyrs in San Marco beside the [Chapel of the] Sacrament, a work as good as he did in that city. He also painted a loggia and other rooms for Sciarra Colonna in the Palace of Santo Apostolo.

'Finally, rich and honoured, [Perugino] took himself to Perugia, where he did a panel in oil in the Chapel of the Signori in which there is *Our Lady with Other Saints*. And in San Francesco del Monte he painted two chapels in fresco. In one of which he did the narrative of the Magi and in the other [365] the martyrdom of some Franciscan brothers. He painted the *Marriage of the Virgin* for the Altar of the Sacrament, where the ring is preserved with which the Virgin Mary was married, and all the audience chamber of the Cambio in fresco. The seven planets are on some chariots drawn by different animals on the vault and the *Nativity* and the *Resurrection of Christ* on the wall opposite the door where one enters. And St John the Baptist with other saints is on a [separate] panel. On the walls he then painted Fabius Maximus and other ancient illustrious men, the sibyls and the prophets, and he did his portrait with his name below in an ornament. And this work was truly the most beautiful that Pietro did in Perugia, where he did many others that time does not allow to be enumerated. He began a work in fresco of no little importance for Castello [Città] della Pieve. But, interrupted by death, which put him under its scythe at the age of seventy-eight years, he did not complete it and was honourably buried in Castello della Pieve in the year 1524.'[48]

Leonardo da Vinci

'The very famous painter Leonardo da Vinci[49] was born of a Ser Piero da Vinci. He was not only most worthy in painting but was very handsome in body and countenance, very great of strength, attractive in speaking, excellent in sculpture, rare in music, sang very well in improvisation, and played sweetly on the lyre. He learned the art of painting from Andrea Verrocchio but not only surpassed his master by a great length but also all the others who had painted up to his time. Among the first things that he did was a cartoon for a door hanging to be made in Flanders of gold and silk to send to the king of Portugal. In this he drew in chiaroscuro, heightened with white, Adam and Eve when they sinned in the terrestrial paradise and a meadow of endless kinds of plants with some animals and the fig tree. The leaves and views of the branches were foreshortened. This was conducted with such very great care that it seemed impossible that a man could do so much. This cartoon, not long ago, was among the very rare things of Ottaviano de' Medici.

'Ser Piero was asked by a farmer to have a shield of fig wood painted for him. Therefore, Ser Piero gave it to Leonardo, asking him to paint something there. He took this to one of his rooms and did crickets, snakes, butterflies, grasshoppers, bats, large and small lizards, and other strange animals on it. From all of these he formed a very horrible and frightful ugly animal that appeared to emit a poisonous breath and turn the air to flame. And he made it to [369] come out of a dark and jagged rock, emitting fire from its mouth and eyes and smoke from its nose so strangely that it was not possible to gaze on it without terror. And this was the painting that he did on the small shield and, arranging it on a stand that had rather confusing light, he called his father who came to see the little shield. He came in not thinking about anything. When he saw that ugly animal, not believing that it was painted on the little shield but real and alive, he turned around frightened, about to run away. Then Leonardo stopped him and told him: "This work serves the purpose for which it was made; therefore, take it and do with it what you like, for this is the goal that was expected of the work." This seemed to be a marvellous thing to Ser Piero. And therefore, he purchased another painted little shield and gave it to the farmer who held it very dear. And [Ser Piero] sold that of Leonardo to some merchants for a hundred ducats, which they then sold to the Duke of Milan for 300 scudi.[50]

'[Leonardo] did a very rare *Our Lady* in a picture that Pope Clement VII would come to have. And, among the other things, he did in it was a glass vase full of water with some flowers in it and the most natural dew drops are seen on the glass vase. He drew a Neptune on his chariot in the sea with monsters and sea gods on a sheet for his very good friend Antonio Segni. He started a picture in oil in which there is a head of the Medusa with the hair on her head of weaving serpents, the strangest invention that it is possible to imagine. [370] But it remained incomplete. And this is among the marvellous things of the Grand Duke Francesco. Another is a head of an angel that raises one arm in the air which, coming forward, is foreshortened from the shoulder to the elbow, and puts its other hand to its breast. He also began a panel of the narrative of the Magi where there are some very beautiful heads, but he did not finish it, and this was in the house of Amerigo Benci.

'Then [Leonardo] went to Milan in the service of Duke Lodovico Sforza, for whom he painted an altar panel in which there is a *Nativity* that the Duke sent as a gift to the Emperor. He also did a *Last Supper* for the Dominican Brothers of Santa Maria delle Grazie in Milan, a very rare and marvellous thing. And he gave so much grace and majesty to the heads of the Apostles that he left that of Christ incomplete, not believing that he would to be able to give it that celestial divinity that is required of the image of Christ. In the same room where the *Last Supper* is, he portrayed Duke Lodovico from life with Massimiliano, his son, and the Duchess Beatrice with Francesco, his other son, both of whom then became dukes of Milan.

'Then, returning to Florence, [Leonardo] did a *St Ann with Christ and the Glorious Virgin* with other saints in a cartoon that would have been used for the high altar of the Annunziata. All the people of Florence flocked to see this cartoon as a miraculous thing, and then it was sent to France to King Francis. As was also the portrait, also by the hand of Leonardo, of Madonna Lisa, wife of Francesco del [371] Giocondo. She was a very beautiful woman, and the portrait was such that it is not possible for art to make more progress. He also portrayed Ginevra d' Amerigo Benci, in that time a young girl of famous beauty. Having to paint the Sala del Consiglio [or Cinquecento] in Florence, he began a cartoon, drawing on it the narrative of Niccolò Piccinino, captain of Duke Filippo of Milan. In this he made a knot of horsemen fighting over a standard, something truly of all perfection, and no one ever made horses more beautiful than he. He painted an Our Lady with Her Child in Her arms in a little picture, and in another little painting he portrayed a little boy who is marvellously beautiful. Not long ago these paintings were still in the house of the Turini in Pescia and perhaps are there still. Cammillo degli Albizi, a gentleman of the grand duke, has a very beautiful little painting, which he holds very dear as a rare thing, in which there is the head of *St John the Baptist*.

'Finally, Leonardo took himself to France, where he was very well regarded and cherished by the king. And there, already old and having been sick for many months, being one day visited by the king, he raised himself in bed out of respect and to tell him his ills when a paroxysm came upon him. Therefore, the king, with a presentiment, taking [Leonardo's] head, to encourage and help him, [Leonardo], aware of his favour, expired in his arms at the age of seventy-five years.

'Leonardo was of very great talent and succeeded in all the things that he put himself to do. He did a book on the anatomy of horses and one on the anatomy of men [372] and wrote some very beautiful precepts concerning the art of painting. These writings, as far as I know, have not yet been seen in print.[51] In conclusion, Leonardo deserves by his excellence his immortal fame. Therefore, moved by his great merit,

Vincenzio di Buonaccorso Pitti, a young student and very beautiful talent, has done this epitaph about him.

Vinci overcame nature, and Time and Death,
With those works, with this fame;
And if with both made envious and sad
The first Painter. Here are his bones in death.

All greatly commended Pitti's verse and concluded it was of lively spirit, ornate of belles-lettres, and of praiseworthy practice. But then, when the praise of him was completed, Vecchietti resumed his discussion, saying:

Giorgione of Castelfranco

'At the same time that Florence was gaining fame through the works of Leonardo, Venice, equally, made its name resonate through the excellence of Giorgione from Castelfranco sul Trevigiano.[52] He was raised in Venice and so attended to design that he passed Giovanni and Gentile Bellini in painting and gave a certain liveliness to his figures that made them seem alive. The Very Reverend Grimani, Patriarch of Aquileia, has three very beautiful heads of his hand in oil that show the excellence of Giorgione. One is of himself as David. Another is a portrait from life holding a red birretta in his hand. And the other is of a boy with fleecy hair, [373] as beautiful as it is possible to do. He portrayed Giovanni Borgherini, and the master who was teaching him, in a picture when [Borgherini] was a young man in Venice. And this picture is in Florence, belonging to the son of that Giovanni, as there is also in the house of Giulio de' Nobili a very lively and spirited head of a captain in armour. He did many other portraits, all very beautiful, that are scattered throughout Italy in the hands of many people. It delighted him greatly to paint in fresco and, among other things, he painted a whole facade of the Cà Soranzo on the Piazza San Paolo in Venice. On this, in addition to many pictures and narratives, a picture is seen done in oil on plaster that has held up to the water and the wind and is preserved up until today. And he also painted the figures in fresco that are at the Rialto [Fondaco dei Tedeschi], where heads and figures are seen very well done, but he only did those narratives that he wanted to do.[53] He did Christ carrying the Cross and a Jew pulling him along in a picture that was then placed in the Church of San Rocco, and today they say it does miracles.[54]

'He disagreed with those who said that sculpture has greater nobility than painting, since it shows different views of a single figure. [Giorgione] proposed that from a single figure in painting he would reveal the front, the rear, and the two profiles from the sides to only one glance, without going around it as is the practice to do with statues. He then painted a nude man whose back was turned. And on the ground there was a pool of [374] very clear water in which he did the reflection of his front part. On one side there was a burnished breastplate that he had taken off, and his profile on the left was seen in the reflection of that armour. And, on the other side there was a mirror that showed the other side, a thing of very beautiful judgment and caprice that was greatly praised and admired.[55] He did many other things that I skip for brevity. And perhaps he would have done many more, and increased his praise, if death had not taken him from the world in his thirty-fourth year, to the endless sadness of whoever knew him.'

Antonio da Correggio

'Before I turn to discuss the Florentine painters, I do not want to avoid saying something about Antonio Correggio.[56] He was a very singular painter and excellent and marvellous in colour. The greater part of his works are in Parma such as the many very beautiful figures with marvellous poses done in fresco in the great tribune in the cathedral. And also two large pictures in oil, in one of which is the dead Christ, which was highly commended. And he painted in fresco in the tribune of San Giovanni in the same city an *Our Lady Ascending to Heaven* among many angels and other saints. This has such beautiful movement of the drapery, and the figures with such a beautiful air and so charming, that it is not possible for art to desire anything better. He painted an *Annunciation* in fresco, in the church of the Observant Brothers of St Francis. When they took down the wall where it was, the wall was encircled with timbers reinforced with iron and cut away [375] little by little to save it. And it was re-erected in another, more secure place. In Santo Antonio he did a panel of Our Lady and St Mary Magdalene. Next to her is a little boy who laughs so naturally that whoever looks at him is moved to laughter. And a St Jerome is there coloured in a manner so marvellous that the painters look at it as a surprising thing that it is not possible to paint better. He did an *Our Lady with Her Child* in Her arms in fresco above a gate of that city that makes the wayfarers marvel.

'[Correggio] did two pictures in Mantua for Duke Federigo II to send to the Emperor. In one of these there was a nude *Leda*. And, in the other, there was a *Venus* done with such softness of colour, of shadow, and of flesh that it did not appear to be painted, but true flesh.[57] There is a panel of his hand in Modena in which there is a *Madonna*. And, in the house of the Erculani in Bologna, a Christ appears in the garden to Mary Magdalene, something very beautiful. And, in Reggio [Emilia], there is a panel of the *Nativity of Christ* from whom goes out a splendour that illuminates the shepherds and the other figures who look on Him. And there is a woman there among the others, who puts her hand in front of her eyes, so well expressed that it is a miraculous thing. There is also a choir of angels singing above the hut, so well done that they seem to have just descended from Heaven, rather than to have been made by the hand of a painter. And, in the same city, there is a little picture of Christ, now in the garden, with little figures painted as at night. [376] There the angel illuminates Christ with its splendour, so well done that it is not possible to compare it with anything else. He did many other things, all beautiful, that time does not allow me to speak of. And, at an age of about forty years, leaving immortal fame, because in colour it can be said that he had passed all painters, he passed to the eternal life.'[58]

Fra Bartolomeo

'A Bartolomeo[59] was born in a town called Savignano in the vicinity of Prato. He was taken in by some of his relatives in Florence, who lived by the Porta a San Piergatolini and was called Baccio della Porta for being next to that gate. He learned the art of painting from Cosimo Rosselli. After he left Cosimo, he gave himself to the study of the things of Leonardo da Vinci and, in a brief time, acquired great credit and reputation as much in colour as in drawing. Piero del Publiese at that time had a small marble *Our Lady* in very low relief by the hand of Donatello, a very rare thing. To enclose it he had commissioned a wooden tabernacle with two little doors. He had them painted by Baccio della Porta, who did two little narratives of little figures in the manner of miniatures on the inner side of the doors. One of these was the *Nativity of Christ* and the other the *Circumcision*, of which it was not possible to see a thing more carefully done nor more beautiful. And, for the outside of the little doors, he painted the *Annunciation* to the Glorious Virgin [379] by the angel in oil in chiaroscuro. This work today belongs to Grand Duke Francesco and is among the most esteemed of his excellent things. Baccio began to paint in fresco the chapel in the cemetery of the Hospital of Santa Maria Nuova where the bones of the dead are. There he did a *Last Judgment*, where care and a beautiful manner are seen in the part that he finished. But being given to the spiritual life and caring little for painting, he left it incomplete and attended to the sermons of Fra Girolamo Savonarola, having adopted a strict practice for himself from him.

'But it happened that one day the party contrary to Fra Girolamo arose to seize him and put him in the hands of the law for the sedition that he had done in that city. And the friends of the monk banded themselves together in good number and shut themselves up in San Marco. Among them, because of his affection, was Baccio. Hearing the battle they were having in the convent, killing and injuring some, greatly fearing their actions, he made a vow to take the habit of that order if he lived through that fury. He fully observed this a little later. Fra Girolamo, being arrested and condemned to death, Baccio took himself to Prato and professed as a friar in San Domenico and was given the name of Fra Bartolomeo. And it was four years – although he was constantly requested to paint something – that he never wanted to take the brushes in his hand.

'Bernardo del Bianco had commissioned a chapel in the Badia [380] of richly carved stone with glazed terra cotta figures in the round in some niches and with friezes full of cherubs with very beautiful decorations. Finally, being in Florence, moved by the entreaties of [Bianco], [Fra Bartolomeo] painted the panel of this chapel. In it there is a St Bernard writing, looking up to see the Queen of Heaven with Her Child in Her arms brought by many angels, a work worthy of great consideration. And above that he also did the arch that is seen there in fresco. Two very beautiful panels are by his hand in San Marco. In one, with good drawing and three-dimensionality, are some angels flying in the air holding open a canopy below which is an Our Lady surrounded by many figures. And Christ as a child marries St Catherine. And among the principal figures in front are St George in armour with a standard in his hand, St Bartholomew standing, and two little boys with very beautiful poses and brilliant colour playing instruments, one the lute and the other the lyre. In the other panel, which is opposite to it, there is a Virgin surrounded by many saints. And in the same church he painted that *St Mark the Evangelist* in a panel that was put up on the wall where the door of the choir is. [He painted] this figure five braccia high, to show that he knew how to work on a large scale. This is a work that for its excellence and for its great drawing deserves every praise. And above an arch of the guesthouse of the convent he did a *Christ with Cleopas and Luke* in fresco. And because he was said by some to not know how to do nudes, he did *St Sebastian* nude in colour. In this picture [381] the appearance of the flesh and the sweet air of the face corresponded to the beauty of this person. And it is said that when this figure was unveiled in the church, the brothers found women in Confession who had sinned in gazing at the loveliness and lascivious manner of that figure. For this reason it was removed from the church and placed in the chapter house, from where it was taken down and sent to the king of France. The panel that is under the organ in the Annunziata is by his hand.

'And in San Martino in Lucca there is another [panel] in which there is an *Our Lady* with a little angel at Her feet playing the lute and other saints. Equally, in San Romano there are two pictures of his on canvas. In one is the *Madonna of Mercy* with some angels holding her mantle. And the people are shown in different poses in appropriate scale, looking at Christ on high sending thunderbolts down at the people. Here excellence is recognized in the invention, in the drawing, and in the colour, and this is among the beautiful works that he did. Christ and St Catherine the Martyr are in the other one, together with St Catherine of Siena, which is a very beautiful figure. His own portrait is seen in a panel, drawn by his hand, in the Chapel of Ottaviano de' Medici in San Lorenzo in Florence that he could not complete as he had drawn it. [Fra Bartolomeo] did many pictures for many gentlemen, among which is one of a very beautiful *Our Lady* in the room of Lodovico Capponi. And a large picture is in the house of Antonio Salviati in which there is the Glorious Virgin, showing very great emotion in Her face, adoring Her Child. [382] And the Child is done with great care. Beside Him is a seated St Joseph putting his hands on his knees and foreshortened in depth, a very beautiful figure. And truly this painting gave him a great reputation as, in having it done, Salviati recognized its great value.

'But if I wanted to recount all of [Fra Bartolomeo's] works the other painters would wait in vain to be discussed. Therefore, I will not say more of him than that, at forty-eight years of age, leaving his body – which was given honourable burial in San Marco – to the earth, his soul was returned to Heaven. Sig. Antonmaria Bardi di Vernio, a young man of very beautiful talent, to whom the Muses are friendly, has done this epitaph about him.

Nature astonished, to her who lived down here
The glory of his art going before her;
And this the Brother was, who set in earth
His body, and wrote his name among the stars. ...[60]

Raphael of Urbino

'Now it should be necessary to allot time to be able to discourse at length, since it suits me to speak of the most excellent Raphael Sanzio of Urbino.[61] But since long discussions are not allowed, I will treat [only] part of his things [and] briefly. Raphael was born in Urbino at three at night on Good Friday the eighty-third year after 1400 to a Giovanni de' Santi, a painter of no great name. And reaching the age to be able to draw, he was taught to draw by his father. And, seeing that he was succeeding in this manner, that he knew how to surpass [his father], and that if he was going to become a capable man in this calling he needed a better master than [his father], [386] [his father] put him with Pietro Perugino. In a brief time, he so imitated [Perugino's] manner, that the things that [Raphael] did could not be distinguished from those of his master. But then he left Pietro, proceeding little by little to improve his style until it became the height of excellence and perfection of the art.

'Three styles are seen in his work. Of the first, very similar to that of his master but rather improved, is a not very large panel of the *Marriage of the Madonna* in San Francesco in Città di Castello and two pictures in Florence in the house of the Taddei. He did these for them to more than thank them for their hospitality. They had taken him in, the first time he came to Florence.

'Of the second style is a little painting of a Christ praying in the garden, in the Hermitage of the Camaldoli, in the room of the principal of that place, so very finished that it looks like a miniature. A panel of *Our Lady and Some Saints* is in the Chapel of the Ansidei in the Church of the Servi in Perugia. There is a Christ in Glory, God the Father with some angels, and some seated saints painted in fresco in San Severo, a little monastery of the Order of Camaldoli, and his name is seen written there. A panel in which there is the Glorious Virgin with Christ on Her lap, St Peter, St Paul, St Cecilia, and St Catherine is in the Church of the Sisters of St Anthony of Padua. These saints have the most beautiful and the sweetest air of face and the most varied hairstyles that [387] it would be possible to see. And above this panel is a very beautiful

God the Father in a half-tondo. And on the predella of the altar are three narratives of little figures, works certainly admirable and devout.

'Returning to Florence the second time, he did two portraits in this manner for Agnol Doni that can be seen in the Casa Doni on the Corso de' Tintori, one of him and the other of his wife. And he painted Our Lady, in a picture for Domenico Canigiani, with Jesus playing with a young St John, who St Elizabeth has in her arms. St Joseph gazes at them, supporting himself with both hands on a staff. This marvellous work is found today belonging to the heirs of this Domenico, who hold it in that respect that is appropriate for such a rare gem. Then, going to Perugia, he did a dead Christ being carried to burial in a panel for Madonna Atalanta Baglioni in the Church of San Francesco. And there Our Lady is seen in a swoon and the faces of all the figures weeping with great emotion and particularly that of St John. This moves to pity whoever sees it. And, in sum, this work, for the air of the figures, for the beauty of drapery, for the charm of the colour, and for an extreme goodness that it has in all its parts, is a very rare and marvellous thing.

'Finishing this work, [Raphael] returned to Florence, where he was commissioned by the Dei to do the panel that was going to the chapel of the high altar of Santo Spirito. And he began it and brought the model to a very good conclusion. And [388] at the same time he did a picture that was later sent to Siena that, with the departure of Raphael, remained with Ridolfo Ghirlandaio. He completed a blue drapery that it lacked. And the unfinished panel of the Dei was then put by Messer Baldassarre [Turini] of Pescia in the pieve of his country, since Raphael had left it unfinished, being called to Rome by Julius II. There, in the Camera della Segnatura, he painted a narrative where the theologians reconcile philosophy and astrology with theology. There all the savants of the world are portrayed debating in various ways and, to the side, in the portrait of Zoroaster, he painted himself, portrayed in a mirror. Many gods are put in their appropriate places there, the Virtues and many saints and Mount Parnassus with the muses and other beautiful inventions. The astrologers, poets, philosophers, and theologians are arranged with very great grace. It would take too long here if I wanted to discuss the excellence of this work piece by piece, because it is endless. And it is enough to know that it is by Raphael of Urbino and that the Pope, seeing it, had all the narratives of the ancient and modern masters pulled down. And he wanted [Raphael] alone to have the credit for all the work that [Raphael] had done or would do in such works.[62]

'[Raphael] then portrayed *Pope Julius* in a picture in oil so alive that it made the portrayed afraid to look at it. Today, this is in Santa Maria del Popolo with a very beautiful picture done by him at the same time of the *Nativity*. There the Virgin covers the Child with a veil [389] that is of the greatest beauty, and the face of the Madonna, besides being very graceful, shows joy and pity together. There also is St Joseph, contemplating the King and Queen of Heaven with admiration, and both of these pictures are shown on solemn feast days.

'All of the things that will be discussed from here forward are of the third manner that, it is said, comes from his having been taken to see the paintings of the [Sistine] Chapel of Michelangelo. [Raphael] first painted a *Galatea* on a chariot drawn over the sea by two dolphins with tritons and other marine gods and the narrative of *Psyche and Cupid* in a very beautiful manner in a loggia for Agostino Chigi, a very rich merchant, for his palace in Trastevere. Therefore, this Agostino had him do a chapel in Saint Maria della Pace, which he did in fresco in his new manner, much more grand and more beautiful than his other. And he painted some prophets and sibyls there of the greatest beauty, and very great lifelikeness is seen in the women and children that are there. In sum, this work was held of as great beauty as any he had done, very beautiful, and it gave to him a great name and reputation in life and after death. He then painted the panel of the high altar in [Santa Maria in] Aracoeli, in which he did an *Our Lady* in the air with a very beautiful landscape and some saints, which it is never possible to praise enough.

'Then, continuing to paint the rooms of the palace of the Pope, [Raphael] did a narrative there of the miracle of the sacramental corporal [390] of Orvieto or, as some call it, of Bolsena. And, on the other side, he portrayed Pope Julius hearing mass with many others, where the Cardinal San Giorgio is portrayed. And opposite this narrative he painted where St Peter, in the hands of Herod, is guarded in prison by men at arms. Very great art is seen in the view that he has done there and in the reflection of the light of a nearby torch that a figure has in his hand. This falls on the armour of those that are around him. And the light of the Moon is shown where that does not reach so that the smoke of the candelabrum, the radiance of an angel that is nearby, the dark of the night, and the light of the Moon appear a natural and not a painted thing. And in painting that imitates the night, never was anything seen more real or better done than that. Other narratives are in this room, such as that of Pope Julius sending Avarice away from the Church. Heliodorus who, at the command of Antioch, tried to despoil the temple of all the savings of the widows and wards, is thrown down and bitterly struck. But it would be much too long if I wanted to recount everything. I will only say that Pope Julius having died, then Leo X being named, he wanted such work to be continued. [Raphael] painted, on the other wall, the arrival of Attila at Rome and Pope Leo III [I], who put him to flight with only a benediction, meeting him at the foot of Monte Mario. Rafael has St Peter and St Paul in the air in this narrative, [391] coming to defend the Church with swords in hand. This was his invention, because the narrative does not say this, and this is the kind of licence that the painters are used to taking to themselves.[63]

'At the same time [Raphael] painted a panel in which there is Our Lady, St Jerome dressed as a cardinal, and the Angel Raphael accompanying Tobias. This was put up in the chapel where the Crucifix is that spoke to St Thomas of Aquinas in the Church of San Domenico in Naples. One of his panels is in the chapel where the body of the Blessed Elena dall' Olio is, in the Church of San Giovanni in Monte in Bologna. There St Cecilia is seen, entranced by the sound from a choir of angels in Heaven, wholly absorbed in the angelic harmony. And, on the ground, there are many musical instruments that do not seem to be painted but real, and other saints in all perfection that appear to be truly alive. Therefore, many verses have been done about this painting. He did a small painting of little figures in Bologna for Count Vincenzio Ercolani, in which there is a Christ in Heaven with the Four Evangelists as the Prophet Ezekiel describes them. And he sent a picture to the Counts of Canossa in Verona, in which there is a *Nativity of Our Lord* with a highly praised daybreak.

'And for Bindo Altoviti he did his portrait when he was young, which is held to be very beautiful. And equally he made him a picture of *Our Lady* that he sent to Florence and today is found in the chapel of the new apartments in the palace of Grand Duke Francesco. There a very old St Anne is painted [292] seated, handing to Our Lady Her Child, of such beauty in His nudity and in His face that His laugh cheers whoever looks on it. And the Virgin could not be more modest nor more beautiful. There is a young nude St John sitting there and another very beautiful saint, and architecture in the background, where he has made a window covered with linen, that illuminates the room that is behind the figures.

'He did another picture in which he portrayed a large-scale Pope Leo, Cardinal Giulio de' Medici, and Cardinal de' Rossi. In this, the figures do not appear imitated on a plane but in three dimensions in the round, with other marvellous considerations, and this picture is today in the collection of Grand Duke Francesco. He also painted Duke Lorenzo and Duke Giuliano de' Medici. These portraits are in Florence belonging to the heirs of Ottaviano de' Medici. And a very beautiful portrait of a woman, greatly beloved by him up to his death, is found belonging to the brothers Matteo and Giovambatista Botti, very well-bred and virtuous young men and children of another Giovambatista.

'Then Raphael did a panel of a *Christ Carrying the Cross*, in which there are the Marys weeping and St Veronica holding out her arms with very great kindness to hand him the cloth. And there are many armed men there on horseback and on foot in varied and very beautiful poses, and it is truly a rare and marvellous thing. And this panel was taken to Palermo in Sicily and put up in the Church of Santa Maria [393] dell Spasmo of the Brothers of Monteoliveto.

'Meanwhile [Raphael] did not, as a result of this, omit working on the rooms of the Pope. Thus, a little later, he unveiled the room of the Borgia Tower, in which he had done a narrative on each wall, two above the windows and two others on the unbroken walls. One sees the fire in the old Borgo in the first where, they not being able to extinguish the fire, St Leo IV puts it out completely with a benediction from the loggia of the [Vatican] Palace. The same St Leo is in the second where the port of Ostia is depicted, occupied by an army of Turks who had come to take him prisoner. In the third is when Pope Leo X consecrates the Most Christian King Francis I of France. And the crowning of that king is seen in the fourth, in which the Pope and King Francis are portrayed from life, one in armour and the other pontifically dressed, in addition to many cardinals, bishops, chamberlains, and squires, all portrayed from life.

'[Raphael] then did the panel for the high altar for the Black Fathers of San Sisto in Piacenza, painting Our Lady there with St Sisto and St Barbara, a truly very rare and singular work. He also did many pictures for France and for its king, particularly a *St Michael* fighting with the Devil, something held marvellous. He began the room where the victories of Constantine are. And he did many cartoons, coloured by his hand, for making gold and silk Arras tapestries that were made in Flanders and then brought to Rome. And they are seen yet [294] today in the [Sistine] Chapel of the Pope. He painted a young St John for Cardinal Colonna on a very beautiful canvas that today is in the hands of Francesco Benitendi in Florence.

'He did a panel of the *Transfiguration of Christ* for Giulio Cardinal de' Medici to send to France, which, working unceasingly, he himself brought to the highest perfection. There a possessed young man is seen led to Christ so that, coming down from the mountain, He would free him. Very great care is seen in this work and faces, which aside from their extraordinary beauty are novel, varied, and beautiful. And it is the common judgment of craftsmen that this work, among the many that he did, is the most celebrated and the best. And it seemed that Raphael wanted to show all of his virtue in this as the last thing that he would do since, having finished it, death arriving for him, he no longer touched the brushes. This panel was then set up in San Pietro in Montorio in Rome.

'He made many other pictures for many people that for brevity I leave behind. I will not extend myself more in advancing his praises since his name alone manifests his virtues. He died on the same day that he was born, that is on Good Friday, having lived thirty-seven years. He was buried in Santa Maria Rotonda, where he had previously ordered an ancient tabernacle restored with new masonry and an altar made with a statue of *Our Lady* in marble. Many epitaphs were done about him but, leaving aside all the others because they are known, [395] I will only come to recite one, recently done about him by Sig. Antonmaria Bardi di Vernio, which is this:

If Phoebus unlocks the ray, or Jupiter strikes down
The clouds, Astraios wheels, or Mars quivers
You will see the Urbinate paint on linen or on paper,
Also, that these and those breathe and move.

Domenico Puligo

'Domenico Puligo[64] of Florence would have his beginnings from Ridolfo Ghirlandaio and was a great friend of Andrea del Sarto. And it gratified [Domenico] to show [Andrea] his things to correct [Domenico's] errors. Painters are not accustomed to do this today, with little praise to them. They suppose each one to be better than the other. But returning to Puligo, he painted his things with softness and not much colour, giving them grace and three-dimensionality with a certain misty veil. Therefore, he was greatly esteemed while he lived. He wanted to do paintings more than anything else. He did a very beautiful picture for Agnolo della Stufa that was put up in his Badia of Capalona in the countryside of Arezzo. He painted another picture of *Our Lady* for Messer Agnol Niccolini, Cardinal and Archbishop of Pisa, which is today in the possession of his son Giovanni. He did another similar to it, which Filippo dell' Antella has. In another, about three braccia high, he painted a full-length Our Lady with Her Child between Her knees, a young St John, and another head. Filippo Spini has this work today, which is among the good ones that he did. [396] He did many very beautiful portraits from life and among the others was that of Barbera of Florence, a famous courtesan in that time and beloved by many, not so much for her beauty, but because she sang music excellently. Giovambatista Deti has that portrait today and to satisfy his wife, who has it in their room, he promoted [Barbera] to her as St Lucy, because she has a piece of music in her hand.

'[Domenico] was celebrated for the best of his works, a large picture where he did an Our Lady with some angels and cherubs and a St Bernard, writing, and I believe this belongs to the Giocondi. Many portraits from life and other pictures of his hand are in the house of Giulio Scali by the Porta a Pinti. In the great tribune in the Church of the Servi in Florence he did a St Francis receiving the stigmata for Francesco del Giocondo in fresco on a panel. This work is very sweet in colouring and done with softness and care. And around the tabernacle of the sacrament in the Church of Cestello he painted two angels in fresco, and on the panel of a chapel in the same church he did the Madonna with Her Child in Her arms, St John the Baptist, St Bernard, and other saints. And for the Badia of Settimo, outside of Florence, he painted in the cloister in fresco the visions of Count Ugo, who established this abbey. The tabernacle of St Catherine is of his hand that is on the corner of the Via Mozza in which there is the Glorious Virgin with Her Child in Her arms [397] marrying that saint. In a confraternity [Santa Trinità] in the Castello of Anghiari he did a *Deposition from the Cross* that it is possible to enumerate among his better works. So is a very beautiful picture of an Our Lady seated with the Child on Her lap and a young St John seated and a St Joseph in a very soft manner, and the figures all done with very great care, that is found today in the house of Messer Francesco Borghini, Auditore of His Most Serene Highness.[65] But it would be much too long if I wanted to recount all the pictures and all the portraits that Domenico did. He was very valued in managing the colours with a good and unified manner. And he died of plague at fifty-two years in the year 1527.'

Andrea Ferrucci

'I will not omit saying something about Andrea di Piero Ferrucci[66] of Fiesole, who received the first principles of sculpture from Francesco Ferrucci. Although, in the beginning he did not learn anything other than carving foliage, nevertheless, he then had little by little so much experience that it did not take long [*sic*] before he was given to make figures. In these, although great design is not seen, there is recognized a certain natural skill and judgment that is pleasing. He was taken to work in Imola, where he did a chapel of grey stone in the Innocenti of that city that was much praised. He did many things in the Castello di San Martino in Naples and in other places of the city. He did the marble chapel where the baptistery is in the Church of Santo Jacopo in Pistoia, and he made the basin for the font with great care. And on the wall of the chapel he did [398] two life-size figures in half-relief in a beautiful manner, that is, *St John Baptizing Christ*.

'He did the marble panel erected between the two stairs that ascend to the elevated choir in the Church of the Vescovado in Fiesole [Duomo]. In this, three figures are seen in the round and some narratives in low relief. And he did the little marble panel that is built into the wall in the middle of the church in San Girlamo in Fiesole. He then carved the marble apostle, which we discussed yesterday, that is in Santa Maria del Fiore and the head of Marsilio Ficino, set above his tomb, which is very beautiful and appears just like him.[67] He made a marble fountain that was sent to the king of Hungary and a tomb that was likewise taken to Strigonia, a city of Hungary, on which there was an Our Lady with other figures. There are two marble angels in the round from his hand at Volterra. But this is enough for him who died in the year 1522 and was buried by the Confraternity of the Scalzo in the Church of the Servi.'[68]

Benedetto da Rovezzano

'Benedetto of Rovezzano,[69] a town three miles from Florence, was in his time a very famous sculptor. The marble tomb in the Carmine in Florence of Pier Soderini, who was Gonfaloniere, is of his hand, done as is seen with great care, and also the marble tomb of Oddo Altoviti in Santo Apostolo with a finely worked ornament of foliage. In competition with Jacopo Sansovino and Baccio Bandinelli he did the marble *St John the Apostle* that is in Santa Maria del Fiore.

'Then, in the year 1515, the heads of the Vallombrosian Order wanted to transfer the body of St Giovangualberto from Passignano to the Church of Santa Trinità in Florence. They had Benedetto do the design and then put his hand to the chapel and tomb, together with a very large number of marble figures in the round and narratives in bas-relief of the life of St Giovangualberto. And he worked together with many other carvers in the house of the Guarlondo, a place near San Salvi outside the Porta alla Croce. There the general of that order, who had him do the work, lived almost continuously. And Benedetto did this chapel and tomb in such a manner that it would surprise whoever saw it. But the government of the convent having changed – whatever the reason – that work remained incomplete [406] until 1530, at which time there was war around Florence. There were so many of these works broken and spoiled by the soldiers and so ruined that what remained that was not stolen was then sold by the monks for a very small price. Therefore, one can clearly understand that not only men and cities but public and private marbles are subject to fortune.

'The Chapel of St Stephen of the Pandolfini family in the Badia of Florence is also of the hand of Benedetto. Finally, he went to England in the service of that king, where he did many works of marble and bronze and particularly his tomb. And then, returning rich to Florence, within a short time he lost his eyesight and after not many years he gave an end to his days.'[70]

Raffaello da Montelupo

'Baccio [da Montelupo] left a son named Raffaello da Montelupo,[71] who not only equalled his father in sculpture but surpassed him by far. He himself was called by Antonio da Sangallo [the Younger] to Loreto, together with other sculptors, to finish the decoration of that chamber according to the directions left by Andrea Sansovino. There Raffaello completed all the *Wedding of Our Lady* started by Andrea. And he brought it to perfection with a very good manner, partly from [Andrea's] models and partly from his own inventions. The very beautiful figure of *St Damian* that is in the [new] sacristy of San Lorenzo in Florence is by his hand.[72] Also his are the two beautiful escutcheons in stone with figures, one for Emperor Charles V and the other for Duke Alessandro de' Medici, put on the bastion of the Fortezza da Basso of Florence. He did two [three] marble figures five braccia tall for the tomb of Pope Julius II in San Piero in Vincoli in Rome. He made fourteen statues of clay and stucco on the Sant' Agnolo Bridge for the entrance of Emperor Charles V into Rome. These were held the best that were done for that display, and he did these with such promptness that there was time to come to Florence, where the Emperor was also expected. [408] In the space of only five days he did two rivers of clay on the Santa Trinità Bridge, each nine braccia high, the *Rhine* for Germany and the *Danube* for Hungary. Then he worked in Orvieto in the chapel where Mosca, an excellent sculptor, had previously done many beautiful ornaments, and there he did the narrative of the Magi in marble in half-relief.

'Then going to Rome in the service of Tiberio Crispo, Castellan of Sant' Agnolo, he was made architect of that great work. There he beautifully organized many rooms and did a marble statue five braccia tall which is that *Angel of the Castle* from which the standard flies that is on top of the square tower in the centre. He also did the effigy of *Pope Leo* that is on his tomb in the Minerva in Rome but this was not greatly praised because he turned the work over to his workers and did little there himself. And there are three marble figures in half-relief of his hand in [Santa Maria della] Consolazione, and in Pescia he did the tomb for Messer Baldassarre Turini of that place. He did many very praised wooden Crucifixes, of which the nuns of Santa Appollonia in Florence have a very beautiful example and another small one is found belonging to Pietro Berti of Florence. [Berti] greatly delights in and is well informed concerning painting and sculpture and, therefore, has put together many drawings by worthy men of the art and has a very great knowledge of ancient medals.

'But returning to Raffaello, in Orvieto, where he was many years, he limited himself finally to caring for [409] the structure of Santa Maria. And he found a new way of finishing chapels – to make them of marble seeming to be too expensive and too wasteful of time – arranging that they be decorated with stucco. And he made the drawings for them as he also made a very beautiful drawing for the ciborium for the sacrament and for a Corinthian temple outside of Orvieto. And in Santa Maria he carved a *St Peter* in marble with the intention of continuing to make all twelve of the Apostles. But finding himself greatly afflicted by the stone, he resolved to have it removed in spite of being sixty-six years of age. But he lost his life in that treatment and was buried with great honour in Santa Maria above the tomb of Mosca.'[73]

Andrea del Sarto

'Now it is appropriate for me to speak of the very excellent Andrea del Sarto.[74] And I am fortunate that the time allows me to say only a little about him because for this reason I will be partly excused. Because, if in every way I said enough about him, I would never be able to say what is necessary.[75] Andrea was born the year of Christ 1478 of a father who always practised the art of the tailor [*sarto*]; therefore, he always took his last name from him. He was put with a goldsmith at seven years of age, where he more enthusiastically attended [415] to drawing than to work with the chisel. This becoming known to Gian Barile, a rough painter of that time, he was put to learn from him. And because [Gian] saw after some time how much Andrea was inclined to painting and hoping he would make a good result in it, he put him to be with Piero di Cosimo. [Piero] was then among the better painters in Florence. Apprenticed to him [Andrea] made great advances in the art.

'But then, annoyed by the strange nature of his master, [Andrea] opened a shop together with Franciabigio by the Piazza del Grano, and they did many works together. But the first painting that Andrea did by himself was for the Confraternity of the Scalzo, of terretta in fresco, containing the narrative of *St John Baptizing Christ*, which gave him much fame. After this he was commissioned to do a panel of Christ when he appeared to the Magdalene in the form of a gardener. This work is very laudable and today is found in the church of the brothers of San Gallo in San Jacopo fra Fosi.

'[Andrea] then did three narratives of St Philip [Benizzi] in the atrium of the Annunziata. In the first, this saint clothes the naked. In the second, a thunderbolt comes from the sky and strikes a tree while he is scolding some gamblers who laugh at St Philip and blaspheme God. Very beautiful and appropriate poses are seen there of the dead, the frightened, the amazed, and of a horse who gets loose and flees from fear. And in the third St Philip removes a spell from a woman, with all the [417] things that could happen about such a thing. And after these three narratives were unveiled, hearing them greatly praised, taking heart, he proceeded to do two others. In one of these, St Philip is dead, mourned by his monks, and a dead child is recuscitated on touching the bier of St Philip. In the other, he shows the monks putting the robes of [the Order of] St Philip over the heads of some little boys. And there he portrays the sculptor Andrea della Robbia as an old man dressed in red, stooped over with a mallet in his hand.

'For the Monks of Vallombrosa [Andrea] painted the arch of a vault in their refectory in the Monastery of San Salvi outside the Porta alla Croce. In this he did, in four tondi, *St Benedict, St Giovangualberto*, the *Bishop St Salvi*, and *St Bernard degli Uberti* of Florence, [Vallombrosian] monk and cardinal. And in the middle, he did a tondo in which there are three faces that are one and the same for the *Trinity*, and this work in fresco was very well done. In a minute scale he then did that *Annunciation* in fresco that is on the path from Orsanmichele [to the Mercato Nuovo]. This was not among his other highly praised things. He did many pictures for many citizens at this time that I will not mention because from time to time they have gone to other people and it would be a very long thing to enumerate [them].

'Then he did the other two narratives in the courtyard of the Annunziata in fresco. One is of the *Birth of Our Lady* with figures very well arranged in a room in the various poses as are needed in such circumstances. And above are some cherubs who are in the air throwing [418] flowers. The other is of the *Magi from the East*, guided by the star. And in this there are three portraits from life. The first is of Jacopo Sansovino looking towards those within [the picture] who are looking at the narrative. The second, leaning on him and making a sign, is of Andrea del Sarto himself, who has an arm foreshortened. And the third is of Aiolle, the musician, with a head in profile behind Sansovino. And there are some little boys there climbing the wall to see the magnificent and the strange animals pass that the three kings brought with them. And these two narratives are such that they can never be praised too much [and] deserve no more than to be more praised and imitated by those who wish to become capable men in painting.

'At the same time [Andrea] did a panel for the Badia of San Godenzo. And he painted the *Annunciation* of the angel to the Glorious Virgin in a panel for the brothers of San Gallo with some heads of angels with a smoky softness, conducted with very great grace and art. He did a picture in which there is the narrative of Joseph, son of Jacob, for Zanobi Girolami, which was held to be a very beautiful painting. He did a little panel in which there is Our Lady, St John the Baptist, and St Ambrose for the men of the Confraternity of Santa Maria della Neve, behind the nuns of Sant' Ambrogio. This was set up on the altar of that confraternity. He painted a picture of a *Virgin Mary* for Giovanni Gaddi, who was then clerk of the chamber. This was held the most beautiful picture that Andrea had done up to then. He did [419] some other pictures at this time that it is not possible to discuss with certainty because they are no longer in the hands of those people for whom he made them.

'There is a panel from [Andrea's] hand in which Our Lady is painted standing on an octagonal base on the corners of which some harpies are seen, in the Church of the Nuns of St Francis in the Via San Francesco. This Virgin holds the Child with Her arm with one hand and a closed book with the other. Looking on are two nude children at Her feet, as decorations. And on the right hand is a very well-studied figure of St Francis, and on the other side, St John the Evangelist in the act of writing his *Revelations* in a very beautiful manner. And there is a transparent cloudy smokiness in this work that appears to move over the buildings and the figures. And truly this painting is miraculous and singular and rare among the things of Andrea.

'[Andrea] then worked in the Confraternity of the Scalzo. And, on entering the door of that confraternity, did a *Charity* and *Justice* and two narratives next to the altar. In one, St John preaches to the multitude. And in the other, being in the water, he baptizes a great number of people where various and beautiful poses are seen. At that time he did the very beautiful portrait of Baccio Bandinelli that today is in the study of Ridolfo, here among his other things. Andrea painted a picture with great art and charming colour of *Our Lady* surrounded by playing little boys for Alessandro Corsini. And for Giovambatista Puccini he did a picture of a [420] *Virgin* to send to France. But [Andrea] succeeded so very beautifully that [Giovambatista] kept it for himself and had him make him another of a dead *Christ Surrounded by Angels* supporting Him. This work was engraved in Rome, although not very well, by Agostino [dei Musi] of Venice and then sent to the king of France.

'Pope Leo X, having to come to Florence at this time, which was the year 1515, a very superb display of arches, statues, colossi, and other beautiful inventions was made. And, among the other things, a facade for Santa Maria del Fiore was constructed of wood, with the architecture by Jacopo Sansovino, and with many narratives painted in chiaroscuro by the hand of Andrea, which were held a marvellous thing. [Andrea] was then sought after to make another picture for the king of France, who had been extremely pleased with the first. And so he did a very beautiful *Our Lady* that was immediately sent off by the merchants, who were paid four times more for it than they paid Andrea.

'He did some panels [*spalliere da cassoni*] for Pierfrancesco Borgherini, in competition with Granacci and Jacopo Pontormo, painting there the narrative of Joseph. These paintings were truly precious gems. And he also did for this Borgherini a picture of *Our Lady,* held to be a very rare thing. The *Head of Christ* that is over the altar of the Annunziata is of his hand, so beautiful that it is held certain to be impossible to make one more alive and more charming. The panel is also his work that was put, where there are others of his, in the Church of San Jacopo fra' Fossi. In this, four standing figures are [421] seen discussing the Trinity: St Augustine, St Peter Martyr, St Francis, and St Lawrence who, as a youth, listens. And St Sebastian is there appearing truly flesh, who, being nude, is shown from the back. The kneeling Magdalene, whose face is the portrait of his wife, is there below with very beautiful drapery. In summary, this panel is marvellous and held the best of the things of Andrea done in oil.

'Then called by King Francis, [Andrea] went to France in the service of His Majesty. There he portrayed the infant Dauphin from life in swaddling clothes and, taking it to the king, he gave him 300 gold scudi. He then did a *Charity* that was held to be a very rare thing and many other pictures that it would be a long thing to discuss. And finally, pressed by his wife by mail, he returned to Florence. There he did four other narratives in the Scalzo. *St John Taken before Herod* is in the first, the supper and *Dance of Salomé* in the second, and the *Beheading of St John* in the third. And *Salomé Presenting the Head* is in the fourth, where there are figures who are astonished, so truly astonished that they astonish others. These figures are the studio of those who want to acquire a name in painting. He then did the tabernacle that is outside the Porta a Pinti, in which there is an Our Lady seated with Her Child in Her arms and a young laughing St John done with very great art. This tabernacle, because of the unbelievable beauty of this painting, was left [422] standing during the siege of Florence in the year 1530 when the Convent of the Ingesuati, which was next to it, was ruined.

'By the hand of Andrea is the panel of the *Assumption of the Virgin* with the Apostles in a little church built to accommodate this panel by Pier Salviati at the Villa Baroncelli a little outside of Florence.[76] The two narratives of the *Vineyard of Christ,* which are at the end of the garden of the Servite Brothers, are also his work. They are done in chiaroscuro in fresco with skill and with marvellous excellence. And in that convent he painted a very beautiful *Pietà* coloured in fresco in a niche at the top of the staircase in the novitiate. And another *Pietà* in a little painting in oil and, at the same time, a *Nativity* are in the room of the general of that order. He did a picture for Zanobi Bracci, in which there is a kneeling Queen of Heaven leaning against a rock. She contemplates Christ, who is lying on some linens looking up at Her smiling. And St John is there making a sign.[77] Behind him is St Joseph resting his head on his hands, which are supported by a rock.

'That narrative where the tribute of all the animals is presented to Caesar in the hall at Poggio a Caiano, villa of the Most Serene Grand Duke Francesco, is of his hand. But whoever wanted to individually discuss the rare things that are there would require a longer time to complete the task than we are now given. [Andrea] then did a very beautiful nude half-figure of a *St John the Baptist* in a picture that I believe is found today belonging to our grand duke. And he painted another [423] similar *St John the Baptist* to send to France, which he then sold to Ottaviano de' Medici. He also did two pictures for him of the *Virgin Mary,* as he also did one for Lorenzo Jacopi and another for Giovanni Dini.

'Then the plague coming to Florence in the year 1523, he took himself to the Mugello with his family. There, for the Nuns of San Piero à Luco of the Order of the Camaldoli, he did a panel in which there is a dead Christ mourned by His Mother, St John the Evangelist, and the Magdelene, figures so alive that they lack only breath. St Peter and St Paul are also there contemplating the dead Saviour of the World. Later, he did the *Visitation* of Our Lady to St Elizabeth for these nuns, which is to the right above the crèche in the church. And he painted a very beautiful *Face of Christ* on canvas, which is today in the monastery of [Santa Maria degli] Angeli in Florence. One of his panels in which there is Our Lady in the air with Her Child in Her arms and four figures below is in Gambassi, a castle between Voltera and Florence. A very beautiful picture of the *Queen of Heaven,* by his hand, is found in the house of Messer Antonio Bracci. He did two other narratives in the Confraternity of the Scalzo. In one of these he painted Zechariah sacrificing and struck dumb by the appearance to him of the angel. And in the other is the *Visitation* of the Madonna.

'Andrea copied the face of Pope Leo from a picture by the hand of Raphael of Urbino. And he made it so similar that the pictures were switched, and it was given to the Duke of Mantua [424] as something by the hand of Raphael. He then portrayed the face of Giulio Cardinal de' Medici, who then became Pope Clement VII, similar to that of Raphael, which was very beautiful. There is a very beautiful panel of his in the Church of the Madonna di Santa Agnesa along the walls of Pisa. This is divided into five pictures where there are some saints, the most beautiful and graceful women that he ever did. But what will I say of the Virgin resting on a sack with Her Child in Her arms and St Joseph beside Her, done in fresco above the side door of the Annunziata that goes out into the cloister? In this Andrea showed his advance over the drawing, the grace, the colour, the lifelikeness, and the three-dimensionality of all the other painters who had painted up to that time. And, in truth, one would never be able to praise it enough.

'The cloister of the Confraternity of the Scalzo lacking only one narrative of being completely finished, Andrea did it, having added grandeur to his manner. And there he painted the *Birth of St John the Baptist* with much better figures and greater three-dimensionality than the others who had worked there before him. One of his panels, in which St John the Baptist, St Giovangualberto, St Michael the Archangel, and Cardinal St Bernard are painted, was put up in the Church of Romitorio beside the cells of Vallombrosa. I saw this to my great pleasure last year, having gone to see that holy and solitary place with Don Salvadore. He was then the general of the Order of the Vallombrosians and today is abbot there, where I received endless [425] courtesies from him. And truly he is a man of great value in administration, well lettered, of praiseworthy manners, and deserving of every dignity and honour.

'But returning to Andrea, another panel is found of his hand in Serazzana, where an Our Lady is seated with Her Child in Her arms and other saints. And there is a half-tondo in the Chapel of Giuliano Scali in the great tribune around the choir in the Annunziata in which there is an *Annunciation*. That marvellous *Last Supper* in San Salvi is his work, which is not only the most beautiful thing that he did but also the most beautiful that could be done. This is facile of manner, observant of design, lively in colour, and has all the parts that belong to good painting. One of his panels is in the Badia of Poppi, in which there is an *Assumption of Our Lady* surrounded by many cherubs and other saints, but not entirely finished because at the death of Andrea it remained incomplete.

'There are some beautiful pictures of his in the house of the heirs of Filippo Salviati. And Baccio here has, among many other things of worthy men that he has put together, a very beautiful little painting in which there is a *Nativity of Christ* of his hand with many little figures. Andrea did a marvellous picture in which there is the narrative of Abraham when he intended to sacrifice his son, with figures in all perfection and a landscape as well done as art can do. This painting was then given to Lord Alfonso Davolos, Marquis of Vasto, which he had taken to the Island of Ischia to some rooms in the company of other very worthy paintings. In another [426] picture, he painted a very beautiful *Charity* with three children that today is found in the house of Bastiano Antinori, a gentleman notable for his virtues and for the reputation of his manners. He did a picture of Our Lady seated on the ground with Her Child in Her lap looking at a young St John supported by St Elizabeth for Ottaviano de' Medici. And another was for Giovanni Borgherini, in which there was the Mother of the Saviour of the World and St John and Christ and the very beautiful face of St Joseph. And he did a narrative of Abraham similar to that above, but smaller, for Paolo da Terrarossa that today is in Naples. Francesco Trosci has a very beautiful picture of his hand in his first manner in which there is the Virgin with Her Child, St John, and St Joseph.[78]

'For the men of the Confraternity of St Sebastian behind the Servi, he did a *St Sebastian* at war that was very beautiful, almost as if to show that it would be the last thing that he would have to do. Soon thereafter he took sick, suspected of the plague, dying at the age of forty-two years, and he was buried with little ceremony in the Church of the Servi. And not long thereafter, his student Domenico Conti had Raffaello da Monte Lupo do a rather ornate tablet of marble with a Latin epitaph constructed by Piero Vettori, who was a young man at that time. And this marble was built into one of the pillars of the church. It was then removed from there by some citizens, wardens of this church, little cognizant of [Andrea's] virtue, saying it had been put there without their permission. [427] But Bernardo Davanzati, a man, as is known by everyone, of great worth in writing and who well understood Andrea's merit has done this epitaph about him.

Dead Andrea, Nature
Says, did you conquer me? And bows her head:
And Painting falls,
Its face veiled, bloodless, and so rests.

Properzia de' Rossi, Sculptress

'It would seem to me to be too great an error, and with respect to women to fall into too great a fault, if I kept silent the virtues of Properzia de' Rossi of Bologna.[79] She, being very rare of talent and very beautiful of form, beside singing and playing instruments that she did better than the other women of her city, gave herself also – being by nature inclined to design – to carving peach pits. On these she did, with very great patience, many narratives so well conducted with graceful little figures that they astonish whoever would see them. On only one pit she once did the whole *Passion of Our Lord,* in which it was almost a miracle to see on such a small thing so great a number of figures and so well composed. But then, taking heart, she put herself to working on marble and portrayed Count Guido de' Peppoli from life, which was held to be a very beautiful head. That artful picture of marble on the facade of San Petronio in Bologna, where there is the narrative of Joseph in Egypt losing his mantle, [428] fleeing from the entreaties and the trap of the enamoured woman, is of her hand. And two marble angels were also done by her on the same facade, carefully worked with very great three-dimensionality. Properzia finally devoted herself to engraving copper printing plates, happily succeeding in everything. The knowledge of the virtue of this rare woman spreading, Pope Clement VII, having crowned the Emperor in Bologna, desirous of seeing things beautiful and ingenious, asked about her. But he found that, to the great sorrow of all the city, she had passed to the other life that same week and that her body reposed in the Hospital of the Dead. Vincentio di Buonaccorso Pitti has done this epitaph about her:

The splendour of two beautiful eyes would increase
From marble to marble, oh new surprise and strange!
Rough marble, delicate hand
Death envied her when she was still alive. ...[80]

Rosso

'Now we will speak of the Florentine painter Rosso.[81] He was not only an excellent painter but a very excellent architect, very beautiful conversationalist, good musician, and learned philosopher. In his youth he drew from the cartoons of Michelangelo. And he was satisfied to be with only few masters, having an individual opinion of his own that conflicted with their styles. He showed this in a tabernacle done in fresco at Marignolle outside the Porta a San Piero Gattolini in which a dead Christ is painted, where that strong and marvellous manner of his is seen that others did not use. Then, being still beardless, he did the arms of the Pucci with two figures above the door of San Sebastiano de'

Servi that were held to be very beautiful. Then, gaining courage, he painted the *Assumption of Our Lady* in the courtyard of the Annunziata. There he did a heaven of all nude angels dancing around the Virgin with very beautiful outlines and a graceful manner. And the poses of the Apostles and their faces are very beautiful, although it seems that their drapery is too agitated.

'He did a panel in which there is a dead Christ for the Lord of Piombino and in Volterra he painted a very beautiful *Deposition from the Cross*. Then he did a panel that is in the Chapel of the Dei in Santo Spirito in Florence, a marvellous work to which it would not be possible to find another to compare to nor to exceed it in three-dimensionality, grace, drawing, poses, and unity of colour.[82] Another altarpiece of his, similar in perfection, representing the *Marriage of the Madonna*, is in San Lorenzo.[83] [435] Here are very well-studied nude figures with all the requirements of anatomy, the women very graceful, the hairstyles new and capricious, and the drapery with very beautiful folds.

'Rosso then going to Rome, he painted a work above the things of Raphael in the Pace. But it was not held to be as great a good thing as his others and, in any case, it was poor compared with the things of Raphael. He did some drawings of the gods, when Saturn turns himself into a horse and when Pluto abducts Proserpina that were engraved and printed. The sack of Rome occurred at this time, where Rosso was made a prisoner of the Germans and very badly treated by them. He fled to Perugia, where he was taken in and clothed by the painter Domenico [Alfani] of Paris. And for this Domenico he made a very beautiful cartoon for a panel of the narrative of the Magi. Then he moved to Borgo [Sansepolcro], where he painted that marvellous panel that is in Santa Croce in which Christ is taken down from the Cross. Then he took himself to Arezzo and was asked to paint a vault of the Madonna delle Lagrime. And he, therefore, did four very beautiful cartoons of narratives from the Old Testament appropriate to the Glorious Virgin and put great study into some nude figures that should have gone in this work, which he did not complete. One notes that, because of the siege which was then around Florence, Florentines were looked on with suspicion in Arezzo. And, not trusting himself there, Rosso left all of his cartoons, taking himself to Borgo Sansepolcro, where he did a panel for those [436] of Città di Castello. In this he showed a multitude and a Christ in the sky adored by four figures. And in this he had Moors, Gypsies, and the strangest things in the world, where the figures are very perfect but the composition very eccentric.

'After this, [Rosso] moved himself to France. There he was very well regarded by King Francis, and he ordered him an allowance of 400 scudi and made him superintendent over all the royal buildings, paintings, and decorations. Therefore, Rosso did many beautiful pictures that were put in the gallery in Fontainebleu. There he had many narratives of the acts of Alexander the Great painted to his designs in fresco, and at the two ends of the gallery, he painted two panels himself in oil. In one is a *Venus and Bacchus* with many vases painted in imitation of gold, silver, crystal, and various very precious stones with so many beautiful inventions as to astonish everyone. And a satyr is there seeming to smile and a little boy riding a bear like a horse that could not be done more naturally nor more beautifully. In the other are *Cupid and Venus* with other figures of a beauty of which it is not possible to speak fully. He then did a hall called the Pavilion, doing very beautiful ornaments there of stucco and figures with little boys, festoons, and various kinds of animals. And in the compartments on the walls in fresco are seated figures representing all the gods and the goddesses of the ancients.

'[Rosso] did many other things for this king that it would be too long to recount. And when Emperor Charles V went to Fontainebleau in France with only twelve men in the year 1540, under the safe conduct of King Francis, [437] Rosso did half of all the decorations that were made to honour so great an emperor. And Francesco Primaticcio did the other half. But those of Rosso were held not only the better but the most beautiful that had ever been seen in any time. He did many pictures and drawings for many lords and a book of anatomy with the intention of having it printed in France. And after his death two cartoons were found among his things. In one there is a *Leda*. And in the other the Tiburtine Sybil, showing to Emperor Octavian the Glorious Virgin with Her Child in Her arms. And in this he did the portraits of the king and the queen and their guard and the people with such a great number of figures and so well done that it is possible to say with truth that this is the most beautiful work that it is possible to see and the best that he had ever done.

'Finally, he found himself favoured by the king and very wealthy from the benefits of fortune. [But], having been robbed of I do not know how many hundreds of scudi, [Rosso] attributed the theft to a Francesco di Pellegrino of Florence, his very close friend and a familiar of his house. [Francesco], being put in prison and tortured severely, was finally discharged from prison as innocent. And, moved by just indignation, it appearing to him that Rosso had unjustly disgraced him, he charged him with the injury of libel. Rosso seeing that he could not help himself and knowing he had done an injury to a friend and stained his own honour, did not want to retract. And pressed in this way, in desperation he took a very powerful poison. [438] This took the life from him in a stroke, to the very great sorrow of the king and of all the craftsmen for having lost so great a man. Messer Baldello Baldelli, called the Lively One [*Il Desto*] in the Academy of the Lively Ones [*Svegliati*], has done this sonnet about him:

To form the beautiful and the perfect,
  More beautiful and perfect than ever done,
  To be able to decorate the world
  Nature looked for her glory:

And searching about in rare
  And divine works, she cared to place
  Great Rosso, and yet incorporating and contemplating him
  She was stopped as by another care;

Then enthusiastically exclaiming: with brush,
  And living colour, Ah by his art
  I find myself defeated: I confess it, and note.

This is the perfect, and this the beautiful;
  Yet since I am also of so much work the part
  I will give him the voice, the emotion.[84]

Franciabigio

'The Florentine painter Franciabigio[85] learned the principles of the art from Mariotto Albertinelli. And then he was the partner of Andrea del Sarto and for a long time they had the same shop. The first works that [440] he did were in San Brancazio, a *St Bernard* done in fresco and a *St Catherine of Siena* on a pilaster in the Chapel of the Rucellai. A picture of his of Our Lady with Her Child in Her arms and St John as a child playing with Him is in San Pier Maggiore. And an *Annunciation* with the angel in flight, where there is a highly praised building in perspective, is by the door to the right entering the church. He did the narrative of the *Visitation* of the Madonna in a shrine in fresco in San Giobbe behind the Servi, and he did the panel of the high altar of this church, portraying himself in the face of St John the Baptist. In the Chapel of St Nicholas in Santo Spirito he painted two angels in oil put on either side of a wooden statue of that saint. And he did the *Annunciation* in two medallions and completed the *Miracles of St Nicholas* in the predella in little figures done with great diligence. But very beautiful is the narrative in fresco of the *Wedding of the Queen of Heaven*, done by him in the courtyard of the Annunziata. There very lively faces are seen, very beautiful poses, and marvellous diligence. However, it is true that, irritated with the brothers because they unveiled this narrative without his permission, he spoiled a part with a mason's hammer, particularly the face of the Madonna. And if not restrained he would have spoiled it all. No matter what prize he was offered, he would never set it to rights; therefore, it is still today a thing spoiled.

'There is a shrine of his hand in which there is a Crucifix with other saints at Rovezzano, outside of Florence's Porta alla Croce. [441] And a *Last Supper* of the Apostles done in fresco is in San Giovannino close to the Porta San Pier Gattolini. And there are two narratives of his done with great care in the Confraternity of the Scalzo. In the first is St John the Baptist taking leave of his father to go to the desert. In the second is the meeting of Christ and St John that occurred in their travels with Joseph and Mary, who are seen to embrace. [Franciabigio] then worked at Poggio à Caino for Duke Lorenzo de' Medici and he did there the narrative where Cicero [Caesar] is carried in triumph by the citizens of Rome with very beautiful views, in which he was highly valued. He painted St Thomas confounding the heretics with his doctrine in a lunette over the door of the library in the Convent of Santa Maria Novella. This work is very well done and of a good manner, and two little boys are holding an escutcheon in the ornament there, done with great care and goodness. He did many pictures, but one among the others is a work truly worthy of great praise in which, in small figures for Giovanmaria Benintendi, David is watching Bathsheba washing in the bath. And one finds there a building in perspective, and under a loggia, he showed a very beautiful regal banquet. Baccio Valori here also has a large picture on canvas in which the entrance of Pope Leo into Florence is painted with many well-arranged figures. But not to be too long I will keep silent of the other things done by him. Ultimately, he died at forty-two years of age, the year of our well-being 1524, and was buried in San Brancazio opposite his house.' [442]

Francesco Mazzola Parmigianino

'Among the excellent painters that Lombardy has had, the most excellent of all has been Francesco Mazzola Parmigianino.[86] He gave a certain liveliness and grace to his figures and a sweet air to his faces that was a marvellous thing and had an individual manner in doing very beautiful landscapes. At sixteen years of age he did *St John Baptizing Christ*, in a panel of his invention that astonished whoever saw it. This was put in the Annunziata where the Observant Brothers are, in Parma. Then, wanting to prove himself by working in fresco, he painted a chapel in San Giovanni Evangelista, the church of the Black Monks of St Benedict. And seeing it turn out well, he was going to do seven more. But in the middle of this [the army of] Pope Leo X being in the field around Parma, Francesco took himself with a cousin of his to Viandana, a place belonging to the Duke of Mantua. There they stayed while that war lasted, and he painted two panels in tempera. St Francis is in one of these receiving the stigmata, and St Clare. This was put up by the Observant Brothers. And the *Wedding of St Catherine* with many figures is in the other that was put up in San Piero. And these works were not those of a beginner, of one learning the art, but rather of an experienced man and a thorough master. Returning to Parma after the war, he did Our Lady with Her Child in Her arms and St Jerome on one side and [443] St Bernardino da Feltro on the other, in a panel in oil, and all these works were done before he was nineteen years of age.

'Coming then to a desire to see Rome, [Parmigianino] painted two pictures. In the largest he did an Our Lady, with Her Child in Her arms handing some fruit from Her lap to an angel. And there is an old man with arms covered with hair. All are done with art and with very great judgment. He painted himself in the other, which was smaller, a ball turned on a lathe divided in half. In this he looks at himself in the mirror with all the things that are seen in a mirror with such lustre, reflections, and lights of the mirror that it was a miraculous thing. And taking himself to Rome, he gave these two pictures to Pope Clement. He, seeing their excellence and the young age of the youth, was completely astonished and he gave him much flattery and many favours. Therefore, Francesco, lured by hope of the Pontiff, painted a very beautiful picture of the *Circumcision* that was held to be a very rare thing for his inventions with light. The figures at the front were illuminated by the radiance of the face of Christ. The figures behind them were lighted by some burning torches carried by other figures going up some steps. And those at the back were illuminated by the brightness of the dawn, which revealed a very beautiful landscape with endless buildings. And he also gave this picture to the Pope, who held it very dear. At the same time he did many other pictures and portraits that I pass by for brevity.

'[Parmigianino] was commissioned by Madonna Maria Bufolini of Città di Castello to do a panel that [444] would have been put in San Salvadore del Lauro. In this Francesco did an Our Lady reading, elevated above the ground, who has the Child between Her legs. There is a sleeping St Jerome. And a St John kneels on the ground on one knee, with [the other] foot lying on the ground foreshortened. He, twisting his torso, motions towards the Christ Child. This unfinished panel was then taken by Giulio Bufolini to their church in Città di Castello. And the reason he did not complete it was the sack of Rome. And Francesco barely avoided losing his life there since he was so intent on working when some Germans entered his house that the noise that they made did not distract him from the work. And they among themselves were so amazed and astonished, seeing him work, that they allowed him to continue. And so, while the very cruel throng of those barbaric people laid waste to the city, stealing and spoiling the sacred and non-sacred things without respect for men or for God, he was provided for and greatly esteemed and defended from every insult by these Germans. However, it is true that he made many drawings for them, which were the payment for his ransom. But then the soldiers changed, Francesco was put in prison, and it was necessary that some money be paid that he had.

'And seeing Rome all ruined and the Pope made prisoner, [Parmigianino] took himself to Bologna. There he had some prints engraved on copper and among the others the *Beheading of St Peter* [sic] *and of St Paul*[87] and a large *Diogenes*. In the Chapel of the Monsignori in San Petronio he painted a *St Roch* [445] showing great emotion of spirit with a very beautiful landscape and a dog that seems alive. He did many pictures for many people at this time. But among the others he painted Our Lady in one, with Christ holding a globe of the map of the world and the Madonna with a very beautiful air. And in an extraordinary way he has dressed Her in a gown that has sleeves of yellowish gauze that almost [look like they were] striped with gold, and her flesh appears very real and her hair could not possibly have been done better. Pope Clement having gone to Bologna at this time, Francesco gave him this picture. It then, I do not know how, came into the hands of

Messer Dionigi Gianni [Dionisio Zani] and it is so much liked by everyone that endless copies are made of it. He also painted *Our Lady, St Margaret, and Other Saints* in a panel for the nuns of St Margaret in Bologna, a work held, as it deserves, in very great veneration. Meanwhile, Emperor Charles V came to Bologna to be crowned by Pope Clement. And Francesco, often going to see him eat but not drawing his portrait [there], did his image in a very large oil painting in which he painted Fame crowning him and a little boy in the form of a tiny Hercules handing him the world. This painting is found today in the collection of the Duke of Mantua.

'Finally, Francesco, taking himself back to Parma, was commissioned to do a rather large vault in fresco in the Church of Santa Maria della Steccata. There, on the arch in front, he did six very beautiful figures, two coloured and four of chiaroscuro. At the same time [446] for the Cav. Baiardo, a gentleman of Parma and his close friend, he painted a picture of Cupid making a bow with his hands. At his feet he did two little seated boys, one taking the other by the arm and laughing, wanting him to touch Cupid with his finger. And [the other boy], not wanting to touch him, cries, showing fear of being burned by the fire of love. This picture is very charming of colour and perfect in every part and has been imitated by many. Then, moving himself to Casal Maggiore, he did a panel in the Church of Santo Stefano in which there is Our Lady in the sky and St John the Baptist and St Stephen below. And after this he painted *Lucretia*, the Roman, in a picture – which was his last painting – that was a divine thing, the best work that left his hands. It is quite true that I have left many things by him behind because the time does not allow me long discussions. In the end he died in Casal Maggiore, 24 August 1540, and was buried as he had directed in the Church of the Servi, called Fontana, a mile from Casal Maggiore.'[88]

Giulio Romano

'Among the many students of Raphael of Urbino, the most excellent of all was Giulio Romano.[89] And thus Raphael was helped by him in his more important things as in the Loggia of the Pope done for Leo X. There is there, by the hand of this Giulio, the creation of Adam and Eve and that of the animals, the ark of Noah, his sacrifice, and the narrative where the daughter of Pharaoh finds Moses in the basket cast onto the river in which there is a marvellous landscape. And also many figures are of his hand in the apartment of the Borgia Tower, and particularly the base done in a bronze colour, the Countess [448] Matilda, King Pipin, Charlemagne, and Godfrey de Bouillon, King of Jerusalem.

'Raphael died leaving his heirs Giulio and Giovanfrancesco, called Il Fattore, with the burden of finishing the works Raphael had started, of which the greatest part they conducted to perfection. Many are the things that Giulio did in painting and in architecture, in which he was greatly valued, but I will briefly make mention of the most excellent of his works of painting, so that I do not trespass the brevity of our purpose. Giulio designed and built a palace below Monte Mario[90] for Giulio, Cardinal de' Medici, who became Pope Clement, in which he painted many paintings worthy of praise, and especially at the head of a loggia, in fresco is a very large *Polyphemus* with many little boys and little satyrs playing around him, a work very well done.

'Then, under Pope Clement, together with other craftsmen, [Giulio] produced the Hall of Constantine begun by Raphael. And there Giulio painted in fresco the narrative where Constantine is addressing his soldiers and the sign of the Cross appears in the sky. And a dwarf who is at the foot of the Emperor putting a sallet on his head is done with much art. And on the largest wall he did the battle where Constantine put Maxentius to rout. There very beautiful and fierce poses, and many portraits from life are seen such that this work deserves greatly to be praised, even if it is a little too much shaded in black. On the other wall he did a *Pope St Sylvester Baptizing Constantine*, where Pope Clement is portrayed from life in the face [449] of St Sylvester. And many other portraits are there, as in the figures that he did under this narrative, finished like bronze. Above the chimney piece on the fourth wall he showed the [old] church of St Peter in Rome in perspective, with the throne of the Pope when he sings the Pontifical Mass with the orders of cardinals and other prelates. In this narrative there are many women kneeling looking at that ceremony and a beggar asking for alms and the mercenaries of the papal guard, very beautiful figures. And there among the others, Giulio himself, Count Baldassare Castiglione, writer of the *Courtier*, and other men of letters are portrayed.

'At this time [Giulio] did a picture of an *Our Lady*, and there he painted a cat so lifelike that this painting was then called *The Picture of the Cat*. And there is a picture by him above an altar in Santa Prassede in Rome, in which there is *Christ Beaten at the Column*. He then painted a panel that was sent to Santo Stefano, a monastery of the monks of Monteoliveto in Genoa, in which St Stephen is stoned. There marvellous poses are seen, and patience is clearly expressed in the saint, and truly this could be called one of the most beautiful works that Giulio did. One of his panels is in Santa Maria dell' Anima in Rome, in which there is Our Lady, St Anne, St Joseph, St James, St John as a child, and St Mark the Evangelist with his lion beside him, which is a very beautiful thing. And there is a building there that curves in a circle like a theatre with some statues [450 as 436] so arranged that it is not possible to see better. And there among the others is a woman, spinning, looking at a brooding hen with chicks of which art in the imitation of nature cannot do more. It is true, however, that this panel would be somewhat better if it were not so painted in black, which has made it very dark and much is lost there of the effort expended. Giulio built a palace to his design on the Janiculum Hill for Messer Baldassare Turini of Pescia [Villa Lante]. He painted narratives of Numa Pompilius there and some fables of Venus, Love, Apollo, and Hyacinthus in the bathroom of this palace.

'Taking himself then to Mantua in the service of the marquis, who was then Federigo Gonzaga, [Giulio] constructed a very beautiful palace to his design outside the Porta a San Bastiano in Mantua at the place called the "T" [the Palazzo del Tè]. And he painted many narratives there such as that of Psyche, where she is seen on a vault when she married Cupid in the presence of all the gods. He has made the figures there foreshortened with the view *di sotto in su*, and some are not more than a braccio tall and they appear to be three braccia in height. And they are done with so much art and with so much judgment, that besides having very great three-dimensionality and appearing alive, they pleasantly deceive the eyes of those who look at them. And these narratives of Psyche were then printed from the drawings by Batista Franco of Venice. In other rooms with very beautiful [451 as 433] inventions, Giulio did the narrative of Icarus [Fall of Phaeton] when, taught by his father to fly and wanting to go too high, he fell into the sea when the wax liquefied, and [also] the twelve months of the year. In another round room and with new inventions of imaginative architecture built by him, he painted Jupiter angered, hurling lightning at the giants. There all the gods are seen running away frightened in various directions and the giants smitten in various ways and dying with fierce and frightful poses. And, in summary, the room for its new inventions and the painting for its great excellence is a very rare and astonishing thing.

'[Giulio] painted all the narratives of the Trojan War, from his drawings, in a hall in the palace where the duke lived in Mantua. And twelve narratives in oil are in an antechamber below the heads of the twelve emperors that had previously been painted by Titian. A panel of his hand in oil is in Sant' Andrea of the same city, where Our Lady is painted in the act of adoring Jesus the Christ Child with many other figures. And on either side of that panel are two narratives painted from his drawings by his pupil Rinaldo. Over a fireplace for his friend, the organist of the Duomo in Mantua, Giulio painted a Vulcan in fresco pumping his bellows with one hand. And with the other, in which he has a pair of tongs, he holds the iron of an arrow that he is making. Venus has already tempered some others in a vase and now puts them in the quiver of Cupid. And this is among the beautiful works that Giulio did, of which few others of his hand in fresco are to be seen.

'In San Domenico is a panel in which Christ is seen dead. Joseph and Nicodemus with other figures try to place Him in the tomb. [452] Many are the very important buildings that he built in Mantua, as he renovated almost all the city, and for himself, he built a very beautiful palace. And he painted so many pictures for the duke and for other gentlemen that it would be too long for me to recount them all. And he did many tapestry cartoons and endless drawings, many of which were printed. He was, to conclude, a rare man in painting and architecture. And ultimately he took sick in Mantua at the age of fifty-four years and passed to a better life and was given burial in San Barnaba. Sig. Antonmaria Bardi di Vernio did this epitaph about him:

If ready had he the art, and the hand
Tell Tebro, and more the ancient Manto,
That anywhere the Sun shines, there is exultation
For Giulio, it is enough to say that he was Roman [Romano].[91]

'It seems to me – as much as I have done – that for my part I have completed my obligation. And, seeing that the sun begins to hide under the tops of the mountains so that its rays, grazing the earth, have lost almost all the power of their random warmth, it therefore, would seem to me time to not stay here anymore.'

Vecchietti getting to his feet as he said this, all the others got up, and took delight in walking among the pleasant hills, discussing various things until the hour of supper. But that arriving, they turned their steps towards the villa where, according to their habit of the other days, being praiseworthily served, they dined. And then, as it was time to give their exhausted limbs rest, all took themselves to sleep.

Book Four

Great judgment induced those learned Greeks, Most Illustrious and Most Excellent Lord, to give place to painting among the Liberal Arts. And by public proclamation they forbade slaves and base men from being able to exercise it, perhaps fearing that this very noble art would lose its charm and reputation from unworthy and vile persons putting it into practice. Therefore, very excellent painters flourished in that time because, being noble men, they practised the art nobly and, more for honour and for glory than for recompense, they industriously put study into their works. And [457] philosophers, gentlemen, and emperors did not disdain to handle the colours and the brush with praise up to the time of the Romans. Painting is not only noble but also very useful since by means of it ... men are made friends of the king and very rich and have obtained prizes that surpass every treasure. Equally, it is necessary because it embraces design, order, and measure, without which, good things would be quite lacking from our affairs. This art being thus very noble, very useful, and necessary, all men should seek to learn it.

Those who do not esteem painting might respond to me that today – it not being forbidden to anyone, no matter how ignoble, to be able to practise it – it might have lost its native nobility, or some part of it become vile. And, in our time, we have seen many unrefined men raised by means of painting to those honours of citizenship and the knightly class where it is hardly possible for nobles of the purest blood to arrive. But while it is very true, as all philosophers know, that no one can give to others what he does not have in himself, how are we able to say that painting has become vile if it makes the lowly climb to a supreme degree? And this which I say of painting is understood equally of sculpture, having already concluded that both are of one art only.

But meanwhile, those who [feel] they cannot actively discuss what pertains to drawing and to painting should [458 as 444] be moved by the authoritative example of Your Excellency. One notes that you, along with the exercise of arms and difficult literary responsibilities, do not avoid the exercise of the art of drawing, putting your hand to it with very great praise to make the concepts of the mind appear with lines, shadows, and light.[1] And those who cannot, whatever the reason, practise painting at this time, at least [should] not avoid loving it as a very beautiful thing, becoming immortal painters in the spirit (which they have every power to do).[2]

Such painters imitate nature, not in its superficial forms, but in the unswerving observation of the order that the Supreme Creator gave it. They do not alter the inventions of others derived from divine precepts and holy constitutions. They explain their inventions appropriately, without injury to anything. They arrange their narratives with good order so the viewer does not find them tedious. There are modest movements, temperate, and full of grace. They do not have discordant or disunited parts. They blush with shame at the adoption of evil. They pale at the cold theme of perpetual punishment. They cover with shadow their own and other people's faults. They illuminate good works and honours done. They paint with the yellow of Faith, the white of Hope, the red of Charity, the blue of Justice, the black of Prudence, the green of Fortitude, and the purple of Temperance. And doing this, they make themselves divine in painting, receiving in payment for their marvellous paintings very great endless wealth [459 as 445] and very bright eternal name.[3]

The four gentlemen discussing at Vecchietti's villa, about whom the things of mine are written above and I am now prepared to write, are of these two kinds of painters. Returning to them, I will say that the fourth morning, after taking their usual recreation over the pleasant hills and afterward having taken their customary meal to restore the body, they moved to a very beautiful *ragnaia*[4] between two verdant slopes a little below the villa. And so thick were its leafy plants that it was not possible for the rays of the sun at that hour to have enough strength to finally penetrate to the ground except in some places where the branches were less dense, broken, and scattered. Very clear water (whose slow course was interrupted in little stages) proceeded through the middle of this, murmuring with great sweetness. The noble brigade seated themselves in relief on some greenery where the coolness was greatest next to [the stream] and, after a while, Michelozzi spoke thus.

'Every day new delights and new pleasures are discovered in this villa such that I, who do not yet know its name, will call it, with the permission of Bernardo, the repose [*Il Riposo*] from worries and from boredom.'

'You will call it by its proper name,' responded Valori, 'and that this should be true, favour us, Bernardo, with that sonnet that you have already composed on the name of this villa.'

'You then desire,' Vecchietti said, 'that I enter the field with my rough verses. But I, to confirm what you say and to show Girolamo that he has guessed well, [460] would not want to fail to recite them, such as they are.'

And he said:

Well was he prescient of my agreeable, animating repose
Who first the green hill,
And my sweet shelter chose to call *Riposo*
For only here I seem to get quietness and rest.[5]

Happy fields, clear waters, and shady woods,
Where now with hook, now with nets, now with bird lime[6]
Now little hares, now fish, now charming and wild
Birds I captured, for which I happily hid snare.

Well cultivated always, and scattered all around
Are beloved seeds; may the green laurel shade the fountain,
And look at it ever brighter.

Let the pine, the fir and the ash never feel the iron;
But let them always keep under their boughs, in the shade,
A singing choir of nymphs and shepherds.

The other three gentlemen praised the verses of Vecchietti when, interrupting them, he said: 'There is no more time now to waste on such things that matter little but rather to pray Ridolfo to begin that discussion that is his turn today.'

Valori and Michelozzi approved the words of Vecchietti and turned towards Sirigatti intending to say something. But he, not waiting for their response, immediately spoke in this manner.

'It is not given to men to bear being asked to do such things as it is necessary for them to do. Therefore, I will quickly say what I need to say since at least [461] the promptness of obeying excuses me where the insufficiency condemns me.' Having said this he kept silent for a moment and, seeing the others attentively waiting for him to speak, he resumed his discussion in this manner ...[7]

The Cavaliere Bandinelli

'Baccio Bandinelli[8] was born in Florence of a Michelangelo di Viviano of Gaiuole, a goldsmith and jeweller very capable in his art. He learned the first principles of design under his fatherly custody, and then was put to work with the sculptor Giovanfrancesco Rustici, who was then the best of the city. With him, in a brief time, he greatly advanced and began to make some heads and figures. But because the works of Bandinelli are many, I will come to speak, because of what time allows, only of the most famous and of the most beautiful. He painted two pictures: when the Saviour takes the Holy Fathers out of Limbo in one; and the *Drunkenness of Noah* in the other, uncovering his shame in front of his sons. But, not succeeding in colour, he returned to sculpture and did a marble statue three braccia high of a young *Mercury* with a flute in his hand, held to be a rare thing and sent to the king of France. Then he did the *St Peter* that today is in Santa Maria del Fiore in one of the niches among the other Apostles. Later, he did the *Orpheus* of marble that is in the courtyard of the Palace of the Medici. The *Laocoön* of his hand is also there at the head of the second courtyard of that palace, a work conducted with great artifice and care. He drew the narrative of the [478] *Martyrdom of St Laurence* for Pope Clement, a truly very rare thing that was engraved by Marcantonio [Raimondi] of Bologna. And Bandinelli received a Knighthood of St Peter from the Pope as a reward. He painted *St John* in a picture as a young man nude in the desert, holding a lamb with his left arm and raising the right to Heaven, which was very esteemed for the drawing but is crude in the colour, and he gave this to Pope Clement.

'He was then commissioned to do the *Hercules*, who has Cacus under him, that is in the piazza. For this he made a great wax model showing Hercules having the head of Cacus fixed with a knee between two stones, restraining him with great strength with the left arm, holding him huddled between his legs and Cacus shows his suffering. And Hercules grinding his teeth with his head bent towards him lifts his arm with great fierceness to smash his head. This model is found today in the collection of Grand Duke Francesco, admired by those of the art as a very beautiful thing. And then it was not done because it could not be done in such a manner in marble. Therefore, Bandinelli then did the work as it is seen today in the piazza that, while it was then criticized, also made known his quality.[9] In this style, he did a narrative of a *Deposition from the Cross* in small figures in low and half-relief and he cast it in bronze. This truly marvellous work he gave to Emperor Charles V in Genoa who, in return, made Baccio a Knight of St James.

'Taking himself then [479] to Rome, they allocated him the tombs of Pope Leo and Pope Clement. For these he made the statues that are seen there except for that of Pope Leo, which is of the hand of Raffaello da Montelupo, and that of Pope Clement, done by Giovanni di Baccio. Then, returning to Florence, he did those marble statues that are in the niches at the end of the Gran Sala of the Most Serene Grand Duke, that is, *Sig. Giovanni de' Medici, Duke Alessandro, Pope Clement, Duke Cosimo,* and *Pope Leo.* He then did the *Adam and Eve* that are behind the choir of Santa Maria del Fiore, figures worthy of praise.[10] And later, he did the dead Christ with the angel supporting His head. This work can with truth be said to be the most beautiful that he ever did and worthy of every praise. Also of his hand is the *God the Father,* six braccia high, seated over the altar and giving the benediction although it is not a figure of such goodness as that of Christ.

'Bandinelli did many other things that time does not allow me to describe, and he was very excellent in drawing, and many of his drawings are seen in print. In the end, he died at seventy-two years and was buried in the Church of the Servi in the chapel where there is the dead Christ of marble supported by Nicodemus whose face represents Baccio from life. And these statues were started and mostly done by Clemente, Bandinelli's natural son, who then died in Rome. And then [they were] completed, where they are seen arranged today, by Bandinelli himself. [480] To exalt the name of the *cavaliere* who had so greatly exalted sculpture, Sig. Antonmaria Bardi di Vernio has done these verses about him:

Decorated by Charles V with the holy insignia
He, who dead lives on today in a thousand poems,
Who gave motion and life to bronze and marble
He could do it with his talent and with his work.

Jacopo da Pontormo

'Jacopo da Pontormo[11] was the son of a Bartolomeo di Jacopo Carucci of Florence, who withdrew to Pontormo and there took a wife, where Jacopo was born; therefore, he was always then called of Pontormo. After the death of his father, he came to be in Florence and learned the art of painting, first from Leonardo da Vinci, then from Mariotto Albertinelli and from Piero di Cosimo, and finally from Andrea del Sarto. Among the first works that Pontormo did were the *Faith* and the *Charity* that are above the door of the first portico of the Annunziata on either side of the arms of Pope Leo. These figures are of all the goodness and grace that it is possible to do and better done painting in fresco, with more three-dimensionality, and with more beautiful colour, was not seen up to then. And Jacopo was not more than nineteen when he did them and if he would have continued painting in this manner he would have passed all the ancient and modern painters.

'For Bartolomeo Landfredini, [Pontormo] painted two beautiful and marvellous little boys in fresco holding up an escutcheon in a niche above a gate along the Arno between the bridge at Santa Trinità and the [Ponte alla] Carraia. [481] In addition to the many other things that Pontormo did for the entry of Pope Leo into Florence, he painted a *God the Father* with many cherubs. And a *St Veronica* who has the effigy of Jesus Christ on the Sudarium was for the chapel where His Holiness heard mass in the quarters of the Pope [Santa Maria Novella]. This work, being done with great speed, was very praised. He then painted in fresco, in the Church of San Ruffello behind the Archbishop's Palace, a chapel in which there is Our Lady placed in the middle of some saints with the Christ Child in Her arms. And, in the lunette of the chapel is a *God the Father* surrounded by some seraphim. He did two very beautiful chiaroscuro figures above the door of the Hospital for Priests between the Piazza San Marco and the Via San Gallo. He then painted the little narratives in oil that are on the Chariot of the Mint [for the annual procession] of St John. And above the gate of the Confraternity of St Cecilia, on the heights of Fiesole, this saint was done by him holding some roses in her hand, coloured in fresco as beautifully as could be desired. Later, he did the narrative of the *Visitation* of the Madonna in the courtyard of the Servi in such a beautiful manner and with so much sweetness of colour that the figures appear alive and of flesh and not painted.

'[Pontormo] then did the panel that is in San Michele Visdomini on the Via de' Servi in which Our Lady is seated, handing the little laughing Jesus to St Joseph. And another very beautiful child is there as St John the Baptist and two other nude little boys holding a canopy [482]. In sum, all the figures that are there are very perfect, and this is the most beautiful panel that this rare painter ever did. In competition with other masters, he painted some narratives of the deeds of Joseph in little figures on two *cassoni* for Pierfrancesco Borgherini. This painting, in all perfection in every part, cannot possibly be praised enough. He also did a picture of the same beauty for Giovanmaria Benintendi, in which there is the *Adoration of the Magi*. By his hand in the Sala Grande at Poggio a Caiano there is the narrative of Vertumnus with his farm workers. There is there a very rare figure of a seated peasant holding a vine pruner and the narrative of Pomona and of Diana with other goddesses. There is a very beautiful picture of his above an altar in the church of the nuns of St Clement on the Via San Gallo in which St Augustine is painted as a bishop giving the benediction, with two nude cherubs flying through the air. A picture from his hand of an *Our Lady with Her Child* in Her arms surrounded by some children is today in the house of Alessandro Neroni. And Carlo Panciatichi has another picture in his house, also of a *Madonna*, but with a different pose.

'Some very beautiful prints of Albrecht Dürer came from Germany at this time. Pontormo gave himself to imitating that German manner, leaving to a large extent his own, given to him by nature, all full of sweetness and grace. And he painted with this altered manner – being called by the monks of Certosa – many narratives of the Passion [483] of Jesus Christ, in their cloister, in fresco. Of these the best, and which had least of that German manner, is that where Christ is with the Cross on his shoulder. In front of Him are the two naked thieves. And St Veronica accompanied by many women is there handing Him the Sudarium, and the Jewish officials of justice are in different poses on foot and on horseback. He did many other works and pictures for these monks, but very beautiful is a picture in his own style in oil on canvas in which he painted a life-size Christ at the table with Cleophas and Luke. And there, among those serving, are portraits that appear alive of some lay brothers of these monks.

'Then, he painted the chapel of Lodovico Capponi the Elder in Santa Felicità, doing *God the Father* surrounded by four very beautiful patriarchs in the ceiling of the vault. And the Four Evangelists are in medallions at the corners, of which one is completely by the hand of Bronzino, who was working with him. And in this work it is seen that Pontormo had returned to his good manner of before. But in the panel of this chapel, where Christ is lowered from the Cross and taken to the tomb, he wanted to do something different. There he made the colouring so bright and unmodulated that one has difficulty distinguishing the bright from the middle tones and the middle tones from the dark. He also did a picture of *Our Lady* for the same Lodovico and he portrayed, in the face of St Mary Magdalene, a child of [Lodovico's] who was a very beautiful young girl. He also painted a panel in that German manner for the nuns of Sant' Anna next to the Porta a San Friano, in which there is the *Madonna and Her Child* in Her arms [484] and other figures. And in the predella he did little figures showing the Signoria of Florence when it goes in procession.

'[Pontormo] painted a very beautiful picture of the *Resurrection of Lazarus* in his [original non-German] manner that was sent to King Francis. And he did another for the sisters of the Hospital of the Innocenti, in which there is the narrative of the eleven thousand martyrs crucified in a wood by Diocletion. Here there is a battle of horsemen and nudes and some very beautiful cherubs flying through the air shooting arrows at the men doing the crucifying, a work truly worthy of endless praise. Michelangelo Buonarroti, having done his famous cartoon of the nude *Venus Kissing Cupid*, Pontormo portrayed this in painting from that cartoon. This, for the drawing of Michelangelo and for the colour of Jacopo, succeeded as a very rare thing, and Duke Alessandro would have it and hold it very dear. He painted in oil on dry plaster the first loggia that is found on the left on entering the palace at Castello, doing some narratives there of the ancient gods and Liberal Arts. And there he portrayed Duke Cosimo at a young age and Madonna Maria his mother from life, which work time and the air consumed little by little. He did many pictures and portraits from life for various people that for brevity I will not mention.

'Finally, he was given the choir of San Lorenzo by Grand Duke Cosimo, on which he was [employed] eleven years and died at sixty-five years before having entirely completed it. [485] One sees there neither worthwhile invention, nor composition, nor perspective, nor colour, although there are some good torsos. And of this choir I will not speak further, confessing either not understanding what he had wanted to do or not having any taste for what is there.[12] One can judge from this that when men want to overreach they do worse and that people when they begin to age do better in giving advice than putting it into practice. Baccio here has, for devotional purposes, a very well-done little drawing of this work. The cover for this has been painted by Giovanbattista Naldini, and a very beautiful garden is shown there with Christ in the guise of a gardener appearing to the Magdalene.

'Pontormo was accompanied to the grave with great honour by all the painters, sculptors, and architects. And his body was put to rest in the first cloister of the Servi under the narrative that he had done of the *Visitation* of the Madonna. Messer Cosimo Gaci, a young man of very beautiful spirit, did this epitaph on Pontormo:

In the thousand faces to which I gave life and motion
My noble colour you will be able to read
Viewer, who I am: you will find here
I broke the earth prison by spiritual will.[13]

Ridolfo Ghirlandaio

'My mother's father Ridolfo di Domenico Ghirlandaio,[14] for whom I was given the name Ridolfo, learned painting under Fra Bartolomeo of San Marco and intensely studied drawing from the famous cartoon of Michelangelo. These works by the hand of Ridolfo are in Florence. The panel in the Monastery of Cestello, in which there is the *Nativity of Christ*, has a very beautiful landscape very like Sasso della Vernia. And above the hut are some singing angels. This panel was very praised for colour and for three-dimensionality. Two panels are in the Confraternity of St Zenobius that is in the corner of the rectory of Santa Maria del Fiore. In these are narratives of St Zenobius resuscitating a young boy in the Via degli Albizzi and [490] when, carried to burial through the Piazza of San Giovanni, [St Zenobius] makes the dry tree bloom. They put these on either side of the *Annunciation* that was already there, done by Albertinelli. That very well-done narrative in fresco where there is the portrait of the dwarf is in the cloister of the [Santa Maria] degli Agnoli monastery. There St Benedict, sitting with two angels at the table, waits for Romanus to send him the bread in the cave and the Devil cuts the rope with stones.[15] An *Our Lady with Her Child* in Her arms and some very beautiful angels are above the holy-water font. And seen in the refectory of the same monks is the very beautiful *Last Supper*. Three very beautiful narratives of the Glorious Virgin, which have the appearance of miniatures, are in a predella in the Church of the Misericordia [the

Bigallo] on the Piazza of San Giovanni. A very beautiful and graceful work of his is that lavish little tabernacle on the corner of the house that belongs today to Zanobi Carnesecchi, where the Madonna with Her Child in Her arms is between St Matthew the apostle and St Dominic. Two panels are in the church of the nuns of St Jerome on the heights of San Giorgio. In one of these is *St Jerome in Penitence* and the *Nativity of Jesus Christ* is in the lunette above. And in the other, which is opposite this, is an *Annunciation* and *St Mary Magdalene Taking Communion* is in the lunette above. In the chapel where the Signori used to hear Mass in the Palace of Grand Duke Francesco is [Ridolfo's] very *Holy Trinity* in the vault, some cherubs holding the Mysteries of the Passion and the heads of the twelve Apostles in the other compartments. The Evangelists are in the four corners and, in [491] the front, the Angel Gabriel greeting the Virgin. In some landscapes, the Piazza of the Annunziata is shown as far as the Church of San Marco. This work was very well conducted and done with great care. And his panel where there is Our Lady, St John the Baptist, and St Romualdo is in the Ognisanti.

'The panel in the Pieve of Prato is by [Ridolfo] in which there is the Queen of Heaven offering Her belt to St Thomas, who is together with the other Apostles. Ridolfo did many other works and many portraits from life that I pass by for brevity. He greatly exhausted himself in the displays and in the scenery for comedies for the weddings of Duke Giuliano and Duke Lorenzo de' Medici and for the entrance of Pope Leo into Florence. And, because he was very beloved by these lords, as an honoured citizen he would have many offices through their efforts.'

Michele di Ridolfo

'[Ridolfo] would have several painting students and among the others, Michael di Ridolfo,[16] very beloved by him. Together with him [Ridolfo] brought many beautiful works to perfection that it would be too long to discuss. Not omitting to say that among the most beautiful paintings that Ridolfo did in fresco was a *Visitation of Our Lady* in the Church of the Madonna delle Vertighe, a place of the monks of Camaldoli outside the township of Monte a Sansovino.

'And [Ridolfo] painted some grotesqueries on the vault and very beautiful landscapes on the walls in the Camera Verde in the palace of our Grand Duke. In the end, aged and plagued by gout, he passed to the better life at seventy-five years and was honourably buried in Santa Maria Novella near [492] his forefathers.'[17]

Fra Giovanagnolo Montorsoli

'The excellent sculptor Fra Giovanagnolo Montorsoli[18] was the son of an Agnolo of Poggibonzi. And, because he was born in the village of Montorsoli three miles distant from Florence on the road to Bologna, he took his last name from there. He was first put by his father with the stone carvers and then with the sculptor Andrea [Ferrucci] of Fiesole. He worked with Michelangelo Buonarotti in the sacristy of San Lorenzo, carving some rosettes and other work. But, stopped from this work by the plague in the year 1527, he, who was very inclined to religion, was made a monk of the Servi. And where up to then he was called Agnolo, he was named Fra Giovanagnolo at his initiation. And the portraits of *Pope Leo, Pope Clement,* and *Duke Alessandro* in the Church of the Annunziata are of his hand.

'Then called to Rome by Pope Clement, who with a brief removed [Montorsoli] from the religious, he restored many ancient statues for that Pontiff and did [496] the portrait of that pope in marble that was very praised. Then, he came to Florence to help Michelangelo finish the Chapel of San Lorenzo and there he did the marble statue of *St Cosmas*, a very beautiful figure, as is known.[19] The grey sandstone tomb of the Brother General Agnolo [Lancini] of the Servi in the Church of San Pietro in Arezzo is of his hand. Here there are some statues and [the effigy of] this general on the sarcophagus and two weeping little boys in the round extinguishing the torches of human life, with other beautiful ornaments.

'Mergellina is a place in the area of Naples at the end of the Chiaia, above the harbour, with a very beautiful view. Sannazaro, a very rare poet, gave it to the Servite Brothers. There [Montorsoli] did the marble tomb of Sannazaro, with many statues in the church, conducted with beautiful artifice. In Genoa, he did many beautiful works of marble such as the statue of *Prince Doria* that is in the Piazza della Signoria and the *St John the Evangelist* erected in the Cathedral Church. The chapel in San Matteo with the tomb of Prince Andrea Doria is his. Here there are many very beautiful statues and, among the others, a *Resurrected Christ* of marble in full relief and an Our Lady with the dead Christ in half-relief. And there are so many other figures that it would be too long to discuss them, in addition to beautiful orders of architecture and various decorations. A very well-done sea monster of marble at the palace of the prince shoots water into a fish pond, and there are two more marble portraits of the same prince.

'In the Piazza of the Duomo in Messina [497] [Montorsoli] did that very beautiful eight-sided fountain that is seen there. It is decorated and enriched with so many marble narratives in low relief, so many statues in the round, and with so many sea monsters that it is a marvel to see them. And in the highest place there is a figure in armour representing the constellation Orion, who has the arms of the city of Messina on his shield. He also did the fountain that is on the shore which, aside from many other statues, has a five braccia tall Neptune in the middle who, with trident in hand, plants his right leg next to a dolphin. In the Duomo of this city there are two marble Apostles of his hand, *St Peter* and *St Paul,* large and very good figures. And he did a marble life-size *Our Lady* in the chapel of Captain Cicala in San Domenico and a marble narrative in low relief done with great care in the Chapel of Sig. Agnolo Borsa in the cloister of this same church. He arranged for water to be conducted by way of the wall of Sant' Agnolo for a fountain and himself carved a large little boy in marble pouring water into a vase, a work very praised. And he made another fountain for the Wall of the Virgin with a virgin pouring water into a basin. He also did a very beautiful marble statue, four braccia high, representing *St Catherine the Martyr* that was sent to Taormina, a place twenty-four miles from Messina.

'Finally, [Montorsoli] had put back on the habit in the Church of the Servi in Florence, having decided to live in quiet serving God, when he was called to Bologna. And [498] it was arranged for him to do the free-standing marble high altar in the Church of the Servi and a tomb with figures and with rich ornaments of variegated stone. There is a nude Christ, two and a half braccia high, in the middle of this altar with some other statues on the sides. Returning to Florence, he did a beautiful tomb in the middle of the chapter house of the Annunziata for himself and for all the men of the guild of design who would not have their own burial place. And Fra Giovanagnolo caused the Accademia del Disegno, which was created in the time of Giotto, to be put back on its feet [*si rimettesse in piede*]. He was helped in this by Grand Duke Cosimo, who was made head of this academy, ordering that a representative named by him represent him there.[20] And with great honour the bones of Pontormo, having been taken from where they were first buried, were the first placed in the tomb done by the monk [Montorsoli]. And then Fra Giovanagnolo, having died at age fifty-six in the year 1563, was buried in it, with common sorrow and with honourable exequies. And Piero di Gherardo Capponi, lover of virtuosi, did this epitaph about him:

The tonsured Angel came, and in Heaven
He saw these forms, where they were on earth
His marbles live, and dead to the world on earth
He lived, now is dead, and lives on earth, and in Heaven. [499]

Francesco Salviati

'The very famous painter Francesco Salviati[21] was the son of a Michelangelo de' Rossi of Florence, a weaver of velvets, and was instructed when small by his father in his trade. But the little boy, who was by nature inclined to painting, never did anything other than draw. Therefore, his father put him with a jeweller, then he put Francesco to painting with Giuliano Bugiardini. He also learned drawing from Bandinelli, was put in the shop of the painter Rafaello [Piccinelli] of Brescia, and finally, with Andrea del Sarto. Among the first paintings that Francesco did are three little narratives in a tabernacle of the Sacrament for the monks of the Badia. In the first of these is the *Sacrifice of Abraham;* the manna is in the second, and in the third the Hebrews, leaving Egypt, eat the Pascal lamb. This work gave great evidence for the success that Francesco would have. Then, he painted *Delilah* cutting Samson's hair and in the distance when he destroys the temple, having it fall down on the Philistines. This picture was sent to France as a rare thing.

'[Salviati] then went to be in Rome with Cardinal Salviati the elder with whom he was some time and acquired the last name of Salviati which he then always maintained. And among the first things that he did for that cardinal was a picture of an *Our Lady* and on canvas a French nobleman racing in the chase behind a hind that, running away, finds refuge in the temple of Diana. These works pleased greatly. He then painted some narratives in fresco of the life of St John in the Chapel of the Palace of [500] this Salviati. He did *Christ Speaking to St Philip,* in fresco, in a niche above the door at the back of Santa Maria della Pace and the Virgin and the Angel of the Annunciation on two corners. And the *Assumption of Our Lady* is in a large picture on one of the eight sides of that temple. This work was judged to be no less beautiful than the others that are there of the hand of Raphael of Urbino, Rosso, Baldassare [Peruzzi] of Siena, and others. He then did the *Arms of Paul III,* with some very beautiful large nude figures, on the facade of the house of Bindo Altoviti at the Ponte Sant' Angelo. He painted in fresco when Our Lady visits St Elizabeth, in the second church of the Florentine

Confraternity of the Misericordia [San Giovanni Decollato] below the Campidoglio. He did this work to astonish all Rome. And of the things Salviati did in fresco, one is able to put this among the best with very beautiful inventions, orderly composition, and with the observation of perspective in the buildings and in the diminution of the figures.

'There is from [Salviati's] hand in Venice a very beautiful *Psyche* to whom many gifts and incense are being offered in an octagon, four braccia high, in a drawing room painted by other painters in the palace of the Patriarch Grimani [at Santa Maria Formosa]. And this was held to be the most beautiful painting in Venice. Some very graceful nude and clothed figures in fresco are in a chamber of this patriarch. The panel for the nuns of Corpus Domini, in which there is a dead Christ with the Marys and an angel in the sky holding [501] the Mysteries of the Passion in his hand, is [Salviati's]. And a panel in which there are many figures was put in the church of the nuns of St Christina [in Bologna] of the Order of the Camaldoli.

'The works done by [Salviati] in Florence included a very beautiful picture of *Our Lady* in the house of Jacopo Salviati and another large picture that is a marvellous thing in which Adam and Eve are eating the forbidden fruit in the terrestrial paradise. There is a coloured *Pietà* with the Madonna and the other Marys on a silver cloth, the beauty of which it is not possible easily to describe, and a very beautiful book of bizarre clothing and of different people's hairstyles and of horses for carnival parades. A picture of a very beautiful *Charity* is in the Udienza della Decima, and a very praised picture of the *Queen of Heaven* is in the house of Simon Corsi. In the house of Piero Bertini is an *Our Lady* painted on canvas with Christ and St John as laughing little boys, a very charming and capricious work. [Salviati painted] a very beautiful picture in the house of Giovambatista Ubaldini in which his father Lorenzo is portrayed in half-length, done with very great care and held very dear by Giovambatista, who delighted in it and understands good paintings very well. A panel is beside the door in the Chapel of the Dini in Santa Croce in which Christ is taken down from the Cross with the Virgin and with the Marys, a work done with great art, with great three-dimensionality, and with charming colour.[22] And the hall that, for being painted by him, is called the Hall of Francesco Salviati is in the palace of Grand Duke Francesco. In this there are many narratives of [502] the deeds of Furius Camillus with other very beautiful inventions, and the task would not end for whoever wanted to speak of the beauty of this work. He also painted the ceiling of the room in this palace, where one eats in the winter, with many devices and little figures in tempera and [also] the study that is over the Camera Verde.

'In Rome, besides the works of [Salviati's] that we have discussed, there is also of his hand the panel that is in the Chapel of the Cherici di Camera in the [Vatican] Palace of the Pope. The chapel in fresco in the German Church where, in the vault, there are the Apostles receiving the Holy Spirit is his and in a picture that is in the middle, *Christ Resurrected* with the unconscious soldiers around the tomb. And in the panel in fresco is Christ dead with the Marys, with other narratives of saints on the walls. The chapel of the Palagio di San Giorgio [Cancelleria] is done with very beautiful compartments of stucco and the vault in fresco with figures and narratives of St Lawrence and the panel in oil in which there is the *Nativity of Christ* where Cardinal Farnese is portrayed. The *Birth of St John* in the Confraternity of the Misericordia is beside his narrative of the *Visitation*. And at the head of that confraternity are the very beautiful apostles *St Andrew* and *St Bartholomew* in fresco on either side of the panel altarpiece where there is a *Deposition from the Cross*, by the hand of Jacopo del Conte. Two angels in fresco holding a canopy are in a chapel of San Lorenzo in Damaso. In the refectory of San Salvadore del Lauro is the *Wedding at Cana* in Galilee in which Jesus Christ made wine from water, with a great number of figures, [503] and, on the side, some saints and Pope Eugenius IV, who was of that order. And above the door of the refectory, on the inner side, is a picture in oil in which there is *St George Slaying the Dragon*, done with great boldness and very charming colour. Two narratives are in fresco in the drawing room that is in front of the great hall in the Farnese Palace. Lord Rinuccio Farnese the elder is in one receiving the baton of the Holy Church from Eugenius IV with some Virtues. And Pope Paul III Farnese is in the other giving the baton of the Church to Lord Pierluigi, but this work was not completely finished by him but by Taddeo Zuccaro. And in the palace formerly of Cardinal Ricci of Montepulciano on the Strada Giulia, in the hall where there are many pictures in fresco is the narrative of David. And there Bathsheba is seen washing in a bath with many other women, very beautiful figures, and in summation all this work is marvellous in design, in invention, and in colour.

'In France [Salviati] painted many narratives with large numbers of figures in some pictures in fresco above the cornices of chimney pieces in the palace of the Cardinal of Lorraine at Dampierre and equally a study where he used great diligence. Salviati did many pictures for many people and portraits and cartoons for tapestries that are not discussed for brevity. He drew very well, and his drawings are held of very great value. In the end he died with great loss to art in Rome at fifty-four years, the year of Christian well-being 1563, and was buried in San Girolamo, the church near the [504] house where he lived. And he has been honoured by Vincentio di Buonaccorso Pitti with these verses:

Here rests, and sleeps the common dream
Who was Salviati, and Earth is cold and dusty:
Alive his fame where others measure
[No longer among us] against our foot his tracks.[23]

Michelangelo Buonarroti

'Now what I will say, it being appropriate for me to speak of the divine Michelangelo[24] in whom is seen all perfection of sculpture, of painting, and of architecture? [510] Only he has wholly obscured the glory of the ancients and surpassed the fame of all the moderns. I will not say anything other than that, if I were not in the act of attempting to speak of him, and I am, the little time that is left to me only suffices to allow me the satisfaction of telling you briefly the works that he did, saying that they are of the hand of Michelangelo Buonarroti. And this will be enough to recognize their excellence and to know that they are of a manner that overcomes all others [and] that cannot in any way compare with them.

'But coming now to discuss [Michelangelo] in more detail, I say that he was born in the Casentino. His father was named Lodovico Buonarroti Simoni and descended from the noble family of the counts of Canossa. That year he was *Podestà* of the township of Chiusi and Caprese near the Sasso della Vernia. Being of suitable age to be able to absorb learning, Michelangelo was put by his father to learn grammar. But he, inclined to design by Heaven and by nature, never did anything other than draw. Many times he was scolded by his father, it seeming to [his father] that to attend to such things would humiliate their house. But Lodovico was finally worn down by his son. And, having been advised by others in the Arte della Lana and della Seta, and seeing that Michelangelo wanted only to rise in design, he put him with Domenico Ghirlandaio. And, in a brief time, [Michelangelo] not only passed all the apprentices in drawing but the master himself.

'[Michelangelo] was then called [511] by the Magnificent Lorenzo de' Medici to be in his garden, a school of virtuosi. He was there four years, given the expenses of his table, and provided with five scudi a month so that he could study, and his father was given a good office. Buonarroti advanced greatly at this time, particularly by drawing for many months from the figures of Masaccio in the Carmine. And he carved the battle of Hercules with the centaurs on a piece of marble, a marvellous work, not by a youth such as he was but as if by a man very consummate in the art. Today, this belongs to his nephew Lionardo Buonarroti, who holds it very dear, as a rare thing and in memory of his uncle. He equally did an *Our Lady* at that time in low relief, a little more than a braccio high, in which he imitated the manner of Donatello. And he imitated it so well that it seems to be of [Donatello's] hand except that there is seen there more grace and more design. And this is in the hands of our Grand Duke, the Most Serene Francesco de' Medici. He holds it in great account as a most singular thing, there not being other low relief in sculpture than this from the hand of Michelangelo.

'The Magnificent Lorenzo then having died, [Michelangelo] took himself back to his father's house, where he did a marble *Hercules*, four braccia high, that was then sent to France to King Francis. The wooden *Crucifix* that is above the lunette of the high altar in Santo Spirito is also of his hand, done at that time. The Arca of St Dominic in Bologna was previously erected by the early sculptors Giovanni Pisano and then by Niccolò dall' Arca. [512] Two marble figures on it, a braccia high, are carved by [Michelangelo]. One is an angel holding a candlestick and the other *St Petronius*. Then, he did a young *St John* of marble for Lorenzo di Pierfrancesco de' Medici, and he did a life-size sleeping *Cupid* that was sent to Rome and sold as an ancient figure and today is found in Mantua.

'Afterwards [Michelangelo] took himself to Rome and did a life-size marble *Cupid* for Jacopo Galli, a Roman gentleman, and a figure of a *Bacchus*, ten palms tall, who has a cup in his right hand and in his left a tiger skin and a cluster of grapes that a little satyr is trying to eat. He then did that marvellous work of the marble *Pietà* in the round that is in San Pietro in the Chapel of the Vergine Maria della Febbre about which I will keep silent, not being able to discuss fully such a miraculous thing.

'But what will I say of the nine-braccia tall marble *David* that [Michelangelo] then did, having returned to Florence, erected by the door of the Palace of the Grand Duke? Who has ever seen or who thinks they will ever see a more perfect figure, done with greater facility and with more beautiful poise? He did *Our Lady* in a bronze tondo that was sent to Flanders by some merchants. In a tondo for Angelo Doni, he painted the Glorious Virgin kneeling who has the Child in Her arms and hands Him to Joseph. And in the background he did many leaning, standing, and seated nude figures, completed with the greatest diligence, nor is it possible [513] to see a thing more beautiful.

'Being then commissioned to paint a part of the Sala del Consiglio by the Gonfaloniere Pier Soderini, [Michelangelo] made a cartoon,[25] portraying in it many nude persons. Bathing in the Arno River because of the heat, they are shown in that instant of the alarm that the enemy was attacking them, hurriedly springing out of the river, dressing themselves in different poses. And this was that famous cartoon that for a long time was put up in the Sala del Papa on the Via della Scala, in the great upper hall of the House of the Medici. It was the studio of all the Florentine apprentices and foreigners who were drawn by the fame of what they went there to draw. Because [Michelangelo] had been sick in his house, Roberto Strozzi had two statues from Buonarroti representing two prisoners. These were to have served for the tomb of Julius II but were then not placed on the work. Roberto sent them as a gift to the king of France, and they are today at Écouen. And a *Victory* above a prisoner that should also have been used for that tomb is in the Sala Regia of the Palace of Grand Duke Francesco, a work of such beauty that it is not equalled either in antiquity or today.

'Then, in the time of Julius II, [Michelangelo] painted the [Sistine] Chapel of the Pope with narratives from the Old Testament. And its unveiling astonished not only Rome but the whole world, craftsmen converging there from every part to see it and to draw it. And in the time of Paul III, he painted and unveiled the miraculous *Judgment* in the same chapel.[26] In this work he passed not only all [514] the others who have painted up to now but he surpassed himself and his so celebrated work that he had painted before. And because this *Judgment* is seen to have been issued in many prints, I will not speak further about it. In the Minerva beside the choir is a marble *Christ* by him, a very wonderful figure.

'In the Sacristy of San Lorenzo in Florence, done by [Michelangelo] himself to his design, are the not completely finished *Our Lady* with Her Child in Her arms, *Duke Lorenzo* and *Duke Giuliano* seated, *Night, Day, Dawn*, and *Dusk*, reclining figures with very beautiful poses. These, while they are of marble, appear to be real flesh, lacking only breath and nothing more. And many poems were done about these statues when they were unveiled, among which I remember a quatrain done about the *Night*,[27] I do not know by which author, and it is this:

The Night, that you see in such a lovely pose
Sleeping, was carved by an Angel
In this stone, and because sleeping she has life,
Awake her if you do not believe, and she will speak to you.

To which Michelangelo, pretending how Night would speak, replied:

I am grateful for the sleep, and more so to be of stone
While last the injury and the shame,
Not to see nor feel are great good fortune to me;
Therefore not to wake me; one should speak low. [515]

'In the chamber of Grand Duke Francesco is a marble *Apollo* of his hand, extracting an arrow from his quiver, a figure, while not entirely finished, very rare. He painted, in tempera on canvas, a *Leda Embracing the Swan* and Castor and Pollux emerging from the egg. He gave this marvellous work to his student Antonio Mini, who sold it to King Francis, and today it is seen in Fontainebleau. And the cartoon of this Leda is the one we have seen in the house here of Bernardo.

'These marble statues are of his hand on the famous tomb of Julius II, done to his design in the Church of San Piero in Vincola in Rome. *Leah*, daughter of Laban, is shown as the active life, holding a mirror in one hand and a garland of flowers in the other. *Rachel* is the contemplative life, with folded hands and bent knee. And *Moses* is a very great and very beautiful figure, and not only as beautiful as it is possible to do but perhaps more than man is able to imagine. Two narratives in the Pauline Chapel were painted by him, one of the *Conversion of St Paul* and the other of St Peter when he was nailed to the cross. Here there are endless very beautiful considerations surrounding the perfection of the design, granted that Michelangelo did not attend to the beauty of colouring nor to a certain charm of the landscape and of perspective and decoration as the other painters do. And these were the last paintings that he finished, being seventy-five years of age.

'Who would wish now to speak of his things of architecture [516] would have to divide up a very wide field. But it is enough to say that the very famous Church of St Peter in Rome is his work and that he was very excellent in this profession, as in sculpture and in design he had no equal.

'He finally passed from this mortal to the eternal life in Rome at eighty-eight years, eleven months, and fifteen days of age, on 17 [19] February, 1563 [1564][28] and was buried in a depository in Santo Apostolo with a great gathering of those of the art, of friends, and of the Florentine colony. But then his body was sent to Florence by his nephew Leonardo. There marvellous and honourable obsequies were performed for him in San Lorenzo, with the favour of Grand Duke Cosimo, by all those of the Accademia del Disegno. And the funeral oration was given in his honour by Benedetto Varchi. And then his heirs had that marvellous marble tomb done with the three statues and with his portrait that is seen in Santa Croce. Many beautiful spirits did not omit writing verse on his death that was collected together to form a book that is seen in print. However, I will not insist on reciting them to you here but rather an epitaph newly done about him by Bernardo that pleases me greatly for containing the principal virtues of Michelangelo, and it is this:

The city having provided, and generously erected,
Palaces and Temples, and yet only one to Peter,
The sovereign Buonarroti
Would leave behind defeated [517]
Archimedes, Vitruvius, and Polygnotus.
In the colouring of his divine concepts
One concedes more beauty than the
Paintings of Protogenes and Apelles.
His bronzes and beautiful marbles move to envy
Myron, Lysippus, Polyclitus, and Phidias.
Nor do the stars prevent him
From speaking brilliantly in a style uniquely his,
He stands erect to his great praise.[29]

'Neither have the stars prevented you also from speaking brilliantly,' Michelozzi said, turning towards Vecchietti, 'and [your] exalted style of celebrating the deeds of others, if I am right, has brought praise upon yourself, particularly since you, with the verses that you have made, have not neglected those beautiful things of theirs of which you speak.'

'You honour me much more than is appropriate,' Vecchietti responded. 'Sirigatti, had you listen to my weak verses concerning a standard of perfection that is higher than would seem to be possible.

Then you, have put me ahead of where I myself am able to go. But I take it all with infinite thanks from you both.'

They courteously and repeatedly conversed about this for some time and then Sirigatti continued his discussion in this way: 'Being gathered at the summit of perfection of sculpture and painting in discussing Michelangelo, it would seem to me, if it does not displease you, that we can bring our discussion to a close. It is not appropriate for us, having climbed to the top of the mountain, wanting to go forward, to go down [518] to a lower part.'

'In fact to remain at this height,' Vecchietti replied, 'continuing to fight the winds that buffet those who pause on the peaks of mountains, would be difficult and perhaps dangerous since it is a place not really ours. [But] rather than finishing our discussion on the heights of Buonarroti, it would seem that we should not so greatly look down on those craftsmen who cannot arrive at such excellence. That would be a great fault, since praise is given to all of those who race with swift steps even though they do not acquire the first prize.'

'Truly Bernardo is right,' added Valori, 'and we would wrong the painters and sculptors who live today, and too greatly dash their hope – being themselves among those who, with great study, try to imitate Michelangelo – if we also do not discuss them. Therefore, if it does not burden you Ridolfo, continue with your discussion until the more rare modern craftsmen are given consideration.'

'I will be ready to obey,' Sirigatti responded, 'although perhaps unfit to satisfy. And before I speak of those painters and sculptors who are alive and of whom I have personal knowledge, so as not to leave behind some others worthy to be named even if dead, I will resume my discussion with.'[30]

Vincentio Danti

'Vincentio di Giulio Danti[31] of Perugia was put as a young boy to the art of the jeweller, doing marvellous things in that. Meanwhile, not omitting to study drawing, in the end he gave himself completely [520] to the casting of bronze figures. Thus, at the age of twenty he cast the six-braccia-high metal statue of *Pope Paul III* seated. This came out very well. And, granted that he had been greatly valued in similar work, carefully done little narratives in low relief are seen on [the Pope's] mantle. And this work was put up in Perugia on a pedestal next to the door of the Duomo.

'Then coming to Florence in the service of Grand Duke Cosimo, [Danti] did, by order of His Highness, the door of the sacristy of the Pieve of Prato. And, above this is the tomb of Messer Carlo de' Medici, natural son of Cosimo the elder, once Provost of that area. And, above the marble sarcophagus is seen a life-size Our Lady with the Child beside Her and two cherubs in low relief on either side of [Carlo's] head which is very like the deceased. He completed the two marble statues, which Andrea dal Monte Sansovino had left unfinished, that are erected above the [east] door of San Giovanni in Florence. The two figures carved from only one marble showing *Honour over Falsehood,* which were erected in the courtyard of the palace of the Cav. Messer Vangelista Almeni, are of his hand, done with great care. And the curly hair of Honour is drilled through in a way that makes it appear natural. The two marble figures representing *Rigour* and *Equity,* which lie in beautiful poses on either side of the Medici arms at the head of the new Uffizi, are also his work.[32]

'With great good fortune [Danti] cast the three bronze figures that one sees [521] above the [south] doors of San Giovanni towards the Misericordia, and they came out so well, so fine and so clean, that it was not necessary to rework them.[33] In the middle, one sees the humility and patience of St John, kneeling with folded hands awaiting the decapitating blow coming to him from above. On the left hand is the ferocity of the arrogant minister with tousled hair, his sword raised in the act of cutting off the head. And, on the right is the cruelty mixed with horror of Salomé waiting with a basin under her arm to carry the demanded gift to her iniquitous mother. A larger than life marble *Venus* of his is in the Baroncelli Palace and a *Virgin with the Her Child* in Her arms, four braccia tall, in the Arcivescovado of Florence. Grand Duke Francesco has some very beautiful low reliefs of marble and bronze from his hand. One among the others is done with little narratives with the greatest care. This serves for a door for a cabinet where His Highness keeps writings of importance. Another, a braccio and a half high and two and a half wide, is in His Highness's collection. In this, Moses is shown raising the serpent on the wood to revive the people bitten by snakes, a work truly very rare, as rare as Vincentio has done in low relief.

'This man was of the highest calibre in almost all the virtues. [Danti] understood fortification and building profoundly, as in the work he did in Perugia on the fortifications of that city. And the Palace of the Signori was reduced, to his order and design, to that good form that is seen today, and he particularly [522] succeeded there in the stairs. And he discovered the way of conducting water into that city without aqueducts that was a wonderful thing. For the temple of the Escorial that King Philip then had decided to build, he did a design in the form of an oval to accommodate the site. This was sent by Grand Duke Cosimo to His Majesty together with another done by the Florentine Accademia based on his design. And if Vincentio had not retired to Perugia and taken a wife he could easily have gone – since he had announced he could do it – to put this design into effect. He did many other designs and buildings that I pass by, to not go too far outside of our interest.

'Finally, [Danti] applied himself to painting, and for the chapel of Sig. Giovanna Baglioni, in San Firenze, he painted the panel in which there is the Crucifix between the thieves and many figures at the foot of the Cross. This is done with good design and beautiful order, a work worthy to be praised even though not very well coloured because he was not yet accustomed to handling colours. And he also did many paintings in his own house where he lived. And he was not little valued in the composition of Tuscan verse and particularly in doing hundreds of verses after Petrarch and other famous authors. He wrote a work about design divided into fifteen books, of which one is seen in print.[34] And it is hoped the others will immediately see the light through the efforts of Brother Ignazio, his brother. [Ignazio] is a very excellent mathematician and cosmographer, over and above his many other virtues, of whose worth the world should one day very greatly take notice. [523] Finally, enjoying himself in his country with some beautiful villas that he had next to the city, Vincenzio died at age forty-six to the great sorrow of all those who knew him. And he was buried with great honour in San Domenico in the Chapel of St Vincent and the Ten Thousand Martyrs that belongs to the Danti family. And Brother Ignazio had a marble tomb made for him above which is the bust of this Vincentio, carved by Valerio Cioli. I will omit reciting for you the Latin epitaph that one reads there. And in exchange I will recite two quatrains that Piero di Gherardo Capponi – who deserves every praise as a lover of the beautiful things of Vincentio and as a friend of Brother Ignazio – has done about him and this is the first:

Superb palaces and sacred temples
Not only Vincentio, to his praise, erected;
But in bronze, in marble, and in colour he expressed
That which he wrote, and others see for all time.

Listen to the second of newer concept:

Envy fills learning and the arts to the brim
In their admiration of Danti. He bared his breast
To show them bare, and one comes to enjoy them less.
Now he lives in bronze, in marble, and on paper.

The verses of Capponi were greatly commended, and it was concluded that they were of very beautiful design, of laudable manner, and ornamented with such virtue that they were [524] notable compared with all others. But ending their discussion of him, Sirigatti resumed his discourse in this way.

Girolamo Danti

'Vincentio had a brother named Girolamo,[35] who gave hope of becoming a great figure in painting but his premature death removed him from working in this world. He painted all the sacristy of the Badia of San Pietro of the Black Monks in Perugia and all the guesthouse in fresco. A completely painted chapel in San Francesco is also seen of his hand in the vault of which it is the *Resurrection of Christ* and other narratives. The very well-done panel, in which there is the *Nativity* of the Son of God in the Church of San Domenico in Gubbio, is his work. He helped his brother Frate Ignazio in beginning that Galleria [della Carte Geografiche] that [Ignazio] began in Rome which is so famous today in which [Girolamo] painted some figures. He was a good draftsman and, although he demonstrated capable mastery in the art, he reached the final end of his life at the age of thirty-three and was buried before Vicentio in the Chapel of the Danti.'

Titian

'Titian[36] of Cador of the family, not as Vasari says of the birds [*uccelli*] but of Veccelli, being ten years of age and recognized as a beautiful talent was sent to Venice and put with the painter Giovanni Bellini. He was with him some time, so that he would learn the art of painting. And, meanwhile, Giorgione of Castelfranco having come to be in Venice, Titian gave himself to imitate his manner, liking it more than that [525] of Giovanni Bellini. And he so imitated the things of Giorgione that many times things done by [Titian] were deemed done by Giorgione himself. Many, many are the works that Titian did, and he was particularly very excellent in portraiture and whoever would want to discuss all [of his work] would require a long time of it. However, I will make brief mention of his most notable things.

'Works of his hand in Venice include the narrative that was left incomplete by Giorgione in the Sala del Gran [Maggiore] Consiglio in which Frederick Barbarossa kneels before Pope Alexander IV who puts his foot on his neck.[37] The panel of the high altar in the Church of the Brothers Minor called the Cà Grande [the Frari] in which there is Our Lady going up into Heaven and the twelve Apostles is his. But of this work, for being done on canvas and poorly cared for, there is little to be seen. In another panel, in the same church, he painted the Virgin with Her Child in arms, St Peter and St George, and the kneeling patrons of the chapel portrayed from life. In the little Church of San Niccolò, of the same convent, is the panel in which there is the *Madonna with Her Child* in Her arms surrounded by many saints gazing at her. Among them is a nude St Sebastian, and this work is seen in prints. In the Church of San Rocco is a picture in which there is *Christ Carrying the Cross* with a rope around His neck pulled by a Hebrew. This work today is the greatest devotional object that the Venetians have; thus, it can be said that the work has earned more than the master.[38] [526] The picture is his done with beautiful grace in Santa Maria Maggiore, where St John the Baptist is in the desert among some stones, a lamb, and a landscape that has some trees above the bank of a river. The Doge and Titian himself are portrayed in the picture in the hall of the Collegio where *Our Lady, St Mark and St Andrew* are seen, a work truly very beautiful. The panel of the altar of St Peter Martyr, in the Church of San Giovanni e Paolo, is his, where this saint, larger than life, within a grove of very large trees with other figures, has fallen to the ground and is wounded in the head by a soldier. [The saint] is seen to be at the point of death, and in the air, two nude angels come from a light in Heaven that illuminates the landscape. And this painting is conducted with more care and is the best studied that Titian ever did.

'Many soldiers fighting while a horrible storm comes down from the sky are in the great narrative of the rout of Chiaradadda in the Sala del Gran Consiglio. Above the door in the Salotto d' Oro, in front of the Sala del Consiglio de' Dieci, is a painting in which there is Christ sitting at table with Cleophas and Luke. In the Scuola of Santa Maria della Carità, the Glorious Virgin climbs the steps of the temple where there are many portraits drawn from life. The panel of the high altar in which there is the *Holy Spirit* in the Church of the Brothers of Santo Spirito is his. Three pictures in oil are on the ceiling of Santo Spirito, in which there are *Abraham Sacrificing Isaac*, David cutting off the head of Goliath, and Cain who has killed Abel. And in the panel finished with the very greatest art that is on the altar of St Lawrence in the church of the Cruciechieri [Santa Maria Assunta] [527] there is this martyr, foreshortened over the grate, who, surrounded by many people, has the fire under him. And the night is portrayed there illuminated by that fire and by two lights that two servants hold and from a light of splendour that, coming from Heaven, separates the clouds and overcomes every other light. And many figures appear at the windows in the background with oil lamps and with lighted candles, and the reflections of the lights make very beautiful effects.

'In Vicenza the *Judgment of Solomon* in fresco, under the loggia, where there are discussions at public audiences, is of [Titian's] hand. He did two pictures in Ferrara to complete a little room of the duke where other painters had painted. In the first is a river of red wine around which there are many intoxicated musicians and singers and a very beautiful sleeping nude woman. And in the other are many cupids and cherubs in different poses, and among the others a little boy is marvellous urinating into a river, and all this work is conducted with very great diligence. At this time Titian developed a friendship with Messer Lodovico Ariosto who then wrote of him:

> ... and Titian, who honours
> Not less Cador, than Venice and Urbino.

In Cador, his country, he painted a panel in which there is Our Lady and the Bishop St Tiziano and himself, portrayed kneeling. In the Cathedral of Verona he did the *Assumption of the Queen of Heaven* with the Apostles at the foot of the facade in a panel [528] which is very esteemed in that city.

'These are the most famous portraits done by him: Emperor Charles V done many times, and the last time that he portrayed him he was made a knight and he was allotted 200 scudi at the beginning of each year by the Camera of Naples and every time he did [Charles's] portrait he would be given 1,000 scudi; King Philip of Spain; Pope Paul III many times; Duke Ottavio; Ferdinand, King of the Romans; Emperor Maximilian and his brother; Queen Maria; the Duke of Saxony when he was a prisoner; King Francis I of France; Francesco Sforza, Duke of

Milan; the Marquis of Pescara; Antonio da Leva; Monsignor Pietro Bembo before and also after he was made cardinal; Fracastoro; and Cardinal Accolti of Ravenna. The Grand Duke Francesco de' Medici has this [last] today, as he also has that of Cardinal Ippolito de' Medici in Hungarian dress. For Monsignor Giovanni della Casa, a very rare poet, [Titian] did a portrait of a Venetian gentlewoman so beautiful that it was illustrated by him with that sonnet which begins:

Titian saw well in new form
My idol, whose beautiful eyes open and turn.

He painted many doges of Venice and, in sum, there has not been a prince, or lord, or gentlemen of any name in the time of Titian who was not painted by him.

'Many very beautiful [529] pictures of his hand belong to King Philip, and among the others a *Last Supper of Christ* with the Apostles in a picture, seven braccia long, of marvellous beauty. And a very beautiful portrait of *Cardinal Ardinghello* is in the house of Baccio here. But it would be much too long if I wanted to recount all the pictures made for individual people. In the end, he died of old age in the year 1576, being ninety-eight or ninety-nine years of age, there being plague in Venice. And he was buried in the Church of the Frari, where he was not given an individual burial according to his merit, the city all troubled by the bad pestilence.'

Jacopo Sansovino

'The excellent sculptor Jacopo Sansovino[39] was the son of Antonio di Jacopo Tatti of Florence but because he learned the art of sculpture from Andrea Contucci from Monte Sansovino, he always derived his last name from the country of his master. He was greatly valued in architecture and did many buildings with great praise that we will not discuss now as only the most famous works of sculpture done by him will be mentioned. The marble *St James the Great* of his hand is in Santa Maria del Fiore in Florence, a figure so celebrated, so alive, and so graceful that nothing more [can be said].[40] A very beautiful marble *Venus* on a seashell in the house of the Cav. Gaddi was done by him and a *Cecero*,[41] also of marble. Two little boys holding an escutcheon, worked by him in marble with all the art that it is possible to do, are in the house of Giovanfrancesco Ridolfi. [530] A marble *Bacchus* of his hand that, lifting an arm in the air, holds a cup in its hand with very beautiful pose is in the rooms of the Most Serene Grand Duke Francesco. And this figure is so beautiful that it is esteemed the most beautiful statue that has been done by a modern master and the grand duke, as a very good judge of this art, holds it very dear.

'The larger than life marble Madonna with Her Child in Her arms is his work in the Church of Sant' Agostino in Rome, a figure very praised. And in the Church of the Spaniards [Santa Maria di Monserrato] is a *St James* of marble, four braccia high, done with great diligence and knowledge. Figures done by him seen in Venice include the *St John* of marble which is above the holy-water font in the Cà Grande [the Frari] and the life-size *Madonna* that is above the door of San Marco. The Madonna who holds Her Child in Her arms is above the gate of the Arsenal, and the two very beautiful statues representing *Neptune* and *Mars*, each seven braccia high, are at the entrance of the staircases of the Palace of San Marco. And he did many figures and narratives of bronze there of which – for it not being our purpose – I will not speak further.

'In Padua there is a great marble half-relief narrative by his hand of a miracle of St Anthony of Padua put in the Chapel of the Santo, esteemed a very rare thing. Sansovino was a very excellent architect as it is not possible to believe the many important buildings that he did in Venice, or, it is possible to say, were returned to life by him [531] and made beautiful. In the end, he died in the year 1570, at ninety-three years of age and was buried in his chapel in San Gimignano and above his tomb is a marble statue done by him while he was alive representing himself. And Messer Doctor Bernardo Baldovinetti, who greatly delights in poetry, has done this epitaph about him:

> Sansovino, who made Adria proud
> Of bronzes and marbles, of palaces and temples
> Who illuminated the Arno, and early removed the effort from the art of sculpture; now here is laid.[42]

Agnolo Bronzino

'The painter Agnolo, called Bronzino,[43] was born in the neighbourhood of Monticelli outside the Porta a San Friano of honest family but of poor and humble fortune. And having learned to read and write at an early age, his father, seeing that he was very inclined to design, put him to be with a painter who painted coarse things, with whom he was two [534] years. Then, he was put to work with Raffaellino del Garbo and, finally, was settled with Jacopo da Pontormo with whom he profited greatly, as was then seen.

'The first works of account that Bronzino did, being still young, are in the Certosa of Florence [at Galluzzo] above a door that goes to the cloister. On the outside is a *Pietà* with two angels in fresco. And, on the inside is a nude *St Lawrence* on the grate, in oil on the wall. He then did two Evangelists in two medallions, in oil, in the Chapel of Lodovico Capponi the Elder in Santa Felicita,[44] and he coloured some figures in the vault. The narrative in fresco, in the upper cloister of the Badia in Florence, of St Benedict when he throws himself naked on the thorns, held a very good picture, is by his hand. He painted a very beautiful shrine in fresco in the garden of the nuns called the Poverine [San Girolamo] in which Christ shows himself to the Magdalene in the guise of a gardener. A picture done by him in oil is on the first pillar on the right towards the high altar in Santa Trinità, where a dead Christ, Our Lady, St John, and St Mary Magdalene are seen in a very beautiful manner.

'Then, having moved to Pesaro, [Bronzino] painted the fable of *Apollo and Marsyas* with many figures on a harpsichord case for Guidobaldo, Duke of Urbino. This work is held to be a very rare thing. He also did the portrait of the duke and some very beautiful figures in oil on the spandrels of the vault of one of his villas [Villa Imperiale]. Returning to Florence, he did many portraits and pictures that it would be a long thing [535] to recount. Two pictures from his hand of the Glorious Virgin with other very beautiful figures are in the house of Carlo di Bartolomeo Panciatichi, chamberlain of the Grand Duke, and portraits of his father and mother, so natural that they appear alive. And the same gentleman has a picture, also by him, in which there is a *Christ Crucified*, done with much study and with great diligence. He did a *Pietà* with some angels in fresco in a tabernacle for Matteo Strozzi for his villa of San Casciano, a work truly worthy of praise. Antonio Salviati has a picture of his of the *Nativity of Christ* in little figures. This work is held dear by that gentleman as a very rare thing, as it truly is, and it is seen in prints and copied in many places, Salviati having courteously allowed this. Bronzino helped his master Pontormo do the work at Careggi, where he himself did five figures in the spandrels of the vault – *Fortune, Fame, Peace, Justice,* and *Prudence* – with some very well-done cherubs.

'[Bronzino] then painted the Chapel of the Ducal Palace,[45] in the vault of which he did sections with very beautiful cherubs, *St Francis, St Jerome, St Michael the Archangel,* and *St John,* figures done with great diligence. And on the walls, he did three narratives of Moses: when the serpents rain down on the people with many beautiful considerations in the figures of those who are bitten; when the manna comes down from the sky; and when the people pass through the Red Sea with the [536] submersion of Pharaoh. This was printed in Antwerp. In the panel of this chapel, in oil, he did Christ taken down from the Cross in the lap of his Mother but Grand Duke Cosimo removed it and sent it as a gift, as a very rare thing, to Granvelle, a man of very great favour next to Charles V. Another, similar, also done by Bronzino, was put up in place of it between two very beautiful pictures by the hand of the same, in one of which is the *Angel Gabriel* and the *Virgin Annunciate* in the other.

'[Bronzino] was excellent in doing portraits and did many of them, among which was that of Grand Duke Cosimo and of his consort Sig. Donna Eleonora, which could not possibly be more beautiful. He also portrayed all the children of this Grand Duke at an early age and then at other older times, and these pictures in all perfection are seen today in the collection of Grand Duke Francesco with many others done by the same. He then designed fourteen cartoons for Arras tapestries for the Sala de' Duecento that came out very beautifully when finished.

'Then [Bronzino] did the panel in the Chapel of the Zanchini in Santa Croce, on the left on entering the church through the middle door, painting there *Christ Descending into Limbo* to deliver the Holy Fathers. Here there are very beautiful nudes and men and women in different and graceful poses and Jacopo da Pontormo and Giovambatista Gelli portrayed from life. And, among the women are Madonna Costanza da Sommaia, wife of Giovambatista Doni, deserving of endless praise for her beauty and modesty, [537] and Madonna Camilla Tedaldi del Corno, no less beautiful and modest. These portraits are, in sum, beautiful and the panel completely of a beautiful manner, good design, and charming colour.[46] Equally of his hand is the panel of the *Resurrection of Our Lord,*[47] put in the Chapel of the Guadagni behind the choir of the Annunziata, in which an angel of all beauty is seen. In the house of Jacopo Salviati there is painted very beautifully, in a picture done by him, *Venus with a Satyr.* The panel in the Duomo in Pisa is his work, where there is a nude *Christ with the Cross* with many other figures among whom is a flayed St Bartholomew that seems to be a true dissection. The panel in Santo Spirito in Florence is of his hand, in which Christ is seen in the form of a gardener appearing to the Magdalene.[48]

'Pontormo having left the choir of San Lorenzo incomplete at his death, Bronzino completed it and did many nudes that were missing in the part at the base of the *Deluge,* and he also painted many figures on the other parts. And below, where there remained an unpainted space between the windows, he did a nude St Lawrence on the grate surrounded by some cherubs and the portrait of Pontormo to the right of St Lawrence. In these figures he showed he had surpassed his master. He then did two panels. In one of these he painted a *Deposition from the Cross,* with many figures, that was sent to Porto Ferraio on Elba to the City of Cosmopolis and put in the Church of the Zoccolanti Brothers. And in the other he painted the *Nativity* of Jesus Christ, and this is in [538] Pisa in the Church of the Knights of St Stephen.

'[Bronzino] painted all the great men of the House of Medici in little pictures all of one size on sheet-tin. He began with Giovanni di Bicci and Cosimo the Elder up to Catherine, Queen of France, of that line and, for the other [line], from Lorenzo, brother of Cosimo the Elder, up to Grand Duke Cosimo and his children. These portraits are in order behind the door of a study in the apartment of new rooms of Grand Duke Francesco. Here there are many ancient statues of marble and of bronze and small modern paintings, very rare manuscripts, and endless medals of gold, silver, and bronze, arranged in very beautiful order.

'Finally, Bronzino painted on a wall of the Church of San Lorenzo the martyrdom of that saint in fresco with an endless number of figures differing in dress and in gesture with a very beautiful view. And many nudes are done there with great diligence and design.[49] The last work that he finished was the beautiful panel of the miracle of Christ when he resuscitates the daughter of the synagogue, put in the rich and charming chapel of the Cav. Gaddi.[50] And, on his death, he left another not completely finished panel in which there is the *Conception of the Madonna* which was given by him to the Monastery [della Concezione] that is being built on the Via della Scala. Sig. Valori has a large picture of his hand in terretta on canvas, in which the wedding of Catherine de' Medici, Queen of France, is seen with many figures in different poses. In summary, Bronzino was [539] an excellent painter and not a little valued in poetry and, particularly, in writing in the style of Berni.[51] In the end, he died at the age of sixty-nine years and was buried with great honour in the Church of San Christofano on the Corso degli Adimari. And his pupil Alessandro Allori imitated his master no less in the excellence of his poetry and in his other virtues than in his painting. [Allori] recited in the Accademia del Disegno a very beautiful oration he composed on [Bronzino's] death and then he did this epitaph for him:

Not dead who lives as Bronzino lived,
His soul is in Heaven, here are his bones, and his name on Earth
Illustrious, where he sang, painted, and wrote.

Tommaso da San Friano

'Tommaso d'Antonio Manzuoli,[52] and not Mazzuoli as Vasari says, was born in the Borgo San Friano and, therefore, was called Tommaso da San Friano. He learned the art of painting from the painter Carlo da Loro but left his master behind by a great distance. The first work that he did was a *Madonna* that is in the Church of the Paradiso outside of Florence, put between *St Bridget* and *St Anthony*. The panel in which there is the *Assumption of the Glorious Virgin* into Heaven in San Donato, in Polverosa, is of his hand. He sent a panel to Ancona, in which Our Lady was painted in the act of mercy, receiving under Her mantle all those who apply to Her.

'Works done by [Manzuoli] in Florence include a panel [540] of the *Nativity* of the Son of God in Santo Apostolo and another in the Church of the Candeli, in which there is a dead Christ in the arms of His Mother and the Marys in mourning poses, a very praised work. A Virgin Mary with four saints is in the Arte de' Coiai [Leatherworkers]. And a very beautiful panel of the *Visitation* of the Madonna is his in San Pier Maggiore of a beautiful manner and charming in colour in which the figures are very well studied, and it is all well composed with a well-done view. There are two pictures of his hand in the Studiolo of grand duke Francesco done with great care. In one are seen those who go naked to some mountains and, lowered with rope in various ways, extract diamonds. And in the other are *Dædalus and Icarus* who, flying, flee from the labyrinth with many other figures.

'Many are the pictures and the portraits that [Manzuoli] did for various people but very beautiful among the others is a small painting of his that Raffael Gucci has, in which *Adam and Eve* are painted with two very beautiful children and a very charming landscape.

[Gucci] is a very gracious young man who, aside from his many other virtues, sings music excellently. Tommaso would have succeeded in becoming a very rare painter if death, at the age of thirty-nine years, had not removed him from the world where he was mourned and buried in the Carmine in the middle of the church under a headstone of marble.'[53]

Giorgio Vasari

'Appearing now before the Aretine painter and architect Giorgio Vasari,[54] if I wanted to recount all of his works, a large field would be handed to me to discuss since he has done so many of them that such a thing would not come to an end. Therefore, as was done with the other painters, [542] I will discuss him with brevity, only making mention of his principal works. He was the son of an Antonio Vasari of Arezzo, and because nature inclined him greatly to drawing, he was directed by his father to the art of painting and had the first principles from Guglielmo Marcilla [Guillaume de Marcillat] of France. Then, coming to Florence, under Michelangelo Buonarroti and Andrea del Sarto, he gave some time to the work of drawing and then, returning to his country, he did some paintings. But Cardinal Ippolito de' Medici passing at this time through Arezzo, he took him to Rome in his service. There he would have occasion to attend to the study of drawing, to then become that worthy man that he became, in his rapidity of painting and in his copying of inventions. Among the first works that he did as his own was a picture for the Cardinal de' Medici, in which there is Venus with the three Graces dressing her and a libidinous satyr among some bushes looking at Venus with very great desire.

'Then coming to be in Florence in the house of Ottaviano de' Medici, [Vasari] painted, in a picture three braccia high, Christ dead, carried by Nicodemus, Joseph, and others to the tomb, and behind there are the Marys weeping. And Duke Alessandro had this picture, keeping it in his room while he was living, and today it is in that of the Most Serene Grand Duke Francesco. By order of Duke Alessandro, he finished the ground floor room of the Medici Palace, left incomplete by Giovanni da Udine. He painted four narratives there of the deeds of Caesar, and when [543] he did this work he was not older than eighteen years. But here it is permissible to make a leap and to come to his more esteemed works, as too much time would be lost to speak of everything, and by now the day has passed its greatest part.

'There is of [Vasari's] hand in Rome a panel, in which there is Christ taken down from the Cross in the Church of Sant' Agostino. His room painted in fresco with narratives of the deeds of Pope Paul III is in the Cancelleria in the Palace of San Giorgio. Here there are very beautiful inventions with great numbers of figures with varied poses in different costume and with very beautiful views. This work was done by him in one hundred days with the help of some apprentices. The panel in which there is the *Conversion of St Paul* is in San Pietro Montorio, and the panel of the high altar, where he painted the *Beheading of St John*, is in the Confraternity of the Misericordia [San Giovanni Decollato]. And in the house that then belonged to Bindo Altoviti, the vault of the ground floor is painted in fresco, and four large pictures in oil of the four seasons of the year on the ceiling of an antechamber and many easel pictures of his are also in this house.

'For the hermitage of Camaldoli in Tuscany, in the church of these fathers, there are three panels of [Vasari's] hand, two on the tramezzo. In one of these is *Our Lady with Her Child* in Her arms surrounded by some saints. And in the other, the *Nativity* of Jesus Christ, where a night is imitated very beautifully, illuminated by the splendour of the Son of God and of the angels that are in the air. And the third is that of the high altar, in which the Saviour of the World is taken down from the Cross, and in fresco on a wall [544] some narratives of St Romualdo. For Monte Sansovino [San Augustino] he did a panel of the *Assumption of the Madonna*. In San Michele in Bosco, outside Bologna, he painted the refectory of that monastery, dividing it into three pictures. Abraham in the Mambre Valley has prepared food for the angels in the first. Christ in the house of Mary Magdalene and Martha telling Mary that she has chosen the better role is in the second. And, in the third, St Gregory is at table with twelve poor men, among whom he recognized one as Christ. And in the face of St Gregory he portrayed Pope Clement VII, and he portrayed Duke Alessandro among the many lords and ambassadors who are around them watching them eat and many brothers of that convent among the servants.

'Moving to Venice, [Vasari] did nine painted pictures in the palace of Giovanni Cornaro that is by San Benedetto. Two panels were done by him in the Duomo in Pisa. In one is Our Lady, St Jerome, St Luke, St Cecilia, St Martha, St Augustine, and St Guy, the hermit. And in the other, Christ is dead in the lap of His Mother at the foot of the Cross, with the Marys and the thieves on their crosses. Having then been called to Naples, he painted the refectory in the monastery of Monteoliveto built by King Alfonso I, doing compartments of stucco on the vault with grotesquerie, figures, and the forty-eight celestial signs and six panels on the walls, in oil. The rain of manna on the Hebrew people is in the three that are above the entrance of the refectory. And narratives [545] of Christ when He dines in the house of Simon are in the other three, with many beautiful inventions and virtues appropriate to the monks. And on six walls down the length of that refectory he painted six parables of Jesus Christ. And on the panel of the high altar in that church he did the Glorious Virgin presenting Her Child to Simeon in the temple. And on the vault of the guesthouse, in life-size figures in fresco, he did *Christ with the Cross* on His shoulder with many saints who long to carry it. For Sig. Don Pedro of Toledo, Viceroy of Naples, he painted a chapel in his garden at Pozzuolo with some stucco decorations. In the sacristy of San Giovanni Carbonaro, a convent of the Observant Hermit Monks of St Augustine, there are twenty-four pictures of his hand of narratives from the Old Testament and a Christ crucified with beautiful stucco decoration in the chapel outside of the church.

'In Santa Fiora e Lucilla, a monastery of the Black Monks of Monte Cassino [in Arezzo], [Vasari] painted the *Wedding of Queen Esther with King Ahasuerus* in the refectory, in an oil panel fifteen braccia long. In this there are an endless number of figures in different poses, conducted with great diligence. He did many paintings in Arezzo, his country, including a *Nativity* of Christ in fresco with many figures for the nuns of Santa Margherita in a chapel of their garden. He has painted completely by himself the choir, of which he became owner, in the Pieve, together with the free-standing panel that can be seen from both sides. A panel for the nuns of Santa Maria Novella is his [546], in which there is the *Annunciation* to the Madonna by the angel and two saints on the sides. And in his house, built to his design, there are endless paintings done by him in public and private rooms.

'Three large panels, works of [Vasari's], are seen in the refectory of the Black Friars of San Piero in Perugia. That in the middle is the *Wedding at Cana* in Galilee. The Prophet Elisha sweetening the very bitter pot with flour is on the right.[55] And in the other, on the left, is St Benedict who in time of very great famine sees the angels who bring him some camels loaded with flour. For Santa Maria di Scolca, about three miles outside of Rimini, he painted the choir in the church, doing prophets, sibyls, and evangelists there, and four large figures in the gallery [of the cupola]. And in the panel, in oil, put in the middle between two pictures, is the *Adoration of the Magi* and horses and giraffes with the people of the three kings among these saints [the Magi]. The panel of the high altar in the Church of San Francesco in Rimini is his, in which he painted this saint receiving the stigmata from Christ, where he portrayed the mountain of La Vernia.

'Principal works of [Vasari's] hand in Florence include the panel of the *Conception of the Madonna* in Sant' Apostolo that was the first panel that he did in Florence and, perhaps, the best and done with most care.[56] The *Last Supper* of Our Lord, in a panel in oil, is in the refectory of the nuns of the Murate. And the panel of the martyrdom of St Gismondo is in San Lorenzo.[57]

'In the palace of the Most Serene Grand Duke Francesco [547] [Vasari] painted the room called The Elements, and on a balcony in the corner of that room he did the deeds of *Saturn and Ops* on the ceiling. And on the ceiling of another great room are all the story of *Ceres and Proserpina*. And on the ceiling of [yet] another are narratives of the goddess Berecynthia and of Cybele with her triumph and the four seasons and the twelve months on the walls. On the ceiling of another is the *Birth of Jove*, with other deeds of his indicated. On another balcony, in the corner of the same room, are other narratives of Jove and of Juno. And in another room that follows is the *Birth of Hercules* and all of his labours.

'And on the level of the Gran Sala of this palace he painted eight newly done rooms, including public and private rooms and a chapel, with various paintings and portraits from life of the deeds of the illustrious men of the House of Medici. He began with Cosimo the Elder, and every room has taken its name from the most famous of those painted. In the first one are the most notable deeds of Cosimo the Elder and those virtues that were most peculiar to him, and his greatest friends and servants and children drawn from life. Lorenzo the Elder follows in the second with this [same] organization. Pope Leo is in the third and Pope Clement in the fourth. Lord Giovanni [delle Bande Nere] is in the fifth, and Duke Cosimo in the sixth. And then follows the chapel, where there is a large picture by the hand of Raphael of Urbino between *St Cosmas* and *St Damian*, figures done by Giorgio. In the apartments of the grand duchess he painted many deeds of illustrious Greek, Hebrew, Latin, and Tuscan women in four rooms. [548]

'But what will I say of the ceiling of the Gran Sala, a work of so much importance and worthy of Grand Duke Cosimo having given it thought? In this there are about forty great narratives, some of them in pictures of ten braccia in every dimension, with very great figures in all styles, with a variety of bodies, of faces, and of clothing where there are different arms, horses, artillery of every sort, voyages, storms, snows, and so many other things that it is a marvel to see it. Although it is true that Vasari was helped by many apprentices in this work, still, all came from him and from his drawings. And on the walls of this hall, which are each eighty braccia long and twenty tall, he painted many wars in fresco that it would be a long thing to recount. But among the others is the taking of the fortress of Siena, done at night, where very beautiful reverberations of lights are seen coming out of the lanterns in the field.[58]

'The panel in the Carmine is by [Vasari's] hand, in which is Christ crucified, Our Lady, St John, and the Magdalene. The panel of the high altar in the Badia, in which there is the *Assumption of the Queen of Heaven* [is his]. Three panels were done by him in Santa Maria Novella. In the first is *Christ on the Cross* surrounded by some virtues.[59] The *Resurrection of the Saviour* of the World is in the second.[60] And the Glorious Virgin with the *Mystery of the Rosary* is in the third.[61] Another three of them are in Santa Croce: that of the *Holy Spirit*;[62] that of *St Thomas Touching Christ*;[63] and that of the Son of God carrying the Cross.[64] Many were the pictures and the portraits that he did for many people and also other works [549] that for brevity I have passed by. But among the other very beautiful pictures is that in the Udienza [del Magistrato] de' Nove [Conservatori] in which there is the face of Our Lord. And very praised was a portrait that he did of Messer *Alessandro Strozzi* before he was Bishop of Volterra. Having seen it, Giambatista Strozzi the Younger, a very virtuous gentleman who explains his concepts very well on paper, moved by its beauty, did two madrigals[65] about Vasari, and this is the first:

From the beautiful Vase, art emerges from his studio
  His vermilion and white drawn so alive,
  And colour natural,
  That will not be found wanting, by time or else.
  Nor even by Apelles for that first honour.
  And it is true that while much
  Richer crowns and more brilliant garlands
  Our Alexander [Strozzi] has, this makes him greater.

Now listen to the second:

There at the beginning of the day
  Flowers, violets and roses, and how many lilies

Pearls, and diamonds
I see; but alive in noble Vase ornate:
Yes alive and clear sparkling,
That never heats nor chills,
Dry wind, nor lightning of the sky
Will not change in them one
Page, so much virtue the Heaven to one. [550]

'Vasari, in summary, was very expeditious in his paintings and very copious of invention. And, in addition to painting, he was very practised as an architect and also delighted in writing. Therefore, he did that great work of the *Lives* of the painters, sculptors, and architects, beginning with Cimabue up to [Vasari's] time, and truly it was written with some felicity and with good style. Finally, he was commissioned to paint the cupola of Santa Maria del Fiore, which he started, and he did there those prophets around the circle of the lantern that are seen there. But, interrupted by death, he was not able to pass further forward, and then Federico Zuccaro finished all of it. He died in Florence at sixty-three years of age and of Christian well-being 1574. His body was taken with great honour to Arezzo and buried in the Vasari choir in the Pieve. The young student Pietro Bertini of Arezzo has done this epitaph about him:

Turn here your eyes, oh you who pass, and halt your step.
Here of Giorgio is the carnal veil,
And his fame fills the world, and flies to heaven.
Honour his temple, his name, his spirit, and his stone.

'Having finished here our discussion of those painters and sculptors who have gone on to a better life, and who appear to us most excellent, and needing now to say something of those who live, I will begin with those foreigners of whom I have [551] some information. Perhaps it could be that there are others, in addition to those of whom I will speak, who would be found worthy of praise and of remembrance. But, not having knowledge of them, I will be excused if I do not make mention of them.'

Tintoretto

'Thus in Venice,[66] the excellent painter Jacopo Robusti, called Tintoretto,[67] has already been born of a Batista Robusti, a citizen of that city who followed the wool trade and was a dyer. Being very inclined by nature to design, he gave himself with great diligence to drawing all the good things of Venice and made a great study of the statues of Jacopo Sansovino representing *Mars* and *Neptune*. And then he took for his principal master the works of the divine Michelangelo, not concerned with any expense in collecting [Michelangelo's] figures from the sacristy of San Lorenzo and equally all the good models of the best statues that were in Florence. Therefore, he himself acknowledged that he did not recognize any except the Florentine craftsmen as masters in the things of drawing. But in colour he said he imitated nature and then, particularly, Titian, so much so that many portraits done by him have been held [to be] by the hand of Titian. He then, by his own natural instinct, is copious in invention, spirited and graceful in poses, and very charming in colour.[68]

'[Tintoretto] has done many beautiful works in Venice but I will only speak of several of the principal ones and they are these. In the Church of Sant' Anna there is a picture in which there is the sibyl showing the Glorious Virgin to the Emperor Octavian. Two panels are in [552] San Benedetto, that of the high altar where he painted *Our Lady with Her Child* in Her arms and the *Nativity* of Our Lord, in the other. And on the shutters of the organ of this church he has painted the *Virgin Annunciate* on the inside and the Samaritan speaking to Christ at the well on the outside. A picture in which there is the serpent raised by Moses is in San Bastiano and a picture sixteen-feet tall and ten wide, in which there is Christ crucified with figures larger than life, is in San Severo. His panel of the high altar in San Cassiano shows the *Resurrection of Christ* with some saints. And this panel is put between two pictures, fourteen braccia tall and nine wide, in one of which is *Christ on the Cross* and, in the other, when He went into Limbo. A *Last Supper* of Christ with the Apostles and two panels with narratives of saints are in San Felice. A Christ taken down from the Cross is in Santa Maria della Carità. In the Church of the Jesuits is a panel of the crucified Saviour with the Virgin and the Marys and five pictures in the Trinità contain narratives of Adam and of Eve and one of *Cain and Abel*. A panel of the *Adoration of the Magi* is in Spirito Santo. And his is the panel on the high altar in San Marciliano, in which there is this saint with other figures. Two pictures, thirty-six braccia tall and twenty wide, with figures larger than life are in Santa Maria dell' Orto, in one of which is the *Last Judgment* and in the other the narrative of Moses when he receives the law and the golden calf is worshiped. And in the [553] cupola of the high altar he finished a very beautiful construction in fresco with angels playing trumpets. And above the altar he has done *Justice, Fortitude, Temperance,* and *Prudence,* and in this church another panel of St Agnes resuscitating the dead child of the tyrant, and a choir of angels playing various instruments, on another ceiling. In Santa Maria Maddalena are two pictures of this saint, in one when she preaches and in the other when, wanting to take communion, she swoons and dies.

'On the shutters of the organ in Santa Maria de' Servi [Tintoretto] painted the *Annunciation* on the inside and *St Augustine* and *St Paul* on the outside and *Cain Killing Abel* on the wall in fresco. A panel of the *Trinity* with some saints is in San Girolamo, and the *Last Supper* of Christ with the Apostles is in San Simeone. Another similar *Last Supper* is in San Polo and a panel of the *Ascension of the Madonna.* Three pictures are in Santa Margherita: in the first Christ washes the feet of His Apostles; in the second He is preaching on the mount; and the *Last Supper* with the Apostles is in the third. In Santa Maria [Assunta] de' Crociferi, the panel of the high altar in which there is the *Ascent of the Virgin* into Heaven is his and a picture of the *Circumcision of Our Lord.* And, in the refectory of these fathers is the narrative of *Canagalilea.* A panel of the *Ascension of Christ* with some saints is in Santa Maria Zubenigo, and he has painted the Four Evangelists on the inside of the shutters of the organ and the *Conversion of St Paul* on the outside. [554] A panel of a Christ crucified and the Magdalene is in San Francesco, and a panel of the *Birth of St John the Baptist* is in San Zaccheria. In San Gimignano is a panel in which there is St Catherine and the angel who comforts her as she goes to debate. A panel is in San Giuseppe, where there is the *Archangel Michael* with the demon underneath him, and the patron who had him do the panel is portrayed from life there kneeling. A panel is in San Gervaso e Protaso in which St Anthony is seized by devils and Christ appears in the sky to help him, and there are two pictures in the Chapel of the Sacrament of this church: when Christ washes the feet of the Apostles in one and when he eats with them in the other. In San Salvestro is a panel of *Christ Baptized by St John* and a picture of the Saviour praying on the mountain. A panel of an *Our Lady and Christ* is in San Moisè, and a picture of the narrative of the *Raising of the Serpent* is in Santi Giovanni e Paolo. In the Scuola di San Marco are four pictures of miracles of that saint where different beautiful poses are seen: the dead raised, spirits freed, the Moors in flight, the coming of the rain from Heaven to extinguish the fire in which they tried to burn a martyr, and dreadful effects of an accident at sea.

'In the Scuola di San Rocco there are thirteen pictures on the ceiling. In the first, that is, that in the middle, which is forty braccia long and sixteen wide, there is Moses with the serpent above him, and the principal figures are ten feet tall. In the second, Moses makes the water come out of the stone with his rod. [555] In the third is the rain of manna from the sky. In the fourth is the *Passover* [the supper of the Easter Angel]. In the fifth, Abraham sacrifices Isaac. In the sixth, Jonah escapes from the whale. In the seventh are *Adam and Eve*. In the eighth is the resurrection of the dead.[69] In the ninth is *Jacob's Ladder*. In the tenth is *Jacob Sleeping*. In the eleventh, the Hebrew people pass through the Red Sea. In the twelfth, the people of Pharaoh are submerged, and in the thirteenth is Moses with the column of fire. And around these pictures there are some little pictures in chiaroscuro in triangles. Then ten pictures, each twenty-five braccia tall, [are] on the walls of this scuola, in which the principal figures are each nine feet tall. In the first one is the *Nativity of Christ*. In the second He is baptized by St John. In the third He gives the *Sermon on the Mount*. In the fourth is the *Resurrection*. In the fifth is the *Last Supper* with the Apostles. In the sixth is the *Pool of Bethesda*. In the seventh is the *Miracle of the Five Loaves and Two Fishes*. In the eighth is the *Resurrection of Lazarus*. In the ninth is the *Ascension of Christ*, and in the tenth He is tempted by the Devil. Four pictures are in the Albergo of this scuola. In the first, twenty braccia in height and forty in length, Christ is crucified with a great number of figures. In the second, He is led to Mount Calvary. In the third, He is seen led before Pilate, and in the fourth, He is shown, beaten, to the people. There is a narrative of St Rocco and God the Father with a choir of angels on the ceiling of this Albergo, and the [556] *Adoration of the Magi* in another picture, with another endless number of figures that I pass by for brevity.

'In the choir of the Church of San Rocco there are four pictures of the deeds of this saint and another picture in the middle of the church containing the *Miracle of the Poor Person* to whom Christ said, "Take up your belongings and go."[70] In the Scuola de' Mercatanti is a picture of the *Ascension of the Virgin* with many portraits from life. In the Spedale degli Incurabili there is a panel in which there is St Ursula with her company.

'Then there are many works done by him in the palace of the Signoria where the prince lives [Palazzo Ducale]. In an atrium [Atrio Quadrato] going into the Collegio, going up the staircases, he has there four pictures with narratives of Vulcan, the three Graces, Pallas, Bacchus, and Ariadne. And Jeronimo de' Priuli, Prince of Venice, is portrayed on the ceiling kneeling before Justice, St Mark, and Venice. In another room that is called the Anticollegio [Sala delle Quattro Porte] a ceiling is painted in fresco that, in the first picture, has Jove coming down from Heaven and, on the advice of the gods, leading Venice to the water. The *Liberty* [of Venice] is painted in the second. And Juno presents the peacock to Venice in the third. Then there are four figures signifying the four cities of the dominion of the Signoria, and another four that denote the four cities of the sea. And in the [Sala del] Collegio there is a large picture in which the Most Serene Lord, Niccolò da Ponte, today Prince of Venice,[71] is painted in a humble posture before the Queen of Heaven with Christ in Her arms and with some saints surrounded by a choir of angels. [557] In the room called the Prega [Sala del Senato][72] there is a picture of the *Resurrection of Our Lord* above the throne of the prince. In the Sala del Gran Consiglio he has painted about a hundred princes of Venice and pictures of the deeds of this city, in the defence of Brescia, in the taking of Gallipoli, and in the victories it had against the Este and Visconti. And there is a picture there of twenty-four braccia, in which the prince of Venice on a royal throne with the Signoria gives audience to many ambassadors and people and receives the offerings and the tribute of many nations. And Venice is there coming down from the sky in the company of many virgins and the winged lion presents her a branch of olive and one of palm, and the prince rises to do her reverence. And in this work there are endless portraits from life done with great diligence and fidelity.

'In the Library [of San Marco] [Tintoretto] painted twelve philosophers and two pictures of narratives of Venice. Above the high altar in the Church of San Marco is the panel done by him of the *Nativity of Christ*.[73] Four pictures of his hand are in the Sala del Collegio.[74] In the first is the portrait of Prince Mozzenigo with the *Ascension of Christ* with many figures. In the second is the portrait of Prince Andrea Griti before the Blessed Virgin who is in the middle of some saints. In the third is the portrait of Doge Donato Francesco in front of Our Lady surrounded by some saints. And in the fourth is the portrait of Prince Piero Lando before the Bearer of the Supreme Good who has St Sebastian, St Anthony, and St Peter beside Her. And in the room of the most excellent [558] lords, heads of the almighty Consiglio de' Dieci, he has painted a narrative of the *Silenzio* [the Prodigal Son] with the four moral virtues.

'Tintoretto has painted many other things as excellently, among which are eight pictures that were sent to King Philip, but time does not allow me to speak of them as would be appropriate. He has been marvellous in portraits and has done many of them. And among the others is one of the excellent sculptor Jacopo Sansovino that is found today belonging to the Most Serene Grand Duke Francesco de' Medici, by whom it is held dear as a rare thing. The king of France [Henry III], when he was in Venice, also wanted to be portrayed by him and, therefore, gave him 100 scudi and made a present of the portrait to Lord Luigi [Alvise] Mocenigo, then Doge of Venice. Tintoretto, today finding himself sixty years of age, neither therefore fails to virtuously do his best but also studies. He takes great pleasure as someone who recognizes good things in having some models of the excellent Giambologna nor, however old, does he tire in imitating them. But enough is said of him.'

Marietta Tintoretta

'Tintoretto has a daughter named Marietta,[75] called Tintoretta by all, who, besides her beauty and grace and knowledge of playing the harpsichord, lute, and other instruments, paints very well and has done many beautiful works. And she did, among the others, the portrait of Jacopo Strada, Antiquarian of Emperor Maximilian II, and the portrait of she herself that, as a rare thing, His Majesty keeps in his room. And [Maximilian], as also King Philip and Archduke Ferdinand, did everything to have this excellent woman with him [559] and sent to ask her of her father. But [Tintoretto], greatly loving her, did not want her taken from his sight. But, having married, she enjoys its virtues and she does not fail continually to paint, finding herself about twenty-eight years. But, because I have no detailed knowledge of her works, I will not move forward in discussing her.'[76]

Jacopo Palma

'In the same city Jacopo Palma,[77] son of Antonio who was the nephew of Palma Vecchio, applied himself to painting to his great praise. After the principles that he had from his father, he was taken to Pesaro by Guidobaldo, Duke of Urbino, and, being seen fit to become a worthy man in painting, he was sent to Rome to study drawing where he resided about eight years. Then, returning to Venice, among the first works that he did, being twenty-three years of age, were two pictures that are in San Niccolò de' Frari. In one is a *Deposition* from the Cross and in the other the *Descent of Christ into Limbo* to deliver the Holy

Fathers. He then did, in the Church of the Jesuits [Crucicchieri], four narratives in two chapels of the life of the Madonna and a panel of the *Coronation of the Virgin*. The sacristy of the Church of San Jacopo dell' Orio was completely painted by him with narratives from the Old Testament, and there are also two pictures there within a chapel of the deeds of St Lawrence. A large picture from his hand is in the Church of Santa Trinità in which there is Christ crucified with a great number of figures, and in San Paterniano, the panel [560] of the high altar in which this saint is painted with other figures.

'[Jacopo's] works include the panel in the Church of Santa Maria Zubenigo, in which there is the *Visitation* of the Virgin to St Elizabeth and the picture above the Chapel of the Sacrament in San Giuliano that shows *Christ Resurrected*. And two pictures represent two visions of the Apocalypse in the place called the Albergo in the Scuola Grande di San Giovanni Evangelista. He has painted three pictures on the ceiling in the Sala del Gran Consiglio. In the largest of these is seen a *Venice Triumphant* with an endless number of nude and clothed figures in different poses, and two deeds of the arms of that republic are shown in the smaller, other two. Then, he has done many paintings for private people such as many narratives of poesies for lords Manno and Armarò Grimani in one of their rooms and a large picture in a hall in which there is *Christ Raising Lazarus* with many figures. Two pictures were for Lord Vettorio Cappello, brother of the Most Serene Lady Bianca, Grand Duchess of Tuscany, one of the *Resurrection* of the Saviour of the World and the other of the killing of the first-born of Egypt. And a picture is his for the Duke of Savoy [Carlo Emanuele I] from the narrative of David, when he cuts off the head of Goliath. And [he painted] for many others that I will pass over for brevity. Today, he has in hand some pictures that will go into the halls of the palace.[78] And a picture forty-six feet high and thirty-three wide will go to the Scuola di Santa Maria e di San Girolamo [Scuola di San Fantin]. In this he is painting an *Assumption of the Glorious Virgin* with a Paradise [561] full of angels and of other figures that has been hoped to succeed as a beautiful work. It is yet believed that Palma, going through life, will attain a very great achievement in art, not being more than thirty-three [forty] today and working so well.'

Paolo Veronese

'Also of great name in Venice is Paolo Caliari[79] of Verona, who was the son of the sculptor Gabriello and learned the art of painting from his uncle, Antonio Baillo [Badile] of Verona. He has done many works but I will make mention only of those that have reached my ears. He did three rather praised panels for the Black Monks in San Benedetto, in Mantua, and a panel in Sant' Andrea in the same city in which there is St Anthony beaten by the Devil. He did this work in competition with many others who are there, and it was held the best. There are two panels of his hand inside the Church of San Giorgio in Verona: that of the high altar showing the martyrdom of St Lawrence [probably St George] and that where a miracle of St Bernabà is seen. In the refectory in San Lorenzo [Santi Nazaro e Celso] of the Black Monks, he did a large picture for them that shows the *Last Supper* of Christ with the Apostles, and the Magdalene is there washing His feet. In Vicenza, in the [Church of the] Madonna del Monte [Berico] in the refectory of the monks of the Servi, he has painted a picture of the Last Supper of the Saviour with the Apostles [Supper of St Gregory], which is very liked, as is also a panel in Santa Corona of the *Adoration of the Magi*. The panel of the high altar in Santa Giustina in Padua, which is seen in prints, is of his hand and another panel of the *Ascension of Our Lord* in [562] San Francisco of the same city.

'These works were done by [Veronese] in Venice. A picture of the miracle of Christ making wine from water is in the refectory of the Black Monks of San Giorgio, and another picture is in the refectory of the monks of [Santa Maria dei] Servi and a panel in the church. A large picture contains a *Supper at Emmaus* in Santi Giovanni e Paolo and a panel of a dead Christ in the church [*sic*]. He did three pictures in the Library of San Marco, in competition with other painters, and it brought him a gold chain as a prize from the Procuratori. And he has painted the ceiling and a great picture above the throne of the prince where the cabinet meets in the palace of the prince. These works are greatly praised by all. The greatest part of the paintings in the Sala del Consiglio de Dieci are of his hand, and he has painted two ceilings where the three greatest *capi* [of the Consiglio de Dieci] are. And now that the ceiling of the Sala del Gran Consiglio is restored, he has done three pictures there worthy of praise, on the side of the dais of the prince.

'[Veronese] has done a panel in the sacristy of San Zaccheria and one at Castello in the Church of the Patriarch [San Pietro]; that of the high altar in Santa Caterina; one in San Giuliano di Merceria; one in the sacristy of San Francesco dalla Vigna and two in the church; and the panel of the high altar in San Bastiano between two rather large pictures. Then, he has done many pictures for princes and for private individuals such as four very beautiful pictures for the Most Serene Carlo [Emanuele I], Duke of Savoy. The Queen of Sheba is introduced to Solomon in the first. [563] The *Adoration of the Magi* is in the second. *David* with the head of Goliath is in the third. And *Judith* with the head of Holofernes is in the fourth. Equally, he has done two for the Emperor [Rudolph II]. In one, Venus, Mars, and Cupid are weeping. And in the other, a Venus is arranging her hair and Cupid holds up a mirror for her, truly done very gracefully. Recently he has painted two very beautiful pictures with life-size figures, one of *Procris* and the other of Adonis sleeping in the lap of Venus. Paolo finds himself today, at fifty-two years, not omitting to continually apply himself with great profit to painting.'

Jacopo Bassano

'Held very rare in colour in the same city is Jacopo Ponte,[80] from Bassano, who spreads the colours with so much liveliness and grace that the things painted by him seem natural, and particularly animals and the varied furnishings of houses. The panel of the high altar in the Church of San Rocco in Vicenza is of his hand, as is also that on the high altar in San Leuterio and one in Santa Croce and a picture in the palace of that city. He did a panel of the *Martyrdom of St Lawrence* put in the cathedral in Cividale. He has painted a ceiling in the Palace of the Podestà in Bassano, his country, and two panels in chiaroscuro in the Church of San Francesco. A panel in Madonna delle Grazie and another of the *Nativity* of Christ in San Giuseppe are his. He has done many works in Venice of which I do not have knowledge. And, today, Jacopo is sixty-six years of age.' [564]

Francesco Bassano

'[Jacopo] has a son named Francesco[81] to whom he has taught his beautiful manner of painting. And today, in Venice, he has painted four very beautiful pictures on the ceiling of the Sala del Gran Consiglio and the taking of a city in another room called the Scortino, which we would call the Squittino (pip squeak).[82] There he has shown the night with reflections of light that are a marvellous thing. He has done two pictures for the Most Serene Carlo, Duke of Savoy, which greatly please for their beautiful colour and charming manner. His pictures are in Florence, Rome, and almost every part of the world, and it is true that in colour he is most worthy. And it can be said that these Venetian painters put very great study into the charm of colour, much more than they put into the excellence of their drawing.'

Annibale Fontana of Milan

'But now it is time to pass to Milan where an Annibale Fontana[83] of Milan is praised as a worthy sculptor. He, in competition with the Florentine sculptor Stoldo Lorenzi, has done two prone larger than life marble sibyls above the pediment of the middle door in the new construction of the Church of Santa Maria di San Celso. And a narrative of the *Nativity* of Christ is above this door with three angels over the hut in a marble picture carved with great care, four braccia high. And two very beautiful prophets are in two niches on the same façade, one done as *Jeremiah* and the other as *Isaiah*.

'Besides working in marble he is very rare in carving crystal. He has carved the four times of the year in relief, a half-palm high, on a vase [565] with two heads of the Medusa. On another oval vase he did the narrative of Jason stealing the Golden Fleece. He carved narratives from the Old Testament on six pieces of square crystal that served to decorate a little chest. *Adam and Eve* eat the forbidden fruit with many animals on the first. *Noah's Ark* is on the second. Moses receives the law from God, with the people of Israel, on the third. Abraham sacrifices his son on the fourth. *David Killing Goliath* is on the fifth, and the *Babylonian Exile* is on the sixth. And he did the *Creation* of the world with figures half a palm high on a large oval, about two palms long, that was also used for the same chest. The Duke of Bavaria [Albert V] purchased this for 6,000 scudi. [Annibale] also attached twelve pieces of crystal onto another little chest, carving the twelve labours of Hercules on them. But it would be much too long if I wished to recount all of his works, not only on crystals but on agates, carnelians, emeralds, sapphires, and carved on other precious stones. In this work he is, in summation, a rare man and not little valued also in casting bronze, but this not being our interest, I will not speak more of it.'

Bartolomeo Passerotti

'The painter of illustrious name, Bartolomeo Passerotti,[84] is in Bologna. Initially, he learned the art from the architect and painter Jacopo Vignola, who took him to Rome where he made a great study of drawing. But Vignola, prompted by his business, [566] returned to France, where he had come from, and Passerotti to Bologna. And, shortly thereafter, he returned to Rome and put himself to work with Taddeo Zuccaro, and for some time they resided together. But Taddeo's brother Federico coming to Rome, Passerotti took housing above him. And he did the portrait of Pope Pius V and of Cardinal Alessandrino, and then portrayed from life Pope Gregory XIII and Cardinal Guastavillano. These portraits were marvellously like them. There are many works done by him in Bologna: one of his panels is in San Bastiano, another in San Jacopo, one in San Giuseppe Fuori le Mura, one in San Pietro Martire, one in the Grazie, one in Santa Maria Maddelena, one in San Girolamo, one in the Duomo [San Petronio], and one in San Pietro. And his paintings are seen in many other places, all worthy of praise.

'[Passerotti] is doing a book of anatomy, of bones and tissues, in which he wants to show how one can come to learn the art of drawing by putting it into practice. And it is possible to hope that it will have to be a beautiful thing since he draws very well. And among his other drawings he has done two heads on imperial sheets, one of *Christ* and the other of the *Virgin Mary,* completed in all perfection with the pen, and he has left the lights [to be shown by] the paper. And these are found today in the hands of Brother Ignatio Danti, mathematician of His Holiness, who has put them in a book of drawings that he made from the hand of all the worthy men of art. In Florence, Giovambatista Deti, a man who greatly delights in the belles-lettres, [567] has a large picture on canvas by the hand of Passerotti, vigorously coloured in oil. Here there are sailors in a boat proposing the enigma to Homer, who is on the shore, and a gypsy woman is on the other side. And Passerotti portrayed himself in the face of Homer and the waters of the sea and some seashells and a dog that appears alive are very naturalistically seen there. [Deti] also has eight sheets drawn with pen in which a vigorous manner is seen with great three-dimensionality. And Deti gave a very beautiful head of a *Gypsy Woman,* also drawn with pen by the same master, to Sig. Don Giovanni de' Medici who, as someone who understands good things, holds it dear. It can be believed that Passerotti has done many other things but, not being known to me, I cannot speak of them. Today, I understand that he has in hand a panel that is going to the Dogana in Bologna, in which he is painting the Glorious Virgin presented at the Temple. And he, as I was going to say, has come to be about fifty-three years of age and always proceeds in art with his praise advancing.'

Prospero Fontana

'Equally, in Bologna, is the experienced and careful painter Prospero di Silvio Fontana,[85] who worked in Genoa in the palace of Prince Doria. And then [he worked] with Perino del Vaga in the halls of the Palagio della Signoria and, particularly, in that of the Consiglio. And he made small drawings of the narratives that are there that have gone out in print. There are many panels of his hand in Bologna: two in the Church of San Jacopo [San Giacomo Maggiore], one in the Church of the Gesuati, one in the monastery of [Santa Maria] degli Angeli, one in the [568] monastery of San Giovambatista, one in that of Santa Caterina, and one in Santa Maria Maggiore. He painted the Cappella Grande in the Palagio de' Signori and the gallery of the choir of the cathedral church. And he has done many other works that I cannot talk about for not having detailed knowledge of them. Fontana finds himself today at the age of seventy-two years.'

Lavinia Fontani

'And, to proclaim his name he has a daughter named Lavinia,[86] who paints very well and has done many paintings in public and private places. And these have gone to Rome and other cities where they are held of great merit.'

Federigo Barocci

'But it is appropriate for me at this time to pass to Urbino, where there is the very excellent painter Federigo Barocci,[87] whose works, for drawing, for composition, and for colour make whoever see them marvel. Among the first paintings that he would do was a *St Margaret* with the serpent that is in the Church of Corpus Christi [Corpus Domini] in Urbino. There are these paintings by his hand in that city. A *St Cecilia* with three [four] saints and a *St Sebastian* shot with arrows are in the cathedral. A Madonna with Her Child, St Simone, and St Taddeo is in San Francesco, and for the high altar in this church, a *St Francis* receiving the stigmata [*The Pardon*]. And a Christ on the Cross, the Virgin, and St John is in the Church of the Crocifisso. Being in Rome, he painted in fresco on the vault of a room in the Boschetto [Casino of Pius IV] the *Queen of Heaven with Four Saints* and other figures in compartments of that room. And on the [569] vault of another room is the

Virgin Annunciate, and in a room of the Belvedere [today, the Etruscan Museum] he began a *God the Father Speaking to Moses*. But, interrupted by an illness, he was not able to finish it and was forced to return to Urbino, where he was ill for four years. And as a votive offering he did a little picture of *Our Lady with Her Child and St John* that is in a church of the Cappuccini [Crocicchio], about two miles from Urbino.

'The panel is [Barocci's] work in the Church of San Lorenzo in Perugia, where Christ is taken down from the Cross. The panel of the *Madonna of Mercy* in the Pieve of Arezzo was done by him with many figures pertaining to that mystery, and this work is very famous and done with great art. But not less esteemed is another of his panels that is in the Church of the Confraternity of the Cross in Singaglia, in which Christ is seen carried to the tomb, done with so much diligence and with such grace of colour that is a marvel to see. One of his panels, of the *Martyrdom of St Vitale,* is also in Ravenna. He did a Crucifixion with the Madonna and other saints for the Cardinal of Urbino [della Rovere] that he sent to the area around Rocca [Arcevia]. And a small picture is his for Sig. Duke Giudobaldo [II della Rovere], in which there is the Glorious Virgin returning from Egypt, and this lord gave it to the Duchess of Urbino [Lucrezia d' Este], and today it is found in Ferrara. He painted a panel in the Confraternity of Sant' Andrea in Pesaro, in which Christ is seen on the shore of the sea, St Andrew kneeling, St Peter leaving the boat, and someone going [570] to the shore, where there are very beautiful considerations. And, in summary, Barocci is a rare man in painting but is not able to work a great deal because of poor health and finds himself at forty-five years of age.'

Federico Zuccaro

'Federico Zuccaro[88] of Castel Sant' Agnolo in Vado learned the art of painting from his brother Taddeo ...[89] and advanced little by little in it so that to his great honour he has been able to do the works of importance that he has done. Being seventeen years of age, he worked under the guidance of his brother in the choir of Santa Maria dell' Orto in Rome. He himself did the angel announcing to the Madonna, the narrative of the *Visitation* of St Elizabeth, and the narrative of the Hebrew people fleeing from Egypt. The other paintings are of the hand of Taddeo. Then, reaching the age of eighteen years, Federico painted the facade of the Dogana and inside did the narratives of St Eustachio, his conversion, baptism, and death.

'Then he worked four continuous years in the Papal Palace during the pontificate of Pius IV, not refusing any undertaking and taking on every sort of work, doing it with experience and to a high standard. And, among the other things, he painted five narratives from the New Testament on the vault of a room in the little palace of the Boschetto. These included the *Transfiguration* of the Lord, the *Faith of the Centurion*, the *Wedding of Cana* in Galilee, the *Multiplication of the Five Loaves and Three Fishes*, and the *Expulsion of the Pharisees* from the temple. They are compartmentalized with grotesquerie [571] and with very beautiful decorations. In this work very great art and diligence are recognized. Then, he painted some little narratives of *Venus and Adonis* and the *Birth of Bacchus* and other fables in a gracious manner in the loggia above the pond. He painted some narratives of Pharaoh in a hall in the Belvedere and a frieze in another room with many figures and narratives about various subjects. The *Justice* that is painted in the Office of the Rota is of his hand, and the *St Paul* and the *St Matthew* in chiaroscuro in the Sala de' Palafreniere with part of the frieze, done of foliage and cherubs, that is under the ceiling.

'Meanwhile, the fame of the value of Federico spreading, the Patriarch Grimani called him to Venice where he resided two years and a half. And he painted a chapel in San Francesco della Vigna for this patriarch, doing two narratives in fresco there, one of the *Adoration of the Magi* and the other of the *Resurrection of Lazarus*, and a narrative in oil of the conversion of the Magdalene. And he painted some narratives in the palace of this Grimani [at Santa Maria Formosa], among which is seen, in the principal hall, the delivery of Justice that, with other little narratives, went out in prints. He did some large narratives in chiaroscuro for the Confraternity of the Calza that served as very rich scenery used for acting a tragedy. He also painted, inside a loggia in the villa of the very illustrious Giovambatista Pellegrini, the narrative of Horatio when he held the bridge against all Tuscany and the narrative of Curtio when he threw himself [572] into the abyss of fire.

'Leaving Venice and coming to Florence for the wedding of the Most Serene Francesco de' Medici, Grand Duke of Tuscany, when he married Queen Joanna of Austria, [Federico] did seven narratives in chiaroscuro for the arch of the Dogana. And he painted that very beautiful canvas that is today in the great hall of the new Uffici, where the council meets. This initially served as a background for the marvellous scene of the comedy that was performed for that wedding.

'Then, returning to Rome, [Federico] painted an *Annunciation* for the Jesuits at Guglia di San Mauritio, and under it the *Nativity* and the *Circumcision of Our Lord*. But his brother Taddeo died at this time and left some works incomplete. The picture in oil of the *Coronation of the Madonna* set above the high altar in the chapel on the right in Trinità [dei Monti] and the two prophets on the side in fresco were finished by Federico. The other paintings are of the hand of his brother. The panel in oil of the *Coronation of the Virgin* and the *Martyrdom of St Lawrence* in San Lorenzo in Damaso were done by him. At Caprarola, the place of Cardinal Farnese, he painted the chapel, the great loggia, and other rooms, therefore, making use of the help of many painters as he also did at Tivoli [Villa d' Este] for the Cardinal of Ferrara. He painted the *Adoration of the Magi* in a picture in fresco in the Church of Sant' Alò degli Orefici, another picture of the *Flagellation of Christ at the Column* in [Santa Lucia del] Gonfalone, and in Santa Caterina de' Funari, two narratives of that saint. In the Sala Regia [573] he did the narratives of Gregory VII when he blesses King Frederick [Henry IV] returning to obedience, and he finished the *Taking of Tunisia* that was begun by his brother. At the same time, he did two large pictures in oil for the Cardinal of Urbino. In one, St Peter is in prison, and this was sent to Fossembrone. And in the other is the *Virgin Ascending to Heaven,* and this was for the chapel of the palace of that cardinal in Rome. There are also two pictures in oil of his hand in Orvieto, one of the one born blind who recovers the light and the other of the resuscitated son of the widow.

'Having done these works, Federico took himself to France, where he did many paintings for the Cardinal of Lorraine. And, in the gallery of one of his villas, he painted ten large narratives of the deeds of this cardinal within very beautiful compartments of stucco. Then, going to Flanders, he did two canvases [*tele*] for Arras tapestries, in one of which he portrayed *Immaturity* and in the other, *Youth*. These canvases are found today in Florence. Moving to England from there, he did the portrait of *Queen Elizabeth* and that of her favourite Milord [*Milord*] *Leicester*, both standing and life-size.

'Finally, returning to Italy, [Federico] came to Florence where the Most Serene Grand Duke Cosimo commissioned him to do the very great work of the cupola, already started by Giorgio Vasari and gone little forward at his death.[90] Therefore, Zuccaro then brought to completion in a few years what is seen today that, for its great size, would not have been [574] unlikely to have occupied the whole space of the life of one man. Rapidly finishing this work, he was called to Rome by

Pope Gregory XIII, where he was put to the work in the Cappella Paolina. But for his own reasons he left Rome, and today, I believe, is found doing some pictures for the Duke of Urbino. But for now this is enough said of Federico, who is truly a worthy man of great invention and expeditious in his work.'

Girolamo Muziano

'Girolamo Muziano[91] of Brescia is employed in Rome in painting to his great praise. He had his first principles in drawing in Venice and moved to Rome as a youth, where he advanced so much in art that his name already resounds everywhere as an excellent painter, as he truly is. Among the first works that he did were some saints finished as bronze in the Chapel of the Gabrielli in Santa Maria sopra Minerva. Then he painted the *Resurrection of Lazarus* as an exercise on a canvas done with very great diligence in which very beautiful faces are seen. And it is recognized in this that he understands good composition. Therefore, he acquired much [credit] among those of the art for that work. A *St Francis* of his hand is in Santo Apostolo with a landscape in fresco in a very charming manner and the *Virgin Annunciate* on a wall in oil within a chapel.

'[Muziano] was called at this time to Orvieto, where Raffaello da Montelupo had done the chapels in Santa Maria, and in one of these he painted [575] the panel in oil and the walls in fresco with narratives of the life of Christ with prophets and with other saints. Finishing this work, which was very praised, he took himself to Fuligno, and there he did a narrative in fresco of St Elizabeth receiving some patients, and this is seen in prints.

'Returning to Rome, [Muziano] went to be with Ippolito d'Este, Cardinal of Ferrara, and did endless paintings in his famous garden of Monte Cavallo [Quirinal] and, among the others, some very beautiful landscapes in fresco. He painted an *Annunciation* in oil in the chapel of the Palace of Monte Giordano [Palazzo Taverna]. And many rooms with various narratives are at Tivoli that it would be a long thing to recount. But, among the other paintings there, are marvellous landscapes in fresco in the execution of which Muziano is very rare. He did a canvas in oil at this time in which there is Christ washing the feet of the Disciples where very great emotion and very beautiful poses are seen. And there is Judas lacing a shoe, showing that he was hurrying to go to accomplish the betrayal that he committed.

The Cav. Gaddi has a picture from the hand of Muziano in chiaroscuro of this same invention and also a *St Jerome* in oil, a head of *St Francis*, and many drawings.

'Finally, leaving the Cardinal of Ferrara and having taken a wife, he began to work for himself. And he painted some narratives of the life of Christ within a chapel of Abbot Ruizzo of Venice in Santa Caterina at the Torre de' Melangoli [Santa Caterina dei Funari] and all the vault in oil and a dead Christ on the panel. He did a panel of the *Assumption of the Virgin* for [576] Monsignor Mattio Contarini, the Datary,[92] in San Luigi dei Francesi. He painted St Paul, the first hermit, and St Anthony in a panel for the current Pope, Gregory XIII. And one cannot easily describe the majesty and the reverence with which he has represented these two old men while they are taking the food that the raven brought them daily, nor how very beautifully he has depicted the loneliness of that desert with a marvellous landscape. The narrative of the *Coming of the Holy Spirit* with a large number of figures is by his hand on the ceiling in the Stanza del Concistoro [afterwards Parimenti]. At this time Giovambatista Altoviti had the sculptor and architect Giovanantonio Dosio construct a chapel at Loreto, which had stucco decorations in the vault, and Altovito desired that Muziano do the paintings there. But not being able to go there because of the many works that he had in Rome, he painted some narratives of the life of St John the Baptist on canvas that would fit there. And he sent his student Caesar Nebbia of Orvieto there with his drawings and cartoons to paint the vault. He himself did a very beautiful *St Francis* in oil in the church of the Nunziata [Collegio Romano], where the Jesuits are and another similar one is over an altar in the Church of the Capuchin Brothers below Monte Cavallo.'

Cappella Gregoriana[93]

'But what will I say of the mosaics that [Muziano] has composed with so much diligence in the famous Cappella Gregoriana [in St Peter's in Rome]? Pope Gregory XIII had this rich work done. Finished mixed stone of many different kinds and very lustrous columns of African stone are seen there in very beautifully compartmentalized orders. [577] He has decorated the vault of gilded stuccos with very charming paintings. Very fine foliage decorations, the devices of the Pope, and other significant things are seen on the gallery. St Gregory of Nazianzus, whose sacred body reposes in this chapel, St Jerome,

St Gregory, and St Augustine are within the lunettes. An *Annunciation* in mosaic appears on the wall above the altar, truly a marvellous thing. And all the mosaics that are there are integrated in such a beautiful manner and with so much art that they seem painted with the brush and with colour. Muziano has achieved from it very great and maximum praise, having found a new way of making stucco different from that which the ancients used, and with which to more easily and better compose mosaic.

'That gallery of the Belevedere, in which Brother Ignatio Danti lays out all the provinces of Italy with beautiful order, is done to [Muziano's] direction with so many decorations of stucco and painting. Many are the pictures Muziano has done for private persons and many the works of his that are seen in prints engraved by the excellent engraver Cornelius Cort but our brevity will not allow discussion of all his things. I will only say that, finding himself around fifty-five or fifty-six, he has in hand two panels that will go to the Cappella Gregoriana. And having made himself known with drawing and with colour as a rare man, [578] today – [doing] whatever anyone wants done – in celestial drawings at every turn, he decorates the heavens with his beautiful pictures.'

Scipione Pulzone

'Scipione Pulzone[94] from Gaeta is very excellent in the same city in doing portraits from life, so done by him that they appear alive. Therefore, he is required to portray all the principle lords of Rome and all the beautiful women, so that it would take a long thing to recount all of his portraits. But it is enough to say, especially, that he has portrayed Pope Gregory XIII, Cardinal Farnese, Cardinal Granvela, Cardinal Ferdinando d'Medici,[95] and the Lord Don John of Austria who, to be portrayed by him, had him come to Naples where he brought usefulness and honour. And, in summary, in the making of portraits Scipione is held marvellous by all.

'But [Pulzone], to also show that he is no less worthy in doing narratives and other paintings, has done two very beautiful panels in oil. In one, the Glorious Virgin is on a cloud with angels and below some male and female saints and a little boy, son of the Marquis of Riano, patron of the panel, portrayed from life, and this was put in the Cappuccini in Rome. Christ is carrying the Cross in the other, with the throngs and the Madonna with the Marys weeping behind, and this has gone to Sicily for Lord Marcantonio Colonna. And these two works are very praised, and today he finds himself with many others in hand that are awaited as very beautiful things.

'But it is now time that we take ourselves back to Florence, where the art of design is practised every day and has been in great supply [579] from Cimabue up to now and perhaps in greater excellence than is known in other cities of the world. But before we discuss the Florentine craftsmen, who are many, we will, however, treat some worthy foreign men. They, having advanced greatly in Florence and demonstrated their virtue in this city into which they have continually been welcomed, almost make it their own country.'

Giovanni Strada of Flanders

'Among these is Giovanni di Giovanni Strada[96] of Flanders, born in the city of Bruges, who was under paternal instruction up to the age of twelve years, working on painting, then was two years with Frans Maximiliaen, a painter of some name in that country. But Giovanni, becoming free because of the death of his father, took himself to be in Antwerp with the painter and teacher Lungo Piero of Holland [Pieter van Aertsen], with whom he lived three years to great advantage. And, after several months in this city, working for himself he [began] doing many paintings and other pictures. But hearing the excellence of Italian painters discussed, he decided to proceed to Italy and, therefore, took himself to Lyons and stopped with Corneille of Lyons, painter of King Henri [II], doing various paintings.

'And after six months, [Strada] moved to Venice where he put himself to work by himself. But not supporting himself in that city [because he was not] accepted as a master, he did tapestries for Grand Duke Cosimo. And it was convenient for him to come to Florence, where he did many different cartoons for tapestries with narratives, [580] grotesquerie, foliage, and animals. And, among the others, there are hangings there that contain narratives of the *Four Seasons*, the *Chariot of the Sun*, the *Deeds of Joshua*, and other inventions. Called then by a commissioner of the Pope, he passed to Reggio [Emilia] and painted a hall and two private rooms, in fresco, and did some portraits. Completing these works, he returned to Florence where he drew other cartoons for tapestries. But Pope Paul [III] was dying at this time, [and it] being the year of the Jubilee, he took himself to Rome where he drew all the things of Michelangelo and of Raphael of

Urbino and portrayed with three-dimensionality a great part of the antiquities of Rome. And then he was put to work in the Belevedere with Daniele da Volterra. And after some months he was called by Francesco Salviati and greatly advanced in painting working in his company, to a large extent taking on his manner.

'The Holy Year ending, [Strada] returned to Florence, where he was commissioned to do other cartoons for tapestries, and he painted the principal cities of Italy on a balcony for the Duchess Eleanora of Toledo. Meanwhile, the deeds of arms having occurred in the Chiane between the Marquis of Marignano and Piero Strozzi, and the forces of Grand Duke Cosimo having the victory, Giovanni painted that day in a panel in oil. This picture is still seen today on the ceiling of the new rooms [Stanze of Pope Leo] of the Ducal Palace. Then Giorgio Vasari having come to be with Grand Duke Cosimo and having taken over all the work of painting, Strada was called [581] by him to work with him. And he painted four panels in oil by himself on the ceilings in four rooms on the level of the Sala dell Orivolo. In the first is the narrative of the *Sabines* putting themselves in the middle between their husbands and their angry fathers, making them make peace, and a frieze below in fresco with other narratives. In the second is the narrative of *Queen Ester with King Ahasuerus* and the frieze below that accompanies it. In the third is *Penelope* when she weaves the tapestry, with the deeds of Ulysses on the frieze. And in the fourth is the narrative of the beautiful *Gualdrada Berti*[97] of Florence with a frieze of various narratives.

'Then parting from Giorgio, [Strada] put himself to work for himself and he did two small panels in oil in the monastery of Chiarito, one of the *Assumption of the Madonna* and the other of *Christ in the Garden*. In San Clemente he painted in fresco the *Passion of Our Lord* in an oratory. In the Annunziata he did the very beautiful panel of Christ on the Cross speaking to the thieves that is held the best work that he has done.[98] The panel of the *Ascension* in Santa Croce is of his hand,[99] that of the *Baptism* in Santa Maria Novella,[100] and that in Santo Spirito in which Christ is expelling the Pharisees from the temple.[101] He did a very beautiful *Last Supper* for Monticelli in oil on canvas and a panel in oil in which there is the *Annunciation* in the villa of Messer Giovambatista Capponi, canon of Santa Maria del Fiore. And then he painted the chapel that is in the garden of the Servite Brothers in fresco. He did four very beautiful pictures of *Lasciviousness, Lust*, the *Samaritan Woman*, and *Christ* that were [582] sent to Spain. He did the triumphal arch at the Tornaquinci corner with two canvases, each thirty braccia high, in which there are views, fountains, women on horseback, and other figures for the arrival of Queen Joanna of Austria into Florence. And four narratives of the emperors in chiaroscuro were twelve braccia wide.

'Endless are the narratives that [Strada] has done in cartoons for various tapestry hangings for Grand Duke Cosimo such as the narrative of the *Goddess Pomona* and of the *God Terminus*, of *Saturn*, of the *Life of Man* in nine pieces, of the *Sabines*, of *David*, of *Queen Esther*, of *Ulysses*, of *Solomon*, of *King Cyrus*, of the *War in Siena* in nine pieces, of the deeds of the Magnificent *Lorenzo de' Medici*, of *Lord Giovanni* [dalle Bande Nere], of *Cosimo the Elder*, and of *Pope Clement*. He then did cartoons for more hangings for Poggio [a Caiano], villa of our grand duke: one of the hunting of the *Wild Boar*; one of the *Lion*; one of the *Ostrich, Sylvan Goat, and Chamois*; one of the *Bucks, Fallow Deer, and Roe*; one of the *Bears*; one of the *Wolves*; one of the *Hares and Rabbits*; and one of the *Otter and Sylvan Cats*. Lord Don John of Austria, returning to Naples, sent to call him so that he paint his wars, and he took him with him to Flanders and [Strada] resided with him until this lord died. Returning to Florence after this, he was called to Naples by the *visitatore* of the Order of Monteoliveto. There he painted, for [583] Lord Fabbrizio di Sangue, the *Mysteries of the Madonna* in a chapel in fresco, and *Our Lord's Miracles* in the vault of this, and the *Assumption of the Queen of Heaven* in the panel in oil. And he began another chapel above the dormitory of the brothers that his son Scipione then finished. And before leaving Naples, he painted four canvases in oil containing the narratives of *Rebecca*, *Bathsheba*, *Susanna*, and *Venus with the Graces*. These paintings are in Naples in the house of Giovambatista del Rosso.

'Returning finally to Florence, because his virtue is known through all the world, [Strada] has done many sheets that are seen going out in prints such as six royal sheets of various fantasies of hunting surrounded by borders, an *Academy of Design*, a *Crucifixion*, an *Ascension*, a *Christ Expelling the Pharisees from the Temple*, a *Baptism of Our Lord*, a *Neapolitan Horse* on a royal sheet, and a book of twelve hunts on small sheets. Finally, greatly expanding his ambition, he has done six books of drawings that are being engraved in Antwerp by the hand of the excellent engraver Philippe Galle. The first book, which will be named for its different narratives, will contain examples of the good government of princes, illustrious Roman women, the four seasons with the Sun, the life of man, and the Judgment of God in four medallions. The second will show the wars of Lord Giovanni [delle Bande Nere] de' Medici, the wars of Siena, and the coronation of Grand Duke Cosimo. The third will have within it the different ways of hunting four-footed animals, [585] fish, and birds. The fourth will show all the kinds of horses of every province. The fifth will represent all the acts of the Apostles, and this in great part is already seen in print. And the sixth, and last, will show all the Mysteries of the Passion of the Saviour of the World in forty pieces. Now, he is putting three sheets in order with some figures: the first of the *Nativity of Christ*, the second of *His Death*, and the third of the *Resurrection*. And three other sheets of narratives of saints – *St Agatha*, *St Agnes*, and *St Lucy* – that will all be engraved in Antwerp by the same master. He has done many pictures for many people that it would be a long thing to recount. But, among the others, Baccio Valori has one in which there is a life-size *Cupid and Venus* coloured with great softness.'

Chapel of the Cav. Messer Girolamo Pazzi at Monte Murlo

'Today [Strada] is painting a chapel in fresco in the villa of the Cav. Messer Girolamo de' Pazzi at Monte Murlo. In the vault of this, he is doing a *God the Father in Glory* and when He creates the world, the *Last Judgment*, and the *Inferno* and the *Twelve Apostles*. And in other narratives, on the walls, he portrayed from nature the *Hermitage of Camaldoli*, *La Verna*, *Impruneta*, *Certosa*, and *Loreto*. And [he also did] a *Crucifixion* with some saints on the panel, in oil.

Giovanni Strada is truly very copious in invention and excellent in composition and with his many works has greatly enriched the art of design in putting together men, animals, landscapes, and cityscapes in new and beautiful inventions. He finds himself at sixty years of age, never ceasing to study nor tiring in the art.'

Giambologna

'Also in Florence in the service of the Most Serene Francesco de' Medici is the excellent Flemish sculptor Giambologna,[102] born of honest parents in the territory of Douai. In his first years, his father directed him into the study of letters with the intention of making him a notary. But he, not having an inclination to that, took himself from such studies and, against the will of his father, went to be with Jakob de Breuck, a sculptor and engineer, who had already been in Italy.

And residing with him some time, desirous of seeing the things of Italy, he took himself to Rome. He was there two years, and there he studied very industriously, portraying in clay and wax all the praised figures that are there.

'Then, intending to return to his country, [Giambologna] passed through Florence and was received here kindly by Bernardo. Seeing his studies done in Rome, and recognizing that he was succeeding in becoming a worthy man, [Bernardo] recommended that he not return immediately to his country but stay in Florence and study yet a few years. Here, surrounded by many figures of Michelangelo and other rare sculptors, he would not lack occasion to be able to copy them. And because he understood that Giambologna did not have the means to linger in Florence, [Bernardo] offered him his house for two or three years without any expense. Therefore, considering the good counsel of Bernardo, and the friendly offer to take him in and feed him in his house, [Giambologna] accepted his offer and applied himself to study with great diligence. For this reason, having made great progress, he began to be known among the other craftsmen [586] as a person of very beautiful spirit, although they said he was greatly accomplished only in clay and wax. But he, to show that he also knew how to demonstrate his talent in marble, begged Vecchietti to give him the marble to make something and, having this, in a brief time made a very beautiful Venus.

'Then, introduced by Bernardo into the service of Lord Don Francesco de' Medici, who was then prince, [Giambologna] began to draw a salary. And soon thereafter, in competition with Ammanati and Benvenuto Cellini, he did the model of Neptune that he wanted to make for the fountain of the piazza. In this he showed clear sign of his excellence and if the Neptune had not first been promised to Ammanati, it would not have fallen to be done by anyone else but [Giambologna]. He did a *Galatea* of marble, two and a half braccia high, that was sent by Bernardo to Germany. He did a bronze *Bacchus*, four braccia high, for Lattanzio Cortesi. Then, he did the very beautiful figures of marble representing Samson, who has a Philistine under him, that are on the fountain in the courtyard where the simples are in the Casino of Grand Duke Francesco.[103] And he cast three little boys of bronze for another fountain.

'Therefore, the fame of [Giambologna's] value spreading, Grand Duke Francesco was begged by the community of Bologna that he be pleased to concede such a man to make a fountain in their principal piazza. And so, the Bolognese having obtained the favour, Giambologna did that very beautiful [587] fountain that to his great praise and with great decoration and usefulness to the city is seen in the piazza opposite the palace of the governor.

'At the same time [Giambologna] did a bronze *Mercury* the size of a fifteen-year-old boy that, together with a bronze narrative and a figurine, also of metal, was sent to the Emperor [Maximilian II]. Afterwards, he did a marble figure, five braccia tall, as a *Florence* who has a prisoner under her and at the same time another seated marble figure, the size of a sixteen-year-old girl. This statue was sent to the Duke of Bavaria [Albert V]. Then he did a standing figure of marble, six braccia tall, as the sea *Ocean,* in the middle of that very large basin of granite in the Pitti. At the feet of this crouch three very beautiful figures of marble that, if they were standing, would be five braccia tall. They are done as the rivers *Nile, Ganges,* and *Euphrates,* and on the plinth are three narratives in low relief. At this time, he also carved a marble figurine that belongs to Grand Duke Francesco and another, three braccia high, for Jacopo Salviati.

'[Giambologna] was then given an altar for the Duomo in Lucca, all of marble, which he conducted with great diligence, doing many ornaments there and five marble statues larger than life and two boys looking ten years of age. These figures were marvellous to whoever contemplated them. He carved *Grand Duke Cosimo* in marble. This was placed on the new Uffici, where it replaced [588] that of Vincentio Danti of Perugia. He then did the marvellous work of the group of three statues that is in the piazza of which, since in previous days we have spoken enough, I will not speak further.[104] I have omitted discussing the great infinity of very graceful marble and bronze figurines that he has done, and thousands are seen, over and above those modelled [larger, for others] to walk around. Nor have I made mention of the many bronze portraits done from life that are in the Grotto at Castello, the villa of the our grand duke.[105] And of his are some figures done at Pratolino and particularly a seated colossus, done as the *Apennines,* a figure partly of wall and partly of *pietra serena* that if it were standing on its feet would be fifty braccia tall. Today, he has in hand a chapel [the Grimaldi in San Francesco di Castelletto] for Genoa, in which there will be six bronze statues and six narratives in low relief.'

Salviati Chapel

'But a very rare thing will be the chapel that is being done by him in San Marco for Antonio and Averardo Salviati that he will construct of composite orders with six columns of mixed marble, each six braccia high. And there they will make compartments of many fine stones of many sorts, and three painted panels will be seen on the three walls of the chapel, that in the middle by Alessandro Allori and one of the other two by Batista Naldini and the other by Francesco Poppi. Around that rich ornament there will be six larger than life marble statues representing *St John the Baptist, St Philip, St Anthony, St Adovardo, St Dominic,* and *St Thomas Aquinas,* and six narratives in bronze of the deeds of St Antonino, [589] Archbishop of Florence. And three partly nude and partly clothed life-size bronze angels will make a rich and charming composition above the pediment of each of the three inside chapels. Outside, above the arch of the great chapel, a four-braccia-tall marble *St Antonino* will be seen. And all these figures will be by Giambologna himself. It would be a long thing to recount the compartments of gilded stucco, the paintings by the hand of Allori, and the thousand other ornaments that will go in the vault. Also, there will be a beautiful mixture of different marbles in the pavement, the oriental stones like gems in [people's] rings arranged in many places, and endless beautiful measures to make the work appear very orderly, very rich, and very charming. This comes from Giambologna who, never forswearing any labour, proceeds to advance in his art every day with great praise, his life having run fifty-four [about sixty] years of age.

'Now, needing to speak of the Florentine craftsmen, I would not wish that you wait for me to methodically proceed [progressively] step by step concerning the more excellent in my discussion, because it would be very difficult for me to make such distinctions. However, leaving the more or less excellence of these to others who intend to judge their work, I will instead first move to discuss the older, as memory serves me, and then, little by little, come down to the younger who have been recognized with praise as good masters.' [590]

Bartolomeo Ammanati

'And beginning with Bartolomeo di Antonio Ammanati,[106] I say that he was born in Florence the year of Christian well-being 1511 and learned the first principles of drawing from the Cav. Bandinelli. And then he made himself a worthy man in sculpture in Venice, under the instruction of Jacopo Sansovino, and later, returning to Florence, he gave himself to study the statues of Michelangelo that are in the sacristy of San Lorenzo. The first figures that he did of marble were a *God the Father* with some angels in half-relief for a tomb of holy bodies in the Duomo in Pisa. And, in Florence, a *Leda,* two braccia high, is his that today is found in the hands of the Duke of Urbino [Giudobaldo II] and three life-size marble figures that were taken to Naples and erected on the tomb of Senazaro. Then, he took himself to Urbino, giving himself first to a tomb and did many stucco narratives. But the duke dying at this time, he returned to Florence and did that marble tomb of Mario Nari of Rome, who fought with Francesco Musi. On this he had done the *Victory* with a prisoner underneath him, two little boys, and the statue of Mario above the casket. This should have gone in the Annunziata. But this work – because it was deemed uncertain which one of the two was the *Victory* and because Ammanati was not very favoured in this by Bandinelli – was not otherwise unveiled. And the statues were transported to various places, and the two marble little boys are today in front of the high altar [591] in the Church of the Servi, representing two angels.

'For this reason Ammanati, being poorly satisfied, took himself to Venice where he did a four-braccia-tall *Neptune* of striped stone that is seen in the Piazza of San Marco [on the Library]. And from there, he was taken to Padua by Messer Doctor Marco Mantova, in the courtyard of whose house is seen an *Apollo* and a *Jove* of stone from his hand. And a colossus, forty palms high, of pieces of joined stone is [Ammanati's] representing *Hercules,* and on the plinth are four narratives in half-relief of the deeds of that god. This work, having been engraved, is seen going out in prints. And for this Marco he did a stone tomb with six figures and two little boys in the Church of the Eremitani, done with great diligence.

'Expeditiously finishing this work, [Ammanati] passed on to Rome in the time of Pope Paul III and put himself to studying the ancient things. But then Pope Paul having died, he was much used in the coronation of Pope Julius in the ornaments that were done on the Campidoglio. And, not much later, Giorgio Vasari having gone to Rome, they encountered each other and together did the tomb of Cardinal del Monte the Elder [Antonio], in San Pietro in Montorio. There, the statue of *Religion* with little boys all in the round and other ornaments of marble are of the hand of Ammanati. This work was the cause of also having them do the tomb of the brother [Fabiano] of this cardinal, who was a doctor, on which he carved *Justice* with angels and other beautiful works. Vasari then departing, [Ammanati] remained in the service of the Pontiff [592] and did that beautiful fountain decorated with various ancient and modern figures in the Vigna of Pope Julius [Villa Giulia]. And some little boys and many other things of marble there are of his hand.

'But the death of the Pope then occurring, [Ammanati] returned to Florence and put himself in the service of Grand Duke Cosimo, by whom he was allocated a fountain that should have gone in the Gran Sala [dei Cinquecento] of the palace opposite the figures of Bandinelli. And, therefore, Ammanati did six marble statues much greater than life that signified the generation of water. Above a great arch of marble he did *Juno*, signifying air, and, under the arch, *Ceres*, shown as Earth, pressing her breasts so that water comes out from them, intending to show that the rivers and springs surge from the Earth helped by the air. And, therefore, he did the statue of *Arno* there and a woman signifying the fountain of *Parnasus*. And the other two figures were a *Temperance* and a *Florence*, identified by the anchor and by the dolphin, the device of Grand Duke Cosimo, that she holds in her hands. But because it did not then seem their intention to put this work in that room, Grand Duke Francesco made a fountain of all these statues at his marvellous Villa of Pratolino that is called the fountain of Ammanati.

'The marble [bronze] *Hercules Crushing Antaeus*, from whose mouth a great abundance of water goes up seven or eight braccia into the air, above Tribolo's fountain in the Villa of Castello is also of [Ammanati's] hand. Equally his work is the bronze statue portraying [593] the Apennine Mountain that is seen in the middle of the pond of that villa. At the same time he did a *Mars*, a *Venus*, and two little boys all together of bronze.'

Fountain of the Piazza

'Then having to do the *Neptune* that is in the middle of the rich fountain of the Piazza,[107] [Ammanati] made his model in competition with Benvenuto Cellini, Vincentio Danti, and Giambologna. And Duke Cosimo allocated the statue and all the work of the fountain to him. But because the marble he received was narrow in the shoulders, he was not able, as he desired, to show his figure in a pose with the arm raised but was forced to do it with great difficulty, as is seen today. This *Neptune* as you know, ten braccia high and with three marble tritons placed between its legs, is placed on a great seashell. This serves it as a chariot that four horses, two of white marble and two of mixed stone, are in the act of pulling. The great basin – in which the crystalline water goes up and comes down in the air from many jets – is made of mixed marble with eight sides. The four smallest of these are decorated with bronze children with many sea things, some cornucopias, and an epitaph in the middle. And above their level are placed – raised higher than every other around them – four metal statues larger than life, two women shown as *Tetis* and *Doris* and two men representing two sea gods. And eight bronze satyrs sit in various poses at the foot of these sides. Then the larger sides are built low so that the clear water [594] that comes rippling into the large basin can be seen. But it would be too long if I wished to describe the grades of marble, the low basin, and the endless ornaments of this fountain that sends out its waters through seventy openings.

'However, continuing with the other works of Ammanati, I say that at the command of Pope Gregory XIII, who rules today, he has done the tomb of Lord Giovanni Buoncompagno in the Campo Santo in Pisa. There Christ is seen showing his wounds between *Justice* and *Peace*. These three statues, each four braccia high, are of marble. He would have done many more works of sculpture than those that I esteem if he had not given himself to architecture in which, in truth, he is greatly valued. It is not possible to believe the buildings that he has directed, among them the superb and marvellous palace of Grand Duke Francesco, called the Pitti Palace, and the very beautiful bridge at Santa Trinità that was built to his design and order.

'And the world will even more greatly recall his virtue if God gives him enough life so that he can bring to light a useful and beautiful book composed by him about architecture. In this he shows a large and perfect city, making one see in drawings – and discoursing about them – the royal palace with all its appurtenances, the [government] offices, the temples, the guilds, the houses of gentlemen and those of artisans, the piazzas, the streets, the shops, the fountains, and all the other things pertaining to a well-understood city. And then he also describes and draws the [595] royal palace in the country, with gardens and with all the conveniences that are looked for and the dwellings of gentlemen and farm workers, with all the necessary and beautiful requirements that it is possible to desire in country houses. And he has already drawn and described everything so that it lacks nothing except to review and to have it printed. But today, being seventy-two years of age and not very healthy of sight and in the head, he attends more to other things, to obtain eternal health with holy and pious works.'

Vincenzio de' Rossi

'But it is time to proceed to mention the sculptor Vincenzio de' Rossi[108] of Fiesole, who learned the art from Bandinelli and was with him in Rome when he did the tombs of Pope Leo and Pope Clement. The first works that Vincenzio did were a marble narrative in half-relief, where St Peter the Apostle was freed from prison by the angel and a larger than life marble *God the Father,* [and they] are in San Salvadore del Lauro in Rome. Then, coming to Florence with Bandinelli, he did, following what [Bandinelli] ordered him to do, that marble male term that holds up the chain in front of the door of the Palace of the Grand Duke.

'Having done this, returning to Rome, [Vincenzio] carved an almost life-size *Leda with the Swan* in marble. Pierluigi Farnese, Duke of Castro, had this work. Then, he did a life-size *Bacchus and a Satyr* between his legs taking grapes from his hand, and this was put in the Vigna of Pope Julius III. But when Grand Duke Cosimo went to Rome, this statue [596] was given to him by Pope Pius IV, and he had it taken to Florence. He did a marble *Christ* and a *St Joseph* in Santa Maria Ritonda, figures twice life-size. At the same time, he did a *Virgin Annunciate* in half-relief with very beautiful views, and a *Saturn* larger than life eating one of his four children. He was then given the Chapel of the Cesis lords in Santa Maria della Pace, where he did two marble tombs with six larger than life figures all in the round and some prophets and angels in half-relief outside of the chapel; that work gained him a great name. Then, he did Theseus seated and he has the abducted Helen in his lap and a Trojan under his feet, all in only one marble, a work greatly celebrated and done with maximum diligence. Today, this is found in the Pitti Palace and is not only the best that he did but of the best that has been done by the moderns. And Vincenzio, being recognized as an excellent sculptor because of this, was commissioned by the Roman people to do the statue of Pope Paul IV. He did this, five and a half braccia tall, being seated with the very rich ornament of four statues, of which two are very well worked by his hand. And this work was erected on the Campidoglio, where it did not reside for long because the Pope died, and the plebes who had erected the statues threw them to the ground, and they did poorly.

'Vincenzio, then coming to Florence in the service of Grand Duke Cosimo, was ordered by him to do [597] the twelve labours of Hercules in marble, of which he has completed seven which are: when he kills Cacus, when he crushes Antaeus, when he kills the centaur, when he throws Diomede to the horses who devour him, when he carries the live boar on his shoulders, when he helps Atlas hold up the heavens, and when he conquers the queen of the Amazons. And these are all nude figures, four and a half braccia tall, in which very beautiful and vigorous poses are seen and very great care in the art. And they are, today, in the *Opera* of Santa Maria del Fiore, and the models of the other five labours are seen partly in Livorno and partly on the Ponte a Signa. At the same time, he also did a larger than life marble *Mercury* putting a horn to his mouth with his right hand and holding a purse with his left. This was sent to Palermo. And he also did a marble *Bacchus with a Satyr*[109] and an *Adonis*. These statues were purchased by Lady Donna Isabella de' Medici for her Villa Baroncelli.[110] A bronze statue of his hand of a *Vulcan* making the lightning bolts for Jove is in the Studiolo of Grand Duke Francesco. And in Santa Maria del Fiore is the apostle *St Matthew* in the act of trying to write, putting his pen in the inkwell that is brought to him by the angel.[111] He has carved endless portraits in Rome and in Florence for many lords and gentlemen. But, among the others, the marble portrait of Baccio Valori, rather greater than life, and very like him, done by [Vincenzio] without Baccio knowing it and then [598] given to [Baccio] in recompense for the many benefits received.[112] Today, he has in hand a somewhat greater than life-size *Laocoön* of marble with his sons all knotted up by serpents. He is doing this work for Giovanni da Sommaia. He also pleases himself with architecture, and many buildings are built from his designs. And finding himself at fifty-six years of age, he does not avoid continually to practise his art with praise, in which it can be said in truth that he is very practised and industrious.'

Batista del Cavaliere

'But leaving him, I find myself before the sculptor Giovambatista di Domenico Lorenzi[113] who, because he became a worthy man in the art [of sculpture] under the discipline of the Cav. Bandinelli, is always called Batista del Cavaliere. His first works of marble were four statues representing the four seasons that were held to be very beautiful and are in France in a garden of the Guadagni, Florentine gentlemen. At the command of Grand Duke Cosimo, he then did a marble fountain that was sent by His Highness as a gift to a Spanish lord, and this was a basin of marble with a foot of mixed stone in the middle of which a larger than life triton sat on three dolphins. Two graceful marble figures of his are seen on the fountain in the beautiful garden of Messer Almanno Bandini, Knight of Malta, in his villa called Il Paradiso, one done as the *Alfeo River* and the other as the *Spring of Aretusa*. He also did a little boy, about three braccia high, that served for the ornament of the statue [599] of Pope Carafa that was erected in the Campidoglio. The beautiful statue that represents *Painting* on the tomb of Buonarroti is his work that, besides the other well-done parts, shows a very great affect of sorrow in the face. And the portrait of *Michelangelo*, which is above the casket, was equally done by him. Then, he did to his great praise the marble *Perseus*, four and a third braccia high, that is seen in the house of Jacopo Salviati. For that gentleman, he also carved a twice life-size sandstone *River* at play. Today, he is completing a marble *St Michael* over the Demon that he is doing at the instance of Lord Giulio Riccio of Montepulciano who wants to send it to Spain. And here [we] finish with Batista, happily tiring himself in the art, fifty-six years of his life having passed.'

Valerio Cioli

'Valerio di Simon Cioli[114] of Settignano learned the art up to fifteen years under the supervision of his father, who was also a sculptor. Then, he was put to be with Tribolo who was working at Castello, the villa of our Grand Duke. And after four years he took himself to Rome, where, favoured and helped by Raphael da Montelupo, he began to make himself known. And he was some months in the service of Lord Giuliano Cesarini, making busts for some ancient heads and restoring many antiquities for him. Then, leaving him, he did good things on his own, repairing many statues for various people until he was called to serve the Cardinal of Ferrara with whom he resided up to the year 1561. At this time [600] he came to Florence, called by Grand Duke Cosimo to whom in Rome he had given a not very large *Venus* of marble and received, by the liberality of that lord, 100 scudi in recompense. And so he put himself to serve him, restoring all of his antiquities to good condition.

'Then, for the satisfaction of the Grand Duke, [Cioli] portrayed a completely nude *Morgante* the dwarf in marble and equally *Barbino*.[115]

These two statues were done with great diligence and so much verisimilitude that they appeared alive, and these are seen, greatly to his praise, in the Pitti gardens. Of his hand is the marble statue representing *Sculpture*, sitting in a pose of sorrow in the middle of the tomb of Michelangelo in Santa Croce. A braccia-high marble *Crucifix* [figure] on a touchstone cross that Lady Camilla Martelli has and holds dear is also his work, and a similar *Crucifix* and a smaller than life marble Venus together with Cupid is found belonging to Giovanni da Sommaia. He then did for Grand Duke Francesco a marble satyr milking a ewe and water flows from the udder instead of milk. And he did a larger than life-size woman in stone squeezing a marble cloth, carved as if it were wet, making water come out of it, and a little boy is in the corner lifting his shirt in front of him as if to jokingly urinate. And he has also carved a greater than life-size reaping farmer. These figures are at the marvellous villa of Pratolino. Today, Valerio has not stopped continuously serving the Grand Duke by [601] practising his art, finding himself at the age of fifty-four or fifty-five years.'

Giovanantonio Dosio

'Giovanantonio di Giovambatista Dosio[116] was born in Florence the year of the salutary Incarnation of the Son of God 1533, and in the year 1548, his father having died many years before, moved to Rome and was put to the art of the jeweller. And spending a year not liking such work, he was put with Raffaello da Montelupo, with whom he was until his eighteenth year of age, at which time he withdrew to work for himself. And part of the time he worked for a living and part of the time he drew the ancient and modern good things of Rome. The first work that he did of marble was a statue done as *Hope* that is in Santo Apostolo in Rome on the tomb of Giulio the Elder. Then, being very poor, he gave himself to restoring antiquities and working in stucco to earn a living. And in the Boschetto of the Belvedere [Casino of Pius IV], in the time of Pope Pius IV, he did many statues of stucco and figures in half-relief and narratives and repaired many statues of marble. Then, he went into the service of Lord Torquato Conti and did many things of stucco and marble for his castle and served this lord as architect on the Fortress of Anagni since he understood the things of architecture very well and made devices of marble and other works for this fortification.

'Then, returning to Rome, [Dosio] was given the tomb of Anibal Caro, which is seen in San Lorenzo in Damaso, above which he did

[602] [Caro's] portrait in marble. And also of his hand in the same church is the tomb of Messer Giovanni Pacini, physician of the Cardinal Sant' Angelo. The tomb of Messer Doctor Antonio Gallese in San Pietro Montorio was done by him, where he carved [Gallese's] portrait in marble and two little boys and other ornaments. And the tomb of the Marquis of Saluzzo with his portrait in marble is in the Church of the Popolo. For Giovambatista Altoviti, he did his chapel at Loreto with very beautiful compartments of stucco. Then, coming to Florence, he organized the rich chapel of Cav. Gaddi [Santa Maria Novella] and composed the stuccos that are seen there on the vault. Returning after this to Rome, he attended much to architecture and did many buildings there.'

Chapel of the Niccolini

'Called finally to Florence by the very rich and very cultivated gentleman Giovanni Niccolini, who greatly delights in the honour of an undertaking, he was commissioned to do [Niccolini's] chapel in Santa Croce. This will be a marvellous work and every day advances forward to the design of Dosio. This will be of the Corinthian order and will be compartmentalized with great design by twelve pilasters of white marble. In the voids of these will be seen bound up in gold, almost jewel-like, much elegant oriental stone, alabaster quinces of different colours, and black and white octagons surrounded and outlined by very pure white marble. The altar will be put on the wall that faces the east. Above this he will place the panel in which the *Assumption of the Glorious Virgin* will be painted by the hand of Alessandro Allori. [Allori] will also do [603] all the other paintings that will be seen in this rich and well-ordered chapel. On the opposite wall, there will be a low tomb, in place of the altar, with the painted panel above corresponding to that which is opposite. On the other two walls, there will be two tombs of African stone with rich ornaments and epitaphs stating the names of those of the house of Niccolini whose bones repose within. There will be two niches above the tombs, placed between columns of yellow marble with black stone Doric capitals and bases, very beautiful to see. And two devices of the Niccolini held up by marble angels will be placed in the middle of the pediment. But where shall I leave the five large statues that, set in appropriate places, will give the work grandeur and a marvellous aspect? He will make the moulding above the niches of marble, surrounded very beautifully by the frieze of elegant mixed stone. Above this, many painted narratives will be placed between the windows to delight the sight. Stuccos done with gold, where there are various works of low relief, are compartmentalized in the vault with great judgment. And the pavement, which will appear almost as a mirror of mixed marbles on the charming floor, will correspond to these. But it would be too long if I wanted to describe all the decorations, all the charms, and all the considerations that will be within there.'

'However, returning to Dosio, I say that in this work he will broadly demonstrate his virtue as also in the fabric [604] of the Arcivescovado of which he is the architect. But for now enough is said about him.'

Girolamo Macchietti

'At ten years of age Girolamo di Francesco Macchietti[117] was put to the art of painting with Michele di Ridolfo [Tosini/Ghirlandaio] and resided with him quite a few years. And he then was put to work with Giorgio Vasari, helping him paint many rooms in the Palace of the Grand Duke. And after he would have worked with him six years, he took himself to Rome, where he continued to attend to study for two years, meanwhile doing some portraits and pictures as the occasion offered it to him. Then, returning to Florence, after having done many things for private people, he painted a panel for Francesco Lioni. This he had put in the church of one of his villas in which *St Salvadore* is painted with some little angels and St John the Baptist and St Catherine below. Afterwards, he painted the panel in which there are the *Magi* offering gifts to Our Lord, put in the chapel of the Stufa [family] in San Lorenzo. This work is worthy of praise, and the face of the Madonna shows endless beauty and modesty.[118] He then did a small panel that is in the Church of Santa Agata in which the Glorious Virgin is seen in the sky handing her belt to St Thomas who is kneeling, next to whom are St Benedict and St Monica. There are two pictures of his hand in the Studiolo of Grand Duke Francesco. In one, Medea is painted reviving Jason, and the cartoon of this is in the house of Baccio Valori. And, in the other, the *Baths of Pozzuoli* [605] are shown. That very praised panel of the *Martyrdom of St Lawrence*, in Santa Maria Novella, is his work, where a copious and very beautiful composition is seen with very appropriate poses and with charming colour.[119] And St Lawrence, besides the devotion that he shows, is a very well-studied figure. And he who is stoking the fire is done with very good foreshortening, and the king sitting above and those surrounding him are portrayed with all perfection. And not only is this work the best that Giolamo has done but it is also among the best paintings that the moderns are seen to have done.

'[Macchietti] then did two saints for the high altar in the Church of Santa Maria Corte Nuova, within a mile of Empoli. And he did the device of the confraternity of the men of that country, and he painted *St John the Baptist* and *St Michael the Archangel* for the high altar in the church in Pontormo. The panel where the *Trinity* is painted for the Chapel of the Risaliti in Santa Croce, in Florence, is his work.[120] And Ser Matteo Bruneschi, notary to the Mercatantia, had him do that in the Carmine, where the Glorious Virgin is seen ascending into the sky with the Apostles on the ground.[121] And in this he has shown the great spirit of that notary, and it should be a spur to those who are more able than he to do [pay for] pious and laudable works. But, returning to Girolamo, he did a panel in the Pieve of Empoli, in which St Lawrence is carried to Heaven by the angels. And he painted another of the Madonna with some saints for Messer Giovanni Conti that was put [606] in the chapel of his house. This house was then sold by his heirs to Jacopo Salviati. The panel in the Carmine in Pisa in which Christ is portrayed on the Cross with Our Lady and other saints is of his hand.

'Having done these works [Macchietti] moved to Naples and painted a panel in the Church of San Giovanni de' Fiorentini, in which there is the Samaritan woman speaking to Christ. And another panel is his in Santa Chiara, in the same city, showing St Thomas surrounded by other Apostles putting his finger in the wound of the Lord. Then he was taken to Benevento, in the Lands of the Church, thirty-two miles from Naples, where he painted a panel for the Chapel of the Sacrament in the Duomo. There Christ is taken down from the Cross and, above the panel, the Saviour of the World is pouring his blood into a chalice. And the *Last Supper* of Christ with the Apostles [is] below the panel. And *St Lucy* and *St Catherine* [are] on the plinth. Completing this work, he returned to Naples, where he painted *St John the Baptist Baptizing Christ* in a panel that was taken to Messina and put in the Church of the Fiorentini. And in San Giovanni, in Naples, he did another panel representing St Michael the Archangel, who has the Devil underneath him and a God the Father with angels above him and two prophets on the sides. At this time he was called to a place fifty miles from Naples towards Puglia, called Buonalbergo, where in San Niccola, the principal church of that place, he painted two panels. In one is the *Rosary of the Virgin* with all of its mysteries. [607] And in the other is the Queen of Heaven with the Saviour of the World in Her arms and other saints. Then he was brought back to Benevento with prayers where he did a panel in San Francesco, in which there is the Conception of the Bearer of the Ultimate Good with angels appropriate to this mystery.[122]

'Finally, he has returned to Florence and gone to making some portraits for private gentlemen, meanwhile waiting for the occasion of showing his virtue more greatly in public. And truly, they who are able, should not waste time in employing him in paintings for all to see before he, who today finds himself at forty-nine years of age, is worsened by time and loses that vigour that in all men, and particularly in painters and in sculptors, at a certain time in their life is seen to be consumed.'

Stoldo Lorenzi

'Stoldo di Gino Lorenzi[123] learned drawing in company with Girolamo Macchietti, with the intention of turning to painting. But the facility that he had in handling the tools in the shop of his father, who worked in carving, was cause to direct him to sculpture, in which he has then had very good success. The first figure that he did of marble was a *St Paul* that was sent to Lisbon. Luca Martini having seen this figure, he took him to Pisa and took him into his house for six years. Stoldo did a statue for him that was then given by the Duchess Elenora to her brother Lord Don Grazia di Toledo, who put it in his garden of Chiaia in Naples. [608] He also did a marble narrative in low relief for this Martini, in the middle of which Grand Duke Cosimo is seen, and on one side the River Arno and on the other the Arbia,[124] with all the cities of both these regions bringing tribute to their prince with vases in hand. The marble escutcheon of the grand master of the Order of Saint Stephen that is on the facade of the Palace in Pisa is also of his hand, where there are two very beautiful statues in the round, one done as *Religion* and the other as *Justice*.

'Then, returning to Florence, [Lorenzi] was commissioned by Grand Duke Cosimo to do the bronze *Fountain of Neptune* in the garden of the Pitti. This statue is placed above some marble sea monsters, and this work has been highly praised by those with understanding. Then he was called to Milan, where these marble statues are seen of his hand on the facade of the Madonna di San Celso.

Adam and *Eve* are figures done with very great diligence. There are the *Glorious Virgin* and the *Angel* making the celestial embassy to Her. Two narratives are in half-relief. In one, the Magi are seen offering gifts to the Saviour of the World, and the *Madonna Fleeing to Egypt* is in the other. And there is the *Prophet Ezekiel,* greater than life. All these figures are worthy of praise, and in them many considerations of the art are seen. Four statues within the church, representing *Moses, Abraham, David,* and *St John the Baptist,* were also done by him and held to be in great repute. And many others are given to him to do for that church which he will be able to do if God will lend him life. [609] It is hoped that they will be as very beautiful as the others done by him since the excellence of his work is also expected to be seen in Pisa. He has returned to Florence and been put by Grand Duke Francesco, who well knows his virtue, in charge of the works of the cathedral in Pisa. There he is found at present, putting in order the marbles that he is working on, having passed the forty-nine solar cycles from his birth until now in good use.'

Bernardo Buontalenti

'While it is true that Bernardo Buontalenti[125] did not have the art of painting as his principal aim, nevertheless, because those few works that he has done are worthy of praise, I will not avoid saying something about him. Giorgio Vasari gave him the wrong surname, calling him Bernardo Timante Buonaccorsi. Put young in the service of Grand Duke Francesco, who was then prince, he was, having been recognized for his beautiful talent, favoured and helped by His Highness to make himself a worthy man. And [Francesco] had him learn painting from Francesco Salviati, from Bronzino, and from Vasari, and finally under the instruction of Don Giulio Clovio, he learned miniatures in which he greatly imitated his master and became excellent. At the age of fifteen, he did a life-size Crucifix of wood that today is in the church of the nuns of the Agnoli in Burgo San Friano. And at the same time he did the head of *St Monica* of wood that is above the street door of the monastery of that saint. The first work [610] that he did in painting was a *Pietà* in a picture for Bishop Marzi, who sent it to the Emperor [Ferdinand I]. Then he painted a life-size *Madonna* for Lord Mondragone, a Spaniard, and, in a picture the same size for Grand Duke Francesco, Abraham intending to sacrifice his son. He painted a vault in oil with many beautiful inventions for

Marcantonio da Tolentino in his house on the Via de' Ginori. He did a picture of the *Glorious Virgin* with a portrait of Grand Duke Francesco for Don Miniato Pitti, Abbot of Monteoliveto. And another life-size portrait of his hand of the same prince was sent to the father [Ferdinand I] of Queen [*sic*] Joanna of Austria, and Filippo Spina has another smaller of it. He painted the severed *Head of St John the Baptist* in a basin, done with great diligence, that is found today belonging to Jacopo Mannucci. In the Studiolo of our Grand Duke is a picture done by him representing water, in its natural state and [also] put to use, where rivers, fountains, mills, and other charming and beautiful inventions are seen, and a very graceful nude woman is among the other figures there.'

Studiolo of the Grand Duke Francesco

'Grand Duke Francesco has had a studiolo of ebony made to his design that is composed of all the orders of architecture with columns of lapis lazuli, bloodstone, agate, and other fine stones. And some gold terms are on the wall done in competition by Benvenuto Cellini, Bartolomeo Ammanati, Giambologna, Vincentio Danti, [611] Lorenzo della Nera, and Vincentio Rossi. There are marvels of art and richness in this work with many precious gems in beautifully ordered compartments. And some little narratives of Pallas are carefully miniaturized by the hand of Bernardo in compartments. And there are several portraits of the most beautiful Florentine gentlewomen, a very charming thing to see. But whoever would wish to recount in detail all of the decorations put before them, all the friezes, and all the considerations that are there to make it of the greatest beauty, together with the clever closures, the hidden secrets, and a little panel of marble all composed of elegant stones, would have a difficult enterprise, not immediately brought to a conclusion.

'However, returning to Bernardo, I say that he has done in miniature for Grand Duke Francesco: an oval in which there is *Venus* with the sensations of love; a *Christ Carrying the Cross;* and a Madonna with St John playing a pipe whistle, the Christ Child in Her arms, and a little angel to the side. Passing through Spain in the year 1563 with the Grand Duke, then the Grand Prince, King Philip took notice of his virtue in miniaturizing. [Philip] wished that he make him many little paintings in miniature of portraits and of Madonnas, and he also did many of them for the Queen. And he was greatly compensated by them. He has done today, in a picture still in drawing, the mystery of *Christ at the Column* with endless figures so well organized that almost all are seen complete.[126] For each he shows the level where it is placed with very beautiful varied poses, [612] and he intends to complete this immediately.

'This man is not satisfied only with painting but, giving himself to the things of the mind, [Buontalenti] has succeeded in a rare way in finding new inventions: in raising weights, in lifting water, in the laying down of bridges, and in fortifications. Therefore, in the year 1556, in the time of Grand Duke Cosimo, he was sent to Naples to the Duke of Alba as an engineer. He built a bridge on boats on the Tiber at Ostia and built a fort on the river and the battery followed his plans. And then he was sent by the Duke of Alba to Civitella del Tronto to construct that fortification. There, against the opinion of many, with the Count Santa Fiore they held that fortress against the forces of Monsieur Guise, and [Buontalenti] was the reason that great damage did not follow to Italy. He has also given great attention to architecture and to his design were done the fortification and the growth of Livorno, the fortifications of Pistoia, and those of Siena. And the superb palace of the marvellous Villa of Pratolino, beginning with the plan, was built to his design with so many beautiful and charming ornaments that not only show the virtue of Bernardo but the grandeur and the magnificence of Grand Duke Francesco. He has written a book on fortifications where all things allowing a good soldier to direct every enterprise to a good end are shown in drawings and taught in writing. [It includes] all the things, with very beautiful refinements, that are appropriate to the architect of fortifications on all sites. This book he should immediately [613] bring to light as a beautiful thing.

'Grand Duke Francesco understands a great deal in the careful consideration of the things of engineering and of the secrets of nature and of art. It is said that with his advice and help [Buontalenti] has found what up to now has not been seen, and what many do not believe it is possible to discover. This is perpetual motion in a machine in which there are the four elements. This machine, independent of how it is put together [or put in motion], is moved by itself continuously. But enough is said for now of Bernardo who, finding himself forty-eight years of age, does not avoid every day working virtuously in painting, in architecture, and in the discovery of new, beautiful, and useful inventions.'

Batista Naldini

'At twelve years the painter of illustrious name, Batista di Matteo Naldini,[127] was put to the art of painting under the instruction of Jacopo da Pontormo with whom he was many years. And after the death of Pontormo, having worked some time for himself, he moved to Rome and being there to study the things of design, was called by the Prince of Massa to do decorations for his wedding. Having resided with him eight months, he returned to Florence and, encountering Giorgio Vasari, worked in the Sala Regia of Grand Duke Francesco, on which work he occupied himself about four years. Then, parting from Vasari, he put himself to working by himself.

'And among the first works that [Naldini] did was a chapel in fresco adjacent to the side door in San Simone. There a *God the Father* with angels holding the Mysteries of the Passion is seen above the cornice of the chapel [614] and, under the cornice, *Our Lady* who has the dead Christ in Her lap with other figures. Then he painted the panel, in oil, in which Christ carries the Cross accompanied by the throng, put in the first chapel on the left in the Badia. Afterward, he did the portrait of *Cardinal Ruberto Pucci,* at the request of Messer Alessandro Pucci. He did a *St Anthony* with two angels above him in fresco on a pillar next to the high altar in San Pier Maggiore. Two pictures done in competition with many other painters are of his hand, in oil, in the Studiolo of Grand Duke Francesco. One of these is on stone slab in which there appears the way that it is believed ambergris is made. And the other, on wood, represents *Sleep* surrounded by dreams with very beautiful considerations of invention as of art.

'At the same time [Naldini] did two other pictures. The first is of a *Crucifix,* which is found today in the house of Messer Donato Minorbetti, Archdeacon of Santa Maria del Fiore. And the second is of a *Deposition from the Cross,* similar to that which is in the Minorbetti panel in Saint Maria Novella, and the Pucci have this. Then he painted that panel, put in Santa Maria Novella in the Chapel of the Minorbetti,[128] that has made him so famous. In this the dead Christ is in the arms of the Marys who show a very great sense of sadness in their faces, and the Virgin is in the act of fainting and the body of Our Lord could not be desired to be done with more art nor represented more naturally. Then there are appropriate poses in the other figures there with [615] a facile and beautiful manner, and very charming colour is seen there in all the work, and it is in truth the best work that Naldini has done. Also of his hand is the other panel that follows next to that, done for Jacopo Mazzinghi, in which the *Nativity* of the Saviour of the World is shown and there the night is rather well done.[129]

'Sig. Lodovico da Diacceto has two large canvases of [Naldini's] in his gallery in Paris: one of the narrative of *Acis and Galatea* with Polyphemus, the other of *Helen Abducted by Theseus*. He did a panel in which there is the *Glorious Virgin* with Her Child in Her arms and some angels lifting a drape and other saints for the Pucci in their Church of Saint Maria à Granaiuolo, in Valdelsa. The panel in the Pieve of Uzzano, where the Genetrix of the Supreme Goodness, is greeted by the angel is his work. And he did two panels that they put on either side of the door on the tramezzo that passes into the choir of the church in the Hermitage of Camaldoli in which are seen the *Visitation of Our Lady* and the Same seated, surrounded by many saints. The panel of the *Ascension of Our Lord* with many figures in the Carmine in Florence was done by him.[130] For Monsignor Messer Alessandro de' Medici, Archbishop of Florence,[131] he painted a chapel in fresco in San Salvatore, the Church of the Arcivescovado. He did some prophets and angels there and a St Salvador in the air with the Madonna at whose feet is St John indicating the city of Florence, which is portrayed there, which he recommends to Her as its protector. [616]

'For the Most Serene Queen Joanna of Austria, Grand Duchess of Tuscany, of very happy and very holy memory, [Naldini] portrayed a *Christ Praying in the Garden* with the three Apostles in a small panel and some little narratives of the Passion of the Son of God. Then he did the third panel in Santa Maria Novella for Giovanni da Sommaia, where the *Purification of the Madonna* is seen with all those things that pertain to that narrative.[132] The panel in Santa Croce in which St Francis is painted receiving the stigmata is his, a very well-conducted figure showing very great emotion of devotion. He painted two panels in San Quirico à Capalle, Church of the Arcivescovado of Florence: *St Anthony* is shown beaten by devils in the first, and *St Jerome* in penitence in the second. The paintings that are seen in Santa Croce above the tomb of Michelangelo Buonarroti are also of his hand. A panel is seen in the Confraternity of the Trinity in the church in Limite, near Empoli, in which there is the *Trinity.* And another is in Pistoia in the [Church of the] Madonna del Letto representing the *Martyrdom of St Catherine* with the wheel and another equally in the monastery of Santa Caterina in Colle [Val d' Elsa] showing the dead Christ in the lap of His Mother with many figures. Then he did *St Thomas* when he touches the wound of Christ and the Glorious Virgin with the Marys and other figures grieving the death of the Saviour of the World, in two canvases in oil. These works were sent to [617] Palermo by Giovambatista Cini. The panel of the *Resurrection* of the Son of God in the Confraternity of Santa Maria Nouvella in Marti is of his hand.

'These works are seen by [Naldini] in Rome. A picture in which there is *St Matthew* writing his Gospel was done for Alessandro de' Medici, Archbishop of Florence, and today is in the hands of the Datary. A *St John the Evangelist* writing is in a panel in the Church of San Luigi [dei Francesi]. A chapel in fresco is in the Misericordia [San Giovanni Decollato] with some Apostles and some little narratives, and, in the panel in oil, *St John the Evangelist* in the cauldron over the fire with many figures.[133] Another chapel is in the Trinità [dei Monti], where St John is seen baptizing Christ in the panel. And on the facades of the wall and on the vault in fresco are the dance of Herodiana, the beheading of St John, and all the deeds of his life, which work he did for Giovambatista Altoviti. *Christ Expelling the Pharisees from the Temple* is on a canvas for the Roman citizen Antonio da Gallese. And a picture, in oil on canvas, in which there is a *Crucifix* with other figures is found belonging to Messer Andrea Spinola, then Cherico di Camera and today a priest of the Jesuits.

'[Naldini] has painted narratives from the life of the Virgin Mary in fresco on the facades of the walls for the Chapel of the Rospigliosi in Madonna dell'Umilità in Pistoia. Alfonso Strozzi in Florence has a very beautiful picture of his in which Bathsheba is washing in the bath with other women. In the tomb under the chapel that the Salviati built in San Marco, he has done, above the altar in fresco, *Christ Raising Lazarus*, [618] and, under the altar, a little narrative of the Visitation [*Vision*][134] *of the Prophet Ezekiel*. For Paolo Lavoratori of Scarperia he has done everything in fresco for the inside of an oratory placed on the side of his land on the road that goes to Bologna. On the walls, there are many narratives of the Queen of Heaven and the *Trinity* in the gallery with many ornaments.

'Today, Naldini finds himself painting to great praise at forty-seven years of age. And he has almost completely finished the panel that will go into Santa Croce for Lodovico da Verrazzano in which he has painted a dead Christ in the arms of the Marys and the Thieves who appear in the distance still on the cross, very well done. And this panel is very copious of figures and very charming of colour and I believe it will please a great deal. He is also doing a panel for Jacopo Carucci that will be put up in the Carmine, in which he shows Christ resuscitating the widow's son. And another will be placed in the same church that he painted for Bernardo Martellini with the narrative of *Christ Praying in the Garden*. He has another in hand for Bernardo Davanzati of the *Resurrection of Lazarus* that will go in Santa Marta à Montughi. And he has started one of the *Purification of the Madonna* with many figures for Amerigo da Verrazzano that will have a place in San Niccolò oltr' Arno. But it is expected that the panel that he is doing for the Salviati Chapel in San Marco, in competition with Alessandro Allori and Francesco Poppi, in which he paints [619] *Our Lord Calling St Matthew* from the counter [*banco*] to be an Apostle will be a very beautiful work. Batista has a facile and beautiful manner and charming mode of colour, thus his works universally please everyone.'

Santi di Tito

'Santi di Tito Titi[135] learned the first principles of design under the instruction of the painter Bastiano da Montecarlo. Then he was introduced by Bronzino into the art of painting. And, finally, he had much direction in drawing from the Cav. Bandinelli. At the age of twenty-two, he went to Rome and painted some Apostles in fresco and narratives in the vault and a Crucifix on the wall above the altar in a chapel in the palace of Cardinal Messer Bernardo Salviati in Trastevere. And in the Boschetto of the Belvedere, in the time of Pope Pius IV, he did the narrative of the *Vineyard* in a vault above the staircase and, in a room next to it, the *Glorious Virgin Ascending to Heaven* with other sacred narratives and grotesquerie in gilded stuccos. Four large narratives in the great hall of the Belvedere are painted by him and the others are from the hand of Niccolaio dalle Pomarance.

'Then at twenty-eight, Santi returned to Florence and did that panel that is in the Ognissanti in which the Virgin Mary is seen with other figures. A panel of his hand is in San Giuseppe a' Guardi, in which there is the *Nativity of the Lord*, and that in Santa Maria sul Prato where there is the *Pietà* and, above, the *Resurrection*. Two very beautiful panels of his hand are in Santa Croce. That in the chapel of Francesco de' Medici in which Christ is seen resurrected[136] [620] is, perhaps for drawing, the best work that Santi has done. And that showing Christ breaking bread in Emmaus is in the chapel of Antonio Berti, and in this he has exceeded himself in colour,[137] as he has done in San Marco in that picture where are the *Angel Raphael and Tobias*, figures done with great art. He sent a panel to Ragusa, in which he had painted the *Holy Spirit*. A panel of his representing the *Annunciation* with many angels and new inventions is seen in Florence in the Church of the Jesuits [San Giovannino degli Scolopi].

'These are the many works [Santi] has done that have gone outside of Florence to different locations. Two canvases in oil are at Scrofiano, the *Annunciation* is painted in one and a *Pietà* in the other. Two others serve as panels for Borgo Sansepolcro, one in the major church shows the narrative of *St Thomas* when he touches the chest of Our Lord and in the other, which the relatives of Tito have, Christ is seen resuscitating the son of the widow. Two canvases are in Città di Castello, one has the Virgin Mary in it with four saints and the other has St Peter and St John when, putting their hands on the heads of others on the road from Samaria, they infused in them the virtue of the Holy Spirit. A large panel in which there is the *Circumcision of Our Lord* is in the Castle of Casciana, in the area of Pisa. Two canvases are in France in the hands of Sig. Lodovico da Diacceto in which the narrative of *Aeneas and Dido* and that of *Hippomenes and Atalante* are seen. A panel of the *Assumption of the Virgin* with some saints is in the Pieve [621] of Gambasi. Another panel of the same narrative of the Virgin was for Castelnuovo di Carsagnana [Duomo]. A panel in which the triumphal entrance of Our Lord into Jerusalem is shown was for [San Bartolomeo di] Monteoliveto, outside of Florence. A panel of a *Pietà* is in the nunnery of the nuns of the Agnolis in Prato. A panel representing God the Father, the seven gifts of the Holy Spirit, and other mysteries pertaining to the Virgin was for [the Church of] Maria Vergine [Madonna del Soccorso], outside of Prato. A panel of the *Assumption of the Virgin* is in the Carmine at Pisa. A little panel, in which there is a *Madonna with two Saints,* was for one of those little hermitages in the Hermitage of Camaldoli. A panel is in the villa of Luigi Puccini in the Valdarno, where Christ is seen talking with Martha and with the Magdalene. A panel in which there is a *Last Supper* is in the Badia in Fiesole. A canvas for a panel in which he painted the Genetrix of the Ultimate Blessing rising up to Heaven is in the Church of the Servite Brothers at Pistoia. And a panel, four braccia high, of a *Pietà* was for Alicante in Spain. He painted two altars in fresco in two little churches of the nuns of St Luke in the Mugello, in one of which the *Virgin Mary* is seen with some saints and in the other a *Christ on the Cross* with other figures.

'These works are seen done by [Santi] in Florence. For the chapel of the painters in the convent of the Servi, a narrative on the wall in fresco shows when Solomon had the Temple built, and many painters and sculptors are portrayed from life there. And the very well-finished cartoon of that narrative is found completed as a picture on canvas in [622] the house of Baccio Valori. And in the refectory of the same brothers is the supper of the Lord in the house of Simon, where the Magdalene is seen in a beautiful pose at the feet of Christ. The panel of the *Nativity* of the Saviour of the World is in the chapel of the Cav. Michelozzo in the Carmine. Two narratives in oil on plates of stone are in the Studiolo of Grand Duke Francesco, one shows the ways in which amber is found and the other, purple. And a small panel is in a chapel in the house of Simon Corsi in which Christ is portrayed on the Cross with two saints. The Cav. Gaddi has a picture of his on canvas of the *Fable of Semele.* Maestro Pier Conti has a picture done with great diligence in which his wife *Madonna Caterina* is portrayed, a woman who, besides the highly prized beauty that shines from her, is of very cultivated manners. [Conti] is a very excellent doctor and very valued, as you know, in negotiating, in which he is used meritoriously in so many important needs of Grand Duke Francesco. Santi has done many other portraits such as that of *Pope Pius IV,* of the Lord Don *Ferdinando Cardinal de' Medici,* of the Lord Don *Pietro* [*de' Medici*], of the Lady *Isabella de' Medici,* of the Lord *Paolo Orsini,* of *Pier Vettori,* so famous in letters, and of many others that it would be too long to recount.

'Therefore, concluding my discussion of Santi, who today finds himself forty-six years of age, I say that he is a very experienced painter and that he very well understands the things of design, and about him his relative Messer Ruberto Titi has done this sonnet: [623]

You conquer Nature who now defends herself,
 And who, with acts and words
 Competes within design with you alone
 Tempering with living colour open and displayed.

You complect the bashful damsel's face,
 As if timidity flees, and wants,
 The beautiful cheek to appear of violet;
 Where in the face the pale colour is shown.

As if the height of love was withheld before
 Portraying you, whose voice expresses
 The scorn of Saffo, Enone, or Dido,

What muted them to speak before?
 When every other of you keeps silent the cry.
 Of it the walls will never tire.

Alessandro Allori

'Being left without his father at five, the Florentine citizen Alessandro di Christofano Allori[138] was introduced to drawing by his uncle Agnolo Bronzino and then to painting, in which he then had that great success which everyone recognizes. Many are the works worthy of being considered that he did from drawings of his master [or] copied from other capable painters while he was still a boy. But to come to our intention of speaking briefly of the most excellent things, I say that at seventeen years of age he did the first work of his invention. This was a panel in which there is a *Christ on the Cross* and St John and the Magdalene at the foot. Alessandro di Chiarissimo de' Medici put this in the chapel of one of his villas.

'At nineteen [624] [Allori] moved to Rome, where he was for two years, studying the ancient statues and the works of Michelangelo and of other capable men. And at the same time he did many portraits such as that of *Tommaso di' Bardi* and of his wife Madonna *Ortensia Montauti*, and these are found today in Florence in the houses of the above-mentioned Bardi. He also portrayed Madonna *Aurelia Mannelli* and Zanobi and Benedetto Montauti in Rome. And, after having obtained the painting of the Chapel of Bastiano Montauti in the Annunziata, through the help of Tomasso di' Bardi, he brought himself back to Florence. And he did the panel in oil there, taking the invention from the *Judgment* of Buonarroti, and on the wall he painted many narratives where very well-done nudes are seen in fresco. He then did a panel in oil, in which Christ is shown taken down from the Cross, with many figures and the Madonna fainting, which is seen in the Confraternity of Jesus below the Church of Santa Croce. For Grand Duke Francesco, who was then prince, he painted Hercules introduced by the Muses, going to the reward for his labours, in a little picture of small figures done with great care. And at the same time he completed a picture of the *Nativity of Our Lord* with shepherds and with a choir of angels that was sent to Palermo, where it is held in great merit in a confraternity. He did three large pictures for Alamanno Salviati that were put in the great hall of his villa at the Ponte alla Badia. [625] *Pluto Abducting Proserpina* is seen in the first. *Aeneas Carrying Anchises* to safety from the burning of Troy is in the second. And *Narcissus Mirrored in the Spring* is in the third. He also painted many little narratives, friezes, and grotesquerie with various decorations in this villa, but very beautiful was a picture of a *Deposition from the Cross*, portrayed from a drawing by the Cav. Bandinelli. Of his hand in Santa Maria Novella is the panel of the *Samaritan Woman* in the Chapel of Messer Anton Bracci, which work is very worthy of praise.[139] The panel where the women are gathered in Santa Maria Nuova was done by him where the Madonna is seen above with the little Child, and St John is put in the middle with the active and contemplative life, with six virgins at the foot. The panel of the martyrs in the Chapel of the Pitti behind the choir in Santo Spirito is his work, in which there are very well-studied nude figures.[140] And equally is the other panel in the Chapel of the Cini, where the adulteress is shown repentant for her sin,[141] and in truth this work is organized with good composition, with appropriate poses, and with many beautiful considerations.

'Then [Allori] painted three pictures for Sig. Lodovico da Diacceto that are in the gallery of his palace in Paris. *Venus and Cupid* are seen in one and the cartoon of this, finished with care, belongs to Baccio Valori. *Venus and Mars* are in the other, and *Narcissus* looking at himself in the spring is in the third. [Allori] did many paintings for Jacopo Salviati in fresco in two loggias of one of his courtyards in Florence. [626] Sixteen narratives of the deeds of Ulysses are seen there with ornaments of gilded stucco. And in a chamber beside that he painted, in oil, trellises of grapevines with little boys playing, a very charming thing to see. And in a room he did a frieze in oil of the war of the cats and the mice described by Homer.[142] And in a very beautiful grotto richly decorated with sponges, coral, mother of pearl, and many kinds of marine shells, he did some grotesquerie and figures in fresco compartmentalized with great judgment. The same Jacopo Salviati has a picture of his in which Christ is shown liberating the Holy Fathers from Limbo that is done with very great care and perhaps the best work that Alessandro has done.

'Andrea del Sarto, Jacopo da Pontormo, and Franciabigio had already worked in the Gran Sala at Poggio a Caiano, the villa of the Most Serene Grand Duke Francesco. Andrea [del Sarto] began a narrative there, where Caesar is seen in Egypt presented with various gifts by many people. He wanted that this invention be found to signify when the Magnificent Lorenzo de' Medici the Elder was presented with various and foreign animals. This narrative of Andrea [del Sarto], left unfinished, has now been completed by Alessandro [Allori], partly continuing with the figures of Andrea and partly of his own invention. Pontormo painted some nymphs and shepherds there around a circular window. And Franciabigio left the narrative unfinished there where Cicero, being brought to the Campidoglio after his exile, was proclaimed Father of his Country. And this [627] narrative alludes to the return of Cosimo Medici the Elder to Florence.

'Opposite the paintings of Pontormo, Allori has painted the apples of Hesperidis, guarded from Hercules by the nymphs, and [also] Good Fortune. [He painted] *Fame, Glory, and Honour* in large figures under the cornice over the two windows. And *Fortitude, Prudence, and Vigilance* are in a picture above one of the two doors that give entrance to the apartments of the private rooms and *Magnanimity, Magnificence, and Liberality* are above the other. Facing the work of Andrea [del Sarto], [Allori] has painted a great narrative, where the banquet of King Syphax of Numidia is shown, given by him for Scipio after he had routed Asdrubale in Spain. He wanted to show in this narrative, the visit to the king of Naples by the Magnificent Lorenzo who was, despite the ill will that he [the king of Naples] had towards him, greatly honoured. And facing the paintings of Franciabigio, [Allori] has done the narrative of Titus Quintius Flamininus who, speaking in the Council of the Achaeans against the ambassadors of the Aetolians and of King Antiochus, prevents the league that these ambassadors tried to make with the Achaeans. This narrative refers to the Diet of Cremona, in which the Magnificent Lorenzo frustrated the designs of the Venetians, who aspired to make themselves masters of all Italy.[143]

'At this time [Allori] did more panels. One was put in the monastery of Montedomini, where he painted the *Annunciation* for Sister Laura de' Pazzi. One was on canvas in which there is the *Nativity of Our Lord* for Giovambatista Gini, who sent it to his sister in Palermo. [628] And another shows Christ dead in the arms of the angels, and other figures, that is in the Church of Sant' Egidio in [the hospital of] Santa Maria Nuova.[144] Then he painted a chapel for Jacopo Salviati in his palace with narratives, in oil, of St Mary Magdalene and, on the vault that has a background completely of gold, he did six prophets and six sibyls with friezes and other very rich ornaments. At the command of Grand Duke Francesco, he copied the divine image of the *Annunciation of Florence*,[145] the size of the original. This was sent by His Highness as a gift to Cardinal Charles Borromeo. Don Aurelio da Forlì, then Abbot of Passignano, had him do, to his design, the chapel of that place, where the glorious body of St Giovangualberto is buried. And the miracles of this saint are painted there and, on the panel, by the hand of Alessandro is a dead Christ with three angels and the Madonna in the act of fainting. The panel was done by him in the Church of the Carmine, in Pisa, in which Our Lord is seen ascending to Heaven [in fact a *Resurrection*] with figures appropriate to that mystery.

'Endless are the portraits painted by Alessandro for princes, lords, and gentlemen, such as the portrait of *Almanno Salviati*, of his wife *Madonna Isabella*, of Cardinal *Giovanni Salviati*, of Sig. *Vincenzio Vitelli*, of Sig. *Sforza di Piombino*, of *Queen Joanna* of Austria, and of all the princely children of Grand Duke Francesco many times, and the portrait of the Most Serene Lord Don *Filippo de' Medici* of very happy memory [629] who, since that prince was very handsome alive, so it is a precious thing to see his image.'

Today, Prince of Campestrano[146]

'He has also portrayed Lord Don *Antonio de' Medici*, Marquis of Campestrano, and finally Grand Duke Francesco and the Grand Duchess, Lady Bianca Cappello, in life-size figures. Who then wanted to recount all the portraits and paintings made for individual gentlemen would be too long.

'Finding himself today forty-six years of age, [Allori] has in hand and already almost brought to completion a large *Last Supper* [dated 1582] with figures larger than life that is going to Bergamo to the Badia of Astino. Half of this is taken from the *Last Supper* that is in San Salvi by Andrea del Sarto and the other half is of his invention. But it appears to me that that part done by Alessandro [Allori] comes from Andrea [del Sarto], so well has he counterfeited the manner of that excellent painter. He is also doing a picture for the Cardinal Montalto where Our Lord as a child is standing on a bed that is thrown in perspective going away towards the head board, a direction finely done. And the Virgin, who has the most beautiful face that it is possible to see, binds the stomach of Christ and two angels bring something to eat and lower down are St Francis and St Lucy in devout poses. He has been allocated the panel in the middle of their chapel [in San Marco] by the Salviati and all the paintings that go there in fresco. He has also been commissioned to do the two panels and all the paintings for the Chapel of the Niccolini [in Santa Croce]. And the Chapel of the Carnesecchi in Santa Maria Maggiore will be built to his design, and [630] he will do the panel there himself. He has agreed to do, without any reward for his work but only for the benefit of his soul, the Chapel of the Spedal Nuovo of Santa Maria

Nuova. And he has the responsibility of doing the designs and the cartoons for the tapestry works of Grand Duke Francesco.

'Allori is very studious and industrious in his art and has composed a book in dialogue where he demonstrates the art of drawing figures, starting with the small details of the parts and coming little by little to form the whole human body. And all those things that he talks about will be seen in drawings. And I have seen a great part of these drawings, and they are as marvellous to me as industrious, because he has portrayed every nerve, every vein, every bone, and every muscle. And he has made many beautiful anatomies [écorché figures] in different poses and many nude figures of complete beauty. Thus, I strongly believe that this work of his, which he hopes to send into light immediately, will be both of great profit to the students of art and of great pleasure to gentlemen who please themselves by drawing. Considering the virtue and the excellence of Alessandro, Piero Capponi, who we have discussed at other times, has done this sonnet about him as a great courtesy:

Even of great name, and of immortal laurels [allori]
Worthy are you, that while today shamed
Sinner you paint, and today laboured,
Moved by the same emotion our hearts; [631]

Wherein to see her beautiful colours
Which repeat others revealed, others concealed
It covers in charming pallour the native rose,
Tempering, to God to turn, one's own ardour.

What more does nature do? Is made a handmaid
Where it was woman, and from them here the shadows, overcome,
In those the sense, and the motion to the eye believes.

And not only for you to the art the merit surrenders;
But your works from beautiful desire suspended
She contemplates with pleasure, and then every hour becomes more beautiful.

Giovanni Bizzelli

'Among the many apprentices who have been introduced to the art by Alessandro [Allori], Giovanni di Francesco Bizzelli[147] has awakened great hope. He went to Rome in the Holy Year, where he did a panel in which Christ is portrayed on the Cross with the Madonna and with St John for the Florentine Confraternity of the Misericordia. This was put in the Torre di Nona. Then, returning to Florence, working for himself, he painted a panel for Sig. Sansonetto de' Bardi di Vernio of a *Deposition from the Cross*, with many figures appropriate to this mystery, that was sent to Vernio by this *Signore*. He then did the panel that is above the high altar in the church of the nuns of St Agatha, in which the Glorious Virgin is seen with the Child in Her arms and some angels who hold up a canopy, surrounded by St Agatha, St Ursula, St John, and other saints. And because this panel pleased, two narratives in fresco on either side of it were allocated to him [632] that he conducted with commendable diligence. The *Martyrdom of St Agatha* is in one, and this is the best. And, in the other one, this saint dies with other figures. For the Princess, Lady Donna Leonora,[148] daughter of Grand Duke Francesco – a girl not only endowed with rare beauty and of singular virtue but of a marvellous modesty and of an unbelievable [*incredibile*] gentility – he did a little painting, in which there is the *Annunciation* to the Virgin by the angel. She keeps this in her room as a dear thing. Thus, for these works and for the studies that Giovanni, who finds himself at twenty-eight years of age, does every day, one is able to make a judgment that he will advance himself greatly in painting. But this is enough for him and we return to the principle masters.'

Alessandro del Barbiere

'Alessandro di Vincentio Fei, called del Barbiere,[149] practises among these to his great praise. He had his first principles in drawing from Ridolfo Ghirlandaio, being resident in his house some time, then learned to handle colours from Pier Francia, and finally, he worked with Tommaso da San Friano. The first work that Alessandro did of his own invention was a panel of the narrative of St Catherine when she was married to Jesus Christ; with other figures, seen in the Confraternity of St Catherine behind the Annunziata. He then did a St Francis, above a sphere done as the world, in fresco in the convent of the Zoccolanti Brothers at San Miniato al Tedesco. A panel from his hand representing the *Rosary of the Glorious Virgin* is in the church at Vicchio in the Mugello. [633] Another of this mystery is in the Church of the Brothers of St Dominic in Peccioli. He has painted a facade of a cloister in chiaroscuro in which there is the *Last Judgment* in the Pieve of the monks of Monteoliveto at Chiusure, in the area of Siena. And *Christ in the Act of Judgment* is in a little chapel that is in the middle of it. And a dead Christ is above the door of that pieve. He has done three chapels in fresco for the Ricasoli in the Church of Brolio in the Chianti. The *Virgin with the Child* in Her arms and other figures is in the first. Some *Doctors of the Church* debate in the second. And [he painted] some saints to satisfy the patrons in the third. In the Pieve of San Brancazio [Pancrazio] in [Colle di] Val d'Elsa he did a not very large panel in which the *Queen of Heaven* is shown with some saints. A panel of his is in the monastery of the nuns of Lapo [San Giovanni Battista], outside of Florence, showing the Madonna with Her Child and some saints in the lower part and God the Father in the midst of Paradise in the upper part.

'In three instances several of [Alessandro's] works were sent to Messina. The first was a panel for the major church [Duomo] in which he painted *Our Lady with Jesus*, two angels, and some saints. The second is a picture, three braccia high, of the *Adoration of the Magi*. And the third are twelve narratives of St John the Baptist, in oil on canvas, that were put in the church of the Florentines, who had sent to Florence to have him do them. Then he painted two pictures. In one he portrayed *Antonio del Bene* in the dress of the Gonfaloniere, with a page beside him, [634] holding a standard with the insignia of the city in his hand. And in the other he did a *Florence*. And these were sent to France. A chapel is done by his hand in fresco in the [basilican sanctuary of the] Madonna dell'Umilità in Pistoia, where there are eleven narratives of the life of the Glorious Virgin. And on the panel, in oil, is an *Annunciation* and a *Paradise* with angels and God the Father. And equally done by him in that city is the panel of the *Assumption of the Virgin* with the Apostles put in Madonna del Letto [Santa Maria delle Grazie]. He has done a panel of the *Conception* with many figures for Lord Pierantonio de Bardi in the Badia at Vernio, and this Lord Pierantonio is portrayed there from life kneeling in armour.

'These works are of [Alessandro's] hand in Florence. A panel is in the Confraternity of St Bridget, in which there is a *Christ on the Cross* with four saints. The panel in which the Virgin is shown receiving the angelic salutation is in a chapel [Guardini] done to his design in St Niccolò oltr' Arno. The panel of the narrative of *St Sebastian* is in San Brancazio and the *Resurrection of Christ* with many figures in various poses is in a chapel painted in fresco at the head of the garden in the monastery of Crocetta. The panel in the Chapel of the Corsi in Santa Croce is his in which Christ is seen at the column with many figures very well arranged and a perspective done with very great art.[150] And, in truth, this work is worthy of consideration for being well observed in every part and the best that Alessandro has done. Some pictures in oil with narratives of the Madonna are placed [635] on a column in the same church and the ornament with the canopy and angels in fresco that is above Donatello's *Annunciation*. The Most Serene Grand Duke Francesco has a picture in his Studiolo, done by [Alessandro] in competition with the other painters, in which are seen, imitated very vividly, all the ways in which jewellers work. Another little picture of his in small figures, showing the season of winter, is found in the study of the Cav. Gaddi, for whom he has also done many other paintings in certain friezes in his new house in the garden [Paradiso dei Gaddi]. There are two pictures of his hand in my study of very beautiful views that I had him do to accompany some pictures of Francesco Salviati. And he also painted the ceiling of this room for me where there are the nine Muses, the narrative of Zeuxis when he took the beautiful parts of many Croton maidens to depict his famous Venus, and many grotesquerie.'

Study of Matteo Botti

'[Alessandro] has painted a study for the very cultivated young man, Matteo Botti, whose virtues delight many, where he has done the seven Liberal Arts on the octagon of the lantern, in oil. And in the corners are other Virtues pertaining to these arts surrounded with grotesquerie with little birds playing and other charming things. Prints of Albrecht Dürer, arranged between very beautiful decorations in a frieze under the lantern, are placed between some shelves on which little wax models by the most capable men are put. And under this is another frieze with heads of emperors and globes of elegant mixed stone of [636] many kinds placed on a carved and gilded cornice under which are hung about eleven pictures, in oil, representing ancient games, hunting, fishing, and other country pleasures. And between each picture, the twelve months of the year and the four elements are painted with beautiful order on some pillars.

'Finding himself at forty-six years of age, Alessandro today has in hand an almost completed very beautiful painting that is going to Germany in which St John the Baptist is shown with his lamb at his feet in the desert next to the Jordan River in the act of showing himself unworthy of Christ. He is commissioned to do four narratives in the Church of the Jesuits that he has already started: the first of the *Last Supper of the Lord*, the second of the *Transfiguration*, the third of St John the Evangelist showing St Peter to Christ, and the fourth of the Apostles mending their nets. And all these narratives will be done with friezes decorated with little boys.'

Chapel of Cammillo Albizzi

'The Chapel of Cammillo Albizi, the honoured gentleman who pleases himself so much in doing courtesies, will be done to [Alessandro's] design in San Pier Maggiore. On the principal wall of this chapel, there will be a large panel that Alessandro has already completely sketched. And Christ is seen there above, rising into Heaven ingeniously veiled with a cloud, and the Apostles are below with two angels dressed in white in mid-air speaking with them. Four marble tombs will be seen on the side walls. Two rest on the floor, one of which was done by the hand of Donatello and there a dog is seen carved in [637] very beautiful low relief, and the other one shows evidence of being done by a more ancient hand. The other two will be arranged above, halfway up the walls, and they will be decorated above with two carefully worked canopies of gilded stucco around the balls of which some painted little boys will play. Grotesquerie will appear in the vault within very beautiful compartments of gilded stucco. And *Paradise* will be shown in the tondo in the middle with God the Father surrounded by many angels in various poses. And in four ovals that will be constructed as corbels for the vault they will do beautiful views of four figures illustrating *Mercy, Truth, Peace,* and *Justice*. But it would be too long if I wanted to recount all the little narratives, all the friezes, and all the decorations that Alessandro has planned to do here. He is very practised and copious in the inventions of his art, with great facility in handling colour in oil and fresco, and not of little value in painting views and in making many different things appear together in good order in a picture.'

Giovanni Bandini of Castello

'Giovanni di Benedetto Bandini from Castello,[151] called Giovanni dell'Opera for having worked many years in the Opera of Santa Maria del Fiore, was a student of the Cav. Bandinelli, and after his death did the greatest part of the marble low reliefs that are around the choir of Santa Maria del Fiore. The first portrait that he carved completely in the round in marble was of *Girolamo Lucchesini* of Lucca. He then did a life-size statue [638] showing Jason and two sea monsters, and a portrait of *Monsignore Altopascio* [Mon. Ugolino Grisoni], and these figures are seen in the house of this monsignore on a fountain that is at the head of his garden. That beautiful statue on the tomb of Michelangelo in Santa Croce that represents *Architecture* was done by him.[152] The apostle *St James the Less* portrayed, four and two-thirds braccia high, in Santa Maria del Fiore, very well studied and of a beautiful manner, and the apostle *St Philip* of the same size are of his hand.[153]

'Grand Duke Francesco has a bronze figure of his done as *Juno*. Then, he did a greater than life-size marble *Hercules Killing the Hydra* that shows very savage poses and strong and robust parts, and it is truly a statue worthy to be greatly praised, and it is found in the courtyard of the palace of Giovanni Niccolini on the Via de' Servi. He then did a *Bacchus* and two [statues of] *Venus*, two braccia high, that were bought by foreigners and sent away from Florence. Five marble heads of *Grand Duke Cosimo* are seen by his hand in our city: the first above the door of the Opera of Santa Maria del Fiore, the second above the door of the Cav. Minorbetti at Santa Trinita, the third above the door of the new house of the Cav. Gaddi, the fourth in the house of Giovanni Niccolini, and the fifth in the house of Bernardo Soderini. Five others equally are seen of *Grand Duke Francesco*: one above the door of Giovanni Benci, one above the [639] door of Carlo Martelli, one for the Magistrati Nuovi next to the Mint, one in the house of Giovanni Niccolini, and one in the piazza above the door of Benedetto Uguccioni. Sig. Giovan Alberto Princistano has a marble *Venus with Cupid* of his, a very beautiful work, and the very well-done life-size portrait of this *Princistano*; these things were sent by him to Germany. And truly Giovanni does portraits that mimic very excellently, and none of the so many sculptors who have portrayed Grand Duke Francesco have done him as accurately as he has. At different times he has done twenty marble heads representing emperors and other famous ancient men, of which some have gone to France and five are in the house of Jacopo Salviati. One of *Christ* is found in the choir of San Vincentio in Prato, and the others are in Florence in the houses of many gentlemen.

'Today, Giovanni is in Pesaro in the service of Francesco Maria Feltrio della Rovere [II], Duke of Urbino, where he has done the larger than life marble portrait of *Duke Francesco Maria the Elder* that is in the room of this present duke. And two half-life-size marble figures are still in Giovanni's possession: one representing *Venus with Cupid*, who has a fish under his left foot, and the other of *Adonis* with a hunting spear in hand and a dog beside him. At present, he is preparing to cast in bronze a figure on a leaping horse wounding a wild boar and two dogs are there, one of which has [640] the wild animal by an ear and the other is in the act of baying. It is hoped that this work will be done very beautifully as are all of his others since he understands design very well and is very experienced in working and carefully observing all the good considerations that the sculptor is given to have. And finding himself at forty-four years of age, it can be believed that he will come to greater perfection in working so that he will be able to climb a little higher.'

Francesco Poppi

'The excellent painter Francesco di Ser Francesco Morandini from Poppi, commonly called Il Poppi,[154] very industrious and very charming in colour, was sent as a child to learn grammar by his father, who was a notary, with the intention of introducing him into his occupation. But he, who was inclined to drawing by nature, went on his own, portraying now one thing and now another until he had occasion to portray some prints that were sent to one of his relatives, which he copied so well that he astonished everyone who saw them. Some of these were brought to Florence by an uncle of his. And having seen them, Piero Vasari, understanding that they had been done by a little boy, directed that Francesco be sent to Florence. And he took him into his house and put him to learn the art with his brother Giorgio Vasari, with whom he was not able at that time to make much progress. Then various accidents transpired. He was called by his father to Pietrasanta and then he went to the Casentino. Ultimately, he was brought back to Florence by a Felice della Campana and returned to work with Vasari. [641] But, having had some dissension with this Felice, desperate to be able to stay in Florence, because he did not have a way of living, he asked permission to go with God from Giorgio. [Giorgio], understanding the cause of his departure [from Felice], kept him [in his studio] and settled him with Don Vincentio Borghini, Prior of the Innocenti, who took him in most courteously and provided him with every convenience so that he was able to study. Therefore, continuing with great attention to learn all the things of art under Vasari, Il Poppi worked quite a long time for Giorgio, so that he was experienced and industrious in all the manners of painting.

'Finally, leaving [Giorgio] to work for himself, [Poppi] has done many praiseworthy works, among the first of which was a panel of the *Coronation of the Madonna* and four little pictures with angels and saints that are where the women are in the Spedale degli Innocenti. Many other are the works done by him that are found outside of Florence, and perhaps it is well that I remember that they are these. A panel of the *Nativity of Our Lord,* done at night, was for the Badia of Colle di Val d'Elsa, and a panel of the same mystery is at Altopascio. A panel with three saints is in the convent of San Francesco of the Conventual Brothers at Certomondo in the Casentino, and a panel of the *Assumption of the Virgin* and other pictures with saints are in the monastery of Santa Chiara in Castiglione. For the Confraternity of the Angel Raphael in Prato was a panel in which there is this angel. And a picture on canvas in which there is *Liberality with Fortune and Friendship* [642] belongs to Sig. Lodovico da Diacetto in France. A panel shows *Christ on the Cross* with some saints in San Salvi [in Florence], and in San Jacopo at San Miniato al Tedesco is a panel in which there is a *Deposition from the Cross.* A little panel of the *Rosary* is in the Badia in Poppi, and in the same church a panel of St John in front of the Porta Latina, in which this saint is seen in the cauldron of boiling oil with very beautiful care in the reflections of the fire and of the light. A panel of the mystery of the *Holy Spirit* is in the Confraternity of the Holy Spirit and a panel of the *Rosary* is in the Hermitage of Camaldoli. A panel in which there is the Madonna, St Lawrence, and St Francis is at Fronzola in the Casentino, and a panel of the *Virgin* with many saints is in the house of Monsignor Altopascio at Saminato. Two canvases are in Pratolino, in one the *Baptism of Constantine* and the other representing the people of Florence that was done for the baptism of Grand Prince Don Filippo de' Medici of most happy memory. A not very large panel of a dead Christ in the arms of His Mother and some saints is at Faenza and a panel of the *Annunciation* in Santa Verdiana is at Castel Fiorentino.

'Grand Duke Francesco has a picture from [Poppi's] hand in which the *Golden Age* is shown, another on Genoese plate showing the craft of foundry, and an oval in which Campaspe is seen being given to Apelles by Alexander the Great. And he also painted some pictures in fresco of the *Elements* and of *Prometheus with Nature* for His Highness in his Studiolo. Messer Antonio Serguidi, Knight of St Stephen and, because of his very favoured merits, secretary of our Grand Duke, has a very beautiful picture of his of a *Charity.* [643] The Florentine Senator Simon Corsi has a very devote *Crucifix* done by him, and equally Francesco della Fonte has one, Francesco Rondinelli one, and Messer

Caesar Nati one. He has done a *Virgin Annunciate* in the chapel in her house for the Most Serene Lady Bianca Cappello, Grand Duchess of Tuscany, and a picture of a dead Christ with the Virgin and other saints and a large picture of a *Crucifix* for Sig. Pandolfo Bardi di Vernio. Vincenzio di Ambra has two pictures of his hand: one of Christ taken down from the Cross and the other of the *Wedding of the Madonna*. Francesco de' Medici has one in which there is *Our Lady*, and Lord Marquis Antonmaria Malespina has one of a *Crucifix*. Francesco Rucellai has three [pictures]: in the first is *Virtue and Fortune*, in the second his portrait, and in the third *St Mary Magdalene*. Lord Marquis Ottaviano Malespina has a little panel done by him, in which there is a dead Christ, the Madonna, and other saints. Pier Nasi has a canvas in which there is painted the *First Age of Man* and *Spring*. Francesco del Nero has a picture of *Charity*, and the jeweller Regolo Cocapani has another similar to it. The Cav. Gaddi has a picture of the *House of the Sun*, and the Cav. Agnolo Bissoli has a picture of an *Our Lady* with many figures. Niccolò Bissoli has a *Crucifix* and one of his portrait. Messer Camillo Attavanti has a picture in which there is *St Verdiana*, and Ottaviano Conti, a very cultivated young man, has a [644] picture of a *Venus* and his portrait. And Giulio de' Nobli has a picture of the *Judgment of Paris* and his portrait.

'The panel in St Niccolò oltr' Arno is [Poppi's] work in which there is the *Wedding of the Madonna*,[155] a work worthy of praise, and also of his hand in this church is the picture showing the *Angel Raphael and Tobias*. And in San Michele Visdomini in the Chapel of the Treasurer Francesco Buontalenti is the panel of the *Conception* in which very beautiful women's faces and some very agreeable little boys are seen.[156] In the Agnoli he painted a *St Jerome* and a *St Francis*. And he has done endless pictures and portraits for various people among which was one of *Suliman*, Emperor of the Turks, and one of the *Marchese of Pescara* that Grand Duke Francesco had him do and sent it to the Emperor. For Sig. Vettorio Cappello he painted a very beautiful picture on canvas of the narrative of Joseph fleeing from the love-struck woman and a portrait of *Pope Leo*. And [he painted] a *Crucifix* for Stefan Galli that today belongs to the Most Serene Carlo, Duke of Savoy. But it would be too long if I wanted to recount all of these.

'A panel of the *Purification*, which goes to San Piero Scaraggio, is today found in [Poppi's] shop,[157] and a great panel on canvas in which there is the *Nativity of Christ*, conducted with great diligence, done for Niccolò Bissoli who wants to send it to Naples. And [also there] is a portrait of

Lord *Silvio Piccolomini* of which it is not possible to see anything more like him nor more lifelike. And these works are entirely finished. An almost-completed panel that seems to me the most beautiful work that I have seen of his is found in hand today. [645] This is going to be put in San Francesco in Pistoia, and it represents the mystery of the *Purification*. And the Madonna is seen there, a very beautiful figure in a blue gown who seems to rise out of the panel, and there are very beautiful and varied faces there and a view that appears very distant, and the whole work is of a sweet manner and charming colour. He is also doing a panel, which is going to the chapel of Lutozzo Nasi in San Niccolò oltr' Arno, of the miracle of Christ when He resuscitates the son of the widow and a panel of the *Last Supper* of the Apostles that will be taken to Castiglione. A panel of the *Baptism of Christ* is for Braccio de' Ricasoli. And the panel is his for the chapel that the Salviati are doing in San Marco, in which he is commissioned to paint when the Saviour of the World cleanses the leper. This work is expected to be very beautiful because he is doing it in competition with Batista Naldini and Alessandro Allori and because he is resolved to do many drawings for it, something that he has not greatly used in other works of his. Being greatly helped by nature in this art, he has up to now done his panels without doing drawings other than throwing a few chalk lines on the panel and then finishing it with colour without having cartoons or other examples before him. He is painting for Messer Girolamo Minucci, Cup Bearer of the Grand Duke and Knight of St Stephen, a picture in which there is a dead Christ with other figures and another picture for Lionardo Alessandrini [646] of Moses showing the laws to the people.

'But it is time to end the discussion of Poppi, as whoever wanted to take note of all of his things would go on too long. It is enough to say only that he finds himself at thirty-nine years of age and working very well and with very great facility, and his paintings have a marvellous charm, and, being still young, it can be hoped that he will climb to a greater excellence. Having seen some of his beautiful works, Piero Capponi has done this sonnet about him in order, by honouring him, to honour all virtuous men and those who appear to have any singular part in them that is worthy of praise. But hear his verses:

He curbs so much the great desire, that serves
  In gentle hearts, to satisfy only the eyes,
  Contemplating limbs nude, soft, and charming,
  Thus, the free spirit is made a servant;

The women, beautiful, lascivious, and arrogant
Look from Poppi, and if for their less brilliant side
He does not want that work the heart to charm,
Then he preserves it for a Gnido outside of earthly Love.

But he to give place to the senses has trained the soul
In his sacred images establishing the appearance,
Then if he can he ordains the shadowed edge.

Sad, and pleased is the man, fast and slow
Of him (to whom natural beauty surrenders)
The outlines, the colours, the lights, and the shadows. [647]

Giovanni Caccini

'Before I finish my discussion that it is already time to end, the sun having departed from our hemisphere, I do not want to omit saying that today Giovanni di Michelangelo Caccini gives hope of achieving great results in sculpture as [would be expected of] a Florentine.[158] He is the brother of that Giulio called Giulio Romano, who is so excellent in singing. Having learned the art from Giovanantonio Dosio, and not being more than twenty-two, he already works very well. He has restored several antiquities for the Cav. Gaddi and many also for Grand Duke Francesco, and truly, he is greatly valued in carefully joining pieces together and imitating the antique. Inside the chapel where the glorious body of St Giovangualberto is, in the Badia of Passignano, the marble reclining statue of this saint is of his hand, and he also did the stuccos that are seen in the vault. Today he has in hand two rather larger than life statues representing *St Zanobius* and *St Bartholomew* that will go in the Chapel of Zanobi Carnesecchi in Santa Maria Maggiore. Equally, he is doing another larger than life marble figure done as a *Temperance* for Monsignore Messer Giovambatista del Milanese, Bishop of Marsi. And if he – as he is seen to do every day – proceeds continually advancing in the art, it will not be a long time until he can be put in the number of the most excellent masters that sculpture has had.

'But enough for now what is said of him and also enough for you, as I have [648] done what should not fail to satisfy you in discussing the sculptors and painters up to now, not being able to recall any other names right now to memorialize. Besides, the fresh breeze that makes these green branches tremble, together with the late hour, invites one to amuse oneself somewhat before the time of supper supervenes to call us laughing to the villa.'

All got to their feet at the end of these words and, having discussed some things again and added others, wandering with slow footstep, enjoyed themselves in the fresh spirits of the trees. But as the sky towards the west reddened, it was transformed into a blue colour and was decorated with a thousand lucid little flames, and in the villa where the tables were prepared those attending collected.

Appendix: The Artists Described by Borghini

The space Borghini gave to the artists he described
(lines per artist in the 1st edition)

Artist	Lines	Artist	Lines
Andrea del Sarto	358	Beccafumi*	137
Raphael	298	Mantegna	136
Vasari	275	Leonardo da Vinci	135
Alessandro Allori	242	Fra Bartolomeo	134
Tintoretto	233	Santi di Tito	133
Michelangelo	227	Federico Zuccaro	130
Giotto	206	Buontalenti	128
Francesco Poppi	205	Vincentio Danti	122
Perino del Vaga*	200	Girolamo Muziano	116
Giovanni Strada	177	Fra Angelico	115
Battista Naldini		Polidoro Caravaggio	
Bronzino	176	and Maturino*	112
Pontormo	173	Domenico Ghirlandaio*	111
Ammanati	165	Andrea Sansovino*	110
Francesco Salviati	162	Fra Giovangnolo	110
Alessandro Fei	162	Montorsoli	109
Giambologna	155	Il Sodoma*	108
Giulio Romano	154	Girolamo Macchietti	108
Donatello	152	Giovantonio Dosio	103
Titian	146	Masaccio	101
Parmigianino	145	Filippo Lippi*	101
Rosso	143	Baldassare Peruzzi*	99

* Lives omitted in this edition.

Taddeo Zuccaro*	98
Baccio Bandinelli	95
Cimabue	93
Taddeo Gaddi*	
Vincentio de' Rossi	
Perugino	89
Botticelli	83
Ridolfo Ghirlandaio	81
Giovanni Bandini	80
Sebastiano del Piombo*	79
Niccolò Tribolo*	78
Daniele da Volterra*	76
Antonello de Messina	73
Giulio Clovio*	73
Pierino da Vinci*	72
Uccello	71
Francesco Francia*	71
Raffaello da Montelupo	71
Paolo Veronese	70
Andrea del Castagno*	68
Franciabigio	68
Signorelli*	67
Domenico Puligo	67
Lorenzo di Bicci*	66
Piero di Cosimo*	63
Antonio and Piero Pollaiuolo*	62
Jacopo Sansovino	60
Timeteo da Urbino*	59
Palma Giovane	59
'Giottino'*	58
Giovanni da Udine*	58
Correggio	58
Passerotti	57
Luca della Robbia	55
Giorgione	55
Giovanantonio Sogliani*	55
Stoldo Lorenzi	55
Lorenzo di Credi*	54
Spinello Spinelli*	53
Federigo Barocci	53
Verrocchio*	51
Raffaellino del Garbo*	50
Cosimo Rosselli*	49
Valerio Cioli	47
Benozzo Gozzoli*	46
Giovanfrancesco Rustichi*	45
Brunelleschi	43
Benedetto da Rovezzano	43
Gentile Bellini	42
Tommaso da San Friano	42
Albertinelli*	41
Annibale Fontana	41
Giovanfrancesco Penni*	40
Properzia de' Rossi	40
Il Fattore*	40
Desiderio da Settignano*	38
Benedetto da Maiano*	38
Scipione Pulsone	38
Battista da Cavaliere	38
Andrea Ferrucci	37
Bartolomeo Bagnacavalo*	37
Giovanni Bizzelli	35
Giovanni Bellini	34
Michelozzo*	33
Vincentio da San Gimignano*	32
Gherardo Starnina*	32
Primaticcio*	31
Giovanni Caccini	31
Francesco da San Gallo*	29
Masolino*	27
Granacci*	27
Gentile da Fabriano*	23
Antonio Rossellino*	23
'Lorenzo Costa'*	23
Baccio da Montelupo*	21
Girolamo Danti	19
Jan van Eyck	18
Marietta Robusti	18

Jacopo Bassano	18	Francesco Bassano	16
Prospero Fontana	18	Lavinia Fontana	5
Ercole di Roberti*	17	Michele di Ridolfo	5
Ghiberti	16		

Notes

Translator's Preface

1 'Introduction' (New York: Macmillan, 1968; Princeton: Princeton University Press, 1984), xxviii.

2 (Florence: Giunta, 1568; ed. Gaetano Milanesi [Florence: Sansoni, 1906]).

3 'Raffaello Borghini's *Il Riposo*: A Critical Study and Annotated Translation' (Case Western Reserve, 2002; Ann Arbor: UMI, 2003); hereafter 'my dissertation.'

4 Two print facsimile editions of the first edition of *Il Riposo* are available (Milan: Labor, 1967, and Hildesheim: Olms, 1969). The first edition of *Il Riposo* is also available in the microfiche of Count Leopoldo Cicognara's collection, *Catalogo ragionato dei libri d'arte* ... (Pisa: Capurro, 1821), no. 2217; microfiche (Cosenza: Editrice 'Casa del Libro' Dott. Gustavo Brenner, 1960). The first edition has also been intermittently available to some online (http://visualiseur.bnf.fr/Visualiseur?Destination=Gallica&O=NUMM-26872) or (http://gallica.bnf.fr/), but I have been unable to access either from Cleveland.

5 This more legible second edition is available on microfiche as no. 2218 in the Cicognara collection.

6 (Rome, 1754; Milan: Silvestri, 1822).

7 For a review of the various editions of *Il Riposo*, see the Annotated Bibliography of my dissertation.

8 (Milan: Ricciardi, 1971–7). Barrochi carefully examines the derivation of the important sections that she extracts from *Il Riposo*.

9 Dedication of Borghini's translation of Jean de Maconville's *Traité contenant l'origine des temples des Juifs, Chrestiens et Gentilz* ... (Paris, 1563) into the *Trattato di Giovanni di Marco Villa sopra l'Origine de' Tempi de' Giudei, de Christiani, e dei Gentili* ... (Florence: Marescotti, 1577).

Introduction

1 Because Borghini knew only one Grand Duke Cosimo and one Grand Duke Francesco, they will not hereafter be identified by number.

2 See Marcia Hall, *Renovation and Counter-Reformation. Vasari and Duke Cosimo in Sta. Maria Novella and Sta. Croce, 1565–1577* (Oxford: Clarendon, 1979).

3 Marco Rosci, e.g., edited *Il Riposo* (Milan: Labor, 1967). In his 'Saggio Biobibliografico,' in *Il Riposo*, vol. 2, ix, Rosci characterizes Borghini's treatise as very much part of the 'reactionary and conformist climate in which the suffocating moralism of the Counter-Reformation was implemented more in the letter than in the spirit ... allied with the immoral acquiescence and mediocrity of the Grand Dukes, underlined with dark memories of the ferocity of Alessandro ... [so that] the cult of the Florentine artistic tradition, from an effective and positive interlace of great and astute critical and historical judgement over three centuries of Italian art, as in Vasari, becomes simple hagiography or simply gossip.'

4 See 'Eindeutiger und eindeutig,' in Thomas Frangenberg, *Der Betrachter. Studien zur florentinischen Kunstliteratur des 16. Jahrhunderts* (Berlin: Mann, 1990), 79.

5 A number in brackets, here [458], refers to a page number in the first edition. These first edition page numbers appear in the text of this translation.

6 '... il quale [the Puligo painting] si trova oggi in casa M. Francesco Borghini, Auditore di S.A.S.'

7 By way of comparison, the Vasari-Zuccaro frescoes (approx. 38,750 sq. ft.) are about twice the size of all of the frescoed components of the Sistine Chapel: Michelangelo's vault (12,916 sq. ft.); Michelangelo's *Judgment* (2,112 sq. ft.), and what remain of Sixtus IV's *Lives of Christ and Moses* (2,553 sq. ft.).

8 See Cristina Acidini Luchinat, 'Per le pitture della Cupola di Santa Maria del Fiore,' *Labyrinthos* 13–16 (1988–9): 153–75, and Zygmunt Wazbinski, 'Artysci i publicznosc w szesnastowiecznej Florencji "Cane mordente,"' in *Théorie de l'art* (Congrès Varsovie, 1974) (1976), 46–76; reprinted as 'Artisti e pubblico nella Firenze del Cinquecento. A proposito del topos "cane abbaiante,"' *Paragone* 28/327 (May 1977): 3–24.

Elizabeth Pilliod, however, in her *Pontormo, Bronzino, Allori: A Genealogy of Florentine Art* (New Haven: Yale University Press, 2001), 146, notes that Borghini and Allori would have known each other well, as members of the same confraternity, the Compagnia del Gesù, a fact that may qualify the enthusiasm with which *Il Riposo* is described as a stridently pro-Medici–Federico Zuccaro, anti-republican–Allori, polemic. Furthermore, Borghini gives Allori's frescoes at Poggio a Caiano a generous review in Book IV [626–7].

9 'Su "Il riposo" di Raffaele Borghini,' *Rivista d'Arte* 27/3/II (1951–2): 221–6.

10 For a comprehensive listing of Borghini's literary work, see Rosci, *Il Riposo*, vol. 2, xxiii–vi. For a detailed modern review of Borghini's literary accomplishment, other than *Il Riposo*, and an understanding of the relation of that accomplishment to *Il Riposo*, see Giulio Ferroni, 'Le commedie di Raffaello Borghini,' *La Rassegna della letteratura italiana* 73/7 (1969): 37–63.

11 Marescotti had purchased the Torrentino Press. Cosimo established the Torrentino Press in 1546 to restore the reputation of Florentine publishing and end the unproductive monopoly enjoyed by the Giunta Press. The Torrentino Press, which published the first edition of Vasari's *Vite* in 1550, did not flourish as Cosimo had hoped. Vasari would turn to Giunta for his second edition in 1568. 'Lorenzo Torrentino' (Laurenx Leenaertsz van der Beke) ended up wandering about northern Italy, imprisoned at one point on suspicion of heresy for having translated Calvino's *Nicomediana*. He left his press to his sons who sold it to Marescotti in 1570.

Marescotti (Georges Marescot or Mareschot) had come to Florence from France in 1553 to manage the bookstore associated with the Torrentino Press. Marescotti specialized in what Fernanda Ascarelli and Marco Menato describe as '*opere volgari*, works of locale and religious interest' and never achieved his goal of becoming the Ducal Printer.

See Fernanda Ascarelli and Marco Menato's *La Tipografia del '500 in Italia* (Florence: Olschki, 1989), 284–5 and 294–5, and Ascarelli's *Tipografia Cinquecentina Italiana* (Florence: Sansoni, 1953), 139.

12 Ferroni, 'Commedie,' 63.

13 *Rime inedite di Raffaello Borghini e di Angiolo Allori detto il Bronzino*, ed. Domenico Moreni (Florence: Magheri, 1822).

14 Elena Avanzini, *Il Riposo di Rafaello Borghini e la critica d'arte nel '500* (Milan: Gastaldi, 1960), 18–19, versus Rosci, *Il Riposo*, vol. 2, viii; Ferroni, 'Commedie,' 39; and Remo Ceserani, 'Borghini, Raffaello,' in *Dizionario Biografico Degli Italiani*, ed. by Alberto Ghisalberti (Rome: Società Grafica Romano, 1970), vol. 12, 679.

15 Paola Barocchi, ed., *Scritti d'arte del Cinquecento*, vol. 1, 1065.

16 Avanzini, *Il Riposo di Raffaello Borghini*, 19.

17 From a prominent Venetian family, Bianca Capello eloped to Florence with a husband who seamlessly accommodated himself to her relationship with Francesco, a relationship that long predated the death of her predecessor as grand duchess. After her husband, who reveled in his position as the legal consort of the illegal consort, was conveniently murdered in the street by

resentful Florentines, Francesco established Bianca in a house adjacent to the Pitti Palace. Bianca may have been the only person in Florence with a genuine affection for the difficult Francesco and may have been the only human being he was ever able to relate to on a personal basis.

18 Rosci, *Il Riposo*, vol. 2, vii.

19 See his *Print Culture in Renaissance Italy: The Editor and the Vernacular Text, 1470–1600* (Cambridge: Cambridge University Press, 1994), 155–81, in which Vincenzio Borghini appears as the literary hero of the resurrection of the Florentine press in the second half of the sixteenth century. Richardson's more recent and more comprehensive *Printing, Writers and Readers in Renaissance Italy* (Cambridge: Cambridge University Press, 1999) is essential to understanding Borghini's print culture.

20 As Janet Cox-Rearick notes in her *Bronzino's Chapel of Eleonora in the Palazzo Vecchio* (Berkeley: University of California Press, 1993), 256: 'The upheavals of the previous decade [1527–37] and the alliance of Florence with Charles V had put the Golden Age of Lorenzo [the Magnificent] forever out of reach.'

21 Cosimo had hurriedly redecorated the Palazzo Vecchio as a home for Francesco and Johanna of Austria in time for their wedding in 1565. Although Cosimo died ten years before the publication of *Il Riposo* (and Eleonora had died twelve years before that), the Palazzo Vecchio continued to be the home of Francesco while Borghini was writing *Il Riposo.*

22 Edward Olszewski's annotated translation of *On the True Precepts of the Art of Painting*, by Giovanni Battista Armenini (New York: Franklin, 1977), should be consulted concerning this subject, particularly 9–18. See also Anthony Blunt, *Artistic Theory in Italy, 1450–1600* (London: Clarendon, 1940; Oxford: Oxford University Press, 1968), and Liana Cheney, *Readings in Italian Mannerism* (New York: Lang, 1997).

23 'was of white marble and adorned with carvings
so accurate – not only Polycletus
but even Nature, there would feel defeated.'

Purgatorio, trans. Allen Mandelbaum (New York: Knopf, 1995), x:31–3, 260.

24 *Decameron*, trans. and ed. G.H. McWilliam, 2nd ed. (London: Penguin, 1995), vi:5, 457–9.

25 Karen-Edis Barzman, 'The Florentine Accademia del Disegno: Liberal Education and the Renaissance Artist,' in *Academies of Art between Renaissance and Romanticism*, Leids kunsthistorisch jaarboek, ed. Anton W.A. Boschloo ('s-Gravenhage: SDU, 1989), 27n5.

26 'These things being very difficult and taking a great deal of time to understand, I will leave them aside.'

27 Cicero and Quintilian divide *rhetorica* into five parts: *inventio* (the choosing of arguments); *dispositio* (the initial arrangement of the material); *elocutio* (the final polishing of the speech and its decoration with antitheses, metaphors, and rhetorical figures); *actio* or *promuntiatio* (the technique of speech-making, including gestures and voice command); and *memoria* (the necessity of learning the speech thoroughly). See Allan Ellenius, 'Development of the Categories of Painting during the Fifteenth and Sixteenth Centuries,' in *De Arte Pingendi: Latin Art Literature in Seventeenth-Century Sweden and Its International Background* (Uppsala: Almquist and Wiksells, 1960), 60–70.

This rhetorical organization would be mirrored, see Rensselaer Lee, *Ut Pictura Poesis: The Humanistic Theory of Painting* (New York: Norton, 1967), in many of the art treatises of the sixteenth century: Francesco Lancilotto's *Trattato di pittura* (1509) (*disegno, colorito, compositione, inventione*); Paolo Pino's *Dialogo di pittura* (1548) (*disegno, invenzione, colorito*); Lodovico Dolce's *Dialogo della pittura* (1557) (*inventione, disegno, colorito*); *Il Riposo* (*inventione, dispositione, attitudini, membri, colori*); and Giovanni Battista Armenini's *De' veri precetti della pittura* (1586) (*disegno, lumi, ombre, colorito, compimento*). Lee notes that the artists frequently begin with *disegno* and the non-artists with *inventione*.

28 It would be almost 150 years after the circulation of *De pictura*, however, before Borghini became the first author to specifically criticize an artist for departing from the *historia* of a classical myth. See Borghini's criticism of Titian's *Venus and Adonis* [64–5].

29 *Leon Battista Alberti on Painting*, trans. John Spencer, 2nd ed. (New Haven: Yale University Press, 1966), 91.

30 Carlo Pedretti discusses the availability of variant Leonardo manuscripts in Florence, in *The Literary Works of Leonardo da Vinci, Compiled and Edited from the Original Manuscripts by Jean Paul Richter* (Berkeley: University of California Press, 1977), 1:32.

Marco Rosci compares Leonardo's *Trattato* with *Il Riposo*, in 'Leonardo "filosofo," Lomazzo e Borghini 1584: Due linee di tradizione dei pensieri e precetti di Leonardo sull'arte,' in *Fra Rinascimento Manierismo e realtà. Scritti di Storia dell'arte in memoria di Anna Maria Brizio*, ed. Pietro Marani (Florence: Giunti Barbèra, 1984), 53–77. Rosci's study shows the extent to which Borghini adopts Leonardo's remarks unchanged into *Il Riposo*. Rosci establishes that Borghini used a manuscript different from that which was the basis for the 1651 first edition of the *Trattato della pittura*. See also Book II, nn54 and 60, and Book III, n50.

31 'We pass forward,' Michelozzi said [195], 'as we have seen enough of his things and will see more of them in Santa Maria Novella.' There is a

difference of opinion concerning Borghini's evaluation of Vasari. The sense of Marcia Hall's reading of *Il Riposo* is that Borghini was strongly hostile to Vasari and the Maniera painters (*Renovation and Counter-Reformation*, 59). Reading the same passages in *Il Riposo*, Frangenberg finds Borghini less hostile to Vasari and stresses Borghini's appreciation for the style of Vasari's *Immaculate Conception* in Santi Apostoli (*Der Betrachter*, 94 and n74).

32 Citations to Vasari throughout this book are to the 2nd ed. (1568), ed. Gaetano Milanesi (Florence: Sansoni, 1906), unless otherwise noted.

33 Julius Schlosser (-Magnino), *Die Kunstliteratur* (Vienna: Schroll, 1924), 307; as *La Letteratura artistica*, ed. Otto Durz, trans. Filippo Rossi (Florence: La Nuova Italia, 1964), 349.

34 *Vasari on Technique …* trans. Louise Maclehose, ed. Baldwin Brown (London: Dent, 1907; New York: Dover, 1960), 208.

35 See: Frangenberg, *Der Betrachter*, 19–35; Richardson, *Print Culture*, 155–81; Robert Williams, 'Vincenzio Borghini and Vasari's "Lives"' (doctoral dissertation, Princeton University, 1988) and *Art, Theory, and Culture in Sixteenth-Century Italy* (Cambridge: Cambridge University Press, 1997). See also Vincenzio Borghini, *Carteggio, 1541–1580: censimento*, ed. Daniela Francalanci and Franca Pellegrini (Florence: Accademia, 1993).

36 Vincenzio Borghini: 'And in the same way in which high and deep voices, composed together with reason and rule, produce the sweetest harmony and consonance, so in the composition of a picture there should be a composition of larger things with small ones, of distant things with things nearby, so that there results a most pleasant consonance and harmony for the eye,' *Selva di notizie*, in Barocchi, *Scritti*, vol. 1, 611–13.

Raffaello Borghini: '… it is necessary to arrange everything so … that it is created in agreement and unity. As agreement which delights the ears results from varied voices and from different cords, in the same way pleasure and content for the eyes are created from the many parts arranged in the painting' [179].

Vincenzio Borghini, surprisingly, found the best practitioner of such composition, not in Florence, but in the north in the small-scale engravings of Lucas van Lyden, giving Lucas the supreme complement: 'e tenuto quasi cosa divina Luca d'Olanda.' *Benedetto Varchi – Vincenzio Borghini. Pittura e scultura nel cinquecento*, ed. Paola Barocchi (Livorno: Silabe, 1998), 120.

37 Vincenzo Borghini, *Selva*, in Barocchi, *Scritti*, vol. 1, 629.

38 Richardson, *Printing*, 141.

39 Mosche Barasch, *Theories of Art from Plato to Winckelman* (New York: New York University Press, 1985), 272.

40 Armenini, *On the True Precepts*, 120.

41 Avanzini, *Il Riposo di Raffaello Borghini*, 79.
42 *After Raphael: Painting in Central Italy in the Sixteenth Century* (Cambridge: Cambridge University Press, 1999), 247.
43 Richardson, *Print Culture*, 155.
44 Creighton Gilbert, 'The Archbishop on the Painters of Florence, 1450,' *Art Bulletin* 41 (1959): 75–87.
45 G. Gruyer, *Les Illustrations des écrits des Jérôme Savonarole* (Paris, 1879), 207; quoted in Blunt, 46.
46 The Pope and his sister, Margarita de' Medici, were from a Lombard branch of the family so distantly related to the people in Florence that he had to ask Cosimo's permission to put the Medici *palli* (balls) on his coat of arms.
47 Thomas Puttfarken, *The Discovery of Pictorial Composition* (New Haven: Yale University Press, 2000), 171–2.
48 *Renovation and Counter-Reformation*, 56.
49 *Burlington Magazine* 124 (1982): 512–14.
50 But Schlosser, *Letteratura*, 349, compares *Il Riposo*, not to a Platonic dialogue, but to the *Saturnalia* of Ambrosius Theodosius Macrobius (fl. 395–423). The *Saturnalia* was a dialogue compendium of little dramatic character with a great variety of historical, mythological, critical, and grammatical material. As in *Il Riposo*, one of the participants took a leading part in each book, and the remarks of the other participants only serve to bring out new displays of erudition.
51 Avanzini, *Il Riposo di Raffaello Borghini*, 31–2. Lewis Einstein, 'Conversations at Villa Riposo,' *Gazette des Beaux-Arts* 2 (July-Aug. 1961): 6–20, refers to Borghini's dialogue as 'in a half conversational style.'
52 In the extreme case, not letting someone know that you are not letting them know how difficult it is to do what you are doing.
53 Rosci, *Il Riposo*, vol. 2, xii.
54 (New Haven: Yale University Press, 1990).
55 Detlef Heikamp, 'The Grotto of the Fata Morgana and Giambologna's Marble Gorgon,' *Antichità Viva* 20, 3 (1981): 12–31.
56 This report is part of a *Mappe di Popoli e Strade dei Capitani di Parte Guelfa* published in 1584. Claudia Lazzaro, *The Italian Renaissance Garden* (New Haven: Yale University Press, 1990), 121, reads Borghini's description of the landscape at Il Riposo as describing an estate that is more wooded than intensely cultivated: 'the *boschetto* occupied the largest area, although there were also flowers, vines, and fruit trees.' For a discussion of the less ordered character of some Italian Renaissance garden practice, see her Chapter 5, 'Nature Without Geometry: Vineyards, Parks, and Woods,' 109–30.

57 Lazzaro notes that 'a flat terrace, often a major expense, was an important characteristic of the sixteenth-century garden.' *Renaissance Garden*, 83–4.

58 The *Guardaroba* was an administrative concept embracing the grand ducal collections, not a description of the contents of a particular place. 'A recording system kept by members of the duke's own staff accounted for the entrance and withdrawal of the pieces stored first at the Palazzo Vecchio and later also in the Pitti Palace in special rooms and cupboards.' Anna Maria Massinelli and Filippo Tuena, *Treasures of the Medici* (New York: Vendome, 1992), 58.

59 Rosci, *Il Riposo*, vol. 2, xi.

60 Avanzini, *Il Riposo di Raffaello Borghini*, 41.

61 For Don Giovanni see Gaetano Pieraccini, *La stirpe de' Medici di Cafaggiolo* (1925; Florence: Vallecchi, 1986); Franco Borsi, 'Don Giovanni de' Medici, Principe Architetto,' in *Firenze del Cinquecento* (Rome: Editalia, 1974), 352–8; and Malcolm Campbell, 'Family Matters. Notes on Don Lorenzo and Don Giovanni de' Medici at Villa della Petraia,' in *Ars naturam adiuvans. Festschrift für Matthias Winner* (Mainz am Rhein: Zabern, 1996), 505–13. See also Karla Langedijk, *The Portraits of the Medici* (Florence: Studio per Edizioni Scelte, 1983), vol. 2, 1020–6, particularly 55.1 and 55.1a.

62 T.C. Price Zimmermann, *Paolo Giovio* (Princeton: Princeton University Press, 1995), 201.

63 Schlosser, *Letteratura*, 352.

64 Norman Land, 'The Elder Philostratus's Response to Art,' in *The Viewer as Poet* (University Park: Pennsylvania State University Press, 1994), 27–48.

65 This is not an opinion shared by all. Rosci, *Il Riposo*, vol. 2, xii, speaks of 'the unbearable and by now already Spanish abundance of ceremonious formulas, of courtly adulation on all sides.'

66 Avanzini, *Il Riposo di Raffaello Borghini*, 34–5.

67 Blunt acerbically comments: 'The one point worth noting about the book is that Borghini is writing not only for artists but also for those who, without actually painting themselves, yet want to be in a position to judge works of art. No writer of a full-dress treatise on painting before Borghini had set out with this intention' (*Theory in Italy*, 101).

Frangenberg points out (*Der Betrachter*, 78–9) that while Pino, Doni, and Dolce had all previously written treatises that, in their dialogue format and accessible language, are obviously directed to the layman, and while Vasari had directed his *Vite* to artists and laymen at the same time (Vasari, vol. 1, 105), *Il Riposo* was the first treatise that made it its primary goal to provide the layman with the necessary speech and judgment to step before a work of art.

68 Schlosser-Magnino, *Letteratura*, 351; Orienti, 'Su "Il Riposo" di Raffaele Borghini,' 222.

69 See Williams, *Art, Theory, and Culture*, 91–4.

70 In the very helpful review of Borghini's tours of Santa Croce and Santa Maria Novella, Hall, *Renovation and Counter-Reformation*, emphasizes that the value of *Il Riposo* is that it is a contemporary critique of the Counter-Reformation visual reform of these churches by Cosimo and Vasari.

Charles Hope strongly disagrees in his review of Hall's book. He points out that these redecorations mostly dated from a period significantly preceding *Il Riposo.* For Hope, Borghini's vigorous criticism of these paintings represents a different and subsequent iconographic and stylistic aesthetic: 'Far from reflecting recent taste, he was rejecting it and enunciating new standards for religious imagery' (Review, 513).

No one knows when Borghini wrote *Il Riposo* but the assumption of Ferroni, the most thorough examiner of Borghini's literary remains, is that the dialogue was written at some time between Borghini's return to Florence in 1580 and its publication in 1584. This timing could support either Hall or Hope. I think the tone of *Il Riposo* supports Hall's view, that Borghini wrote his dialogue-treatise as a review of his contemporaries.

71 Borghini describes, e.g., the cat as a cat and not as the Devil or a symbol of Christ in Giulio Romano's *Madonna of the Cat*, now in Naples. In the background of Giulio's *Madonna and Child with St James, St John the Baptist, and St Mark* in Santa Maria dell'Anima in Rome, Borghini describes 'the brooding hen with chicks of which art in the imitation of nature cannot do more' [449] as a hen with chicks, instead of Jesus protecting the people of Jerusalem, 'as a hen gathers her chicks under her wings' (Matthew 23:37).

72 Jole Tognelli reminds us of the importance colour has for Borghini in his 'Tra Lingua e Colore. "Vaghezza" cromatica del Borghini,' *Letteratura* 7/37–8 (Jan.–Apr. 1959): 7–14.

73 Avanzini, *Il Riposo di Raffaello Borghini*, 86.

74 Hall contrasts this inconsistent attitude with that of 'Paleotti, who would prohibit even the private collecting of mythological paintings.' *After Raphael* (Cambridge: Cambridge University Press, 1999), 247.

75 Hall, *Renovation and Counter-Reformation*, 57, sees a conflict between Borghini's Maniera-inspired desire for *grazia* in a figure and his Counter-Reformation desire for accurate representation. Hall emphasizes that 'Borghini's rejection of the aesthetic of Maniera art is not total. He demands the glowing colour, the gracefully posed figures, and the beautifully rendered textures of the Maniera, and he criticizes [in the tour in Book II] any lapse from these standards' (59).

76 Hall, *Renovation and Counter-Reformation*, 55.
77 'Review of *Renovation and Counter-Reformation*,' 513.
78 *Der Betrachter*, 85–8.
79 *Italian Renaissance Sculpture* (New York: Thames and Hudson, 1992), 199–200.
80 'The Erotics of Absolutism: Rubens and the Mystification of Sexual Violence,' *Representations* 25 (1989): 7–11.
81 Frangenberg points out (*Der Betrachter*, 94n69) that such single-mindedness was not unlike Svetlana Alpers's characterization of Vasari: 'the astonishing fact that wherever one opens the *Lives*, whether at the beginning of art with Giotto or toward the end with Raphael, the descriptions are alike.' See Alpers, '*Ekphrasis* and Aesthetic Attitudes in Vasari's *Lives*,' *Journal of the Warburg and Courtauld Institutes* 23 (1960): 191.
82 'Review of *Renovation and Counter-Reformation*,' 513.
83 Among the artists who Borghini omits and Vasari includes are Nanni di Banco, Pinturicchio, Jacopo della Quercia, Francesco di Giorgio Martini, and Piero della Francesca.
84 Frangenberg, *Der Betrachter*, 100.
85 Giulio Ferroni, who has studied all of Borghini's literary effort more carefully than anyone else, disagrees. He sees an increasingly censorious attitude in Book IV. See his 'Review of the facsimile *Il Riposo*, by Raffaello Borghini, ed. Marco Rosci,' *La Rassegna della letteratura italiana* 73/7 (1969): 122–4.
86 Schlosser, *Letteratura*, 310–11: 'There is an absolute absence of new material and this comes out clearly in the biography of Ridolfo Ghirlandaio, put in the words of his grandson, Sirigatti, from whom, if ever, we would expect something new … Instead we are given only a meager summary of the more detailed life written by Vasari.'
87 Frangenberg (*Der Betrachter*, 99–100) suggests this but was not as definite as I am saying it is.
88 See Orienti, 'Su "Il Riposo,"' 226.
89 Borghini continues 'but in colour he is said to have imitated nature and then particularly Titian.'
90 See Book I, n16.
91 For Bocchi's guidebook, see *The Beauties of the City of Florence*, trans. and ed. Thomas Frangenberg and Robert Williams (London: Brepols, 2006). Their book is particularly valuable to students of Borghini for its many excellent illustrations of the paintings that Borghini discusses. Frangenberg and Williams do not entirely agree with Schlosser-Magnino concerning Borghini's influence on Bocchi. They find Bocchi much more positive than Borghini:

'Bocchi seeks to assist his readers in the recognition of objects displaying beauty rather than in the assessment of artistic success and failure' (11).

92 Schlosser, *Letteratura*, 351.

93 *La Veglia* (Florence, 1690); reprinted in *Raccolta di Alcuni Opuscoli* … (Florence: Bonducci, 1765), 51, and *Opere*, ed. Domenico Manni (Milan, 1808; Milan: Società tipografica de' Classici Italiani, 1975), 14. Cicognara no. 2196. But in a disagreement with an unnamed critic, Baldinucci speaks of the '*accuratissima* pen of our Raffaello Borghini,' *Decennali o notizie intorno ai profess. Del disegno* (Turin, 1768), ed. Paola Barocchi (Florence: S.P.E.S, 1974) and, elsewhere in his *Decennali*, Baldinucci relies extensively on Borghini for information on Giambologna, Ammannati, and Buontalenti.

94 (Ferrara: Pomatelli, 1722).

95 *El Museo Pitòrico* (Madrid: publisher unknown, 1724; Madrid: Aguilar, 1947), 3, 895.

96 Francesco Maria Gabburri was Superintendent of the Accademia del Disegno. Eric Cochrane, in *Florence in the Forgotten Centuries* (Chicago: University of Chicago Press, 1973), 369, describes him as 'the nearest thing Florence had to an art critic' but really more a connoisseur than a critic.

97 (place and publisher unknown, 1772; Venice: Antonelli, 1824), 7/3/2, 761, and 7/3/3, 1413.

98 *Lettere Sanesi* (Rome: Generoso Salomoni, 1785), 23. Comolli subsequently misquotes della Valle to the effect that the title of *Il Riposo* was appropriate to the dialogue since Borghini was apparently asleep when he wrote it.

99 *Bibliografia Storico-Critica* (Rome: Stamperia Vaticana, 1788), 33–40; facsimile, ed. Bruno Della Chiesa (Milan: Labor, 1964).

100 In the eighteenth century, the dialogue was discussed by Palomino di Castro y Velasco (see n95 above) and in two letters from Pierre Jean Mariette, see Giovanni Bottari, *Raccolta di lettere* … (Rome, 1754; ed. Stefano Ticozzi [Milan: Silvestri, 1822–25], vol. 2, 266–77 and 306–10. In the nineteenth century the dialogue was discussed by Abel Desjardins, *La vie et l'oeuvre de Jean Bologne* (Paris: Henry May, 1883), 17–19 and 32–3.

101 Blunt, 101.

102 For a detailed enumeration of citations and use of *Il Riposo* in the twentieth century, see the 'Annotated Bibliography' of my dissertation.

103 'Commedie,' 37n3.

104 For example: Fredrika Jacobs, 'Aretino and Michelangelo, Dolce and Titian: *Femmina, Masculo, Grazia*,' *Art Bulletin* 82/1 (March 2000): 57n53, and Andrea Bolland, '*Disiderio* and *Diletto*: Vision, Touch, and the Poetics of Bernini's *Apollo and Daphne*,' *Art Bulletin* 82/2 (June 2000): 319n82.

105 See Leonard Barkan, *Unearthing the Past* (New Haven: Yale University Press, 1999), 96.

Personae

1 For Vecchietti, see Michael Bury, 'Bernardo Vecchietti, Patron of Giambologna,' *I Tatti Studies* 1 (1985): 13–56.

2 *Alessandro Filipepi, Commonly Called Sandro Botticelli, Painter of Florence* (London: Bell, 1908); republished as *Botticelli – Painter of Florence* (Princeton: Princeton University Press, 1980), 24.

3 Eric Cochrane, *Florence in the Forgotten Centuries, 1527–1800* (Chicago: University of Chicago Press, 1973), 148.

4 For Valori, see Robert Williams, 'The Façade of the Palazzo dei Visacci,' *I Tatti Studies* 5 (1993): 209–44.

Book I

1 This refers to the seven concentric shells, plus the fixed stars, of the Aristotelean–Ptolemaic universe.

2 This is the page number in the first edition (Florence: Marescotti, 1584).

3 I have used brackets to add a word or phrase to clarify meaning, as here, or to make a brief correction where a footnote does not seem warranted. As seen above, Borghini frequently uses parentheses in his dialogue. In the prologues these are retained. In the spoken passages, Borghini's parentheses are replaced with dashes. I have used brackets in three other ways: (1) to give the Italian word for a translated English word, e.g., serpent [*serpente*]; (2) to give the English word for an untranslated Italian word e.g., Botticelli [Little Keg]; or (3) to clarify the meaning of a phrase, e.g., joining together wood dyed many colours [intarsia], or, the room painted by Francesco Salviati [Sala dell' Udienza].

4 Ellipses indicate an omission from the original 1584 text, in this case, six pages from [3] to [9] concerning *The Excellence of Man*. Omitted is a derivative prose preface, in which Borghini attempts to combine elements derived from astrology, Plato, Aristotle, and the Cabala into an introduction to the study of painting and sculpture. This material is translated on pp. 202–9 of my dissertation.

5 Borghini uses this phrase, not in recognition of Leonardo's ideas, but in the sense that in Renaissance images figures were frequently seen flying through or hovering in the air.

6 Borghini organizes the first edition with italicized marginal headings. These are rendered here as italicized subheadings.

7 For a detailed discussion of items in the Vecchietti collection enumerated by Borghini and their subsequent fate, see Bury, nn37, 39, and 41.

8 Not, as sometimes stated, the cartoon of Leonardo's *Leda*.

9 This was a fragment of the lost *Battle of Cascina* cartoon.

10 Such precious personal workshops were very popular among the upper classes of this period. The most famous was the exquisitely decorated tiny Studiolo of Francesco I, where he played with his chemistry set, his perpetual motion machine, and pursued other pseudo-scientific interests. See Schlosser, *Letteratura*, 350–1.

11 Vecchietti's collection, and that subsequently described as belonging to Sirigatti [19–22], have been assumed by all students of *Il Riposo* to represent real collections rather than collections imagined by Borghini. The basis for this assumption is Borghini's familiarity with the surviving structure of the villa.

12 Lazzaro (*Renaissance Garden*, 123) notes that woods had been considered an appropriate setting for chapels ever since they were recommended for this purpose by Francesco di Giorgio in the late fifteenth century. She mentions Buontalenti's chapel, constructed in a grove of fir trees at Pratolino four years before the publication of *Il Riposo*.

13 Primaticcio and Daniele da Volterra made plaster casts of the Medici tomb figures. Titian and Tintoretto [551] owned casts of Michelangelo's figures.

14 A *braccio*, an 'arm,' was twenty-three inches or fifty-eight centimetres long.

15 For Borghini, 'ancient masters' are those most active before 1500 in contrast to the 'moderns,' beginning with Michelangelo and Raphael.

16 Twenty-six pages are omitted, from [25] to [51]: *Regarding the debate over which is more noble, painting or sculpture; Arguments in favour of the sculptors; Response of the painters; Image of Serapes thrown to the ground; Tale of a priest of Canopus; Arguments in favour of the painters; Response of the sculptors; Conclusion concerning the nobility between the painters and the sculptors; The human mind and its divisions; The goal of science; Definition of the arts in general; Nobility of the sciences from what is known*; and *Of what is known of the nobility of the arts*. This omitted material is Borghini's discussion of the *paragone*, the relative nobility of painting and sculpture. Bottari recognized in 1730 that Borghini's discussion repeats, almost exactly, the discussion of Benedetto Varchi in his *Lezzione della maggioranza delle arti* of 1547 (Florence: Torrentino, 1549). See Barocchi's discussion of Borghini's *paragone* in *Scritti*, vol. 1, 674–90; Varchi in Barocchi's *Trattati d'arte del Cinquecento* (Bari: Laterza, 1960–2), vol. 1, 1–82, and my dissertation, 226–53.

17 Barocchi carefully traces Borghini's sources in her generous annotation, in *Scritti*, vol. 1, 936, of this paragraph and the next, spoken by Vecchietti.

18 See also [82] and Book IV [513–14].

19 While Borghini cited Gilio, he does not use Gilio's vocabulary exactly as Gilio has. Gilio gives 'poetic painters' (Gilio uses Raphael's paintings in the Farnesina as an example) considerable iconographic latitude. Borghini holds the 'poetic painters' to the same standard of iconographic fidelity as the 'history painters,' criticizing Titian [64–5] for the liberties Titian took with the story of *Venus and Adonis.*

20 *... Pittoribus atque Poetis*
Quidlibet audendi semper fuit aqua potestas.
(Painters and Poets
Have always had an equal right in hazarding anything)
Ars Poetica 9, in Horace, *Satires, Epistles and Ars Poetica*, trans. Rushton Fairclough (Cambridge, MA: Harvard University Press, 1926), 450 and 451.

21 Borghini's argument would have been easier to understand if he had quoted the entire passage by Horace (as translated by Fairclough): 'Painters and poets,' you say, 'have always had an equal right in hazarding anything.' We know it: this licence we poets claim and in our turn we grant the like; but not so far that savage should mate with tame, or serpents couple with birds, lambs with tigers' (*Ars Poetica*, 9–13).

22 *Decameron*, IV: 2, 301–12. Fr. Alberto convinced Monna Lisetta that the Angel Gabriel was secretly in love with her and would come to her in the night disguised as Fr. Alberto. In the fullness of time Fr. Alberto appeared in a Gabriel costume complete with wings. Borghini is referring to Boccaccio's report of what follows: 'he flew without wings several times before the night was over, causing the lady to shriek with delight at his achievements, which he supplemented with a running commentary on the glories of Heaven.' Subsequently Fr. Alberto, who was a Venetian, was surprised by Monna Lisetta's brothers and, abandoning his wings, jumped out of the window into a canal.

23 The Romans often identified the Muses, who had originated with the Greeks as water deities, with the Camenae, who were water deities and sometimes connected to prophecy. Borghini seems to be saying that it would be appropriate for water deities, in the sense that they hovered over water, to gather above the scene of Marsyas's trial and execution.

24 It is this fidelity to natural law that leads Borghini to reject 'the fantastical abstraction the Maniera had so often invented. The taste of his time found no virtue in the complex multiple meanings the Maniera artist had sought.' Hall, *Renovation and Counter-Reformation*, 58.

25 I have translated Borghini's frequent use of *tavola*, in this case *tavole*, as 'panel' or 'panels.' In the technical section of his treatise, Borghini devotes a

subsection to the preparation of the wood ground for a panel, *Come si preparano le tavole per dipignervi sopra* (How panels are prepared for painting on). When Borghini discusses sixteenth-century painting, he usually distinguishes between a *tavola* and a *quadro in tela*, a painting on canvas.

In the course of his dialogue, however, it becomes obvious that for Borghini a *tavola* is also a painting of a religious subject in a church, and 'altarpiece' might be a better translation. This is particularly obvious in Borghini's discussion of *tavole* by Venetian painters.

26 Ferroni ('Le commedie,' 44n36) cites this passage together with the prologue of the *Donna Costante*, in his discussion of how Borghini uses a 'heroic' form that involved a 'rigorous distinction between different episodes' in his poetry and in his comedies.

27 For a discussion of this Mannerist tendency in other arts, the *ostentatio artis* of polyphonic music and *epiphoneme* (language that adds ornament rather than carrying sense) in literature, see John Shearman, *Mannerism* (Harmondsworth: Penguin, 1967), 164.

Frangenberg (*Der Betrachter*, 84) uses this interchange as an example of: (1) the increasing dichotomy in the sixteenth century between the discussion of content in the arts and the discussion of their form; (2) the emphasis that the Counter-Reformation put on content at the expense of form; and (3) the clearly subordinate position that form frequently holds in Borghini's discussion of an image.

28 See also Book IV [513].

29 See also Book II [196] and Book IV [538].

30 It is important to remember, whenever Borghini discusses poetry and poets, that he makes his way among his contemporaries with his poetry. Ferroni reminds us ('Le commedie,' 45n37) that in this phrase, 'far con ordine apparire i concetti dell'animo,' Borghini is talking about his own poetry, 'framed on a platonic base by the necessity of a formal order.'

31 An example would be Leonardo Bruni's program for the east doors of the Baptistery in Florence, submitted at the invitation of the *Arte di Calimala* and subsequently ignored by Ghiberti: 'I have chosen twenty stories … It will be necessary for whoever does them to be well instructed about each story, so that he can render well both the persons and the actions which occur in it … Now I do not doubt that this work, as I have planned it, will succeed excellently. But I would very much like to be with whoever has the job of designing it, to make sure that he takes into account the whole significance of each story.' David Chambers, *Patrons and Artists in the Italian Renaissance* (Columbia: University of South Carolina Press, 1956), 48; Italian text in Richard Krautheimer, *Lorenzo Ghiberti* (Princeton: Princeton University Press, 1971), doc. 52, 372–3.

32 See Book II [163] and Book IV [514].

33 Edith Balas argues that the identity of Michelangelo's *Night* was never made clear and identified this figure as Cybele in her *Michelangelo's Medici Chapel* (Philadelphia: American Philosophical Society, 1995). Paola Barocchi sees Borghini's criticism of Michelangelo as a prelude to academic neoclassical criticism. *La Vita di Michelangelo nelle redazioni del 1550, e del 1568* (Milan: Ricciardi, 1962), vol. 3, 1023–4.

34 See also Book IV [520].

35 See also Book II [164–5] and Book IV [593–4].

36 The humanist Pierio Valeriano (1477–1560) was the author of *Hieroglyphica* (Basel: Palma Ising, 1556; New York: Garland, 1976).

37 Vincenzo Cartari (1531–ca. 1569) published the *Imagini degli Dei* in 1556 (Venice: Ziletti; Venice: Pozza, 1996).

38 Benoit de Court, also known as Benedictus Curtius, *Hortorum Libri Triginta* (Lyons: Joannes Tornasius, 1560).

39 In addition to his *Parallel Lives*, Plutarch was an exceedingly prolific essayist who wrote the nine-book *Symposiaca* (Paris: Iacobus Gazellas, 1547), a very large collection of information and discussion on almost everything.

40 Theophrastus (371–287 BC) succeeded Aristotle as head of the Lyceum. His nine books *On the History of Plants* and six books *On the Causes of Plants* were the first systematic written classification of flora. Theophrastus is known to artists for his brief discussion of pigments in *Theophrastus' History of Stones*, trans. John Hill (London: C. Davis, 1776).

41 The ecliptic (Borghini's *eclittica*) is the seasonal path the sun traces across the sky (to be distinguished from the daily path the sun traces from east to west). It runs through the centre of the region astronomers call the zodiac whose length is divided into twelve thirty-degree segments named after the constellations straddling the ecliptic and which is now considered eighteen degrees wide. Art historians may be content with the four-page discussion of this subject in *Wikipedia*, s.v. 'Ecliptic,' www.en.wikipedia.org/wiki/ecliptic (accessed 14 March 2007).

42 See also Book II [165–9] and Book IV [588].

43 Borghini may, in part, have framed the following discussion to recognize the historical Vecchietti's role as a patron of Giambologna and to recognize Vecchietti's part in the writing and publishing of *Alcune Composizioni di Diversi Autori in Lode del Ritratto della Sabine* (Florence: Sermarteli, 1583), the second book ever published about a single work of art. Five of the twenty-three poems in *Alcune Composizioni* were by Vecchietti, and three more by others were not about the statue but about Vecchietti's poems about the statue.

44 This is the most frequently quoted passage from *Il Riposo*, because in the absence of any other documentation it is very difficult to discuss the naming of Giambologna's statue without at least alluding to Borghini's telling of the story. For another translation, see John Pope-Hennessy, *Italian High Renaissance and Baroque Sculpture*, 4th ed. (London: Phaidon, 1996), 490. See also Shearman, *Mannerism*, 162–4.

45 See Jonathan Riess, 'The Civic View of Sculpture in Alberti's De re Aedificatoria,' *Renaissance Quarterly* 32 (1979): 1–17.

46 Frangenberg (*Der Betrachter*, 88) finds this a particularly telling remark from an author who treats the theory of invention from more points of view than anyone before him. For Borghini to endorse separate content for independent art works which were conceived as an ensemble should, Frangenberg suggests, give pause to twentieth-century iconographic researchers.

47 'Equestrian Neptune' refers to Neptune in a chariot.

48 *Epist*. 9: 9, in *Letters of Gregory the Great – Registrum Epistularum*, trans. and ed. John Martyn (Toronto: Pontifical Institute of Mediaeval Studies, 2004): '*Quod legentibus scriptura, hoc idiotis praestat pictura*.' In his description of what St Gregory said, Borghini paraphrases Gilio. See Barocchi, *Scritti*, vol. 1, 314. For a recent discussion of the place of images in a religious context, see Naomi Yavneh, 'Dal rogo alle nozze': Tasso's Sofronia as Martyr Manqué,' in *Renaissance Transactions: Ariosto and Tasso*, ed. Valeria Finucci (Durham: Duke University Press, 1999), 271–4.

49 See also Book II [195–6] and Book IV [484–5]. For Vasari's criticism of Pontormo at San Lorenzo, see Vasari vol. 6, 284–7. For other criticism of these frescoes, see Eugenio Battisti, 'La critica a Michelangelo dopo il Vasari,' *Rinascimento* 7 (1956): 135–57.

More recently, David Franklin in his *Painting in Renaissance Florence, 1500–1550* (New Haven: Yale University Press, 2001), 205, suggests that Borghini, in the discussion of these frescoes that follows here and Borghini's further discussion of the frescoes in Book II [195–6] and Book IV [484–5], 'criticized the fresco explicitly for its apparently heretical content, implying presumably that it was pro-Lutheran in its message.' For Borghini, according to Franklin's analysis, any departure from stylistic or iconographic orthodoxy was heretical and, in the context of the 1580s, suspiciously Lutheran.

50 See also [53] and Book IV [513–14].

51 *Bambocci* can describe either plump babies and very young children, or bodiless children's heads with wings.

52 Isaiah 6:6.

53 Ezekiel 10:19.

54 See also Book IV [573–4].

55 Marcia Hall (*After Raphael*, 249–50) recalls Vincenzo Borghini's struggle reconciling the eight segments of the dome with his program that emphasized the doctrinal sevens: the seven gifts of the Holy Spirit, the seven Virtues, the seven Beatitudes, and the seven Mortal Sins.
56 *Iesus Nazarenus Rex Iudeorum*, written by Pilate (John 19:19–22).
57 The *primum mobile*, which carried the fixed stars, was conceived as the outermost sphere of the universe.
58 A sallet is a light helmet with a projection over the neck.
59 See also Book II [199] and Book IV [548].
60 Borghini ignores the iconography of this painting, which is so complex and obscure that the bishop who commissioned the painting had to write Vasari after it was completed asking the painter to repeat his explanation because the bishop had forgotten it. See Hall, *Renovation and Counter-Reformation*, 61.
61 See also Book II [199] and Book IV [538].
62 This quote does not appear in the story of Jarius (Mark 5:35–42). In the story of the healing of the son of a government official (John 4:46–54), Jesus says 'Go, your son will live.'
63 Frangenberg (*Der Betrachter*, 95–6) devotes considerable attention to what he sees as Borghini's emphasis on proximity and distance as important criteria with respect to the correctness of content. Frangenberg cites three examples in Santa Maria Novella. Here, in Bronzino's *Revival of the Daughter of Jarius*, 'these people though who appear in the distance striving to want to see, to be able to be there, since they are not in the same place where Christ is, perhaps it would have been better for them not to be there.'

In Giovanni Strada's *Baptism of Christ* [97–8], Borghini accepts 'those figures that are seen above the bank of the river in different poses, since they appear very distant from the place were Christ is baptized. But those three figures that are here close by, with faces drawn from life, one of whom motions towards the baptism, are a very inappropriate thing and discordant from the truth, and I am amazed that the painters are induced to make such great errors.' The third example that Frangenberg gives is Naldini's *Nativity of Christ* [101–102] which Borghini criticizes because the ox and the ass, which Borghini considers essential for a proper Nativity, are so far away that they are difficult to see.

64 See also Book II [199–200] and Book IV [548].
65 See also Book II [200] and Book IV [548].
66 A decade is ten Hail Mary's and one Our Father. A Rosary is fifty Hail Marys and five Our Fathers. A Full Rosary, which Borghini defines twice, is 150 Hail Marys and fifteen Our Fathers. Each of the three Rosaries in a Full Rosary is dedicated to one of the Mysteries of the Rosary: the Joyful Mysteries (Annunciation, Visitation, Nativity, Presentation, and Discovery after

being lost for three days); the Sorrowful Mysteries (Agony in the Garden, Scourging, Crowning with Thorns, Carrying the Cross, and Crucifixion); and, the Glorious Mysteries (Resurrection, Ascension, Descent of the Holy Ghost, Assumption of the Virgin, and Coronation of the Virgin). Thus, there are fifteen decades for meditation during the recitation of a Full Rosary. For a comprehensive discussion of the Rosary see Anne Winston-Allen, *Stories of the Rose – The Making of the Rosary in the Middle Ages* (University Park: Pennsylvania State University Press, 1997).

67 Borghini is referring to Alanus de Rupe (de la Roche, van der Clip) (1428–1475), who founded the first Confraternity of the Rosary at Douai in 1470, five years before Jacob Sprenger founded the influential one at Cologne.

68 A quarantine is forty days. It is frequently described as originating with the number of days 'foreigners' were required to wait outside medieval cities, particularly Florence, as a precaution against plague, but it obviously goes much further back in the Judeo-Christian tradition, predating the forty days of Lent, to when it rained on Noah for forty days and forty nights.

69 Pope Gregory the Great (590–604) decreed fixed ceremonies in certain Roman churches called *statis diebus*, Station Days. There are eighty-four days in forty different churches, usually on Wednesdays or Fridays. A station consisted of a meeting at a church near the station church, a procession to the station church, and a mass. Subsequently, many of the processions were moved inside the destination church, for safety.

70 See also Book II [200–1] and Book IV [625].

71 Hope ('Review of *Renovation and Counter-Reformation*,' 513) takes Hall to task because Hall assumes that all of the opinions in Borghini's dialogue are Borghini's. Hope suggests that some of the ideas that Vecchietti, Valori, and Sirigatti express are ideas of the historical Vecchietti, Valori, and Sirigatti, who would probably, in the argumentative Florentine tradition, have had opinions that differed from those of the author. As a specific example, Hope reads this statement by Valori as an ironic comment on Borghini's condemnation of lasciviousness. (See also Valori's perhaps droll comment on Bronzino's *Christ in Limbo* [187].)

72 See also Book II [201] and Book IV [581].

73 Frangenberg explains, (*Der Betrachter*, 96–7) why Borghini is so adamant about these donor figures. Borghini, according to Frangenberg, believes that the appropriate devotional and reverential reaction of the viewer depends on a temporal and physical separation from the religious image so that it is clear to the viewer that the religious image exists in a different space and time from that of the viewer. This requires not only a unity of action, place, and time within the religious image (for the sake of verisimil-

itude, to convince the viewer of its historical reality) but also that nothing invade the border separating the image from the viewer. Such invasions, in Strada's painting, include both contemporary figures and figures communicating directly with the viewer by gesture or eye contact.

A further implication of Borghini's discussion of the Strada painting, Frangenberg continues, is Borghini's rejection of Alberti's visual pyramid which unites the eye of the viewer with the 'window' of the frame of the image. Borghini's devotional requirements sever the viewer from the image. Borghini insists that the viewer, instead, be presented with an image, perhaps divorced from reality but demonstrating intelligibility and clarity. As Frangenberg concludes, 'the picture opens and closes itself before the viewer at the same time' (das Bild öffnet und schliesst sich zugleich vor dem Betrachter).

Frangenberg believes that Borghini's discussion of the Strada painting not only reflects the viewing habits and critical conversation of Borghini's peers but also explains some 'formal peculiarities of numerous Florentine panel paintings of the second half of the Cinquecento.' Frangenberg uses Strada's *Accession of Christ* in Santa Croce as an example ([114] and [188–9]). There is a non-visual clarity in the painting, focused on its periphery as well as its centre of interest with figures carefully disposed in a circle so that they, including the figures in the foreground, do not impinge on an unobstructed view of themselves and of the central activity. None of the participants look out of the picture or attempt to draw the attention of the viewer to the action of the image. The image is largely closed on itself. Another example Frangenberg gives is Strada's *Expulsion of the Dealers from the Temple* in Santo Spirito [203], where the resulting visual tumult is remarkable for only one instance in which a figure violates the edge of the picture surface.

74 Bottari points out (see his note in *Raccolta di lettere*, 76) that, in this painting, St Vincent Deacon and Martyr (ca. 3–4th century) is conflated with St Vincent Ferrer (1350–1419).
75 See also Book II [196–7] and Book IV [605].
76 In other words, by good works and by living a holy life.
77 See also Book II [197–8] and Book IV [615].
78 See also Book II [198] and Book IV [616].
79 See also Book IV [644].
80 See also Book II [198] and Book IV [614].
81 Frangenberg (*Der Betrachter*, 90) discusses the tension in *Il Riposo*, as seen here in the representation of the body of Christ, between iconographical fidelity and desirable form. See also Borghini's discussion of Alesso Allori's *Deposition* in Santa Maria Nuova (directly below) and of Francesco

Salviati's *Deposition* in Santa Croce [110]. Borghini is influenced by, but does not entirely succumb to, the admonishments of Gilio, who enthused, on imagining a painting of a very battered body of Christ: 'This would be the genius, this the force and the virtue of art, this the decorum, this the perfection of the artifice.' *Dialogo*, in Barocchi, *Scritti*, vol. 1, 842.

82 See also Book II [191–2] and Book IV [628].

83 Wazbinski attributes Borghini's criticism of this painting to Borghini's partiality to Federico Zuccaro, as against Alesso Allori, in the debate over the cupola of Santa Maria del Fiore. 'Artisti,' 6. (See Introduction, pages 4–5).

84 Santi di Tito is the painter most closely associated with the patronage of the historical Bernardo Vecchietti.

85 See also Book II [198].

86 Petrarch, Sonnet 82, *The Sonnets of Petrarch*, trans. Joseph Auslander (London: Longmans, Green, 1931), 82.

87 See also Book IV [638].

88 Ibid. [600].

89 Ibid. [599].

90 Bottari comments (*Raccolta di lettere*, 84), from an eighteenth-century Florentine perspective: 'Many worthy men, most excellent in this art, maintain that the art in which, more than any other, Michelangelo was miraculous was architecture because in this he was greater than the Greeks, while in sculpture he equaled them and in painting remained yet inferior to some that surrounded him in his time.'

91 Pope-Hennessy, *Italian High Renaissance and Baroque Sculpture*, 476–7, quotes most of these two paragraphs in his discussion of Michelangelo's tomb. Pope-Hennessy notes that Borghini's story is confirmed by a letter from Vincenzo Borghini to the grand duke of 23 March 1573.

92 Bottari notes (*Raccolta di lettere*, 85) that Amannati's letter was printed by Bartolommeo Sermartelli in 1582 and reprinted by Piero Matini in 1687.

93 Bronzino's painting of *Christ in Limbo* is favourably discussed stylistically in Book II [187]. The painting is praised without qualification in Borghini's biography of Bronzino in Book IV [536–7]. What made the painting so pornographic was the nudity of identifiable upper-class Florentine women, the spectacularly attractive Costanza da Sommaia, wife of Giovambatista Doni, and Camila Tedaldi del Corno. Some three hundred years after the painting was installed in Santa Croce, Borghini's opinion prevailed and, in the nineteenth century, Costanza and Camila were removed from the church to the Museo di Santa Croce, where the Arno finally covered them up in 1966. The ladies remain in restoration, protected from public view by the Fortezza da Basso.

94 See also Book II [185–7] and Book IV [501].
95 See also Book II [191] and Book IV [548].
96 See also Book II [188] and Book IV [548].
97 See also Book II [189] and Book IV [548].
98 See also Book II [190] and Book IV [634].
99 See also Book II [189] and Book IV [605].
100 See also Book II [205] and Book IV [605].
101 See also Book II [195] and Book IV [604].
102 See also Book II [194–5] and Book III [434–5].
103 See also Book IV [644].
104 See also Book II [202] and Book IV [434].
105 See also Book II [202–3] and Book IV [537].
106 See also Book II [203] and Book IV [625].
107 See also Book II [188–9] and Book IV [581].
108 See also Book II [203] and Book IV [581].
109 See also Book II [205] and Book IV [615].
110 See also Book II [205] and Book IV [622].
111 This portrait of Michelozzi was lost in a fire in 1771.
112 Borghini needed to be careful in his discussion of the inappropriateness of donor figures in religious pictures. In her discussion of the altarpiece Bronzino painted for the Chapel of Eleonora in the Palazzo Vecchio, now in Besançon, Janet Cox-Rearick identifies the Virgin as a portrait of Cosimo's mother, Maria Salviati, and the woman in green leaning over the Virgin in the centre of the picture as Eleonora. Cox-Rearick identifies the left altar wing of John the Baptist, now in the Getty Museum, as a portrait of Cosimo's father, Giovanni delle Bande Nere, and speculates that the lost right altar wing of St Cosmas was probably a portrait of Cosimo.

Closer in time to *Il Riposo* is the *Madonna and Saints* in the Uffizi from Bronzino's shop, now attributed to Francesco Butteri (ca. 1535–1606), where Cox-Rearick identifies a posthumous portrait of Cosimo and portraits of Francesco and Ferdinando with their sister Isabella and her husband Paolo Orsini. See Cox-Rearick, *Bronzino's Chapel*, 260–71.
113 See also Book II [187–8] and Book IV [619–20].
114 See also Book II [188] and Book IV [620].
115 See also Book II [194] and Book IV [537].
116 Hall (*After Raphael*, 247) considers this interchange to be a particularly good example of the difference between the lay Florentine Borghini and his clerical Counter-Reformation contemporaries in Rome, Bologna, and elsewhere: 'The exquisitely sensuous angel standing next to

Christ was condemned as lascivious, of course, but then it was praised as a work of art that one would love to have in one's home – a position we do not find articulated by his clerical counterparts. Contrast this opinion with Paleotti who would prohibit even the private collecting of mythological paintings.' Frangenberg (*Der Betrachter*, 90) emphasizes the hypocrisy and Philistinism of this passage. Rosci considers this interchange (*Il Riposo*, vol. 2, xiii) to be 'the most unbearable pages of the book' (*le pagine più insopportalili del libro*).

117 See also Book II [193] and Book IV [108].

118 See also Book IV [644].

119 See also Book II [191] and Book IV [546].

120 St John the Evangelist was said to have been unaffected by a beverage made of snake's venom concocted by the high priest of Ephesus.

Book II

1 'conciossiacosachè non poco doni colui, che tutto quello dona, che è in poter suo di donare.' Bottari notes, *Raccolta di lettere*, 88, the derivation from Ludovico Ariosto, *Orlando Furioso*, ed. Lanfranco Caretti (Milan: Ricciardi, 1954), 1:3:

Nè che poco io vi dia, da imputar sono;
Che quanto io posso dar, tutto vi dono.

2 Borghini explicitly says that the essence of painting and sculpture is mimesis.

3 While Borghini is defensive, he has finally clearly defined his audience of amateurs. Rosci (*Il Riposo*, vol. 2, xi) notes this 'is in effect, the first historical mention of a figure, a creature of Florence, who had certainly existed for some time but could only come forward in a progressively more restricted cultural parochialism of consolidating academicism and courtly art to proclaim his right to enter the artistic literature as a dilettante or amateur.'

4 An *uccellare* is an elaborate planted construction for catching birds.

5 Six pages are omitted, from [129] to [135], concerning *Vecchietti's Uccellare*. See my dissertation, 337–41.

6 Barocchi has annotated the next ten pages [136–46] of the first edition, *Scritti*, vol. 2, 1982–91. Much of this material is omitted in this translation but is available in my dissertation, 343–51.

7 This was Vasari's definition in Chapter 15 of the 'Introduction to the Three Arts of Design' at the beginning of Vasari's *Vite* (vol. 1, 168–69). The only difference between Vasari and Borghini is Borghini's replacement of Vasari's *'expressione e dichiarazione'* with *'dimostrazione.'*

8 Responding to the urging of the others, however, Sirigatti discusses these technical details anyway. We will omit his discourse from [137] to [139] concerning *Way of preparing little panels and sheets for drawing on; Drawing stylets; Watercolours;* and *Lead for drawing*. See my dissertation, 344–5.

9 Omitted is Borghini's description of the preparation and gluing together of the large paper sheets for cartoons. See my dissertation, 346–7.

10 Even Alberti abruptly ends his discussion of perspective by advising artists to use a reticulated net, cautioning 'I doubt if much will be understood by the reader, either because of the newness of the material or because of the brevity of the commentary.' *On Painting*, 58.

11 Five pages are omitted, from [141] to [146], concerning *Ways of colouring sheets with many colours; Drawing charcoal made in many ways;* and *Tracing paper of many kinds, how it is made and how it is used.* See my dissertation, 347–52.

12 Pliny, *Natural History*, 35.85–6. My translation of Borghini's translation, which he probably took from a variant Latin text, differs from H. Rackham's: 'Apelles would politely advise him to drop the subject, saying that the boys engaged in grinding the colours were laughing at him.' Pliny, *Natural History*, vol. 9, *Books 33–35*, trans. H. Rackham (Cambridge, MA: Harvard University Press), 325.

13 *Belletta* is clay that contains decayed animal matter, the protein from which gives it a tacky character.

14 In addition to the iron-toothed spatula, Borghini refers to *stecchi*, small spatulas of wood, bone, ivory, or similar material of a variety of shapes.

15 See *Vasari on Technique*, 149–51.

16 Erwin Panofsky, *Idea: A Concept in Art History*, trans. Joseph Peake (1924; Columbia: University of South Carolina Press, 1968), 74–5, uses this paragraph to illustrate the sixteenth-century move away from attempts by Piero della Francesca and Dürer to fix human proportions in a mathematical construction. Writers were moving towards the irrationality of Lomazzo's *figura serpentinata*.

17 Although elongated *maniera* proportions were still stylish in painting in 1584, the proportions that Borghini describes are completely imaginary and unlikely to match those of any reader or bear any relation to what Borghini may have seen in a classical or Renaissance statue. His use of the measurement of a 'head,' which is actually a 'face' ('from the chin to the top of the forehead'), could have been, but probably was not, an attempt to compensate for Vasari's error, described by Brown, in *Vasari on Technique*, 146n4: 'For Vasari, a practical artist, to commit himself to the statement that figures are made nine heads high, is somewhat extraordinary, for eight heads, the proportion given by Vitruvius (III, I) is the extreme limit for a normal adult,

and very few Greek statues, let alone living persons, have heads so small.' Brown noted that Vasari, in his 'Introduction', at 8, and Borghini following him, derives his proportions from Filarete.

18 Three pages are omitted, from [156] to [159], concerning *Putty to attach parts of marble* and *Ways of giving colour to the marble so that it is similar to the antique*. See my dissertation, 361–3.

19 See also Book IV [529].

20 Blunt states (in *Artistic Theory in Italy*, 154) that 'Raffaello Borghini appears to be the first critic to say simply that a painter possesses or lacks "manner."' Marco Treves, '*Maniera*, the History of a Word,' *Marsyas* 1 (1941), cited Borghini's use of *maniera* in this particular passage of *Il Riposo*, but only at the end of a discussion (69–76) of the use of the word going back to Boccaccio and continuing through Cennini, Ghiberti, Filarete, Manetti, Raphael, and Vasari.

21 See also Book IV [398].

22 Ibid.

23 Ibid. [477].

24 Ibid. [405].

25 Ibid. [638].

26 Ibid. [479].

27 Bottari notes (*Raccolta di lettere*, 126) that much of Borghini's criticism of this statue was repeated by Giovanni Cinelli in his edition of Bocchi's *Belleze di Firenze*.

28 Again see Book IV [479].

29 Ibid.

30 Ibid. [597].

31 Bottari notes (*Raccolta di lettere*, 127) that Borghini passed by eighty-eight statues and reliefs in the choir of Santa Maria del Fiore.

32 See also Book IV [403].

33 Ibid. [520-1].

34 For Michelangelo's sculpture in the new sacristy, see also Book I [65–6] and Book IV [514].

35 See also Book IV [496].

36 Ibid. [407].

37 Ibid. [512]. Bottari notes (*Raccolta di lettere*, 128) almost three hundred years ago, that 'this superhuman statue should deserve being in a niche or in another covered place, along with the Hercules of Bandinelli, because, exposed to the water as it is, it has done poorly, been all ground down and covered with a black scale, and also so that it could be studied.'

38 See also Book IV [478].

39 See also Book I [66–71] and Book IV [593–4].

40 See p. 112.
41 Amannati's Neptune looks to its left shoulder, which is higher than its right, without its torso turning. Borghini is describing the apparent problem with respect to the figure, not the spectator.
42 See also Book I [71–5] and Book IV [580].
43 *Alcune composizioni di diversi autori in lode del ritratto della Sabina ...*, ed. by Michelangelo Sermarteli (Florence: Sermarteli, 1583), 1; quoted by Bury, 'Bernardo Vecchietti,' 43.
44 *Alcune composizioni*, 4; quoted by Bury, 44.
45 *Alcune composizioni*, 13; quoted by Bury, 45–6.
46 See *Vasari on Technique*, 221–39.
47 Hall points out, in noting this passage of *Il Riposo*, that a 'plaster containing a grayish tint would, in fact, serve to desaturate the colors without dirtying them and would pull the tones together into a harmonious balance.' She suggests that this might explain Raphael's ability to 'adjust his tones so that they connect and harmonize as they do' in the *School of Athens*. If, if fact, this was the purpose of adding black to the intonaco, *Il Riposo* is the only place that this is documented in the sixteenth century. See her *Color and Meaning: Practice and Theory in Renaissance Painting* (Cambridge: Cambridge University Press, 1992), 102 and 109.
48 Gum tragacanth was obtained from various species of shrubs native to Asia Minor. See Ralph Mayer, *The Artists Handbook*, 5th ed., rev. Steven Sheehan (New York: Penguin, 1991), 427.
49 *Limbellucci* glue is made by boiling strips of parchment or vellum.
50 One page is omitted, from [172] to [173], concerning *Limbellucci glue* and *How panels are prepared for painting on*. See my dissertation, 378–9.
51 An earth suitable for painting.
52 A total of one page is omitted in two places, here, and at the ellipses immediately below, from [174] to [175], where Borghini describes the preparation of walls for oil painting. See my dissertation, 380–1.
53 The following soliloquy concerning composition, poses, parts, and colour is the formal essence of *Il Riposo*. In this discussion Borghini lays down the Counter-*Maniera* criteria that are the formal counterpart to his Counter-Reformation discussion of invention in Book I. Barocchi has compulsively annotated this important section, in *Scritti*, vol. 1, 936–44.
54 Rosci ('Leonardo "Filosofo,"' 72) believed that Borghini began copying at this point from a now lost manuscript version of Leonardo's *Trattato della Pittura*. See also Introduction, n30 and Book III, n50.
55 See Vincenzio Borghini, *Selva di notizie* in Barocchi, *Scritti*, vol. 1, 611–13.

56 Borghini's use of pose includes not only the position of the trunk and limbs of a figure but also its facial expression.
57 Edward Olszewski discusses this phenomenon and its role in the elongation of the figure in Mannerist practice. 'Distortions, Shadows and Conventions in Sixteenth-Century Italian Art,' *artibus et historiae* 11/6 (1985): 101–24.
58 Borghini seems to be anticipating the tenebrism of Caravaggio.
59 For a discussion of such contrast, *chiaroscuro* or *contrapposto*, see David Summers, 'Contrapposto: Style and Meaning in Renaissance Art,' *Art Bulletin* 59 (1977): 336–61.
60 This concludes the material that Rosci (see n54) believes Borghini copied from a lost manuscript version of Leonardo's *Trattato della Pittura*.
61 At this point Barocchi concludes her annotations of Borghini's formal Counter-*Maniera* principles (see n53).
62 See also Book I [110] and Book IV [501].
63 The lingering persistence of the hierarchic Gothic meets the naturalistic Counter-*Maniera*.
64 See also Book I [109–10] and Book IV [536–7].
65 This is another example where Hope ('Review of *Renovation and Counter-Reformation*,' 513) believes that Borghini allows the historic Valori to speak in the ironic voice.
66 See also Book I [116] and Book IV [619–20].
67 See also Book I [116] and Book IV [620].
68 See also Book I [111] and Book IV [548].
69 See also Book I [114] and Book IV [581].
70 In the discussion that follows, despite his attempt to separate the two, Borghini frequently conflates the form and meaning of an image.
71 See also Book I [111] and Book IV [548].
72 See also Book I [112] and Book IV [605].
73 See also Book I [112].
74 Ibid. [111].
75 Ibid. [111–12] and Book IV [654].
76 See also Book I [111]. The importance of copiousness is emphasized by Alberti: 'That which first gives pleasure in the *istoria* comes from copiousness and variety of things.' *On Painting*, 75–6.
77 See also Book I [110] and Book IV [548].
78 See also Book I [118] and Book IV [546].
79 See also Book I [103–6] and Book IV [628].
80 See also Book IV [480].
81 Ibid. [416–17].
82 Ibid. [434].

83 Ibid. [440].
84 Ibid. [624].
85 See also Book I [116–17] and Book IV [581].
86 See also Book IV [381].
87 Ibid. [363].
88 See also Book I [116] and Book IV [537].
89 All three paintings by Fra Bartolomeo are described favourably and at greater length in Book IV [380].
90 See also Book IV [620].
91 See also Book I [112] and Book III [434–5].
92 See also Book IV [546].
93 See also Book I [112] and Book IV [603].
94 See also Book I [78–83] and Book IV [484–5]. For criticism of Pontormo's fresco by Vasari and others, see Book I, n49.
95 See also Book I [62] and Book IV [538].
96 See also Book I [100–1] and Book IV [605].
97 See also Book I [101–2] and Book IV [615].
98 See also Book I [102] and Book IV [616].
99 Wazbinski believes this criticism of large knees represents a criticism by Borghini of mannerist anatomical deformation. 'Giorgio Vasari e Vincenzo Borghini come Maestri Accademici: Il Caso di G. B. Naldini,' in *Giorgio Vasari tra decorazione ambientale e storiografia artistica*, ed. Gian Carlo Garfagnini (Florence: Olschki, 1985), 294.
100 See also Book I [103–4] and Book IV [614–15].
101 See also Book I [106].
102 Ibid.
103 Ibid. [91–3] and Book IV [538].
104 See also Book I [90–1]and Book IV [548].
105 See also Book I [93–4] and Book IV [546].
106 See also Book I [94–6] and Book IV [548].
107 See also Book I [96–7] and Book IV [625]. Wazbinski attributes Borghini's subsequent criticism of this painting to Borghini's partiality to Federico Zuccaro versus Alessandro Allori in the debate over the cupola of Santa Maria della Fiore. 'Artisti,' 6.
108 See also Book I [97–9] and Book IV [581].
109 See also Book I [99–100].
110 Ibid. [112–13] and Book IV [434].
111 See also Book I [113] and Book IV [536].
112 See also Book I [114] and Book IV [625].
113 See also Book IV [625].
114 See also Book I [114] and Book IV [581].

115 See also Book IV [548].
116 Ibid. [501–2].
117 See also Book I [112] and Book IV [605].
118 See also Book I [115] and Book IV [622].
119 See also Book I [114–15] and Book IV [615].
120 Eighteen pages are omitted, from [206] to [224], concerning *Of the colours; Blacks of various sorts; Whites; How Sangiovanni white is made; How white lead is made; Yellows; Reds; How red ochre is made; Minium; held by the Ancients to be of great merit; Who discovered minium and how it is made; Common minium; How cinnabar is made; How fine lake is made; Ordinary lake; How porporina is made; Greens; What Verdigris is made from; Blue; How ultramarine blue is made; More ways to make blue; Advice concerning colouring; Varnish that dries in the sun; Varnish that dries in the shade; Two ways of applying gold; Two ways of gilding with mordant;* and *How to gild with bole*. See my dissertation, 413–32.
121 Borghini may be using the word *giornata* as a pun. In fresco painting a *giornata* is the new patch of *intonaco* laid down at the beginning of each day which usually has to be completed that day or the incomplete parts taken down before the next day's *giornata* is applied.
122 Ludovico Ariosto, *Orlando Furioso*, ed. Lanfranco Caretti (Milan: Ricciardi, 1954), 32: 46.
123 See [241].
124 Lamentations 4:7.
125 Bartolus (1313/14–1357) was an Italian jurist and the most famous master of the dialectical method (a system of reasoning juxtaposing opposed ideas and seeking to resolve their conflict, as in the Socratic or Platonic dialogues) of teaching law.
126 Song of Songs 1:5.
127 Ibid. 5:11.
128 Borghini has already claimed this distinction for green and black.
129 Pliny, *Natural History*, vol. 9, 36. Diocletian (245–315) was the first emperor to reserve the purple for imperial usage.
130 St Isidore's monumental *Etymologies* were intended as an encyclopedia of all knowledge, for which he is currently recognized as the patron of computers and proposed as patron of the Internet.
131 Giason Maino (1435–1519) was a jurist and author of a *Trattato dei colori*.
132 Ariosto, *Orlando Furioso*, 32: 47. See [232].
133 I cannot determine the translation of this colour but it may be related to *cangiante* (changing) colours, such as those Michelangelo used in the ceiling of the Sistine Chapel, in which two separate colours optically mix into a third colour.
134 Borghini attributes contradictory qualities to several of these mixed colours. The 'jealousy' of deep blue is not consistent with its other qualities of

'goodness, courtesy, friendship, [and] good manners.' The 'coldness and melancholy' of purple violet is inconsistent with its qualities of 'friendship, love, loyalty, integrity, gratitude, and sweetness.' For Borghini 'tan commonly signifies great heart, courage, harsh thoughts, grief, rage, and suffering' and purple-tan denotes 'troubled love, simple courtesy, and false loyalty.'

135 The omitted phrases refer to the fact that Michelozzi actually divides the remaining material into three parts. The first part, the material concerning the ancients, which Borghini paraphrases from Pliny, has been excised from this edition.

136 See Boccaccio's description of the dinner party, where the two daughters of Neri degli Uberti, to the delight of his guests, seized 'the finest specimens' of fish out of an adjacent pond and threw them up onto the dinner table. *Decameron*, 10: 6, 733–4.

Book III

1 Presumably Baccio Valori, who installed Borghini in a suburban villa of Valori's where Borghini completed *Il Riposo.*

2 Rosci (*Il Riposo*, vol. 2, ix–x) points out that while 'the major part of the biographies of *Il Riposo* are pure and simple summaries ... without the least addition to Vasari,' this is a debt that Borghini never expressly admits other than this 'hastily paid ... brief mention of the *Lives*.' (Borghini praises Vasari's *Vite* a second time in Borghini's biography of Vasari [550].)

3 Bottari (*Raccolta di lettere*, 199) reported, 150 years later, that the statue was still in the grotto, but moved from its original location into a corner beside an inscription. The statue was lost but may now have reappeared. See Michael Bury, 'Giambologna's Fata Morgana Rediscovered,' *Apollo* 131/336 (Feb. 1990): 96–100, and Charles Avery's dissent, 'When Is a "Giambologna" Not a "Giambologna," *Apollo* 131/340 (June 1990): 391–400.

4 Lazzaro (at 165) points out that 'by tradition and by necessity water that passed through a garden [in this case a grotto although Lazzaro cites Borghini as an example] was often then turned to practical ends, such as kitchen and laundry uses.' See also her 'From the Rain to the Wash Water in the Medici Garden at Pratolino,' in *Renaissance Studies in Honor of Craig Hugh Smyth*, ed. Andrew Morrogh (Florence: Giunti Barbèra, 1985), 2:322.

5 The frescos on the formal garden entrance to the villa are still decorated with scrolls inscribed with similar verses dwelling on old (*vecchio*) for Vecchietti and rest (*riposo*) for his villa.

6 Thirty pages are omitted, from [253] to [287], where Borghini paraphrases from Pliny: *Of the beginning of sculpture; When working with clay was discov-*

ered; Dibutades of Sicily; Lisistrato of Sicyon; Damophilus and Gorgasus; Dipoenus and Scyllis; Melas, Micciades, and Archermus; Phidias, Alkamenes, and Agorokritos; Polykleitos; Skopas; Bryaxis; Timotheos; and Leochares; The Mausoleum; Pythis; Praxiteles; Kephisodotos the Younger; Menestrato; Socrates; Myron; Philiscus; Lysias; Hagesandros; Polydoros and Athenodoros; Myrmecides; Of the beginning of painting; Cleosante; Bularchus; Hygiaenon; Eumarus; and Cimon of Kleonai; Panaenus; Polygnotos; Apollodoros; Zeuxis; Parrhasios; Timanthes; Pamphilos of Macedonia; Apelles; Campaspe; Protogenes; Aristides; Nikomachos; Ludius; Pausias; Euphranor; Nikias; Athenion; Ctesicles; Irene; Martia; and *Aristarete*. See my dissertation, 459–96.

7 (ca. 1240–1302?). See Vasari, vol. 1, 247–67.

8 Vasari was more robust: 'By the infinite flood of evils which had laid prostrate and submerged poor Italy there had not only been ruined everything that could truly claim the name of building, but there had been blotted out (and this was of graver import) the whole body of the craftsmen, when, by the will of God, in the city of Florence in the year 1240, there was born, to give the first light to the art of painting, Giovanni, surnamed Cimabue, of the family, noble in those times, of Cimabue.' *Lives of the Painters, Sculptors, and Architects,* tran. Gaston du C. de Vere (London: Everyman, 1912; New York: Knopf, 1927; 1996), vol. 1, 51.

9 Rosci (*Il Riposo*, vol. 2, 30) attributes Borghini's confusion between the upper and lower churches at Assisi to a misreading of Vasari.

10 Simone Martini also known as Simone Memmi. For this attribution of the *Triumph of the Church* in the Spanish Chapel, see Vasari, vol. 1, 549–52.

11 (1276–1336). See Vasari, vol. 1, 369–428.

12 Presumably from *giocare*, to play.

13 This is a favourite story with Borghini, as with Vasari. Borghini repeats it for Andrea Mantegna [356], Andrea Sansovino [401], and Domenico Beccafumi [468].

14 'Giving light to' or 'bringing to the light' is a favourite turn of phrase for Borghini. He also uses this as a synonym, in Book IV, for the publication of a written work.

15 Giotto did not go to France.

16 There is no evidence that Dante arranged this commission.

17 She died (1356) about fifty years later.

18 Borghini joins Vasari in brushing past the Scrovegni Chapel. Vasari had said, 'having gone again to Padua, besides many other works and chapels that he painted there, he did a Mundane Glory in the precincts of the Arena,' Vasari, vol. 1, 400.

19 Ten pages are omitted, from [297] to [307], concerning *Taddeo Gaddi, Giottino, Spinello Spinelli, Gherardo Starnini,* and *Lorenzo di Bicci.* See my dissertation, 507–17.

20 (1399–1482). See Vasari, vol. 2, 167–85.

21 (1397–1475). See Vasari, vol. 2, 203–17.

22 By 1730, Bottari reported (*Raccolta di lettere*, 249) that 'the base [of this was] particularly wasted and consumed by time.'

23 In Italian 'camel' is *cammello*; 'chameleon' is *camaleonte.*

24 (1381–1455). See Vasari, vol. 2, 221–49.

25 Rosci (*Il Riposo*, vol. 2, 69) attributes this error to a 'hurried and erroneous reading of Vasari,' but it would seem more likely that Borghini, who must have been very familiar with the placement of the doors, simply made a mistake that he did not correct in his draft or in proofreading the first edition.

26 One page is omitted, from [312] to [313], concerning *Masolino da Panicale.* See my dissertation, 521–2.

27 (1401–1428). See Vasari, vol. 2, 287–301.

28 (1377–1446). See ibid., 327–87.

29 (ca. 1386–1466). Borghini repeats a printing error in Vasari of 1303 for 1383. See Vasari, vol. 2, 395–426.

30 What we call the Baptistry of Florence, the ancient round building in front of the cathedral, Borghini called the Temple of San Giovanni. The four discussants of *Il Riposo* originally met while taking the air in the area around the Bapistry, which Borghini called the Piazza of San Giovanni [10].

31 'Flattened relief' is the use of the chisel in a two-dimensional manner as if it were a drawing instrument.

32 One page is omitted, from [322] to [323], concerning *Michelozzo Michelozzi.* See my dissertation, 532–3.

33 (1377–1455). See Vasari, vol. 2, 505–26.

34 Jan van Eyck (ca. 1390–1441). See Vasari, vol. 1, 184, and vol. 2, 565–9.

35 (1430–1479). See Vasari, vol. 2, 563–73.

36 Twelve pages are omitted, from [328] to [340], concerning *Alesso Baldovinetti, Fra Filippo Lippi, Andrea del Castagno, Gentile da Fabriano, Benozzo, Antonio Rossellino, Desiderio, Lorenzo Costa,* and *Ercole of Ferrara.* See my dissertation, 537–50.

37 (1429–1507) and (1430–1516). Like Vasari (vol. 3, 149–73), Borghini treats the Bellini together.

38 A *rochet* is a white linen vestment resembling a surplice with close-fitting sleeves.

39 *Rime*, Venice, 1568, 21.

40 Ariosto, *Orlando Furioso*, 33: 2: 'Mantegna, Leonardo, Gian Bellino.'

41 Seven pages are omitted, from [343] to [350], concerning *Cosimo Rosselli, Domenico Ghirlandaio*, and *Antonio and Piero Pollaiuolo*. See my dissertation, 553–60.
42 (1437–1515). See Vasari, vol. 3, 309–24.
43 There must be few better examples of how much the meaning of virtue has changed in five hundred years.
44 Three pages are omitted, from [353] to [356], concerning *Benedetto da Maiano* and *Andrea Verrocchio*. See my dissertation, 563–7.
45 (1431–1517). See Vasari, vol. 3, 383–409.
46 Four pages are omitted, from [357] to [362], concerning *Filippo Lippi* and *Francesco Francia*. See my dissertation, 568–73.
47 (1445/50–1523). See Vasari, vol. 3, 565–99.
48 Two pages are omitted, from [365] to [367], concerning *Luca Signorelli*. See my dissertation, 576–8.
49 (1452–1519). See Vasari, vol. 4, 17–53.
50 The basis of the currency of Renaissance Italy was a gold coin weighing about 3.5 grams: in Florence this was the *fiorino* (florin) and in Rome, Venice, and Milan, the *ducato* (ducat). This coin is frequently described, usually with many qualifications, as being worth about U.S.$100. In the early sixteenth century, the fiorino and the ducato were replaced by a gold or silver *scudo* of approximately the same value.

On an annual basis, fifty fiorini usually provided a life of comfort and 100 fiorini a life of ease. A good house could be rented for 15 fiorini. Twelve fiorini would feed, clothe, and house an average adult. Professors at the University in Florence earned 300 fiorini, physicians earned 600 fiorini, and attorneys, 1,200 fiorini. Masons and smiths earned 30 fiorini and servants 6 fiorini (plus room and board). See Richardson, *Printing*, xi and 112–13.
51 Rosci ('Leonardo "Filosofo,"' 71) identifies this statement of Borghini as the first 'explicit mention' of the *Trattato della Pittura*. See also Introduction, n30 and Book II, nn54 and 60.
52 (1476/8–1510). See Vasari, vol. 4, 91–100. Borghini follows Vasari in describing Giorgione as the founder of 'modern' Venetian painting, as they both identify Leonardo as the founder of 'modern' Florentine painting.
53 Vasari expands: 'And so Giorgione … thought of nothing save of making figures according to his own fancy, in order to display his art, so that, in truth, there are no scenes to be found there with any order, or representing the deeds of any distinguished person, either ancient or modern; and I, for my part, have never understood them, nor have I found, for all the inquiries that I have made, anyone who understands them.' Trans. by de Vere, vol. 1, 643; Vasari, vol. 4, 96.
54 Subsequently Borghini also attributes this painting to Titian [525].

55 In his discussion of this painting by Giorgione and similar images, Summers ('Contrapposto: Style and Meaning in Renaissance Art,' 343n31) comments: 'The figure seen simultaneously front and rear, whether by reflection or twisting, was a perennial bone of contention, precisely because it connoted extreme artifice and display, which might be either praised or condemned.' Borghini does both. While repeatedly critical of objects purportedly produced only as a display of the artifice of the artist, Borghini repeatedly praises Giambologna for exactly this in the *Rape of the Sabine*. In discussing Giorgione, Borghini clearly relishes the artifice of Giorgione's painting.

56 (1489–1534). See Vasari, vol. 4, 109–22.

57 Rosci (*Il Riposo*, vol. 2, 33) believes that this *Venus* was Correggio's *Danae*.

58 Two pages are omitted, from [376] to [378], concerning *Piero di Cosimo*. See my dissertation, 586–8.

59 (ca. 1474–1517). See Vasari, vol. 4, 175–202. Fra Bartolommeo was the master of Ridolfo Ghirlandaio, Ridolfo Sirigatti's grandfather.

60 Three pages are omitted, from [382] to [385], concerning *Mariotto Albertinelli* and *Raffaellino del Garbo*. See my dissertation, 592–95.

61 (1483–1520). See Vasari, vol. 4, 315–86.

62 Borghini was severely criticized by Francesco Scannelli (*Il Microcosmo della Pittura* [Cesena: Peril Neri 1657]; facsimile, ed. Guido Giubbini [Milan: Labor, 1966], 154) for not devoting more attention to the Stanze. This seems rather harsh considering what follows three paragraphs below and the brevity with which Borghini treats almost everything.

63 Bottari (*Il Riposo*, 318) points out that the painters were not the only ones who took licence with this story. Leo met Attila at Mantovano on the Mincio River. Borghini follows the invention of Giovanni Villani, who confused Attila with Totila (or Baduila), the king of the Ostrogoths who Justinian crushed in 522.

64 (1492–1527). See Vasari, vol. 4, 461–8.

65 Francesco Borghini was the author's father.

66 (1465–1522). See Vasari, vol. 4, 475–84.

67 See Book II [159–60].

68 Seven pages are omitted, from [398] to [405], concerning *Vincentio da San Gimignano*, *Timoteo of Urbino*, and *Andrea del Monte à Sansovino*. See my dissertation, 607–13.

69 (1474–1550). See Vasari, vol. 4, 529–36.

70 One page is omitted, from [406] to [407], concerning *Baccio da Montelupo*. See my dissertation, 614–15.

71 (ca. 1505–1566). See Vasari, vol. 4, 543–7.

72 See also Book II [163–4].

73 Three pages are omitted, from [409] to [415], concerning *Lorenzo di Credi, Baldassare Peruzzi,* and *Gio. Francesco called Il Fattore.* See my dissertation, 617–23.
74 (1486–1530). See Vasari, vol. 5, 5–60.
75 Borghini devotes more space to Andrea del Sarto than to any other artist (see Appendix), more than to his description of, in order, Raphael, Vasari, Alessandro Allori, Tintoretto, Michelangelo, and Giotto.
76 This is an example, noted originally by John Shearman (*Andrea del Sarto* [Oxford: Clarendon, 1959], 128n17) of how some of Borghini's information is seriously out of date. Pilliod (*Pontormo, Bronzino, Allori,* 260n100) notes that 'despite the death of Piero Salviati twenty years before, the confiscation of Baroncelli by the duke, and its occupancy by Orsini, Borghini described the del Sarto painting precisely as Vasari had: in the chapel built by Piero Salviati.'
77 Vasari expands: 'A St John who stands there is making a sign to the Madonna as if to say that her Child is the true Son of God.' Vasari, vol. 5, 35.
78 This is the first, and rather belated, mention by Borghini of the several styles that Vasari distinguished in the painting of Andrea del Sarto.
79 (ca. 1490–1530). See Vasari, vol. 5, 73–81.
80 Five pages are omitted, from [428] to [433], concerning *Giovanantonio Sogliani* and *Polidoro and Maturino.* See my dissertation, 635–40.
81 (1494–1540). See Vasari, vol. 5, 155–74.
82 See also Book I [112–13] and Book II [202].
83 See also Book I [112] and Book II [194–5].
84 One page is omitted, from [438] to [439], concerning *Bartolomeo da Bagnacavallo.* See my dissertation, 645–6.
85 (1484–1525). See Vasari, vol. 5, 189–200.
86 (1503–1540). See Vasari, vol. 5, 217–38.
87 *e fra l'altre la Decollazione di San Piero e di San Paolo.*
88 One page is omitted, from [446] to [447], concerning *Francesco Granacci.* See my dissertation, 652–3.
89 (1492–1546). See Vasari, vol. 5, 523–57.
90 This is the Villa Madama.
91 Three pages are omitted, from [452] to [455], concerning *Sebastiano of Venice* (Sebastiano del Piombo). See my dissertation, 657–60.

Book IV

1 Don Giovanni de' Medici, as previously noted, was the first Medici to attend the Accademia del Disegno, and in later life he practised as a distinguished amateur architect and accomplished military engineer.

2 Borghini repeats the description of his anticipated audience: non-practising connoisseurs and collectors who become 'immortal painters in the spirit' by reading his book.

3 Giulio Ferroni derives, from this paragraph, his idea that Borghini's dialogue is an extended explication of the essence of the artist as Castiglione's courtier, struggling to realize the ideals of *Il Cortigiano* in the unfavourable social and political environment of late sixteenth-century Florence. For Ferroni, Borghini's image of the ideal painter is 'an image of orderly wisdom, measured repression of the social function, [and] the elimination of every anxious and subversive tendency.' See 'Review of the facsimile *Il Riposo*,' 123–4.

4 A *ragnaia* is another type of planted bird trap, less elaborate than the *uccellare,* in which they met the second day.

5 Dr Luigi Federico Signorini, one of the owners of Il Riposo, suggests a metric translation:

He foresaw well my agreeable repose,
The first who this green hill, and my sweet hostel
Riposo has proposed to call where only
Do I appear to find quietness and rest.

Signorini family, *Il Riposo – Villa Signorini* (Florence: Gli Ermellini, 2002), n.p.

6 Bird lime is a sticky substance made from holly bark that is smeared on twigs to catch small birds.

7 Sixteen pages are omitted, from [461] to [477], concerning *Perino del Vaga; Domenico Beccafumi, called Mecherino; Niccolò, called Il Tribolo*; and *Pierino da Vinci*. See my dissertation, 665–80.

8 (1493–1560). See Giorgio Vasari, *Vita di Baccio Bandinelli scultore fiorentino,* ed. by Detlef Heikamp (Milan: Club del Libro, 1964).

9 See also Book II [164].

10 Borghini offers a more reserved opinion in Book II [161].

11 (1494–1556). See Vasari, vol. 6, 245–89.

12 See also Book I [78–82] and Book II [195–6].

13 Three pages are omitted, from [486] to [489], concerning *Giovanantonio Sodoma*. See my dissertation, 688–91.

14 (1483–1561). See Vasari, vol. 6, 534–48.

15 Around the year 500, Benedict retired to a cave near Lake Subiaco. He was sustained by the daily delivery of bread which a monk lowered into the cave in a basket on a rope.

16 (1503–1577). Michele di Jacopo Tosini. See Vasari, vol. 6, 543–6.

17 Three pages are omitted, from [492] to [495], concerning *Giovanni da Udine* and *Giovanfrancesco Rustici*. See my dissertation, 694–7.

18 (1507–1563). See Vasari, vol. 6, 629–60.
19 See also Book II [163].
20 Borghini omits any mention of Vasari as a co-founder of the Accademia. See Vasari, vol. 6, 655–9, for Vasari's expansive description of Vasari's role in this affair.
21 (1510–1563). See Vasari, vol. 7, 547.
22 See also Book I [110] and Book II [185–7].
23 Five pages omitted, from [504] to [509], concerning *Daniello Ricciarelli* and *Taddeo Zuccaro*. See my dissertation, 706–11.
24 (1475–1564). See Vasari, vol. 7, 135–317. Where Vasari provided enough biographical material, Borghini generally paraphrases or copies, cuts, and pastes his lives together from Vasari's *Vite*. In his life of Michelangelo, however, Borghini appears to have rewritten Vasari's life, albeit in much shortened form.
25 See also Book I [13] and [61].
26 Ibid. [53] and [82].
27 Ibid. [65–6] and Book II [163].
28 Borghini follows Vasari in this dating. Vasari notes (vol. 7, 268), that he was using the Florentine calendar (1563) in contrast to the Roman calendar (1564).
29 Borghini devotes less space to Michelangelo (see Appendix) than to Andrea del Sarto, Raphael, Vasari, Alessandro Allori, and Tintoretto. Rosci (*Il Riposo*, vol. 2, x) notes Borghini's 'curiously hasty and reticent biography of Michelangelo' that Rosci attributes to the 'littleness of the author before such a great source as Vasari and perhaps also to the beginning of the decline of Florence itself.'
30 One page is omitted, from [518] to [519], concerning *Francesco Primaticcio*. See my dissertation, 720–1.
31 (1530–1576). See Vasari, vol. 1, 308; vol. 4, 515; vol. 6, 192; and vol. 7, 301–14; and (*Accademico*) 630–33. This biography is the first in *Il Riposo* where Borghini provides significant biographical information absent in Vasari. In subsequent biographies Borghini provides more, and Vasari less, until Vasari is silent and Borghini becomes the only contemporary chronicler.

The penultimate chapter of Vasari's *Vite*, just before his final chapter highlighting the deeds of the illustrious Giorgio d'Antonio Vasari, concerns the *Accademici del Disegno* (vol. 7, 593–641). Most of the articles in this chapter are very short: one to two pages or less. Naldini, 610, and Macchietti, 613, receive only a bold face identification. Bronzino's life, which is the first, is by far the longest.

Il Riposo is valuable, in part, for the information that Borghini provides concerning the sixteen years between the publication of Vasari's second edition (in 1568) and the publication of *Il Riposo* (in 1584). Vasari mentions many of the artists Borghini discusses at greater length, but Vasari's notice is frequently only in passing and is scattered over several volumes of his *Vite*. Frequently, most of the information Vasari provides is in his chapter concerning the *Accademici*. Such references are identified as above for Vincentio Danti.

32 See also Book I [66].
33 See also Book II [162–3].
34 *Il primo libro del trattato delle perfette proportioni* (Florence, 1567); Barocchi, *Trattati*, vol. 1, 209–69.
35 (1547–1580). Vasari does not discuss Girolamo Danti.
36 (1477–1576). See Vasari, vol. 7, 425–69.
37 Borghini also attributes this painting to Giovanni Bellini [342].
38 Vasari clarifies this comment: '[the painting] has received in alms more crowns than Tiziano and Giorgione ever gained in all their lives' (vol. 7, 437). Borghini also attributes this painting to Giorgione [373].
39 (1477–1570). See Vasari, vol. 7, 485–532.
40 See also Book II [159].
41 Vasari uses *cercero* as another word for 'swan.' Borghini misinterprets this as a proper name. *Cercero* is such an obscure word for 'swan' that Milanesi has to explain it in a note to his Italian readers (vol. 7, 492n2).
42 Two pages are omitted, from [531] to [533], concerning *Don Giulio Clovio*. See my dissertation, 733–5.
43 (1503–1572). See Vasari, (*Accademico*) vol. 7, 593–605.
44 Borghini previously reported only one by Bronzino [483].
45 Cox-Rearick (*Bronzino's Chapel*, 90–1), points out that, following Borghini's description, which essentially repeats that of Vasari, the Chapel of Eleonora of Toledo disappeared from public and printed view until the early nineteenth century.
46 This is the painting that Borghini most castigates for its lasciviousness in Book I [109–10]. Subsequently, he heaps praise on its style and execution in Book II [187]. Furthermore, the contemporary portraits, previously denounced (Book I [97–8] and [115]), are described here with enthusiasm.

Rosci (*Il Riposo*, vol. 2, ix) uses Borghini's discussion of this painting to characterize the whole dialogue: 'It has a decidedly provincial aura, in which the nobility of blood and culture spend their time admiring the svelte grace of their noblewomen, a Costanza da Sommaia or a Camilla Tedaldi del Corno, in a great academic machine such as Bronzino's *Descent into Limbo* in S. Croce, even while, like examining a truffle, accusing those "delicate limbs" of arousing "some stimulus of the flesh" unsuitable in the holy temple of God.'

47 See also Book I [116] and Book II [194].

48 See Book I [113] and Book II [202–3].

49 See also Book I [62], where this gathering of nude barons was severely criticized as most improbable, and Book II [196], where the form of the painting is praised.

50 See also Book I [91–3] and Book II [199].

51 Francesco Berni (1497–1536) was greatly admired as the best of the Italian comic or burlesque poets.

52 (1536–1571). See Vasari (*Accademico*), vol. 7, 611–12.

53 One page is omitted, from [540] to [541], concerning *Francesco da S. Gallo.* See my dissertation, 742–3.

54 (1511–1574). For Vasari on Vasari, see vol. 7, 649–728.

55 2 Kings 4:38–41:

> Elisha returned to Gilgal and there was a famine in that region. While the company of the prophets was meeting with him, he said to his servant, 'Put on the large pot and cook some stew for these men.'
>
> One of them went out into the fields to gather herbs and found a wild vine. He gathered some of its gourds and filled the fold of his cloak. When he returned, he put them up into the pot of stew, though no one knew what they were. The stew was poured out for the men, but as they began to eat it, they cried out, 'O man of God, there is death in the pot.' And they could not eat it.
>
> Elisha said, 'Get some flour.' He put it into the pot and said, 'Serve it to the people to eat.' And there was nothing harmful in the pot.

The noxious plant is thought to have been a colocynth, a Mediterranean and African vine related to the watermelon, the spongy fruit of which is a powerful cathartic.

56 See also Book I [118] and Book II [191].

57 See also Book II [195].

58 Ibid. [204].

59 See also Book I [90–1] and Book II [199].

60 See also Book I [93–4] and Book II [199–200].

61 See also Book I [94–6] and Book II [200].

62 See also Book I [111] and Book II [189].

63 See also Book I [111] and Book II [188].

64 See also Book I [110] and Book II [191].

65 Originating in the Middle Ages, madrigals are short lyrical poems that only subsequently began to be set to music.

66 Sandra Orienti submits that she has identified, in the lives that follow, Borghini's 'instant comprehension and admiration for the Venetians which introduces them with boldness into the environment and taste of the Florentines with an assurance that convinces us that a knowledgeable and friendly critical interest had already appeared in their circle of critics.' 'Su "Il Riposo,"' 225.

67 (1523–1594). Rosci (*Il Riposo*, vol. 2, 138), describes the biography of Tintoretto as 'for the most part original information from Borghini.' For a comparison, see Vasari, vol. 6, 587–94, and vol. 7, 621.

68 Borghini has difficulty admitting that an outstanding Venetian painter (he devotes more space to Tintoretto – see Appendix – than to Michelangelo) could have learned much in Venice. Borghini assumes that Tintoretto's success is primarily the result of unschooled native ability. In his appraisal of Tintoretto as a draftsman, Borghini rejects the judgment of Vasari, who had said that Tintoretto 'worked by accident and without sense of design' (vol. 6, 587).
For the increasing importance of the Florentine concept of *disegno* in sixteenth-century Venetian art theory, see David Rosand, 'The Crisis of the Venetian Renaissance Tradition,' *L'Arte* 11–12 (1970): 5–53. Borghini's praise for Tintoretto, with his *disegno* from Michelangelo and his *colorito* from Titian, would be taken up by Ridolfi sixty years later, but Rosand pointed out that, as a formula for excellence, this combination was actually first suggested by Pino.

69 The Prophecy of the Valley of the Dry Bones, see Ezekiel 37:1–14.

70 Matthew 9:6; Mark 2:9, 2:11; Luke 5:24; John 5:8, 5:11, and 5:12.

71 Da Ponte was Doge from 1578 to 1585.

72 Senators were called *Pregadi* because on election they were formally 'begged' or 'invited' by the Doge to take part in sessions of the Senate.

73 Paul Hills points out that Borghini must have mistaken a temporary arrangement for a permanent installation since Francesco Sansovino wrote in 1580 in his *Venetia città nobilissima* that the *pala d'oro* was in place and highly esteemed on the high altar. Hills notes a payment to Tintoretto for 'a *quadro* of the Nativity of Our Lord for placing on the high altar of San Marco on Christmas Day.' See Hills, 'The Renaissance Altarpiece: A Valid Category?' in *The Altarpiece in the Renaissance*, ed. Peter Humfrey and Martin Kemp (Cambridge: Cambridge University Press, 1990), 48.

74 Borghini returns to the Sala del Collegio in which he had previously described Tintoretto's painting of Niccolò da Ponte in the preceding paragraph.

75 Vasari does not mention Marietta Robusti (ca. 1556–1590).

76 Tintoretto, like Titian, kept a huge workshop. Marietta and his sons Domenico and Marco were his chief assistants. Borghini is the first writer to identify Marietta and the fact that Borghini gives her a biography in 1584 suggests that she had a major hand in the workshop. Despite her importance to Tintoretto, it has been almost impossible to distinguish her hand from her father's. For an attempt to do this, see Paola Rossi, *Jacopo Tintoretto: I ritratti* (Milan: Electa, 1990), 13. See also Carlo Ridolfi, *The Life of Tintoretto and of His Children Domenico and Marietta*, trans. Catherine and Robert Enggass (University Park: Pennsylvania State University Press, 1994), 96–9; E. Conrat-Tietze, 'Marietta, fille du Tintoret,' *Gazette des Beaux-Arts* 2 (1934), 258–62, and Sherry Piland, *Women Artists: An Historical, Contemporary, and Feminist bibliography* (Metuchen, NJ: Scarecrow Press, 1994), 82–4.

77 Jacopo di Antonio Nigreti was called Palma Giovane (1550–1628) to distinguish him from his great uncle Jacopo di Antonio Nigreti, called Palma Vecchio (1480–1528). Vasari discusses Palma Vecchio (vol. 5, 243–8), but he does not mention Palma Giovane.

78 This is the first description in *Il Riposo* of work in progress. Borghini's identification of unfinished work in the studio will become increasingly important when he discusses contemporary Florentine artists.

79 (1531–1588). See Vasari, vol. 6, 367, 588, 591, 593, and 595. Borghini adds to Vasari's biography.

80 (1517–1592). See Vasari's brief comment (vol. 7, 455).

81 Called Francesco Bassano the Younger (1549–1592). Vasari does not mention this artist.

82 I doubt that this is a joke at the Venetians' expense because the phrasing is so out of character with the rest of the treatise. The room is called the Sala dello *Scrutinio* (scrutiny or balloting), used after 1532 to record the votes of the great council for the new doge and other officials of the republic. Currently closed, the ceiling is covered and the walls lined with paintings of Venetian battles and victories.

83 (1540–1587). Vasari does not mention this artist.

84 (1530–1592). See Vasari's passing reference (vol. 7, 423).

85 (1511–1597). Borghini expands on Vasari's brief notes. Vasari, vol. 5, 188; vol. 7, 82, 410, and 621.

86 (1552–1614). Vasari does not mention this artist.

87 (1535–1612). Vasari only mentions Barocci as 'a youth of great promise,' working with 'many young men' in the Casino of Pius IV (vol. 7, 91).

88 (1540–1609). See Vasari, vol. 6, 586 and 593; vol. 7, 79, 83, 85, 86, 87, 89–91, 92, 95, 97, 99–102, 104, 107, 131, and 621.

89 Taddeo Zuccaro is omitted from this edition. See my dissertation, 708–11.
90 See also Book I [83–90].
91 (1527–1592). Vasari makes only passing reference to Muziano (vol. 6, 508).
92 The Datary examined candidates for papal benefices and handled claims to pensions. From *datarius*, giving away.
93 At this point Borghini begins highlighting contemporary projects that he considers to be of exceptional interest.
94 (1550–1598). Vasari does not mention this painter.
95 When Borghini was writing *Il Riposo*, Ferdinando, then a cardinal, was living lavishly in Rome.
96 Jan van der Straeten (1523–1605). Vasari, after making clear his relationship with Strada, 'having made much proficience during the ten years that he has worked ... after the designs and directions of Giorgio Vasari,' describes Strada almost entirely as a designer of tapestries (vol. 7, 99, 309, 584, and (*Accademico*) 617–18).
97 Gualdrada Berti was a thirteenth-century Florentine so renowned for her beauty and probity that she was identified as a paragon by Dante (*Inferno* 16: 37).
98 See also Book I [116–17] and Book II [193].
99 See also Book I [114] and Book II [188–9].
100 See also Book I [97–9] and Book II [201].
101 See also Book I [114] and Book II [203].
102 Jean de Boulogne (ca. 1524–1608). Vasari treats only the very first of Giambologna's career (vol. 6, 191, and vol. 7, 584, (*Accademico*) 629–30, but he does take time to note, vol. 7, 630), that 'many works by his hand and very beautiful models of various things, are in the possession of M. Bernardo Vecchietti, a gentleman of Florence.' Giambologna is believed to have been the architect for the villa of Il Riposo as well as for the Palazzo Vecchietti which is now the Florence office of the Deutsche Bank.
103 Simples are plants, the product of which does not need to be mixed with that of other plants to formulate medically active compounds. The Giardino dei Semplici is the third-oldest botanical garden in the world.
104 See Book I [71–5] and Book II [165–9].
105 Bottari (*Raccolta di lettere*, 481), suggests that Borghini is describing 'perhaps portraits of birds, of which this grotto is full, there not being any human figures there.'
106 (1511–1592). Vasari discusses Ammanati relatively briefly (vol. 4, 453; vol. 6, 185, 187, 191–2, 321, 574, 583; and vol. 7, 81, 227, 510, 521–2 and (*Accademico*) 625–6), concluding that 'I could tell many particulars of this sculptor, but since he is my friend, and another, so I hear, is

writing his history, I shall say no more, in order not to set my hand to things that may be related by another better than I perhaps might be able' (trans. by de Vere, vol. 2, 822).

107 See also Book I [66–71] and Book II [164–5].

108 (1527–1587). Vasari discusses Vincenzio de' Rossi (*Accademico*, vol. 7, 626–7), up to the first two of the seven labours of Hercules that Rossi completed for Cosimo.

109 Rosci (*Il Riposo*, vol. 2, 125) notes that Borghini probably confuses this with Rossi's *Bacchus* and a *Satyr* which Borghini had previously located in the Villa Giulia.

110 Isabella de' Medici (1542–1576) was the second daughter of Cosimo I. She married Paolo Orsini, Duke of Bracciano, who murdered her in one of the most sensational crimes of the sixteenth century.

111 See also Book II [162].

112 This portrait is now lost. Rosci, *Il Riposo*, vol 2, xii.

113 (1527–1594). Vasari describes the beginning of Batista's career through the first three of his four *Seasons* (vol. 7, 316 and [*Accademico*] 638–41).

114 (1528/29–1599). Borghini supplements Vasari (vol. 6, 477–78, and vol. 7, 301, 317, and 639).

115 Another dwarf whose name was actually Pietro.

116 (1533–1609). Vasari does not mention this sculptor.

117 (1534–1592). From the evidence of the *Vite*, the six years Macchietti spent with Vasari appear to have made little impression on the older painter, who mentioned Macchietti only twice in passing and did not report that Macchietti ever worked for him.

118 See also Book I [112] and Book II [195].

119 See also Book I [100–1] and Book II [196–7].

120 See also Book I [112] and Book II [189].

121 See also Book II [205].

122 Marta Privitera uses this paragraph in her reconstruction of Macchietti's lost oeuvre in Naples. 'Girolamo Macchietti a Napoli,' *Arte Documento* no. 4 (1990): 112–19.

123 (1535–1583). See Vasari, (*Accademico*) vol. 7, 637.

124 At Montaperti on 4 September 1260, the Florentine Guelphs were so overwhelmed by the forces of Siena, reinforced with Florentine Ghibelline exiles, that, Dante said, the Arbia ran red with Florentine blood. *Inferno*, 10: 85.

125 (1535–1603). See Vasari, vol. 7, 310, and (*Accademico*) 614–17.

126 For Frangenberg's discussion of this peculiarity of many Florentine paintings in the second half of the sixteenth century, see the last paragraph of n73, Book I.

127 (1536–1591). Borghini expands on Vasari's brief notice of Vasari's junior associate (Vasari, vol. 6, 288–9, and vol. 7, 99, 308, and 610), where Vasari only identifies the young *Accademico* as such. Borghini, for his part, does not allude to Vasari's description of the close association between Naldini and Vincenzio Borghini 'who has made great use of him and assisted him.'

128 See also Book I [103] and Book II [198].

129 See also Book I [101–2] and Book II [197–8].

130 See also Book I [114–15] and Book II [205].

131 (1535–1605; Archbishop of Florence after 1574; elected Pope as Leo XI on 1 April 1605 and died 27 April).

132 See also Book I [102] and Book II [198].

133 St John is said, as an old man, to have been arrested and thrown into a cauldron of boiling oil from which he escaped unharmed at the place just inside the Porta Latina in Rome, now occupied by San Giovanni in Oleo.

134 A typographical error in the first edition.

135 (1537–1603). Borghini enlarges on Vasari's brief notes (vol. 5, 124, and vol. 7, 91, 309–10, and (*Accademico*) 619–20). Santi di Tito did the altarpiece formerly in the now suppressed Vecchietti neighbourhood church in Florence and probably did the frescoes that can still be seen under the garden loggia at Il Riposo.

136 See also Book I [116] and Book II [187–8].

137 See also Book I [116] and Book II [188].

138 (1535–1607). Again, Borghini expands on Vasari's notes (vol. 4, 353; vol. 5, 129, and vol. 7, 308 and (*Accademico*) 606–8).

139 See also Book I [96–7] and Book II [200–1].

140 See also Book II [203].

141 See also Book I [114] and Book II [203].

142 Bottari points out that Homer described the war of the frogs and mice.

143 This is a unique instance in which Borghini praises the use of allegory (he mentioned Salviati's *Triumph of Camillus* in the Palazzo Vecchio but not its political significance). In conformity with his Counter-Reformation principles, Borghini otherwise discourages allegory and prefers transparent iconography.

For a different reading of this fresco cycle, see Cox-Rearick, *Dynasty and Destiny in Medici Art*, 92–6, 104, 106, 108, 115, and 122. She reads the frescoes as a celebration of the whole Medici family, rather than primarily a celebration of Lorenzo the Elder.

Borghini's generous description of these frescoes must dampen the enthusiasm with which *Il Riposo* is summarized as a pro-Medici–Federico Zuccaro, anti-Republican–Alessandro Allori polemic.

144 See also Book I [103–6] and Book II [191–2].
145 This is the *Annunciation* in the Tabernacle of the Annunziata. Still highly venerated by Florentines, it is traditionally thought to have been painted by a monk assisted by an angel.
146 I do not understand the logic of this subheading.
147 (ca. 1550–1607/12). This painter was twelve when Vasari published the second edition of the *Vite*.
148 When Leonora's father died, the lack of a legitimate male heir allowed her uncle Ferdinando to accede to the dukedom.
149 (1537–1592). Although Fei was an *Accademico*, Vasari mentions him only briefly (vol. 7, 620), as an assistant in the Palazzo Vecchio.
150 See also Book I [111–12] and Book II [190].
151 (1539–1598). Vasari (vol. 7, 298, 304, and 317), mentions only Giovanni's sculpture on the tomb of Michelangelo.
152 See also Book I [108].
153 See also Book II [160–1].
154 (1544–1597). Vasari mentions Poppi only briefly as an *Accademico* (vol. 7, 610–11).
155 See also Book I [112].
156 See also Book I [117–18].
157 Ibid. [102–3].
158 (1561–1612). Vasari does not mention Giovanni Caccini.

Selected Bibliography

Acidini Luchinat, Cristina. 'Per le pitture della Cupola di Santa Maria del Fiore.' *Labyrinthos* 13–16 (1988–9): 153–75.

Alberti, Leon Battista. *Leon Battista Alberti on Painting*. Trans. John Spencer. 2nd ed. New Haven: Yale University Press, 1966.

Alpers, Svetlana. '*Ekphrasis* and Aesthetic Attitudes in Vasari's *Lives*.' *Journal of the Warburg and Courtauld Institutes* 23 (1960): 190–215.

Ariosto, Ludovico. *Orlando Furioso*. Ed. Lanfranco Caretti. Milan: Ricciardi, 1954.

Armenini , Giovanni Battista. *On the True Precepts of the Art of Painting*. Trans. and ed. Edward Olszewski. New York: Franklin, 1977.

Avanzini, Elena. *Il Riposo di Raffaello Borghini e la critica d'arte nel '500*. Milan: Gastaldi, 1960.

Barasch, Mosche. *Theories of Art from Plato to Winckelman*. New York: New York University Press, 1985.

Barocchi, Paola, ed. *Trattati d'arte del Cinquecento, fra manierismo e Contro riforma*. Bari: Laterza, 1960–2.

– ed. *Scritti d'arte del Cinquecento*. Milan: Ricciardi, 1971–7.

Blunt, Anthony. *Artistic Theory in Italy, 1450–1600*. London: Clarendon, 1940; Oxford: Oxford University Press, 1968.

Boccaccio, Giovanni. *Decameron*. Trans. and ed. G.H. McWilliam. 2nd ed. London: Penguin, 1995.

Bocchi, Francesco. *The Beauties of the City of Florence*. Trans. and ed. Thomas Frangenberg and Robert Williams. Turnhout: Brepols, 2006.

Boase, T.S.R. *Giorgio Vasari – the Man and the Book*. Princeton: Princeton University Press, 1979.

Borghini, Raffaello. *Il Riposo* ... Florence: Marescotti, 1584; edited by Giovanni Gaetano Bottari. Florence: Nestenus e Moüke, 1730; Siena: Pazzini e Carli, 1787; Milan: Tipografica de' Classici Italiani, 1807; and Reggio

Emilia: Fiaccadori, 1826–7. Milan: Labor, 1967, and Hildesheim: Olms, 1969 (1st ed. facsimiles). See also Leopoldo Cicognara, *Catalogo ragionato dei libri d'arte* ... Pisa: Capurro, 1821, vol. I, 381, #2217 (1st ed.) and #2218 (2nd ed.); microfiche Cosenza: Editrice 'Casa del Libro' Dott. Gustavo Brenner, 1960. Translated as 'Raffaello Borghini's *Il Riposo*,' by Lloyd Ellis, doctoral dissertation, Case Western Reserve University, 2002; Ann Arbor: UMI, 2003.

Borsi, Franco. 'Don Giovanni de' Medici, Principe Architetto.' In *Firenze del Cinquecento*, 352–8. Rome: Editalia, 1974.

Bottari, Giovanni, ed. *Il Riposo*. 2nd ed. Florence: Nestenus e Moüke, 1730.

– *Raccolta di Lettere sulla Pittura, Scultura e Architettura, scritte dai più celebri personaggi che in dette arti fiorirono dal sec. XV al XVII*. Rome, 1754. Ed. Stefano Ticozzi. Milan: Silvestri, 1822–5.

Bury, Michael. 'Bernardo Vecchietti, Patron of Giambologna.' *I Tatti Studies* 1 (1985): 13–56.

Campbell, Malcolm. 'Family Matters. Notes on Don Lorenzo and Don Giovanni de' Medici at Villa della Petraia.' In *Ars naturam adiuvans. Festschrift für Matthias Winner*, ed. Victoria V. Flemming and Sebastian Schütze, 505–13. Mainz am Rhein: Zabern, 1996.

Carocci, Guido. *I dintorni di* Firenze. Vol. 2. Florence: Galletti e Cocci, 1906–7.

Castiglione, Baldesar. *Il Libro del cortegiano*. Trans. George Bull as *The Book of the Courtier*. Harmondsworth: Penguin, 1967.

Ceserani, Remo. 'Borghini, Raffaello.' In *Dizionario Biografico Degli Italiani*, ed. Alberto Ghisalberti, vol. 12, 677–80. Rome: Società Grafica Romano, 1970.

Cochrane, Eric. *Florence in the Forgotten Centuries, 1527–1800*. Chicago: University of Chicago Press, 1973.

Cox-Rearick, Janet. *Dynasty and Destiny in Medici Art: Pontormo, Leo X, and the Two Cosimos*. Princeton: Princeton University Press, 1984.

– *Bronzino's Chapel of Eleonora in the Palazzo Vecchio*. Berkeley: University of California Press, 1993.

Einstein, Lewis. 'Conversations at Villa Riposo.' *Gazette des Beaux-Arts* 2 (July–Aug. 1961): 6–20.

Ellis, Lloyd. 'Raffaello Borghini's *Il Riposo*: A Critical Study and Annotated Translation.' Doctoral dissertation, Case Western Reserve University, 2002; Ann Arbor: UMI, 2003.

– *The Signorini and Their Villa of Il Riposo*. Florence: Ermellini, 2004.

Ferroni, Giulio. 'Le commedie di Raffaello Borghini.' *La Rassegna della letteratura italiana* 73/7 (1969): 37–63.

– Review of the facsimile *Il Riposo*, by Raffaello Borghini, edited by Marco Rosci. *La Rassegna della letteratura italiana* 73/7 (1969): 122–4.

Frangenberg, Thomas. *Der Betrachter. Studien zur florentinischen Kunstliteratur des 16. Jahrhunderts*. Berlin: Mann, 1990.

– 'The Art of Talking about Sculpture: Vasari, Borghini and Bocchi.' *Journal of the Warburg and Courtauld Institutes* 58 (1995): 115–31.

Franklin, David. *Painting in Renaissance Florence, 1500–1550*. New Haven: Yale University Press, 2001.

Freedburg, David. 'Johannes Molanus on Provocative Paintings.' *Journal of the Warburg and Courtauld Institutes* 34 (1971): 229–45.

Gilbert, Creighton. 'The Archbishop on the Painters of Florence, 1450.' *Art Bulletin* 41 (1959): 75–87.

Gilio, Giovanni Andrea. *Dialogo nel quale si ragiona degli errori e degli abusi de'pittori circa l'istorie*. Camerino: Antonio Gioioso, 1564. Ed. Paola Barocchi. Florence, 1986.

Hall, Marcia. *Renovation and Counter-Reformation. Vasari and Duke Cosimo in Sta. Maria Novella and Sta. Croce, 1565–1577*. Oxford–Warburg Studies. Oxford: Clarendon, 1979.

– *After Raphael – Painting in Central Italy in the Sixteenth Century*. Cambridge: Cambridge University Press, 1999.

Heikamp, Detlef. 'The Grotto of the Fata Morgana and Giambologna's Marble Gorgon.' *Antichità viva* 20/3 (1981): 12–31.

Hope, Charles. Review of *Renovation and Counter-Reformation. Vasari and Duke Cosimo in Sta. Maria Novella and Sta. Croce, 1565–1577*, by Marcia Hall. *Burlington Magazine* 124 (July 1982): 512–14.

Horne, Herbert. *Alessandro Filipepi, Commonly Called Sandro Botticelli, Painter of Florence*. London: Bell, 1908. Republished as *Botticelli – Painter of Florence*. Princeton: Princeton University Press, 1980.

Langedijk, Karla. *The Portraits of the Medici*. Vol. 2. Florence: Studio per Edizioni Scelte, 1983.

Lazzaro, Claudia. *The Italian Renaissance Garden*. New Haven: Yale University Press, 1990.

Natali, Antonio. 'Candidior animus.' *Antichità viva* 20/4 (July–Aug. 1981): 22–31.

Olszewski, Edward. 'Distortions, Shadows and Conventions in Sixteenth-Century Italian Art.' *artibus et historiae* 11/6 (1985): 101–24.

Orienti, Sandra. 'Su "Il Riposo" di Raffaele Borghini.' *Rivista d'Arte* 27/3/II (1951–2): 221–6.

Pilliod, Elizabeth. *Pontormo, Bronzino, Allori: A Genealogy of Florentine Art*. New Haven: Yale University Press, 2001.

Platt, Susan. 'Villa Il Riposo – The Concept and the Reality.' Master's thesis, Pius XII Institute, Rosary College (now Dominican University), 1968.

Pope-Hennessy, John. *Italian High Renaissance and Baroque Sculpture*. 4th ed. London: Phaidon, 1996.

Richardson, Brian. *Print Culture in Renaissance Italy: The Editor and the Vernacular Text, 1470–1600*. Cambridge: Cambridge University Press, 1994.

– *Printing, Writers and Readers in Renaissance Italy.* Cambridge: Cambridge University Press, 1999.

Rosci, Marco, ed. *Il Riposo* by Raffaello Borghini. Milan: Labor, 1967.

– 'Leonardo "filosofo," Lomazzo e Borghini 1584: Due linee di tradizione dei pensieri e precetti di Leonardo sull'arte.' In *Fra Rinascimento Manierismo e realtà. Scritti di Storia dell'arte in memoria di Anna Maria Brizio*, ed. Pietro Marani, 53–77. Florence: Giunti Barbèra, 1984.

Rubin, Patricia. *Giorgio Vasari: Art and History.* New Haven: Yale University Press, 1995.

Schlosser (-Magnino), Julius. *La letteratura artistica*, ed. Otto Kurz and trans. Filippo Rossi. Florence: La Nuova Italia, 1964. Translation of *Die Kunstliteratur.* 3rd ed. Vienna: Schroll, 1924.

Shearman, John. *Mannerism.* Harmondsworth: Penguin, 1967.

Signorini, Giorgio. 'Vicende generali della proprietà Vecchietti a Vacciano.' Giorgio Signorini, Grassina (Florence).

Signorini family. *'Il Riposo' – Villa Signorini.* Florence: Gli Ermellini, 2002.

Spalding, Jack. 'Santi di Tito and the Reform of Florentine Mannerism.' *Storia dell'arte* 47 (1983): 41–52. Excerpted from his 'Santi di Tito,' doctoral dissertation, Princeton University, 1976.

Summers, David. 'Contrapposto: Style and Meaning in Renaissance Art.' *Art Bulletin* 59 (1977): 336–61.

Tognelli, Jole. 'Tra Lingua e Colore. "Vaghezza" cromatica del Borghini.' *Letteratura* 7/37–8 (Jan.–Apr. 1959): 7–14.

Vasari, Giorgio. *Le Vite de' piú eccelenti Architetti, Pittori et Scultori* … Florence: Marescotti, 1550; 2nd ed. Florence: Giunta, 1568. *Le vite* … (1550), ed. by C. Ricci. Rome: Bertetti e Tumminelli, 1927. *Le vite* … (1568), ed. by Gaetano Milanesi. Florence: Sansoni, 1906. *Le Vite* … (1550 and 1568), ed. by Rosanna Bettarini and Paola Barocchi. Florence: Sansoni, n.d. *Lives of the Painters, Sculptors and Architects*, trans. Gaston de Vere (1912), introduction and notes by David Ekserdjian. New York: Knopf, 1996. See also, *Vasari on Technique – Being the Introduction to the Three Arts of Design, Architecture, Sculpture and Painting, Prefixed to the Lives* …, trans. Louisa Maclehose and ed. Baldwin Brown. London: Dent, 1907; New York: Dover, 1960.

Wazbinski, Zygmunt. 'Artysci i publicznosc w szesnastowiecznej Florencji "Cane mordente."' In *Théorie de l'art* (Congrès Varsovie 1974) (1976), 46–76; reprinted as 'Artisti e pubblico nella Firenze del Cinquecento. A proposito del topos "cane abbaiante."' *Paragone* 28/327 (May 1977): 3–24.

Williams, Robert. 'The Façade of the Palazzo dei Visacci.' *I Tatti Studies* 5 (1993): 209–44.

– *Art, Theory, and Culture in Sixteenth-Century Italy: From Techne to Metatechne.* Cambridge: Cambridge University Press, 1997.

Index

Artworks discussed in Books I and II are indexed. For an index to the 5,000 to 6,000 works discussed in Books III and IV see the Indice analitico prepared by Marco Rosci in vol. 2 of his 1967 edition of *Il Riposo.*

www.ingramcontent.com/pod-product-compliance
Lightning Source LLC
LaVergne TN
LVHW090801070826
844660LV00022B/1054

* 9 7 8 1 4 4 2 6 1 4 9 3 2 *